JA ECONOMICS®

JA ECONOMICS

Copyright © 2016
Junior Achievement USA®
Colorado Springs, Colorado

First Edition 2000

An Invitation to Students

As you read the newspaper, listen to the news, surf the Internet, or just talk to your family and friends, you come face-to-face with economic issues that affect you and those around you.

- Why do workers with more education and experience usually earn more than those with a high school diploma?
- What makes wages rise over the years?
- Why does the price of gasoline rise or fall?
- Is there a cost to watching television?
- Is recycling always worthwhile? Why do people pollute the environment?
- Does a higher minimum wage help workers?
- Why do some businesses close their plants, lay off workers, or move overseas?
- Is there a cost of going to school? Is there a cost of not going to school?
- Why do people develop and introduce new products?
- Why should a person save money? Where should money be saved?
- What is the secret of compound interest?
- What is an entrepreneur?
- Where do people find money to start their own businesses?

Economics will help you answer questions like these because it helps you think more clearly for yourself. As you progress through this course, you will see that economics is largely a way of thinking—about all kinds of things. Like learning to play a sport or a musical instrument, economic thinking is a skill that takes practice to develop.

To help you develop your economic thinking and knowledge, you will be using a new kind of textbook—an interactive text. Because you can keep this textbook, it is designed to allow—and encourage—you to write in it. In your text, you will find these learning aids:

Mark to Remember
* This is important.
? I have a question about this.
! This is a surprise.

This direction prompts you to use the three symbols to highlight information in the text that you want to remember, you don't understand, or that surprises you. Marking up your text in this way will help you review the material at a later time.

Read to Find Out and Why It Matters
On the opening page of every chapter, you will find a series of questions that will help you read with a purpose. By reading to answer these questions, you will focus on the most important information in the chapter. The "Why It Matters" section will help you understand the importance of the chapter's information in your life.

Margin Activities
In the margin of your text, you will find a variety of questions that will help you check and apply your understanding, predict upcoming information, remember information you previously learned, and to think critically about what you are reading. If you take the time

to complete these questions as you read the chapter, your understanding and recollection of the information you are reading will improve significantly.

In-text Activities

Embedded in the text are activities, generally requiring analysis or application of the material you have just read. Like the margin activities, you should complete these activities as you proceed through the chapter. Completing the activities will help clarify the material for you and prepare you for chapter reviews and/or tests.

In addition to the textbook, you will have the opportunity to complete study guide exercises and activities that will enhance and deepen your understanding.

As you study and learn with the *JA Economics* program, you will see that when it comes to questions of economic analysis, economists often agree about the economy's problems. But they disagree as much as others do about the best solutions. In other words, we all have strong ideas about what is good or bad, right or wrong, and fair or unfair. Economics does not make such judgments for you; you have to make them for yourself. Yet economics can help you understand how the world works. You will see that with economic thinking, you can better understand the likely consequences of all kinds of choices made by all kinds of people; including you!

We hope that you will find your semester of *JA Economics* to be an enjoyable and rewarding experience. Please feel free to share your feedback about the course with us. We would be especially interested in knowing if you found your study of economics using the *JA Economics* program valuable.

Junior Achievement USA
One Education Way
Colorado Springs, CO 80906
www.ja.org

Table of Contents

Acknowledgments

Sponsorship

Junior Achievement USA (JA®; JA USA®) gratefully acknowledges MetLife Foundation for its commitment to the development and implementation of the high school program *JA Economics.*

Junior Achievement appreciates its partnership with MetLife Foundation to inspire and prepare young people to succeed in a global economy.

Consultants

Many educators, economists, businesspeople, and consultants have contributed to the development of *JA Economics.* Special thanks to the following individuals who assisted in the development of this edition of *JA Economics* and the accompanying support material.

Contributing Writers

Dr. James E. Davis, Executive Director, Social Science Education Consortium, Lafayette, Colorado

Sharryl Davis, President, Instructional Design Associates, Lafayette, Colorado

Dr. Lewis Karstensson, Associate Professor of Economics, University of Nevada (Las Vegas), Las Vegas, Nevada

Dr. Donald R. Wentworth, Professor Emeritus, Economics and Education, Pacific Lutheran University, Tacoma, Washington

Reviewers

Patricia Ford, Business Teacher, Thomas Jefferson High School, Auburn, Washington

Thomas J. Fugate, Economics Teacher, Homestead High School, Mequon, Wisconsin

Tony Gaetner, Economics Teacher, Bay City Western High School, Auburn, Michigan

Charles N. LeWarne, Economics and American History Teacher, Kamiak Senior High School, Mukilteo, Washington

Christian E. Nordlin, Economics Teacher, North Side High School, Fort Wayne, Indiana

Roger L. Perkins, Economics Teacher, Kenowa Hills High School, Grand Rapids, Michigan

Michael J. Schlitt, Economics, World History, and Government Instructor, Manchester High School North, Manchester, Indiana

Robert J. Wiersema II, Economics Teacher, Hopkins High School, Hopkins, Michigan

Economic Update

Junior Achievement USA and two university economics professors teamed up to produce a series of position papers on the severe economic recession that hit America and Europe in late 2007 and whose effects were still being felt years later.

The position papers examine the causes, implications, and impacts of what has come to be known as The Great Recession. The papers include: "Understanding the Financial Crisis: Origin and Impact"; "High Unemployment: The Recession's Harsh Reality"; "The U.S. Financial Crisis: Global Repercussions"; "The Skyrocketing Federal Budget Deficit: Worrisome or Not?"; and "Understanding Stock Market Fluctuations: The Turmoil at the Heart of the Capitalist System."

To access the online position papers, visit ja.org.

What Is Economics?

Read to Find Out

As you read this chapter, look for answers to the following questions:

What is the nature of human wants, and how are they satisfied?

What are the four factors of production?

What is the meaning of scarcity?

What is opportunity cost, and why is it important?

What are the key ideas in the economic way of thinking?

What does it mean to "think at the margin," and how do marginal costs and marginal benefits affect daily decisions?

What kinds of choices do businesses face, and what is a major goal of a business?

What are the basic economic decisions facing all societies?

What are the two branches of economics?

Mark to Remember

* *This is important.*

? *I have a question about this.*

! *This is a surprise.*

Why It Matters

Economist Alfred Marshall (1842 –1924) stated that economics is about the "ordinary business of life." This chapter will provide you with a tool kit to help you understand this ordinary business. Ordinary business is how people choose to satisfy their wants. Choice making is fundamental in economics, whether it involves a personal choice, a choice made by a business, or a choice made by government. For you, making good choices is important to becoming a contributing, active, and successful citizen in our society.

iStockphoto '07

What Is Economics?

Building On What You Know

You already know more about economics than you may think you do. Do you buy things? If you do, you are a consumer. If you put some of your money aside in a bank, you are a saver. You may earn money by doing household chores or working at a part-time job. This means you are a producer. As a producer, you exchange your labor for an allowance or wages. As a participant in the economy, you are ready to study economics.

"What is *economics?*" Here is a short answer. **Economics** is a social science that studies how people, acting individually and in groups, decide to use scarce resources to satisfy their wants. Economics is a social science because it involves the study of people. It is scientific because it uses many tools of analysis to explain how the economy works. The United States is blessed with ample resources—plentiful land, water, and minerals; educated and skilled people; a history of creative inventions to reduce hard labor; and creative businesspeople. Yet, it is a simple fact of economic life that people want more than our resources can provide. This condition of scarcity actually forces individuals and groups to make choices about how to use resources, all of which have alternative uses. How people choose to satisfy their wants and why they make the decisions they do is an ongoing concern of economics.

Human Wants

Imagine that a magic genie has promised you that you can have anything you want forever—cars, houses, clothes, jewels, trips, concert tickets, and more. If this were the case, you wouldn't have to study economics. However, it is unlikely that you will meet a magic genie. Like most people, you can't have everything you want.

People have both physical wants and psychological wants. Physical wants, such as food, clothing, and housing, occur over and over. At a basic level, meeting physical wants is necessary to maintaining a healthy, safe life. These basic wants change as people grow older. You don't eat the same food or wear the same clothes that you did when you were an infant. Psychological wants aren't necessary to existence, but satisfying psychological wants makes people feel better, perhaps even happier. Psychological wants reflect our own tastes and are often influenced by our culture. Think about your own wants for wearing up-to-date clothes, attending the latest movie, or even owning a special car.

Physical wants and psychological wants often become mixed in our minds. We don't really think much about sorting them out. We want more and more things—things beyond our basic physical needs. Our wants change over time as we acquire tastes for new products. Our wants are influenced by our friends and advertising. Rarely do we stop to decide which are physical wants and which are psychological wants.

The Want-Satisfaction Chain

 Trying to satisfy people's wants is a complex process. In an economy, millions of people work in thousands of businesses to produce and distribute goods and services to satisfy people's wants. Think of the steps of the process of want-satisfaction like links in a chain, as shown in Figure 1-1 below.

People make choices based on physical and psychological wants.

The authors suggest that only a few physical wants are necessary to life. What physical wants do you believe absolutely must be satisfied? Justify your answers.

_____
_____
_____
_____
_____
_____
_____
_____

Check Your Understanding

Number the sentences in the text that describe the steps shown in the want-satisfaction chain diagram. Make Human Wants number 1. Write key phrases in the margins to help you remember the meaning of the steps.

Figure 1-1: Want-Satisfaction Chain

The process begins with a human want. For example, suppose you want a loaf of bread to make toast for breakfast or sandwiches for lunch. First, bread requires farmers to combine the economic resources of land, labor, and capital to produce wheat. Once wheat is produced, it must be milled into flour, which also uses economic resources. The flour is combined with yeast, water, perhaps sugar, and other ingredients. It is then baked and packaged. Here is the important point. For any good or service, economic resources must be combined in a process of *production*. **Production** is a process that combines economic resources so the result is a good or service that is available for sale. (We will study economic resources in more depth later in this chapter.)

Is the want for bread now satisfied? No, not yet. The production process of bread making only results in bread, an economic good. Somehow the bread needs to be distributed. It has to be made available to you and others who want bread. Bread, as well as other economic goods, must go through **distribution**—the process of getting a product or service to consumers—before the human want can be satisfied.

Once a good or product is distributed, it is available for *consumption*. Since you want bread for yourself and your family, you choose to buy it, probably at a grocery store. After you buy the bread and eat it, your want is satisfied. **Consumption**, using a product or service, completes the want-satisfaction chain.

Is our story complete? Not really. The bread satisfies you only temporarily. When you become hungry again and there is no bread in the house, the want-satisfaction process begins all over.

Creating Your Own Want-Satisfaction Chain

List several products you want. Choose one product from the list that you know something about. In the blank diagram below, create a want-satisfaction chain to show the specific steps necessary to satisfy your want for the product you chose. Do some product research if you need more information.

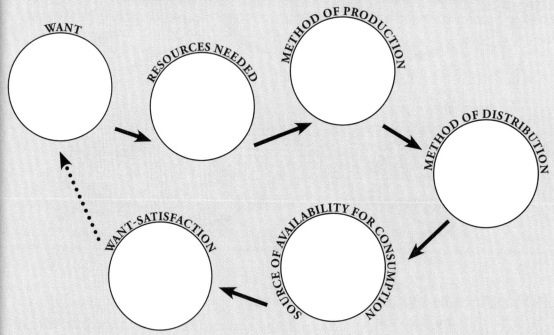

What is the greatest obstacle in satisfying your want? _____

_____

_____

2. production   3. distribution   4. consumption

Resources:
The First Step in Satisfying Wants

In studying the want-satisfaction chain, you learned that resources are the basic elements used to produce goods and services. There are three types of productive resources: natural, human, and capital. Natural resources are unaltered gifts of nature, such as soil, minerals, timber, and fresh water. These resources are referred to as **land**. Human resources, or **labor**, are the physical and mental efforts people use to create goods and services. **Capital** resources are the buildings, tools, and machines people create and use to produce final goods and services. Final goods and services are sold to consumers. A truck that delivers gasoline to a service station is capital. So, too, are a computer and a telephone which deliver information. Producing any good or service requires land, labor, and capital. Economists call land, labor, and capital resources the **factors of production**.

An oil derrick is an example of a capital resource.

Show Your Understanding

Create a graphic organizer to show the relationship among factors of production: land, labor, capital, and entrepreneurship. Use the space below.

Economists call *entrepreneurship* the fourth factor of production. **Entrepreneurship** is the imagination, innovative thinking, and management skills needed to start and operate a business. Entrepreneurs are willing to take risks in hopes of making a profit. Entrepreneurs are important to the success of a business and the U.S. economy. Our economy offers many people the opportunity to become entrepreneurs.

As we look around us, we see ample amounts of the productive resources of land, labor, and capital. Entrepreneurship is not as easy to see, but there is plenty of it around us as well. However, when these resources are put to use in an economy, they come with a cost or a price. This means that the factors of production are scarce as you will learn in the next section.

Scarcity and Opportunity Cost

You may have heard the saying "People are never satisfied." The saying provides a key to greater understanding of the want-satisfaction chain. In the chain, satisfaction is linked to people's recurring wants. There is usually a gap between what people want and the resources available to meet those wants. Economists call the gap *scarcity*. **Scarcity** means that an inequality exists between wants and the resources available to satisfy them.

To discover the inequality, compare wants with resources. The comparison can be stated in a simple formula:

SCARCITY = Wants > Available Resources

The symbol > means "greater than." It is a shorthand way to state the relationship between wants and resources. If, and only if, wants are greater than available resources, then the resources in question are scarce.

For example, a resource, such as water, can be plentiful and still be scarce. It may not be available at the precise time and place it is needed. Water covers about 70 percent of Earth's surface. Yet, everyone has been caught in need of water at some time.

Pause to Think

What images pop into your mind when you hear the word scarce?

_____

_____

_____

_____

_____

Read to find out how economists think about scarcity. Draw a box around the sentences that explain economists' meaning of scarcity.

5. land   6. labor   7. capital   8. factors of production   9. entrepreneurship   10. scarcity

A resource is not scarce simply because there is little of it in existence. A resource is scarce only when there is not enough of it to meet the need for it. A very high-scoring basketball player represents a resource that is pretty rare. Because professional basketball needs high-scorers, this kind of player is considered a scarce resource.

If a small amount of a resource exists, but it is not wanted, it is not scarce. An actor may be very gifted with a unique talent. If theater or movie businesspeople do not want the actor's talent, the actor's resource is not scarce. In order for a resource to be scarce, the demand for the resource must be greater than the amount of resource available. Another example might be a rare jewel. If there is no demand for the jewel, the jewel is not scarce.

Scarce resources have not always been scarce. Today, oil is a scarce resource. When it is turned into gasoline, people agree to pay more and more for it. Two hundred and fifty years ago, oil was not scarce. Why? There was no demand for it. The first successful internal combustion gasoline engines were not built until the late 1800s.

Opportunity Cost

Because resources are scarce, they can only be used one way at a time. For example, if a farmer chooses to use land to grow corn, that land cannot be used to grow soybeans. If you choose to work after school at a bookstore, you cannot use your time to participate in the school debate team. If a family decides to go on a trip, the family cannot use the trip money to purchase a new flat-screen television.

These are examples of alternatives given up when a choice is made. Scarcity forces us to think about our alternatives. Economists have a special term for the highest valued alternative that is given up. It is called *opportunity cost*. **Opportunity cost** is the highest valued alternative given up as a result of making a choice. The farmer's opportunity cost of growing corn is giving up growing soybeans. Your opportunity cost of working in the bookstore is giving up participating in the school debate team. The family's opportunity cost of taking a trip is giving up having a flat-screen television.

Economists think of all costs as opportunities given up. Still, economists most often use the phrase *opportunity cost* to remind us of the most-valued opportunity we sacrifice when we make a choice. How people make choices leads us to the economic way of thinking.

What's Your Opportunity Cost?

Suppose you are given $100. What three things, each costing about $100, would you like to buy?

1. _____

2. _____

3. _____

Now arrange the three items to show your first, second, and third choices. Which items are your opportunity cost?

_____

_____

_____

11. opportunity cost

The Economic Way of Thinking

John Maynard Keynes, a famous British economist writing in the 1930s, said this about economics: "It (economics) is a method ... an apparatus of the mind, a technique of thinking..." In other words, Keynes is saying economics is a way of thinking. Understanding the economic way of thinking will help you understand much of economic behavior. Here are the key ideas.

Scarcity Forces People to Choose

You learned about scarcity in the previous section. Without the scarcity problem, there would be little need for people to make choices. But scarcity is a fundamental fact of life. Making choices is something individuals, businesses, and governments are forced to do. Therefore, choice making is an initial step in explaining much of human behavior and in understanding economics.

All Choices Involve Alternatives

People must give up something important in order to gain something important. People think about their **benefits**, or gains, as well as their **costs**, or losses, in making choices. People try to maximize their benefits and minimize their costs in making economic decisions. For example, if you want to buy some new clothes, you are likely to shop for the best bargain (a benefit) as well as the appropriate style of clothing (also a benefit). You will try to keep your cost as low as possible for an acceptable outfit.

People Try to Make Good Choices

People try to make the best choices they can. They usually don't try to make bad or poor choices. Because people value their time and money, they try to make good choices.

People Respond to Incentives

People respond to *incentives* when making choices. **Incentives** are positive rewards for making some kind of choice or behaving in a certain way. An incentive might be higher wages, lower prices, praise, or a good grade. If a reward is increased, more people are likely to behave in a desired way. If you were promised $100 for receiving an A grade in this course, would you consider this an incentive to study hard?

If a reward is withdrawn or becomes negative, fewer people will pursue a choice or engage in a certain behavior. A negative or withdrawn reward is called a disincentive. **Disincentives** often relate to such things as fines or punishment. Economists can predict how people will respond to incentives and disincentives because they know people try to minimize costs and maximize benefits.

People Gain When They Trade Voluntarily

Trade is exchanging something for something else. Buying and selling goods and services constitute trade. In the U.S. economy, nobody has to trade. Yet, all people trade. When people trade, they believe that they gain. They are better off. Voluntary trade is a foundation of a market economy. If you trade your tuna sandwich for a ham and cheese sandwich with your friend at lunch, you think you are better off as a result of the trade. So does your friend, or the two of you wouldn't trade. If you buy a CD or a soft drink, you exchange or trade your money for these products. You would not buy the products if you did not think you would gain something.

12. benefits   13. costs   14. incentives   15. disincentives   16. trade

Show Your Understanding

As you read each key idea, write one example of a way that the idea operates in your life. Use the lines below and on the next page for your answers. Make sure your examples are different from those in the text.

iStockphoto '07

Choices Are Future Oriented

You cannot choose to change a choice made in the past. Many people have bought a product they found out they did not like, such as a piece of clothing or an appliance. People make choices based on an assessment of what they think is right for them in the future. People operate with limited information about the future and are likely to make mistakes about future choices. How do you know your new DVD player will continue to work? What do you know about the quality of a used car that you are thinking about buying? You must make the best choice based on the information you have.

Our Choices Are Influenced by the Choices of Others

We live in a very large social system, and we are dependent on one another. Others' choices affect us. For example, the actions of foreign oil producers to hold back on the production of oil cause a rise in gasoline prices. The action of the banking system to increase interest rates will cause mortgage rates to increase and result in higher mortgage payments.

Applying the Economic Way of Thinking

The key ideas above are the foundation for the economic way of thinking. All economic study involves choices, but economic choices do not necessarily involve money. For example, you may make the choice to give your time to clean up a park or to take care of a sick friend. You've made an economic choice, but it doesn't require you to pay or receive money.

The economic way of thinking helps us look for clues to answer all kinds of puzzling economic questions. Here are a few. *Why are farmlands turned into housing projects? Why don't cities build high-speed rail systems to cut down on huge traffic jams? Why do people continue to buy gasoline when the price per gallon keeps increasing? Why won't teenagers babysit for $2 per hour? Why don't students keep the school lunchroom clean? Why don't all students always try their best in their school courses?*

iStockphoto '07

Even getting ready in the morning can require trade-offs.

What Are They Thinking?

Select one of the puzzling questions above, and use the economic way of thinking to help you answer the question. Use the economic terms from the seven key ideas above in your explanation.

Question: _____

_____

Explanation:_____

_____

_____

_____

_____

_____

_____

_____

_____

iStockphoto '0

Why don't cities build high-speed rail systems to cut down on huge traffic jams?

Thinking at the Margin

Because resources are scarce and because we must make careful choices about how to use our resources, economists have developed special ways to analyze and discuss choices. As you have learned, every choice involves benefits and costs. Economists, however, focus on *marginal* benefits and marginal costs. **Marginal** simply means the extra or additional costs or benefits of a decision.

For example, you may style your hair each morning. How long you spend combing or brushing depends on the marginal (additional) benefit you get. A look in the mirror tells you it may be awhile before your hair looks just right. The benefit of spending a few additional minutes exceeds the additional cost of your time, so you continue styling.

Soon, however, your hair begins looking the way you want it to look. So the benefit of spending additional time on your hair decreases. Meanwhile, if you're running out of time for breakfast and you don't want to be late for school, your marginal cost of spending additional time in front of the mirror goes up.

As long as you think the marginal benefit is greater than the marginal cost, you keep styling your hair. But at some point, the additional benefit is no longer worth the extra time cost. In essence, you aren't making an all-or-nothing choice: to style or not to style. Instead, you decide how much time to spend combing and brushing and how much time to spend on something else. *You are thinking at the margin.*

Other choices are similar. If you have a car, for example, your decision about buying gasoline is not between buying a full tank or no gas at all. Instead, you decide how much additional money to spend on gasoline versus additional spending on something else. You are using marginal thinking based on the marginal benefits and marginal costs you expect.

Check Your Understanding

Underline and number two examples in the text of people thinking at the margin. Explain why the examples demonstrate marginal thinking.

1. _____
_____
_____
_____

2. _____
_____
_____
_____

What Am I Thinking?

Think of a choice that you currently have, or will have in the near future, that does not involve the immediate exchange of money. It might involve use of your time, knowledge, or skills.

Describe the choice alternatives. _____
_____
_____

Describe the costs and benefits of each alternative.

Alternative _____ Costs _____ Benefits _____
Alternative _____ Costs _____ Benefits _____
Alternative _____ Costs _____ Benefits _____

What choice do you expect to make? _____

Describe the marginal costs and benefits that help you make your choice. _____
_____
_____

17. marginal

Information and Uncertainty

Making choices isn't easy, because information about the costs and benefits of a choice is scarce. When we shop for cars, for example, we want information about what's available. But shopping, too, has opportunity costs because it requires spending time and money. So we shop as long as we think acquiring more information is worthwhile or, in economic terms, as long as our marginal benefit exceeds our marginal cost. Still, information is scarce; we seldom collect all that is available when making a choice. As a result, we may not be fully aware of the benefits or opportunity costs of our decisions.

Furthermore, choices made today can have costs and benefits tomorrow, yet the future is uncertain. You might decide to go to a party but have a terrible time and wish you had never gone.

Despite the scarcity and cost of information and the uncertainty of the future, we must make choices. When doing so, we usually try to make the choices we think are best. This doesn't mean that we behave like human computers, constantly calculating and rationally weighing every possible cost and benefit. It means only that we try, with scarce information and uncertainty, to make decisions we think will make us better off. Economic thinking is a rational way of looking at these choices. By using ideas such as marginal cost and marginal benefit, we can better understand the causes and consequences of the many choices people make in a world full of scarcity.

Does this cartoon illustrate someone weighing marginal costs and marginal benefits to make a sensible shopping choice? Why or why not?

Calvin and Hobbes ©1995 Watterson. Dist. by Universal Press Syndicate. Reprinted with permission. All rights reserved.

Choice Making by Businesses

Thus far in this chapter our focus has been on individual choice making. Businesses face the same scarcity problem as do individuals. Businesses must pay for scarce resources, and businesspeople look for their best alternatives in deciding which resources to buy and how much to pay for them. A business must have a place to do business—an office or a manufacturing plant. A business either owns or pays rent for its space. A business must pay its labor force wages or salaries. A business uses tools and machines, such as trucks and computers, all of which must be purchased. These payments are costs to a business, and good businesspeople look for the lowest opportunity costs when making decisions about where they do business, who they hire, and how they conduct their business.

Because resources are limited, conservation can be important. In this photo, a park ranger is planting a small tree. By practicing conservation, societies can produce more goods and services to satisfy people's wants.

The Profit Motive

A major goal of a business is to make a *profit*—an incentive. To make a profit, the business must sell its product or service. A business wants its sales to exceed its costs. For any business, **profit** is a positive difference between total sales and total costs, meaning that total sales must be greater than total costs (Profit = Total Sales > Total Costs). If the business does not make a profit over time, it will no longer be able to operate. The profit goal causes a business to try to pay the lowest possible prices for the resources it uses and to sell its product(s) at the highest possible prices.

Businesspeople think at the margin. Consider a retail auto parts store. Its managers need to decide how many parts to keep in stock. Retail auto parts store managers know they need to have 16,000 parts in stock to serve their customers. An inventory of 12,000 parts would not be enough to serve their customers. In this case, the marginal benefit of adding an additional 4,000 parts exceeds the marginal cost of putting the parts in stock. Once the number of parts grows to 16,000, however, the additional (marginal) benefit of adding more parts is no longer worth the marginal cost. The store managers then stop adding to the store's stock of parts, just as you decide when to stop styling your hair. In both cases, the choices made are based on marginal benefits and marginal costs.

Basic Economic Decisions in a Market Economy

In the United States we have a market economy, which is also called capitalism or free enterprise. A **market economy** is an economy that relies on voluntary trade as the primary means of organizing and coordinating production. Every day in our country millions of people, including you, members of your family, and friends, make individual choices about using scarce resources. These choices are most often made in *markets*. A **market** is an arrangement that allows buyers and sellers to make exchanges. Individuals weigh the costs and benefits of their choices as consumers. Business owners or managers also must consider the costs and benefits of their decisions to produce and sell goods and services. Similarly, national, state, and local governments must weigh costs and benefits of taxing and providing services.

Thinking Critically

Individuals think at the margin when making personal choices. Business leaders also think at the margin in making business choices. However, business leaders have one consideration when making their choices that individuals do not. What is it?

_____

18. profit   19. market economy   20. market

Taken together, consumers, businesses, and government form our economic system. All three groups in our economy engage in the choice making that is the fundamental aspect of any economic system. We can't possibly identify each of these decisions, but we can put them into three categories. Economists call them the *what, how,* and *for whom* decisions.

What Goods and Services to Produce? Consumers actually help choose the kinds and quantities of goods and services to produce. These consumer choices are made in markets, in which goods and services are bought and sold. Sales in markets send signals to businesses. Businesses use these signals, called sales information, to increase or decrease quantities produced. Producing more of one kind of product leaves fewer resources for producing other products. There are always opportunity costs that producers have to consider when deciding what to produce.

How Should Goods and Services Be Produced? There is more than one way to build a home or a school, to manufacture an automobile, to farm the land, or to provide medical care. Will the school and home be built of brick or wood? Will the automobile plant use flexible work teams or a traditional assembly line? Will farmers use the latest equipment, or will they use older machinery and more workers instead? Will medical care be provided by an individual doctor or a team of doctors? Producers decide how a good will be made or a service delivered.

For Whom Will Goods and Services Be Produced? Since there can't be enough production to satisfy everybody's wants, the goods and services that are produced must be distributed among people who want more than they can possibly have. For example, there aren't enough DVD players to go around for everyone who wants one. So who gets the players that are produced? It probably won't surprise you that those people who have higher incomes are able to buy more goods and services.

The assembly line represents one method of production.

An economy organizes and coordinates all these choices. But the economy is not something apart from the people who participate in it. In our nation, we are the economy. Our individual choices as consumers, savers, workers, and producers determine what is produced, how things are produced, and for whom they are produced. In every country, the way people answer these questions describes the type of economic system they have. In the United States, we rely on markets, or our market economy. Market economies are built on a set of important ideas and principles, often called the "pillars of free enterprise," which you will study in the next chapter.

Consumers determine the kinds and quantities of goods that are produced. Farmers try to meet consumer demands.

What's an Entrepreneur to Do?

An entrepreneur, Maria, is starting a new business of selling fresh fruit drinks in the high school cafeteria. She is considering two business plans for the drinks she will produce, how she will produce the drinks, and for whom she will produce her products. Consider each option described below, then decide which option you think Maria should choose and why.

Option 1 *Produce made-to-order fruit drinks, in which each customer chooses the fruit and flavorings. Made-to-order drinks will require two employees and two drink-blending machines during all the hours the drink stand is open. A variety of fruit will have to be purchased daily. The price of each drink will be $3.00, but customers can have exactly the drink they wish.*

Option 2 *Produce two or three drinks that are made fresh each morning in large quantities. One employee will be able to make the drinks with one blending machine and then sell them. A limited amount of fruit and flavorings will be purchased daily. Each drink will be priced at $1.50 and can be served quickly.*

Which option should Maria choose? _____

Why? _____

_____

Two Branches of Economics: Macroeconomics and Microeconomics

At the beginning of this chapter, you learned that economics is a social science that studies how people, acting individually and in groups, decide to use scarce resources to satisfy their wants. The study of economics is divided into two major branches—*macroeconomics* and *microeconomics*. **Macroeconomics** is the study of the economy as a whole; **microeconomics** is the study of individual consumers and businesses.

Macroeconomics examines questions that lead to an understanding of "the big picture." How fast is the level of production in the nation changing? How fast are prices rising? How many people are unemployed? How has the nation's total income changed? Macroeconomics also seeks to understand economy-wide issues, such as inflation, unemployment, poverty, and long-term economic growth.

Microeconomics examines the choices that individuals, families, and businesses make. What price is an individual willing to pay for a concert ticket? Should we take a family vacation? What wages should we pay our employees? Should we invest in new computers? How will our customers like our new advertising campaign?

Check Your Understanding

Micro and *macro* are prefixes that have opposite meanings. Write the correct prefix for each definition below.

Large, enlarged

_____

Little, small

_____

People just like you have a direct impact on the economy through the choices they make to satisfy their wants.

Summary

Economics is a study of people in their ordinary business of life. Humans have wants, many of which occur over and over again. The process of want-satisfaction—production, distribution, and consumption—helps people satisfy their wants. In the process of satisfying wants, four factors of production are used. These factors are land, labor, capital, and entrepreneurship.

Wants generally exceed available resources, which results in a condition called scarcity. Scarcity demands that people make choices. Opportunity cost, the result of scarcity, is the highest valued alternative given up when a choice is made. The economic way of thinking is a tool of analysis that examines the choice-making process. Of particular interest in the economic way of thinking is the role of incentives and how they affect people's behavior.

Thinking at the margin—thinking about additional costs or benefits—influences individuals' decisions about how they allocate their time and how they earn and spend their money. Businesses, which have a goal of making a profit, also face choices about how to operate, as well as the need to think at the margin.

Taken together, consumers, businesses, and government form an economic system. Any economic system must confront three basic decisions: what to produce, how to produce, and for whom to produce.

Finally, economics is divided into two areas of study—macroeconomics, the study of the economy as a whole, and microeconomics, the study of individuals and businesses operating in the economy.

Looking Ahead

In Chapter 2, "Free Enterprise in the United States," you will see how Americans have used the "pillars of free enterprise" to create their economic system.

FREE ENTERPRISE IN THE UNITED STATES

Read to Find Out
As you read this chapter, look for answers to the following questions:

Why are private property, specialization, voluntary exchange, the price system, market competition, and entrepreneurship considered the pillars of free enterprise?

How does the Circular Flow of Money, Resources, and Products model describe a free enterprise economy?

What activities in the economy contribute to economic growth?

What is money, and what are its three major functions?

What are the goals of the U.S. economic system?

Mark to Remember

* *This is important.*

? *I have a question about this.*

! *This is a surprise.*

Why It Matters

Each day you receive the benefits of living in an economy where more than 300 million people cooperate to help one another get the clothes we wear, the food we eat, the music we hear, and a host of other goods and services. In this chapter, you will learn why it is important for every citizen living in a free enterprise economy like ours to understand how the economy works so that he or she can contribute to the economy for both personal gain and societal benefit. As an American citizen, you are free to make many economic choices; the better you understand our economic system, the better choices you will make.

FREE ENTERPRISE IN THE UNITED STATES

Building On What You Know

Have you thought about what job you'd like to have when you are an adult? In our country, you have the right to pursue whatever job you want. You may need to get a college education or special training to qualify for the job. You may have to earn or borrow money to get the training you need, but no private citizen or government official can tell you that you can't pursue the job of your choice. That freedom of choice comes from our American economic system.

Our economy in the United States is called a *free enterprise* system. **Free enterprise** means that people in their economic roles are free to make choices. Let's look at some evidence of free enterprise at work. You probably have observed that businesses and their employees supply you with electricity, gasoline, TV programs, and laundry or dry-cleaning services. Stores stock their shelves with DVDs, clothes, and many other things you want. Hamburger and pizza restaurants satisfy your food cravings. Think of the millions of choices people in the United States make each day in their roles as consumers, savers, investors, workers, business owners, and government officials. These people are not told what choices to make. They make the economic choices they believe offer them the most benefits.

The Pillars of Free Enterprise

In a building, a pillar is a vertical column that provides strength and support for the entire building. The term is also appropriate to use in describing our free enterprise system. Just as pillars support a building, the laws of a country and the values of its people must support free enterprise if it is to work as an economic system. A free enterprise system functions best when it is supported by six social and legal pillars:

- Private property
- Specialization
- Voluntary exchange
- The price system
- Market competition
- Entrepreneurship

Let's examine each pillar.

Private Property

Private property is the resources and products owned by individuals or businesses. **Public property** refers to the resources and products owned by government. Although the term *property* is often used to describe land, in economics the term also includes buildings, machines, tools, natural resources, and even clothing, appliances, and musical instruments.

The right to own property is protected by the United States Constitution, and the right to decide how private property is used has always been an important part of our American economic system. Do you own a bicycle, a car, or a DVD player? You decide how to use and care for such items. You can lend them to friends, sell them, or give them away. The right to private property allows you to choose the property you buy, but it also makes you responsible for the care of the property. If you don't take care of your car, for instance, you bear the costs of repairs that might have been avoidable. Consequently, the right to own and control private property gives owners a reason to use their property as efficiently as possible.

Businesses, as well as individual citizens, try to use their property efficiently. In the United States, citizens can own property for business purposes and use it to produce income. Privately owned companies, both U.S.-owned and foreign-owned, produce nearly 90 percent of the goods and services available each year in the United States. Just as you want to take care of the things you own, businesses have an incentive, an expected benefit or reward, to maintain their machines and equipment, factories, and shops; to use them wisely to reduce waste; and to make products people are willing to purchase.

iStockphoto '07

Some economists believe the right to private property is the most important pillar of free enterprise. For example, Tom Bethell, author of *The Noblest Triumph: Property and Prosperity Through the Ages,* wrote in 1998, "Without property there can be no prosperity, no peace, and no freedom." [1]

Specialization

Specialization is a process in which businesses and people focus on producing one or a few parts of an entire product. For example, The Gap confines itself to selling clothes, as opposed to selling iPods, televisions, or automobiles. In making this decision, The Gap managers must continually assess the costs of using resources to sell clothes rather than some other good, such as coffee. Starbucks is a good example of a business continually looking for new opportunity. The company started by specializing in coffee products. Now it has included the Starbucks Digital Network and Wi-Fi Service popular music.

Individuals in business also specialize. Some people serve as administrators, some sew clothes, others create advertisements for products, and still others clean the premises when the normal workday is done. Specialized machines are also used in the process. Sewing machines are used to make clothes, scrubbers are used for cleaning floors, trucks transport materials, and computers store information. Specialization allows a business to increase the amount it produces and sells. Generally, specialization contributes to higher wages and profits.

1. Tom Bethell. *The Noblest Triumph: Property and Prosperity Through the Ages.* (New York: St. Martin's Press, 1998).
2. private property   3. public property   4. specialization

Specialization in Schools and Communities

 On the lines below, identify a job in your school and a job in your community that are specialized. Explain why they are specialized jobs.

School

_____

Community

_____

Why? _____

Why? _____

_____

_____

Voluntary Exchange

Specialization leads to voluntary exchange. People must buy and sell products to acquire all the things they want from the economy because they do not have the time and resources to produce everything themselves. Consider an item as simple as a pencil. A pencil cannot be produced by one person. Foresters must grow trees and harvest them to produce the wood for a pencil. Sawmill operators must create the right size wood piece. Other factory workers must produce the glue, the graphite, and the eraser. Assemblers must put together the wood, graphite, and eraser. Finally, truckers must transport these items to a store where the store owner willingly allows you to trade your money for the product. In our economy, everyone is dependent on many other people to voluntarily produce and exchange products. Otherwise, we would have to go without many of the useful and expected products and services that are part of our modern lifestyle.

iStockphoto '07

The Price System

Closely related to private property rights is the *price system*. The **price system** uses monetary prices as a message system to facilitate exchanges between buyers and sellers. As people exchange with one another, they negotiate to establish prices for goods, services, and resources. This is why economists often refer to a market economy as a price system. When buyers and sellers make exchanges, they look to prices for guidance on the perceived value of the product or service. First, prices act as messengers. Prices communicate to businesses how willing customers are to purchase the product. At the same time, the prices of resources tell business owners which resources will be least expensive for them to use in producing their product. Of course, product and resource quality is also of concern to consumers and producers. However, prices are the main messengers in a market economy.

Show Your Understanding

Underline in the text the sentences that describe the two functions of prices in the price system.

5. price system

Second, prices provide strong incentives to businesses and consumers. Increasing prices for a product such as gasoline encourages businesses to increase production of that product. Interestingly, higher prices influence consumers like you to shop for bargains or to reduce your purchases of an item. Falling prices have the opposite effect. Have you ever bought more of an item when it went on sale? Have you resisted buying an item until it went on sale at a price you thought was attractive? These are two examples of how falling prices affect consumer choices.

In determining prices, business owners always have to consider their profit. The prices they set will affect their profit. Recall that profit is a positive difference between total sales and total costs. Firms that make a profit are encouraged to remain in business and produce their products. Firms that cannot make a profit must eventually stop producing or switch to producing a product that does create a profit.

In calculating a profit, the business owner subtracts total costs from total sales (or total revenue). If there is a positive difference, there is a profit. Many business owners like to find out their percentage of profit. To calculate this percentage, the amount of profit is divided by total sales (or revenue). For example, if a business has $1,000 in profit and its total sales (or revenue) are $10,000, the percentage of profit is 10 percent. If the percentage of profit is zero, or a negative percentage, the business owner will need to reconsider his or her product's price and market worthiness.

Prices cannot explain all economic behavior, of course. People have values they act on apart from the price system. A worker may pass up a chance to earn more money because he or she does not want to move to another city. Business firms often contribute money to charitable causes, which may reduce their profits, but improve the quality of life in the community. Some parents give up job opportunities to stay at home while raising their children. For many reasons other than price, consumers may prefer to shop at one store rather than another. Convenience, service, loyalty, and product selection are all factors that consumers consider in their buying choices.

Applying Your Understanding

Ajax Music Company had $1 million in total revenue last year. The company's total costs were $942,802. What was the amount of Ajax's profit?

_____

What was Ajax's profit as a percentage of total revenue?

_____

What's Most Important to Me?

What product are you thinking about buying? _____
Here are five criteria you might use to make a decision about buying the product: price, product quality, product attractiveness, product desirability, and the product's current popularity.

Arrange the criteria from 1 (most important to me) to 5 (least important to me) to show how you will think about your decision.

1. _____ 2. _____ 3. _____

4. _____ 5. _____

Why did you rank number 1 highest? _____

Why did you rank number 5 lowest? _____

Buyers make choices based on the relationship between the cost and perceived value of the product.

19

Pause to Predict

What does the word ***competition*** *mean to you?*

_____

_____

Read to find out what ***competition*** *means in a market economy.*

Think Critically

A trash collector works physically harder than a typical school teacher. Why do most teachers make more money than most trash collectors?

_____

_____

_____

Market Competition

In a free enterprise system, people everywhere compete for resources and products because they are scarce—the want for resources and products exceeds the supply. For example, businesses compete for customers by adjusting their prices or the quality of goods and services they sell. They also compete to buy the lowest cost resources possible. Competition among businesses is called **market competition**. Market competition takes two basic forms: competition in resource markets and competition in product markets.

Competition in Resource Markets. Resources are the land, labor, and capital that businesses use to produce goods and services. Businesses compete against one another in markets for productive resources when they offer money for the resources they need– resources such as skilled workers, oil deposits, and complex machinery. Sellers of resources compete against other sellers by trying to make their resources more productive. You are a potential resource. By getting a good education and developing your talents and skills, for example, you can make your labor resource more desirable, therefore more productive. Not only will you compete more effectively against other workers (sellers of labor), but businesses (buyers of labor) will compete more intensely to employ you. As a result, you are more likely to get a better job and earn a higher wage.

Competition in Markets for Products. Product markets include all the goods and services consumers buy, from running shoes to haircuts. When you spend your earnings, you are competing with other buyers in product markets. Buyers compete with buyers. If you choose to rent an apartment, you will have to pay as much or more than other potential renters, otherwise they will get the apartment. Consider a future decision you may make— someday you may wish to buy a house. Who will you be competing with if you attempt to purchase a house? You will compete with all the other potential buyers of the house. You may want to buy concert tickets in the future. As with the house, you will be competing with other potential buyers of the tickets.

Buyers aren't the only people competing in product markets. Sellers compete with sellers. Sellers compete against other sellers by trying to offer the goods and services at prices buyers are willing to pay. Sellers who cannot compete will fail to make a profit and will go out of business. Those who succeed earn a profit that encourages them to stay in business and perhaps expand the number of products they sell.

Earning a profit isn't easy. Producers continually introduce new products and start new businesses without any guarantee that consumers will buy what they offer. Producers also must constantly try to keep their costs and prices down. They must give people the goods and services they want, when and where they want them. For example, pizza restaurants have been in the delivery business for many years, but Domino's revolutionized the trade by specializing in home delivery and fast service. Many companies have followed Domino's example. Producers know that if they don't satisfy consumer demand, their competitors will. Producers compete against one another to make products more efficiently, conserve scarce resources, increase the number of products they make, and reduce costs and prices. In this way, a free enterprise economy uses market competition to encourage rivalry among consumers and businesses. Rivalry often increases production, productivity, employment, and incomes.

Competing in a Competitive Market

Carmen plans to open a pizza shop in her neighborhood. There are two other pizza outlets within a five-block area, and Carmen has done research to learn that both outlets deliver, have similar pizza toppings and have similar prices. What can Carmen do to overcome the competition when she opens her business? Give Carmen three ideas.

_____

_____

_____

Entrepreneurship

Entrepreneurship is the motivation that drives business leaders to compete and react to changing conditions in the market. As you learned, entrepreneurship is the imagination, innovative thinking, and management skills needed to start and operate a business. Entrepreneurs see opportunities and act on them to introduce new or better goods and services to the market. They develop new ideas and technologies. Entrepreneurs take risks by investing their time and money in innovative ideas and products, knowing they may fail in the market. Entrepreneurs try new methods of management and organization in the hope that they will be able to use scarce resources more efficiently than their competitors.

Through incentives provided in markets, free enterprise encourages and nurtures entrepreneurship. Entrepreneurs have creative, new ideas that they want to sell. They believe in the incentive to make a profit. They want to feel free to make choices to participate in a market. In short, entrepreneurs provide energy and imagination that help our economic system grow and change.

As a mostly free market, the United States economy operates with limited government involvement. Citizens are allowed to own private property and to make most or all of the decisions about what goods and services to produce. Under these conditions, entrepreneurs flourish. The six "pillars"—private property, specialization, voluntary exchange, the price system, market competition, and entrepreneurship—are essential to the success of a market economy. Now let's take a look at a model that will help you understand how resources become goods and services and how money functions to facilitate exchange.

iStockphoto '07

Entrepreneurship captures the imagination, innovative thinking, and management skills needed to start and operate a business.

Think Critically

If you were an entrepreneur, would you prefer to live in a command, traditional, or mixed economy?

_____

Why? _____

_____

_____

Read the feature on the following page to help you answer the question.

Other Economic Systems

 This chapter discusses the free enterprise or market system. This does not mean that there is no government involvement in the U.S. economy, but government involvement is much less than in many countries. In this respect, the U.S. economy is considered a mixed economy. Economists also recognize *command* and *traditional* systems as types of economies.

Command System

In a **command economy**, the government holds most property rights. This type of system is called "command" because the government issues commands to make the what, how, and for whom choices. Until recently, Russia and other Eastern European nations had command economies. In these nations, governments owned and managed most natural and capital resources. Government officials, aided by economists, engineers, and technicians, prepared detailed plans describing how the economy should function.

Essentially, the planners determined what goods and services to produce. If, for example, they decided to increase grain production, they might issue orders to produce more tractors or import more fertilizer. Similarly, the planners might encourage workers to remain on farms by raising wages or issuing orders.

Today, Russia and other nations are struggling to develop new economic systems emphasizing markets and private ownership of resources. China, another once strictly command economy, has also introduced private ownership and allowed markets to grow.

Traditional System

Another type of economic system is a **traditional economy**. As the name implies, people in traditional economies rely on traditions or customs to make the what, how, and for whom choices. Here, long-established customs—not legally recognized and enforced private property rights or government policies—determine what occupations are available, how property is held, and what goods and services are produced.

Traditional economic systems are less common today than in the past. Typically, they are found in remote, rural areas in which people are engaged in agriculture or activities such as fishing or hunting. The goods and services produced in traditional economies meet the needs of the community.

Mixed Systems

Traditional, command, and market economies are different ways of organizing and coordinating people to make the what, how, and for whom choices. In recent years, however, there has been renewed interest in promoting and strengthening market economies throughout the world. Indeed, the world economy is largely a market or free enterprise economy in which people voluntarily exchange with one another.

Still, there are no pure market economies anywhere in the world today. Even in the United States, while markets make most economic decisions, government plays an important role. This blend of voluntary exchange, government command, and even traditional elements has led some economists to describe the U.S. economic system and those of most other democratic countries as **mixed economies**. These economies may emphasize private ownership and voluntary exchange, but they allow the government to play an important role in the economic lives of its citizens.

7. command economy   8. traditional economy   9. mixed economies

Models

Like other social scientists, economists use models. Models represent the real world. Models simplify our complex world and help us understand it. You are already familiar with models. A model airplane shows the basic features of a plane, but it certainly is not the plane itself. A child's doll is a model that shows parts of the human body, but it is not a real body. A map is a model that can help us get from one place to another. A map only represents a land area; it is not the land area itself.

A model can be made to scale, like an airplane, which means the model's size is some fraction of the size of the object that it represents. A model can be a drawing or a diagram that show how something works. A model can be a flowchart, that shows a sequence of events. A model is sometimes a series of numbers or equations that quantify real-world things and show them in number form. A line graph is a model that shows relationships between two sets of numbers that represent real-world phenomena.

Three kinds of models are common in economics—descriptive models, predictive models, and ideal models. The want-satisfaction chain in Chapter 1 is a descriptive model, with a flow chart that shows how wants are satisfied through the processes of production, distribution, and consumption. In this chapter, another descriptive model is discussed. This model is a diagram.

Figure 2-1: THE CIRCULAR FLOW OF MONEY, RESOURCES, AND PRODUCTS

The descriptive model, The Circular Flow of Money, Resources, and Products, shown below, is a simple diagram. It represents economic activity that happens and that you can see every day. The diagram shows in simple picture form how individuals in households and businesses exchange money, resources, and products in markets. Look carefully at the model. The outside part of the model, with arrows pointing in a counterclockwise direction, shows the flow of resources and goods and services in a circular fashion. The inside part of the model, with arrows pointing in a clockwise direction, shows the flow of money in the economy, also in a circular fashion.

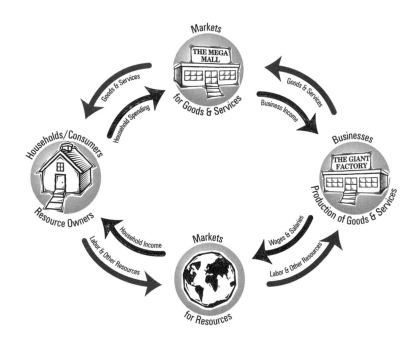

Check Your Understanding

How does the model to the left help you understand the concept of circular flow?

_____

_____

What do the counter-clockwise arrows show?

_____

_____

What do the clockwise arrows show?

_____

_____

Households is the word economists use to describe people living in the United States, regardless of the type of house or apartment they may live in. Households play two important roles in the economy. Members of households are consumers because they buy and use the goods and services that businesses produce. Households are also resource owners. The most obvious resource they own is their labor. They also own other productive resources, such as land and capital.

As consumers, members of households participate in goods and services markets when they buy food, shoes, watches, and countless other products. But where do household members get the money to buy the products they want? They exchange their labor (or other resources) in resource markets for income to spend in the goods and services markets.

Combining the different elements of the economy into the model shows how production and exchange are tightly linked in a free enterprise economy. Households provide labor and other resources to businesses and buy the goods and services businesses produce. Businesses produce goods and services for households and pay the wages and salaries that households use to buy goods and services. The Circular Flow is an illustration of how people in the economy depend on one another.

iStockphoto '07

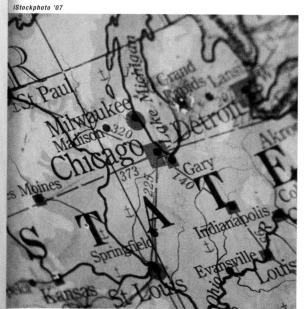

A map is a type of model.

The Circular Flow as a Descriptive Model

The Circular Flow is a descriptive model. Like a simple map, the model uses a few basic images to represent the entire economy. The model leaves out many important details. Just as you would leave out many streets and other features of your neighborhood when drawing a simple map to your home, this model does not include all the goods and services that businesses produce. The model does not show that consumers earn money by selling capital resources and natural resources as well as their labor. Also missing are consumer savings and business investments in new equipment and other capital goods.

Government is an important part of our economy, too. Many people, like public school teachers, work for government agencies, and the government provides many services to its citizens. Further, households pay taxes to the government, and government pays wages and salaries to its employees. Similar flows of money and economic resources move between government and businesses. Goods and services—everything from tanks to paper clips to medical care—flow from businesses to government. Businesses use services such as highways, airports, police protection, and scientific research provided by government. Government pays for purchases from businesses, and businesses pay taxes to government. How the government enters the Circular Flow is described in detail in Chapter 12.

Adding other important elements, such as government, would make the model more realistic—and more difficult to follow. However, if you understand the diagram in this chapter, you can add other elements later to make it more complete.

How Well Do You Understand Models?

Read the following statements and decide whether each is true (T) or false (F).

1. The want-satisfaction chain in Chapter 1 is a model showing how human wants are satisfied. _____

2. The Circular Flow Diagram is a model of a free enterprise economy. _____

3. Both models described in questions 1 and 2 are predictive models. _____

4. Both models described in questions 1 and 2 provide the reader with a complete, comprehensive, detailed description of economic behavior. _____

Making the Flow Grow

Increased production, employment, and income are signs of economic growth. Not only does the circular flow move faster when our economy grows, but the kinds of goods and services flowing around it change, too. Flat-screen TVs, microwave ovens, home computers, and DVDs—and many other products we often take for granted today—were not available a few years ago. Products go away, often because people no longer want them. Record players and manual typewriters are two examples.

Even the demand for resources changes over time. People used to think sand was a nuisance and that it had no practical use as a resource. Today the silicon in sand is made into integrated circuits, solar cells, and transistors. Sand has become a valuable resource. Even the way people make payments has changed. Online banking and "e-billing" have become very popular. Some experts predict that actual money, in the form of coins and paper bills, will become obsolete in the not too distant future.

The Circular Flow model helps us understand the flow of resources into businesses. Businesses produce a flow of goods and services. Households use their incomes from the sale of their resources to purchase goods and services. Incomes and consumer purchases represent the flow of money in the economy. Now we will examine money in the Circular Flow more carefully.

iStockphoto '07

Money in the form of coins and paper bills may someday be replaced by online banking and e-billing.

Think Critically

Do you think a world without coins or paper bills would make our lives easier or more difficult?

_____

_____

Why? _____

_____

Money and the Circular Flow

The Circular Flow model of the free enterprise system of the United States illustrates how voluntary exchange works. However, for voluntary exchange to operate smoothly, households and businesses must be able to make exchanges easily. *Money*, more than any other factor, makes exchange easy. Although we usually think of coins and paper bills as money, in economics **money** is anything that is generally accepted as payment for goods and services. For example, in some parts of the small Pacific island country of Palau, money in the form of beads and shells is generally accepted in exchange for goods and services.

Why is money so important to voluntary exchange? Picture yourself accepting a part-time job at a fast-food restaurant. You and the manager agree to an exchange. You will provide labor at the restaurant, and the manager will give you money in return. Imagine how different this story would be if there were no such thing as money. How would the manager pay you? Suppose you were offered hamburgers as your salary. In this case, you probably wouldn't take the job. After all, you can eat only so many hamburgers, and the rest soon would be cold and stale. Besides, by working at the restaurant, you hope to earn money for new clothes or save for your education. But you aren't likely to find a clothing store that will accept cold, stale hamburgers in exchange for a new pair of jeans. And imagine trying to save hamburgers to pay for your education in a year or two.

Trading goods and services without money is called *barter*. **Barter** is an exchange of goods and services without using money. Barter requires each person to want what the other is offering. Barter would make it impossible for you to get a job in the fast-food restaurant because the manager may want your labor, but you don't want to be paid with the product the manager produces. In other words, you don't want to be paid in hamburgers. Before money was invented, barter was common, but the invention of money made it easier for people to exchange. Today, money has three important functions: (1) a medium of exchange, (2) a store of value, and (3) a measure of value.

Apply Your Understanding

Think of an example of barter in which you were a participant.

What was the barter?

_____

_____

Was the barter satisfactory to both or all participants?

_____

Why or why not?

_____

_____

_____

iStockphoto '07

10. money   11. barter

Medium of Exchange

Instead of exchanging your labor for hamburgers, you can trade it for money. The money is like a coupon indicating that you are owed a specific portion of the goods and services offered in this economy. Then, because businesses and others accept money in return for most goods and services, you can use it to buy what you want. When people agree on the value of money, it becomes a medium, a means of exchange. Exchanging labor for goods and services is much easier when the value of the labor is identified in money terms and the cost of goods and services is also identified in money terms.

Store of Value

Money is an important store of value, which means that you can hold on to it to use sometime in the future. By receiving payment in dollars instead of hamburgers, you can put the money in your pocket or in a bank and save its buying power for future use. It will not lose its value when it becomes cold and stale like an old hamburger.

Measure of Value

Money also indicates the relative value of products and resources. In a barter system, a product has as many different prices as there are other products that can be exchanged for it. For example, the price of a basketball is so many apples, shirts, CDs, oil changes, hamburgers, or any other good or service people could offer in exchange. Without money, then, how would a manager know the value of your labor? How would you know the value of a new basketball? When money is used in exchange, each product or resource has a single money price. People can compare money prices to find the best value for what they are selling or buying. Again, money makes exchange easier, because it allows you to compare values of goods, services, and resources.

Money is the oil in the engine of free enterprise. It makes voluntary exchange efficient, and it reduces the potential for disagreement among buyers and sellers. Without money, a free enterprise system could not work.

Think Critically

When the price of two similar goods, such as two shirts, is the same, what other considerations affect your decision to buy one rather than the other?

_____

_____

_____

What Function Is Money Serving?

Read each statement and identify which of the following functions of money it describes:

    A medium of exchange
    A store of value
    A measure of value

1. The price of a DVD has been reduced to $9.99. _____

2. Your bank savings account statement shows that you have $156.00 in the account. _____

3. You pay $3.99 for a tuna sandwich. _____

4. You have $6.75 in your sock drawer. _____

5. The house next door is listed for sale at $177,500. _____

6. You pay $6.50 to see a movie. _____

Adam Smith

Where would you look to get a glimpse of our economy? Is it under your bed, in your closet, or in your refrigerator? It's in all these places and many more. All the voluntary exchanges we make as consumers, workers, business owners, savers, and government officials are the economy. The economy is everywhere.

Of course, no one invented such an economy. It evolved as people traded with one another. As exchange economies developed, people became curious about how they worked. One of those people was Adam Smith.

A Keen Eye Develops

Born in Scotland in 1723, Smith went to the University of Glasgow when he was 14 years old. That may seem young today, but it was common to go to a university early in those days. After graduating when he was 17, Smith went to England to attend Oxford University, where he studied mostly on his own for the next six years. It was during these years that Smith began to develop his ideas about economics.

Adam Smith probably never used the word *economics* because, although he didn't realize it, he was creating the study. Indeed, when he began teaching at the University of Glasgow, he was a professor of moral philosophy, not economics. For years Smith read, observed, traveled, and worked on the ideas he first developed at Oxford. The conclusion of 30 years of research was a new subject and a book that has influenced people for more than 200 years.

The Wealth of Nations

The new subject, of course, was economics, and the book was *An Inquiry into the Nature and Causes of the Wealth of Nations*. Published in 1776, the same year as the Declaration of Independence in the United States, the book challenged the established thinking of Smith's day. Underlying the book is a question about which Smith thought long and hard. How can people who pursue their own self-interest through voluntary exchange also promote the best interests of society? Smith knew that benevolence among family and friends was important. Here, people willingly provide for others because they know and care for them. But in a large economy, like today's world economy, we depend on the assistance and cooperation of many people we never meet or know. To enlist their cooperation and assistance, said Smith, we rely on a system in which people make exchanges to obtain what they want. "Give me that which I want, and you shall have this which you want, is the meaning of every such offer… It is not from the benevolence of the butcher, the brewer, or the baker, that we expect our dinner, but from their regard to their own interest."[1]

An Invisible Hand

Smith explained that the purpose of production is to satisfy consumers. In an economic system of voluntary exchange, he said, people serve the interests of consumers by following their own particular interests. They identify how best to specialize by working at jobs or owning businesses in which they can produce the most value for consumers. By making their best contributions to producing the total "economic pie," they are likely to receive more slices in exchange. But the gains in exchange also motivate people to develop new products, start new businesses, and invent new ways of producing. Led by the "invisible hand" of the economy, said Smith, we increase the nation's material wealth by using our individual interests, talents, and abilities to serve consumers in the market. Adam Smith had a keen eye to see how voluntary exchange could organize and coordinate people's actions.

Contemporary economists still quote Adam Smith. In the late 1990s, U.S. Secretary of the Treasury Larry Summers said, "What's the single most important thing to learn from an economics course today? What I tried to leave my students with is the view that the invisible hand is more powerful than the hidden hand. Things will happen in well organized efforts without direction, controls, plans."[2]

1 Adam Smith, *An Inquiry into the Nature and Causes of the Wealth of Nations* (The Modern Library, 1937).

2 Virginia Postrel, "After Socialism," *Reason,* November 1999.

Goals of the U.S. Economic System

Free enterprise is not a system that wanders around aimlessly. Although the United States is a large, diverse nation, most Americans agree on a set of basic economic goals. The seven goals are briefly introduced below. You will learn more about these goals in later chapters.

Full employment. Most Americans agree that our country should strive for **full employment**. Full employment means that almost all people in the labor force are able to find work. We agree that there should be a job for everyone ready, willing, and able to work.

Economic growth. Americans agree that economic growth is desirable. **Economic growth** means an increase in output of goods and services in the U.S. economy during a year. The average living standard of people should improve as the output of goods and services is increased.

Price stability. The economic history of our country has convinced most Americans that keeping prices stable is a worthy goal. **Price stability** means that prices of goods, services, and resources do not fluctuate significantly, either up or down, in short periods of time. There have been times in our history when prices, in general, increased or decreased rapidly. Such times create hardships for many people and businesses.

Economic freedom. As Americans, we generally believe that people should have a high degree of freedom to choose how to earn a living and how to spend their income. **Economic freedom** means freedom of choice in employment, buying, selling, use of our time, and other decisions related to our economy.

Economic security. In our country, we believe everyone should have a degree of **economic security**. Economic security means that the basic needs of every person should be met. This includes people who are unable to pay their own way for whatever reason—physical handicap, advanced age, or accidental injury, for example.

Economic equity. Americans believe in economic equity. **Economic equity** means fairness and impartiality. The economic system should offer all citizens equal economic opportunities.

Efficiency. An American goal for our economy is efficiency. **Efficiency** means getting the maximum output from the resources used to produce goods and services. Economic efficiency refers to the entire economy's ability to get the most out of its limited resources, but individuals and businesses also strive to be efficient in using their resources.

Throughout this book, you will have the opportunity to evaluate specific economic decisions and the roles of business, government, workers, and consumers as they contribute to accomplishing the goals of the U.S. economic system. How you view these goals depends on your personal values, but you will have the opportunity to explore these goals and other issues as an economist would, and you can develop your own ideas and opinions.

Think Critically

Beside each goal listed in the text, indicate whether you agree (A) or disagree (D) with the goal, and tell why.

12. full employment   13. economic growth   14. price stability   15. economic freedom
16. economic security   17. economic equity   18. efficiency

Summary

The pillars of free enterprise—private property, specialization, voluntary exchange, the price system, market competition, and entrepreneurship—are essential to the operation and success of the U.S. economic system. The right to own and exchange property and the right to make a profit gives individuals and businesses incentives to use their resources wisely. Prices provide consumers and producers with the information they need to make economic decisions. Specialization increases production and encourages people to exchange goods and services. Market competition, like private property, provides incentives to use resources wisely and produce goods and services that people are willing and able to purchase. Entrepreneurship, the willingness and ability to see opportunities and to take risks to develop new products, is a driving force in the economy and is important for economic growth.

Economists use a Circular Flow model to highlight basic features of a market economy. The model shows how voluntary exchanges between households and businesses answer the economy's what, how, and for whom questions and create a necessary flow of money, products, and resources to help satisfy wants.

Money, anything generally accepted as payment for goods and services, makes exchange of products and resources easier. Money functions as a medium of exchange, a store of value, and a measure of value.

Although we have a large and diverse nation, we agree on several broad economic goals. These goals include full employment, economic growth, price stability, economic freedom, economic security, economic equity, and efficiency. How you view these goals depends on your own value system.

Looking Ahead

In the next chapter, "Demand," you will begin to learn in more detail how the behaviors of buyers in markets help shape behavior in an economy.

Demand

Read to Find Out

As you read this chapter, look for answers to the following questions:

What role do prices play in a market economy?

What is demand, and how does it illustrate the price effect?

Why do people buy more of something at lower prices and less at higher prices?

What is the relationship between individuals' demands and market demand?

What is the price elasticity of demand, and what determines it?

What is the difference between the price effect and a change in demand?

Why It Matters

You are a consumer. Most likely, you have been a consumer for some time. It is certain that you will be a consumer for the rest of your life. Consumers demand goods and services. As a consumer, you want to make good choices because you have limited income. Would you buy a soft drink for lunch if the price were 25 cents? You probably would. You might even buy more than one soft drink at the 25-cent price. Would you buy the same soft drink at a price of $3.00? Maybe yes, maybe no. If the price of the soft drink rose to $10.00, chances are that you and most of your friends would not buy the soft drink. Understanding the behavior of people in a free enterprise market system is important to making good consumer choices.

Demand

Building On What You Know

Two pillars of free enterprise are voluntary exchange and the price system. You participate in voluntary exchange almost daily when you buy a soft drink, a pizza, or another product. You certainly are aware of the prices you pay for goods and services. You have grown up in a price system, but do you know how those prices are set or why prices sometimes change? Think about the prices you pay as you read this chapter.

Entrepreneurs bring new goods and services to consumers, but they are successful only when they offer something consumers are willing and able to buy in a market. As you have learned, a market is an arrangement that allows buyers and sellers to make exchanges. Even people who may not actually buy or sell a product will influence the market if they are interested in the product or service. Sound confusing?

iStockphoto '07

An auto auction illustrates a way in which demand for a product influences its price.

Think about the following example. In most cities you will find an automobile auction house. About once a month, used cars are sold to the highest bidders. The cars being sold are usually owned by used car dealers who want to dispose of the cars because they did not sell when they were on their used car lots.

At an auction, an auctioneer offers each car to potential buyers. The auction price might start at $1,500. Then, bidders bid up the price until only one bidder is willing to pay the highest price bid. If that price is $12,000, for example, the person who bid $12,000 gets the car. Who influenced the final price and sale of the car? The answer is that all of the people who bid on the car influenced the sale, although only one person actually made the purchase. If the other people had not bid up the price, the last bidder could have bought the car for less than $12,000.

The interaction of buyers and sellers in markets drives a free enterprise economy. Wherever markets exist, the interaction of the two groups establishes a market price. Each market price plays a role in guiding buyers' choices in a market economy. How do prices do this?

Demand and the Price Effect

You don't usually think of the stores where you shop as markets or "auctions," but the economic principles are similar. At high prices there are usually fewer buyers for a product than at lower prices. Products are sold to those people willing to pay the market price. Prices influence the "for whom" question in an economy. People willing and able to pay the price for a product get the product. Indeed, prices play such an important role in our free enterprise system that economists often describe it as a "price directed market economy."

What causes prices to rise and fall in a market economy? Learning to use two concepts, demand and supply, will help you find the answer to that question. In this chapter, demand is explained and used to analyze consumer behavior. The concept of supply is explained separately in the next chapter, while Chapter 5 combines both concepts to provide a fuller explanation of market behavior.

If you own a car, then you are probably in the market for gasoline. Does this mean that you will buy all the gas you want at any price? Probably not. Typically, consumers will buy more of something if it costs less, and less of something if it costs more. Economists explain this behavior as the *law of demand*. The **law of demand** is an inverse relationship between the quantity demanded and the price of a product. This means that people will buy more of something, say gasoline, at lower prices than at higher prices.

By now, you probably have learned that some words used in economics have different meanings than in everyday conversation. The word *demand* is one of those. In everyday use, the word *demand* means to order someone to do something. "I demand my money back," says an angry customer. "We demand our rights!" exclaims a group of protesters. When economists use the word **demand**, it means quantities of a particular good or service that consumers are willing and able to buy at different prices at a particular time. You might want a product, which means you are willing to buy it. However, if you don't have the money to buy it, you are not able to. Only consumers who are willing and able to buy the product affect the demand for that product.

Think about the products you typically purchase: T-shirts, hamburgers, ice cream, and DVDs. If the price of your favorite burger soared to $100, you'd probably buy few, if any, burgers. On the other hand, if the price fell to 50 cents, you'd probably increase the number you purchase.

What, then, is your demand for hamburgers? Is it the amount (if any) you'd buy at $100 each? Is it the amount you'd buy at 50 cents each? Or is it the amount you'd buy at other possible prices? Actually your demand for hamburgers is all of these different amounts and prices because demand lists the quantities of what you will purchase at all possible prices.

How Many Hamburgers Would You Buy?

1. If your favorite hamburger's price rose to $100, how many would you buy in a week? _____

2. If your favorite hamburger's price fell to $.50, how many would you buy in a week? _____

3. What price do you feel makes your favorite hamburger a good value? _____

4. What is the highest price you would pay for your favorite hamburger? _____

Check Your Understanding

Explain in your own words the meaning of price directed market economy.

_____
_____
_____

1. law of demand   2. demand

33

Consider a new example, the demand for gasoline. Figure 3-1 shows the amount of gasoline that Althea would buy for her car each week at different prices. At $6 per gallon, Althea would buy 5 gallons per week. At $1.00 per gallon, she would buy 30 gallons per week. All of the different prices and amounts in Figure 3-1, which is a table, represent Althea's demand for gasoline. The table predicts the amount of gasoline she will purchase at different prices.

Figure 3-1: Althea's Demand for Gasoline

Price per gallon	Gallons per week
$6.00	5
$5.00	10
$4.00	15
$3.00	20
$2.00	25
$1.00	30

Figure 3-2 is a graph that uses the numbers in the table above to illustrate Althea's demand. Each point represents one of the rows in the table above. A line connecting the points creates a demand line, which provides a visual model of Althea's demand for gasoline. What, then, is Althea's demand for gasoline? It is *not* a single point on the line. It is the entire demand line that shows you every possible combination of prices and quantities purchased between $1.00 and $6.00. If you wish to be very precise, you could determine from the graph how much gas she is predicted to buy at $2.91 and at $3.44. Don't worry! You will not be required to be that precise in your use of this idea.

Notice the visual clues in the graph. Prices are shown on the vertical axis. The quantity of gasoline measured in gallons per week is shown on the horizontal axis. A demand line slopes downward to the right because Althea is willing and able to buy more gasoline at lower prices than at higher prices.

Check Your Understanding

With a highlighter pen, highlight Althea's demand on the graph.

What is the lowest amount of gasoline shown in Althea's demand?

_____

What is the highest price of gasoline in Althea's demand?

_____

At $3.00 per gallon, how many gallons of gasoline will Althea buy?

_____

Figure 3-2: Althea's Demand for Gasoline

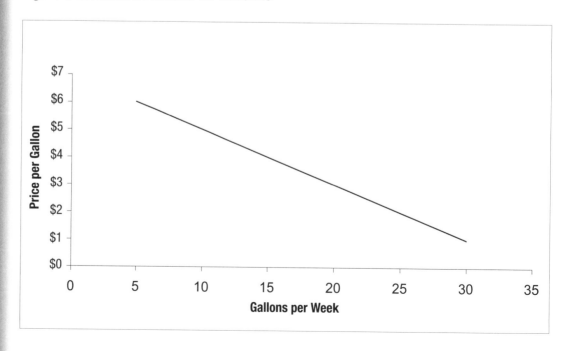

34

Prices serve as both incentives and disincentives to consumers. High prices are disincentives to consumers, discouraging them from purchasing a product. Lower prices are incentives, encouraging consumers to purchase more products.

Prices have a similar effect on decisions made by people other than Althea. In fact, the effect prices have on consumer buying is so common and important that economists have a special name for it. It is called the *price effect*. The **price effect** is the inclination of people to buy less of something at higher prices than they would buy at lower prices.

Why do prices have this effect? Why might Althea buy more gasoline at lower prices and less at higher prices? Four factors explain why people behave this way: buying power, diminishing personal value, diminishing marginal utility, and the availability of substitutes.

Buying Power

For the moment, imagine Althea's gasoline budget is $100 a week. Obviously, if the price of gasoline goes down, Althea's gasoline budget has more *buying power* than before. **Buying power** is the quantity of goods and services a person can buy with a given amount of money. With a price decrease, Althea can buy more gasoline and stay within her budget. If the price of gasoline increases, the opposite effect occurs. Her $100 budget will purchase less gasoline.

Demand for CDs

Here are quantities and prices for CDs demanded by students in one school per month.

Quantity Demanded	Price
300	$ 5.00
250	$ 10.00
200	$ 15.00
150	$ 20.00
100	$ 25.00
50	$ 30.00

On the blank graph below, draw a demand line based on the information in the table above.

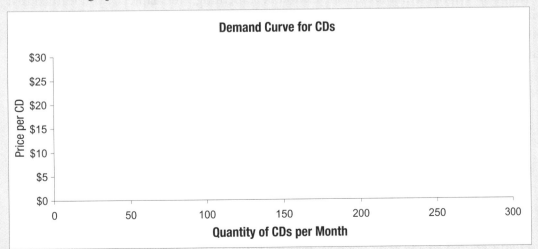

Demand Curve for CDs

Apply Your Understanding

Write a short advertisement for a brand of gasoline that shows the price effect at work.

_____

_____

_____

_____

Check Your Understanding

If the price of CDs is $10.00, how many CDs will students buy?

_____

If the quantity of CDs sold is 200, what is the price students will pay?

_____

3. price effect   4. buying power

Diminishing Personal Value

Althea can use the gasoline she buys for different purposes, such as driving to school, to her part-time job, to the grocery store, or to visit her grandparents. These purposes represent Althea's personal values. However, Althea values some kinds of driving activities more than others. For example, using gasoline to drive to school is more important to her than using it to drive to the store for a single box of cereal. Buying the single box of cereal is a case of diminishing personal value to Althea. The cereal is less important to her than getting to school. If the price of gasoline is $6.00 per gallon, Althea will buy only enough (5 gallons) for her most important trips. But if the price falls to $1.00 a gallon, she will buy more (30 gallons) and use it for less-valuable or less-important trips.

The price of goods and services varies based on demand. Gasoline is especially subject to price fluctuations.

Pause to Predict

You have learned what diminishing personal value means. Predict what you think diminishing marginal utility means. Write your prediction below.

_____

_____

_____

_____

Diminishing Marginal Utility

Althea might love to drive, but there is a limit to the amount she will drive at any one time. Sooner or later, she'll reach a point where enjoyment decreases with every mile, no matter how low the cost of gasoline. What is true of gasoline applies to all products and services. Economists call this change in a consumer's attitude *diminishing marginal utility*. *Utility* refers to the usefulness or satisfaction of something. In Chapter 1, you learned that *marginal* was defined as the extra or additional costs or benefits of a decision. The key term in this definition is *additional*. In this chapter, we apply the word *marginal* to the idea of utility or satisfaction. Thus **diminishing marginal utility** is the point reached when an additional unit of a product consumed is less satisfying than the one before it. How many times do you play your favorite song before you get tired of it? This behavior is a good example of your diminishing marginal utility. You might even get to the point where you can't stand to hear the song again. At this point, the song does not satisfy you at all.

Diminishing marginal utility helps to explain why lower prices are sometimes used to increase the quantity demanded by an individual consumer. For example, many people buy pizza by the slice. If your desire for a second slice of pizza is less than it was for the first slice, you are not likely to buy more than one, except at a lower price. In most cases, you will choose to use your money for something other than pizza to maximize your satisfaction (your utility). How does the pizza seller encourage you to buy more pizza? The seller offers a lower price on the second slice or offers to sell two slices for an average price less than the price of just one slice. For example, you can buy one slice for $2.00 or two slices for $3.50.

Diminishing personal values refers to several possible uses a person has for a fixed amount of money. Earlier you read that Althea has four possible uses for her $100-per-week budget, and she values these uses differently. Diminishing marginal utility refers to only one product. As more and more of the product is purchased and consumed, a person receives less and less utility or satisfaction from it.

Substitutes

Most products have **substitutes**, a good or service that can replace another good or service. However, our willingness to choose the substitute depends on the price of the products. Does gasoline have substitutes? It's easy to think that it does not, but consider Althea's use of gasoline. Instead of driving to school by herself each morning, she could carpool with friends. (Carpooling becomes a substitute for some of the gasoline she currently uses.) She could even take the bus or walk. (Taking the bus and walking become substitutes.) Instead of driving to her grandparents' house each weekend, she could go every other weekend and call them more frequently. (Telephone service provides a substitute for gasoline.) Instead of driving to the supermarket for one or two items, she could plan better and make fewer trips.

These examples demonstrate that there are substitutes for everything, including the use of gasoline. If the price of gasoline rises, Althea is encouraged to seek and use more substitutes, just as you would substitute more tacos, hot dogs, or cheese sandwiches if the price of hamburgers went up. On the other hand, Althea would use more gasoline and fewer substitutes if the price of gasoline decreased. If the price of gasoline falls, the substitutes become less-attractive alternatives to using gasoline.

What Are the Substitutes?

For each of the four items below, name one possible substitute for that product on the adjoining line.

1. Economics textbook _____

2. A full night's sleep _____

3. Saturday night date _____

4. Pizza _____

Check Your Understanding

Below, describe two situations in which you would be inclined to buy more than one product if the seller offered you a lower average price on two or more of the items.

1. _____

_____

2. _____

_____

Think Critically

Name two products for which there is no reasonable substitute.

_____

_____

Market Demand

Price changes affect all of us. We all buy less at higher prices than we do at lower prices. However, this doesn't mean that everyone responds to a price change in exactly the same way. A price change that has a big effect on your behavior may have little or no effect on someone else's behavior. When we want gasoline for our cars and trucks, we express our individual demands in the market. The cumulative result is *market demand*. **Market demand** is the total of all individual demands in a given market at a particular time.

To illustrate with a simple example, suppose the total market for gasoline consists of four people, including Althea. Figure 3-3, a table, shows how each person's individual demand is added to that of others to become a market demand for gasoline. The four individual demands vary widely.

Figure 3-3: How Individual Demands Add Up to Market Demand

Price per Gallon	Althea's Demand		Frank's Demand		Nikki's Demand		Henry's Demand		Market Demand
$1.00	30	+	20	+	35	+	60	=	145
$2.00	25	+	15	+	30	+	45	=	115
$3.00	20	+	10	+	20	+	35	=	85
$4.00	15	+	10	+	15	+	35	=	75
$5.00	10	+	10	+	15	+	35	=	70
$6.00	5	+	10	+	15	+	35	=	65

For example, Henry demands more gas at each price than anyone else does. While a price increase from $5.00 to $6.00 would reduce Althea's consumption, it wouldn't change the amounts of gas that Frank, Nikki, or Henry purchase. Despite these differences, the price effect still applies to each person. They all tend to purchase fewer gallons of gas at higher prices than at lower prices. Figure 3-4 presents the market demand in a graph.

Show Your Understanding

In the table and in the graph, circle the highest price shown.

In the table and in the graph, draw a square around the greatest quantity of gasoline shown.

In the table and in the graph, draw a star to show the market demand for gasoline at $3.00.

Figure 3-4: Market Demand for Gasoline

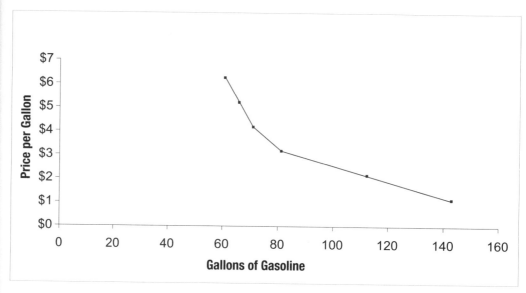

7. market demand

The Price Elasticity of Demand

While demand lines for all products slope downward from left to right, their shape and steepness can be quite different. For example, suppose a quart of milk and a liter of cola each sells for $1.00. If the price of milk rises from $1.00 to $1.50, people will buy less milk. Similarly, if the price of cola rises from $1.00 to $1.50, people will buy less cola. Although the price increases are identical, the decrease in cola sales would probably be far greater than the decrease in milk sales. This change occurs because people find it easier to buy substitutes, goods that satisfy similar wants, for cola than for milk, which is important for maintaining good health.

In such a case, the price effect is greater for some products, like cola, than it is for others, like milk. Economists use a concept called *price elasticity of demand* to measure the impact of the price effect. **Price elasticity of demand** is a measure of the impact of the price effect. It indicates a buyer's eagerness to buy a good or service. When the price effect is large, the demand is said to be elastic. In the case of cola, a small change in price causes a relatively large change or "stretch" in the amount demanded. When the price effect is small, the demand is inelastic, which means that there is little or no stretch. In this case, a price change causes only a small change in the amount demanded.

Study Figure 3-5, a graph, for a moment. Note that the demand lines for both cola and milk cross at a quantity of 70 containers at a price of $1.00. This means that the total revenue for both cola and milk is $1.00 times 70 containers, or $70. Total Revenue (TR) = Price (P) x Quantity (Q) of containers sold.

Suppose the price of both cola and milk increases to $1.50. The same price increase from $1.00 to $1.50 per container of cola brings about a much larger reduction in cola sales than in milk sales. The cola sales drop so much (from 70 to 40 containers per day) that total cola revenue falls from $70 to $60 per day ($1.50 x 40 = $60). This is a clear sign that the price effect is strong and demand is elastic.

Figure 3-5: Price Elasticity of Demand for Milk and Cola Drinks

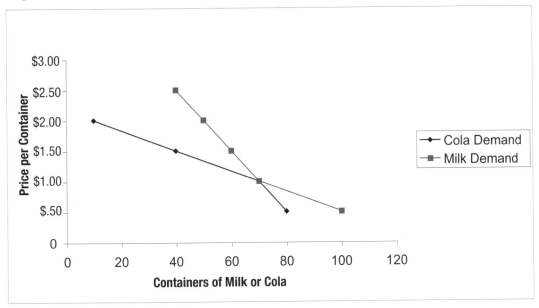

In contrast, the same price increase also causes milk sales to drop, but the sales drop far less per day than cola sales—a drop from 70 to 60 containers. As a result, total revenue for milk increases, rising from $70 to $90 per day ($1.50 x 60 = $90). This is a clear sign that the price effect is weak and demand is inelastic.

The price elasticity of demand is different for different goods and services for several reasons.

Availability of Substitutes
When substitutes are more plentiful, demand is usually more elastic. Cola has an elastic demand because it is easy to substitute fruit juices, mineral water, or other carbonated drinks for cola. But there are fewer good substitutes for the taste and nutrition of milk.

Percentage of Budget
A product's price tends to be more elastic when the price represents a significant percentage of people's household budgets. People are more likely to change their buying habits as a result of a price change when the product is a larger part of their total spending. Such products might include mountain bicycles, automobiles, and household appliances. However, the impact of price changes on these kinds of items may be less on wealthy people than on people with less income.

Time
The longer that people have to adjust to a product's price change, the more elastic the demand for the product tends to be. If the price of gasoline remains high, people have time to make adjustments. They find and use more substitutes. However, when time is short and plans have not been made, demand for gasoline is more inelastic.

Elastic or Inelastic?

Some of the products below are likely to be price elastic; others are likely to be price inelastic. On the line next to the product, indicate whether it is likely to be price elastic or price inelastic. On the adjoining line, identify the reason for its elasticity or inelasticity.

	Elastic or Inelastic?	Why?
1. 52-inch flat-screen TV	_____	_____
2. Table salt	_____	_____
3. A music CD	_____	_____
4. Insulin	_____	_____
5. T-shirts with the logo of the losing Super Bowl team the day after the game	_____	_____

Apple Learns about Elasticity the Hard Way

 Early in 1995, Apple Computer slashed prices on its Macintosh computers in an attempt to increase the company's sales and market share. However, Apple failed to predict how many more computers people would buy at the lower price. The demand for computers soared. Apple had not built enough computers to meet the unexpectedly high number of orders, so many customers went away unsatisfied and unhappy.

Later in the year, Apple produced many more computers, expecting the demand to be strong during the holiday season. However, this time Apple's forecast was too optimistic. The company ended up with costly stockpiles of unsold computers. Unfortunately, Apple learned about price elasticity of demand the hard way.

The Relationship Between the Price Effect and a Change in Demand

If the price of gasoline in Figure 3-4 changes, does market demand change? For example, when the price rises from $2.00 to $4.00 per gallon, the quantity Henry is willing and able to buy falls from 10 to 7 gallons. Is this a decline in demand?

Before you answer, remember the definition of *demand*. Market demand is the various quantities of a product that people are willing and able to buy at different possible prices. This means the demand for gasoline in Figure 3-4 is not one quantity at one specific price. It is *all* quantities at all different prices. Demand is represented by the entire demand line. In this case, the price changed, but the demand line did not change. The price has just moved from one level to another.

For demand to change, the entire demand line must move, or shift. This can only occur if all the possible different price and quantity level combinations change. Figure 3-6a illustrates in a graph just such an example. In this case, demand shifts to the right, from D1 to D2. Here, people want to buy more gasoline at each price. Demand has increased. For example, at a price of $5.00 per gallon, the gallons demanded per week increase from 70 to 90. At a price of $2.00 per gallon, the gallons demanded per week increase from 115 to 135.

Figure 3-6a: An Increase in Demand

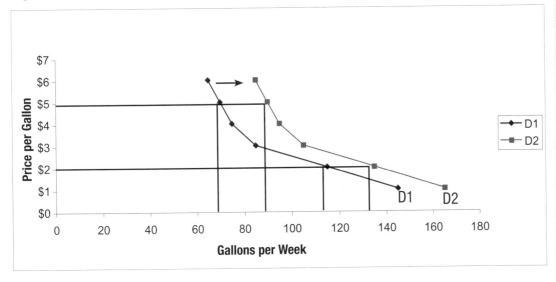

Show Your Understanding

With a highlighter pen, highlight the four sentences in the second paragraph of this section that detail the meaning of demand.

Check Your Understanding

Which demand line, D1 or D2, shows an increase in demand?

If demand shifts to the left, there is a decrease in demand. This is shown in Figure 3-6b, a graph. The demand line has shifted from D1 to D3. In this case, people want to buy less gasoline at each price. Demand for gasoline has decreased. In this example, at a price of $5.00 per gallon, the number of gallons bought per week decreased from 70 to 50. At a price of $2.00 per gallon, the number of gallons bought per week decreased from 115 to 95.

Figure 3-6b: A Decrease in Demand

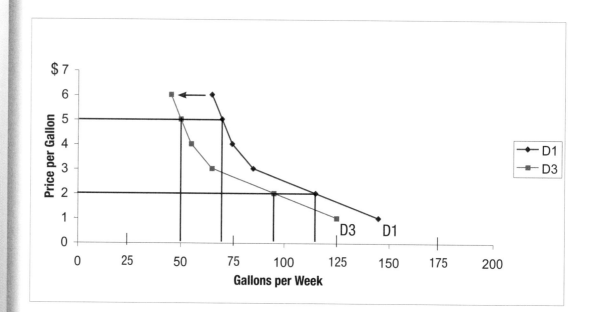

Check Your Understanding

Which demand line, D1 or D3, shows a decrease in demand?

_____

_____

Check Your Understanding

On the lines beside each cause of demand increases and decreases, explain the cause in your own words.

_____

_____

What would cause the demand for gasoline, or any other product, to increase or decrease? There are seven possible causes.

Change in Income

If incomes rise, people have more money to spend. Then they are willing to pay a higher price for the same quantity of a product or to buy greater quantities of a product at the same price. If incomes fall, the opposite is true. Think of some of the products you might buy more of if you suddenly had more income or your allowance doubled.

Money in Our Pockets and Demand

Imagine that you receive $50 for getting good grades this semester. You know that many other students in your school will also receive similar amounts of money for their good grades.

What are two products you would predict that are likely to experience an increase in demand as a result of the additional money students have to spend?

_____   _____

Prices or Availability of Substitutes

What will happen to the demand for gasoline if the price of public transportation increases? A change in the price of one item will result in a change or shift in the demand for a substitute. If the price of public transportation went way up, the price effect tells us that people would use it less often. They would drive their cars more often, so the demand for gasoline would increase and the demand curve would shift to the right. However, ridership of public transportation would predictably increase if gas prices increased or if many more bus routes were added to make public transportation more convenient.

Prices or Availability of Complementary Goods

What will happen to the demand for gasoline if the price of cars increases? Goods that often are used together, like cars and gasoline or popcorn and a soda at the movies, are complementary. **Complementary goods** are products that often are used together. According to the price effect concept, if the price of cars soars, people will buy fewer of them, and the demand for gasoline should fall. Similarly, if the price of cars falls and consumers buy more of them, the demand for gasoline is likely to increase.

Boeing Airlines benefited from a complementary goods relationship in 2006 when the cost of jet fuel increased dramatically. Airline companies with old airplanes that used a lot of jet fuel became very expensive to operate. Boeing's new airplane, the Boeing 787-9, is much more fuel efficient than the older planes. Airline companies decided to ground their fuel-guzzling older airplanes and increased their demand for the newer fuel-efficient airplanes. The higher cost of a complementary good, jet fuel, led to an increase in the demand for new airplanes.

787-9 ©The Boeing Company

When the cost of jet fuel increases, ticket prices go up. What will people do when airfares increase?

Change in the Weather or Season

The demand for gasoline can increase at certain times of the year. During the summer when many people take vacations in cars and motor homes, they usually demand more gasoline at every price. Coca-Cola offers a different example of how the weather affects demand for its product. In 1999, Coca-Cola introduced a vending machine that automatically raised prices for its drinks in hot weather, using a temperature sensor and a computer chip.

Change in the Number of Buyers

The demand for gasoline or any other item is affected by the size of the market, or population, it serves. If the population of a community is growing, there can be a greater demand for gasoline. As more people become comfortable with technology, the number of personal computers and cellular phones increases to meet the new demand. An increase in the number of buyers in a market will cause a demand line to increase or shift to the right.

9. complementary goods

Changes in Styles, Tastes, and Habits

Obviously, fashions change. It's possible that platform shoes and skinny jeans will disappear, only to return at a later time. If the shoe and clothing styles disappear, the demand for them will decrease or shift to the left. Similarly, the kinds of cars people want to drive, their lifestyles, and where they want to live and work can affect the demand for gasoline. If there is a large increase in demand for hybrid cars, there may be a decrease in demand (shift to the left) for gasoline.

Change in Expectations

Consumers sometimes predict that the price or availability of a product is likely to change in the future. For example, if people suddenly expect home computers to be priced higher in the near future, they will probably buy more computers today. In such a situation, the demand for home computers would increase. However, demand may decrease if customers believe that the future price of computers is likely to decrease.

A demand line is quite easy to understand. Demand measures the relationship between the price and amount of a product sold during some time period. In the real world of economics, however, we need to account for change—in income; in prices or availability of substitutes; in prices or availability of complementary goods; in the weather or season; in the number of buyers; in styles, tastes, and habits; and in expectations. Demand and events that cause a demand line to change are useful tools that help us understand consumer behavior.

Changes in Demand

 The list below identifies events, each of which will affect the demand for the product identified beside the event. In the next column, indicate whether the event will cause the demand for the product to increase or decrease. In the final column, identify the possible cause for each shift in demand.

Event	Product	Increase or Decrease	Cause
Increase in price of steak	Hamburger	_____	_____
Low-fat diet becomes popular	Fresh grapes	_____	_____
Disney World admission prices go up	Hotel rooms near Disney World	_____	_____
Hard freeze destroys future orange crop	Orange juice	_____	_____
People's incomes drop	New TV sets	_____	_____

Summary

In economics, demand is the various quantities of something consumers are willing and able to buy at many different prices at a particular time. The law of demand is an inverse relationship between the quantity demanded and the price of a product. Prices influence people's behavior. The price effect is the inclination of people to buy less of something at higher prices than they would buy at lower prices.

When individuals buy goods and services in the market, their demands are combined into market demand. Even though people have different individual demand lines, market demand reflects the law of demand. The impact of a change in price on the quantity consumers will buy is the price elasticity of demand. When a small change in price results in a large change in quantity demanded, the price effect is large and the demand is said to be elastic. In this instance, a higher price decreases total revenue (Price x Quantity Demanded). When the price effect is small, demand is inelastic. In this instance, a higher price increases total revenue.

The price effect shows that people change the amounts they buy at different prices. A change in demand, however, means that people want to buy different quantities of a product at *each and every* possible price. A change in demand is represented graphically by a shift of the entire demand line to the right or left. In contrast, the price effect is movement along an existing demand line.

Looking Ahead

In the next chapter, "Supply," you will learn about the other side of the market where market prices influence the quantities of goods or services that businesses offer for sale.

iStockphoto '07

Demand defines the quantity of a particular good or service that consumers are willing and able to buy at different prices at a particular time.

Notes

Supply

Read to Find Out

As you read this chapter, look for answers to the following questions:

What is supply, and how does it illustrate the price effect?

How is opportunity cost related to the supply of goods and services?

Why do producers want to sell more of something at higher prices and less at lower prices?

What is the relationship between market supply and the supplies of individual sellers?

What is the price elasticity of supply, and what determines it?

What is the difference between the price effect and a change in supply?

Mark to Remember

* *This is important.*

? *I have a question about this.*

! *This is a surprise.*

Why It Matters

As a producer, you do not eat the food you grew, live in the shelter you built, or wear the clothes that you have sewed. How do you survive? To answer this question, you must have a good understanding about the work done by producers. Most people know about being a consumer, but they have little idea about how and why products are made for consumption. Producers are important to everyone in this country. We rely on them for almost everything from food and electricity to gadgets and recreation. Knowing how producers make decisions about the quantities of goods and services that they make available to consumers can help you make better personal economic decisions. This knowledge can also help you better understand ups and downs in the marketplace.

Supply

Building On What You Know

Have you ever gone to the store to buy a specific product only to find that the product was "out of stock"? Maybe that happened when you wanted to buy an electronic toy at holiday time. Or maybe you wanted a particular doughnut but found that kind sold out when you arrived at the bakery. How do producers decide at what price to sell the toys or doughnuts? This chapter will help answer those questions.

Nutritional food is needed for the good health of children and adults. Yet, many people in poor countries do not have enough nutritional food. Food is produced in abundance today, especially in the United States. In some countries, farmers are paid not to grow food products. Why don't farmers just provide food free of charge to all hungry people? Why should anyone have to pay farmers for food production? Doesn't the price of food prevent hungry people from getting the food they need to meet their nutritional requirements?

What good purpose does the price of food serve? You may have figured this out already, but the answer is that price serves as an incentive to farmers. Prices farmers receive for supplying food become their income. Farmers bear opportunity costs for producing food. They could be directing their work to other important tasks if they did not produce food. The prices they receive for their crops serve as incentives for them to continue working as food producers.

The same principle works for you. Think of things you do to earn money. Would you be willing to supply your time to do them if you were paid nothing for your efforts? The money you earn helps compensate you for the opportunity cost of working, and it serves as an incentive to encourage you to work in the future.

Other sellers behave the same way. They want to be paid for the costs of designing, producing, and selling the goods and services we demand. This is true for the French fries you eat, the shirts you wear, and the movies you watch. It is also true for the gasoline you use when driving.

Think Critically

If you earn money by working, about how much per hour do you earn?

_____

_____

Do you think the amount is appropriate for the work you do?

_____

_____

Why or why not?

_____

_____

Supply and the Price Effect

Imagine a business called First Oil Company that drills for oil to make gasoline. Oil is the main resource that is refined into gasoline. To simplify this expensive and complicated process, assume the company uses one oil well for each million gallons of gasoline it produces each week. The company has six wells, so it can produce a total of 6 million gallons per week. The trouble is that some wells are better than others. The best one has the lowest cost of production because its oil is the easiest to extract. The next best one has a higher production cost because the company must use more labor and other resources to get the oil. For the same reason, the third well has an even higher production cost, and so on.

This means the company's marginal cost (the change in cost for an additional output) of producing additional gallons of gasoline increases with each additional well it brings on line. These marginal costs are also considered opportunity costs as the oil company gives up the opportunity to produce other possible oil-related products. The cost of production increases as it produces more gasoline. Its second million gallons cost more to produce than its first million, and its third million gallons cost more than its second. An economist would observe that the company's marginal cost of producing additional gallons of gasoline increases with each additional well brought on line.

Figure 4-1, a table, presents the supply of First Oil Company. The amount of gasoline the company wants to sell varies with the price. If the price of gasoline is $3.00 per gallon, the company uses its best wells and produces 3 million gallons per week. It has little incentive to use any of its other wells because its marginal costs are all higher than $3.00 per gallon. But if the price rises to $4.00 per gallon, it is advantageous for the company to use its fourth-best well, too. It is advantageous because the higher price covers the higher marginal cost of producing gasoline from this well. Consequently, the company produces more gasoline at $4.00 per gallon than at $3.00 per gallon. And if the price rises still higher, First Oil will bring into production higher-cost wells and produce still more gasoline.

Figure 4-1: First Oil Company's Supply of Gasoline

Price per gallon	Gallons per week
$1.00	1 million
$2.00	2 million
$3.00	3 million
$4.00	4 million
$5.00	5 million
$6.00	6 million

iStockphoto '07

Notice the company is willing and able to produce various amounts of gasoline at different possible prices at a particular time. Economists call this relationship between price and amount produced *supply*. **Supply** is the quantity of a good or service that producers are willing and able to sell at different prices at a particular time. This relationship identifies the *law of supply*. The **law of supply** is a positive relationship between the quantity supplied

Pause to Predict

Considering what you learned about the effect of price on demand, how do you think the price of a product affects the supply of that product?

_____

_____

Check Your Understanding

Explain in your own words why marginal costs are opportunity costs.

_____

_____

_____

Apply Your Understanding

Suppose you regularly babysit for one child at the rate of $25.00 for three hours. Your client asks you to babysit for two children, at the same location, for three hours. Will you charge more for two children? _____ How much more? _____ How did you determine the marginal cost for the second child?

_____

_____

The law of supply is a positive relationship between the quantity supplied and the price of the product.

Check Your Understanding

Is the information in Figure 4-1 and Figure 4-2 the same or different?

_____

_____

How do you know?

_____

_____

_____

Which figure, 4-1 or 4-2, do you find easier to understand and why?

_____

_____

_____

and the price of the product. As the price rises, the quantity supplied will tend to rise. As the price declines, the quantity supplied will tend to decline. Supply is not a particular quantity for sale today in the market. It is a list of prices and the quantities that a company is willing and able to supply at each price.

Be careful about the meaning of words in this section. Most people use the word *supply* to refer to the physical amount of a product on the market at a specific time. Physically, we can count the number of gallons of gasoline stored in storage tanks and filling stations at any time, but that number will not help us understand the economic supply of gasoline. To understand *supply* in the context used by economists, you need to understand the definition of supply and use it accurately.

Graphing Supply

Supply can be graphed to provide you with a visual form of the concept. Figure 4-2 is a graph that presents the numbers from the table in Figure 4-1. By connecting the points, it creates a line that depicts First Oil's supply of gasoline. Remember, the company's supply is the entire line, not a particular point on it.

Notice the visual clues in the graph. Prices are shown on the vertical axis. The quantity of gasoline measured in gallons per week is shown on the horizontal axis. A supply line slopes upward to the right because First Oil Company is willing and able to sell more gasoline at higher prices than at lower prices.

Figure 4-2: First Oil Company Supply of Gasoline

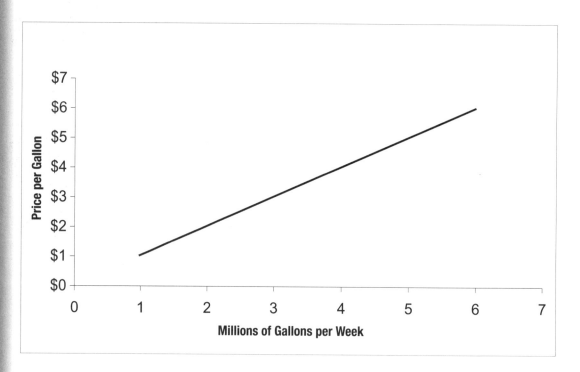

Just as there is a price effect for demand, so too is there a price effect for supply. At higher prices, First Oil is willing and able to offer more gasoline for sale than at lower prices. A higher price is then required to provide the company managers with enough incentive to pay their higher marginal costs.

Supplying Tortillas

Below is a supply table that shows the prices and quantity of tortillas supplied in dozens each day by the company Casa de Tortillas.

Supply of Tortillas Produced by Casa de Tortillas
(quantities in dozens per day)

Price	Quantity Supplied
$ 0.60	500
$ 0.80	1,500
$ 1.00	2,000
$ 1.20	2,500
$ 1.40	3,000

iStockphoto '07

On the blank graph below, draw a supply line for Casa de Tortillas based on the information in the table above.

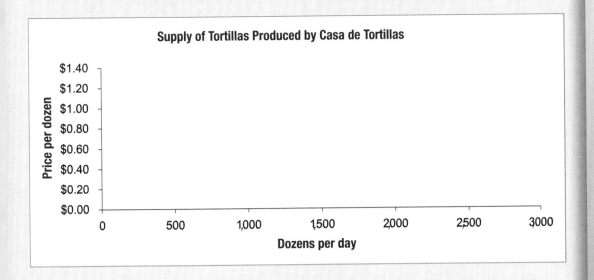

Market Supply

The price effect also applies to other gasoline producers. Of course, they may not respond to a given price change in the same way as First Oil. After all, marginal costs (the change in costs for additional output) differ from producer to producer. Still, other producers also experience higher marginal costs at higher rates of production. So they, too, want to sell more gasoline at higher prices than at lower prices. For example, Figure 4-3 is a table that identifies the supplies of several companies, including First Oil. As each company adds its amount supplied to the gasoline market, the cumulative result is called *market supply*. **Market supply** is the total of all individual suppliers' products in a market at a particular time.

Think Critically

Compare the law of supply with the law of demand that you studied in Chapter 3. In your own words, describe the difference in the two laws.

_____

_____

_____

_____

_____

_____

_____

Check Your Understanding

Circle the correct explanation of market supply.

a. the amount of a product that a company produces

b. the total amount of product put into the market by all suppliers at any given time

c. the amount of product that a company holds in reserve until the price reaches a desired point

Check Your Understanding

Based on Figure 4-3, at $2.00 per gallon, which company adds the most gasoline to the market supply?

First Oil _____
Second Oil _____
Third Oil _____

At $6.00 per gallon, which company adds the most gasoline?

First Oil _____
Second Oil _____
Third Oil _____

Figure 4-3: How Individual Supplies Add Up to Market Supply of Gasoline
(quantities in millions of gallons of gasoline per week)

Price Per Gallon	First Oil's Supply		Second Oil's Supply		Third Oil's Supply		All Other's Supply		Market Supply
$1.00	1	+	0	+	0	+	3	=	4
$2.00	2	+	0	+	1	+	8	=	11
$3.00	3	+	1	+	3	+	12	=	19
$4.00	4	+	2	+	3	+	14	=	23
$5.00	5	+	2	+	4	+	16	=	27
$6.00	6	+	3	+	4	+	17	=	30

As the table shows, the supplies of the three companies differ. Second Oil Company offers no gasoline at $1.00 or $2.00 per gallon because its marginal cost of producing gasoline is higher than those prices. But if the price rises to $3.00 per gallon, the company begins production. Also, a price increase from $3.00 to $4.00 causes First Oil Company to raise production from three million to four million gallons per week, but it has no effect on the amount supplied by Third Oil Company. Despite these differences, each company's supply illustrates the price effect or law of supply. They'll produce more gasoline at higher prices than they will at lower prices.

Figure 4-4 shows the market supply in a graph. The supply line slopes upward to the right because the marginal cost of producing gasoline rises for all companies as they produce more gasoline. Higher prices provide the necessary incentive for companies to bear higher marginal costs and provide more gasoline.

Show Your Understanding

With a highlighter pen, highlight the market supply data in Figure 4-3.

With a highlighter pen, highlight the market supply data in Figure 4-4.

Figure 4-4: Market Supply of Gasoline

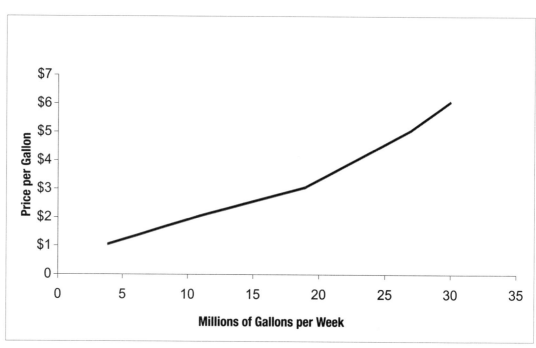

Market Supply of Gasoline

Use either Figure 4-3 or Figure 4-4 to answer the following questions:

1. At a price of $2.00, how much will the market supply of gasoline be? _____

2. At a price of $5.00, how many million gallons will Third Oil Company supply per week? _____

3. If the market supply is 23 million gallons per week, what is the price per gallon? _____

4. Which Figure, 4-3 or 4-4, did you use to answer the questions? Why? _____

_____

Pause to Remember

Before you begin the next section, write in your own words the economic meaning of elasticity *and* inelasticity.

Elasticity _____

_____

_____

Inelasticity _____

_____

_____

iStockphoto '07

Why is the supply of chicken elastic?

The Price Elasticity of Supply

Like demand lines, supply lines can have different shapes depending on their elasticity. If a change in price causes a large change in the amount supplied, the price effect is significant and supply is elastic. For example, the number of chickens provided by chicken producers can increase greatly when the price of chickens goes up. This elastic response happens because ranchers can quickly increase the number of chickens being raised without big increases in marginal costs. A small increase in chicken prices can then bring about a big increase in the number of chickens offered for sale. So in this case, supply is elastic.

Other products have inelastic supplies. In these cases, a change in price has much less influence on the quantity supplied, so the price effect is small and the supply inelastic. Gasoline illustrates an inelastic supply. If the price of gasoline increases, producers can sell some of their stocks of gasoline. They also can try to squeeze more oil from their wells and hire overtime workers. Each of these strategies results in large increases in the marginal cost of production. But despite these efforts and higher costs, increases in gasoline production are relatively small. The price effect is small in this case, so supply is inelastic. Other products that tend to have inelastic supply include custom-made furniture, speedboats, and top-of-the-line motorcycles.

As you can see, an important element in determining the price elasticity of supply is the ease and speed of bringing new resources into production in response to a higher price. The quicker and easier it is for businesses to expand production, the more elastic the product's supply will be. Not surprisingly, the price elasticity of supply depends greatly on the time businesses have to make such adjustments. The more time producers have to change the kinds and amounts of resources they use, the greater the elasticity of supply.

Electrical energy production is an example. When the price of energy soared in 2006, producers couldn't quickly and inexpensively bring big new supplies to the market. Building new power plants and installing new cable lines for service can cost billions of dollars and take years to complete. Just to repair and replace old and deteriorated electrical lines in 2006 was estimated to cost between $8 billion and $10 billion.[1] Over time, if the prices remain above the marginal costs of expanding power production and delivery, the supply of energy will become more elastic as utilities increase the resources necessary for greater production. Products that tend to have elastic supply include home computers, DVDs, and garden tools.

The term *responsiveness* is the key to understanding elasticity of supply. If a business can respond quickly and easily to a price change of the product, supply is elastic. If the business is unable to respond quickly and must buy and install new resources, such as complex manufacturing machines, supply is inelastic.

1. *The Wall Street Journal*, August 18, 2006.

Elastic or Inelastic Supply?

If prices rose sharply, which of the following products would you expect to have an elastic response and which would you expect to have an inelastic approach?

Product	Elastic or Inelastic?	Why?
1. Bottled water	_____	_____
2. Airplanes	_____	_____
3. Autos using alternative fuels	_____	_____
4. Camera cell phones	_____	_____

Show Your Understanding

Reread the section, "The Price Elasticity of Supply." Underline each specific product that is identified as being price elastic. Circle each product that is identified as being price inelastic.

54

Can Supply Be Shifted?

You can't see supply curves, but you can see what happens when they change. You also can observe the visionary people who cause them to change. One of those people was Sarah Breedlove. Born in 1867 to Louisiana sharecroppers, she was only a teenager when her parents died of yellow fever. Later, she married and had a daughter, but her husband died suddenly. She and her daughter moved to St. Louis, where Breedlove worked washing clothes. She also worked part-time selling cosmetics.

C.J. Walker
A'Lelia Bundles/Walker Family Collection/
madamcjwalker.com

At age 37, Sarah Breedlove moved to Denver. There she worked as a cook and married a newspaper salesman, C.J. Walker. When she discovered that she was losing her hair, Breedlove created her own hair conditioners with the help of a drug store pharmacist. The conditioners were so successful that she began selling them door-to-door. She became known as Madam C.J. Walker, and the C.J. Walker Manufacturing Company eventually employed more than 2,000 women. Like other entrepreneurs, Madam Walker had a maverick spirit and was willing to work hard and take risks to reach a goal.

Other entrepreneurs have the same independent spirit and eagerness to innovate and take risks in pursuit of something better. For example, when Steve Jobs and Steven Wozniak formed Apple Computer in 1976, computers were found only in government and industrial laboratories. Yet they had a vision of making the computer into an easy-to-use and inexpensive device for homes.

Steve Jobs
David Paul Morris/Getty Images

Jobs sold his Volkswagen van and Wozniak sold his scientific pocket calculator to raise $1,300 to start their business. Wozniak was the electronic whiz. Jobs had the entrepreneurial drive. After Jobs left Apple Computer in 1985, he started NeXT Computer Inc. He hoped to create another computer "miracle" as he had done at Apple, but NeXT computers didn't sell well. Then, in 1986, Jobs bought Pixar, a part of George Lucas's movie production company. Pixar had helped to create the *Star Wars* movies in the 1980s. Jobs's idea was to use computers to make novel forms of entertainment. The company lost money, but Jobs never gave up. After nearly 10 years, his vision turned into success. By giving cartoon characters a 3-D look, Pixar helped Disney create the first computer-generated feature film, *Toy Story*, in 1995.

Despite this success, Jobs didn't give up on NeXT computers—or Apple. NeXT stopped manufacturing computer hardware in 1993 and shifted its focus to developing its operating system. In 1996, Apple bought NeXT, and a year later Jobs returned to Apple as CEO. The next 14 years would see Jobs and his company scale new heights with the introduction of a string of wildly popular concepts and products, including the iMac, the iPod, Apple retail stores, the iPhone, the iPad, and the iCloud. In 2003, Jobs was diagnosed with pancreatic cancer, which he fought for eight years. He died in October 2011 at age 56.

Steve Jobs and Madam C.J. Walker show how entrepreneurs make our economy grow. As they do, they increase supplies, raise employment, and push incomes higher. By changing supply, these people create positive changes in our economy.

Sources:
Kathy Robello, "The Next Frontier," *Business Week*, December 18, 1995.
"The National Business Hall of Fame," *Fortune*, March 23, 1992.
Bro Uttal, "Behind the Fall of Steve Jobs," *Fortune*, August 5, 1985.

Shifting supply results in changes in production.

Check Your Understanding

In one sentence, explain what the graph in Figure 4-5a shows.

_____

_____

_____

_____

The Relationship Between the Price Effect and a Change in Supply

The relationship between the price effect of supply and a change in supply is similar to the price effect of demand and a change in demand. Keep in mind that when a supply price changes, we are talking about the price effect of supply.

Look back at Figure 4-4. When the price of gasoline rises from $2.00 to $4.00, the amount of gasoline supplied rises from 11 million to 23 million gallons per week. Has supply increased? No, the change in the amount supplied represents a movement along the supply line. Only the amount supplied changed in response to the increase in price.

Movement along a supply line refers to the price effect. A higher price of $4.00 per gallon increases the amount of gasoline that producers want to sell. Supply, however, has not changed because the law of supply already stated that the amount supplied would change at different prices.

Price increases and decreases send messages to suppliers of goods and services. Prices encourage producers to increase or decrease their output. As prices rise, the increase attracts additional producers, while price decreases drive producers out of the market.

The graphs in Figures 4-5a and 4-5b illustrate changes in supply. Sometimes supply does change. That is, the entire supply line shifts. This means that at every price there has been a change in the amount supplied.

In Figure 4-5a, for example, the supply line has shifted to the right, from S1 to S2. The shift represents an increase in supply. It shows that producers are willing and able to offer more gasoline for sale at each and every price. Study Figure 4-5a for a moment. With the increase in supply, at a price of $2.00 per gallon the millions of gallons offered for sale per week increased from 11 to 17. At a price of $4.00 per gallon, the number of gallons increased from 23 to 29 million per week.

Figure 4-5a: An Increase in Supply of Gasoline

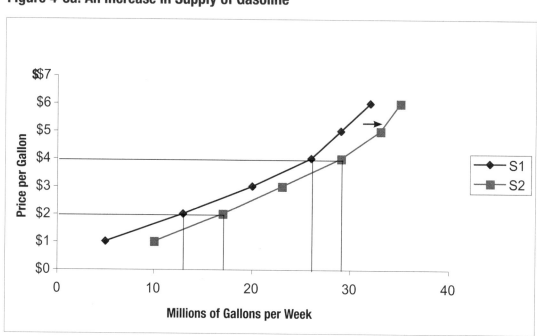

On the other hand, the supply line's shift to the left, from S1 to S3, in Figure 4-5b, represents a decrease in supply. It shows that producers are offering fewer gallons of gasoline for sale at all possible prices. In this case, at a price of $2.00 per gallon, the millions of gallons offered for sale per week decreased from 11 to 5. At a price of $5.00 per gallon, the amount of gallons offered for sale per week decreased from 27 to 22.

Figure 4-5b: A Decrease in Supply of Gasoline

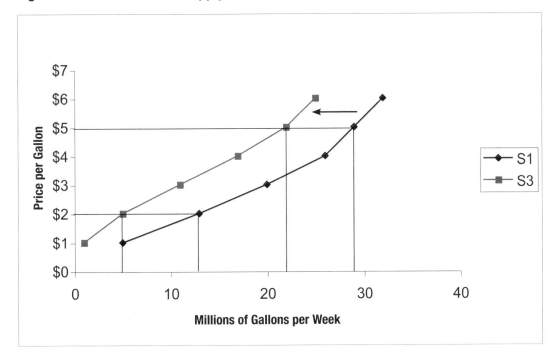

Check Your Understanding

In one sentence, explain what the graph in Figure 4-5b shows.

_____

_____

_____

_____

Changes in Supply

What might cause changes in supply? Economists expect shifts in supply if marginal production costs change, if the total number of firms in the market changes, or if producers have major changes in the expectations for future sales.

Changes in the marginal cost of production. Many businesses invest in research to discover ways to improve production strategies, find better and less-expensive materials, and design more efficient tools and equipment—all to reduce production costs. In addition, many workers suggest ways to reduce costs and improve efficiency. If, as a result of these efforts, the marginal cost of production falls, sellers will be able to supply more at every possible price.

The electronics business is a good example of falling marginal costs of production. All computers, cell phones, iPods, and flat-screen televisions are produced at much lower cost today than five years ago. In general, the supply of electronics equipment has increased in the last 10 years, reflecting the lower production costs at every level of operation. Lower production costs mean that producers can offer their products for sale at lower prices.

Pause to Predict

Before you start reading the next section, predict two situations that might cause changes in the supply of a certain product.

1. _____

_____

2. _____

_____

Changes in the number of producers. When new businesses enter a market, the supply will increase. For example, when in-line skates, bottled water, and mountain bikes became more popular, the number of businesses producing and selling them increased. In each market, these new producers helped increase the supply and shifted the supply curve to the right in these industries. As a consequence, the increases in supply allowed producers to offer more of their products at the same price as they did before new businesses entered the markets.

Change in expectations. If producers expect higher or lower future prices for their products, they may change the amount supplied today. For instance, if oil producers expect much higher prices for their oil in coming years, they might tend to leave more oil in the ground today so they can sell it in the future at the higher price. As a result, today's supply lines of oil and gasoline would decrease or both shift to the left. Another example might be SUVs. If producers of SUVs expect future prices to fall, they may lower their prices now, increasing their supply and shifting the supply lines to the right.

Just as price changes can cause a change in demand, so can price changes cause a change in supply. In a free market, prices play a very important role in what products are produced and sold.

Show Your Understanding

Underline the key sentence in each of the three subsections in "Changes in Supply" that will help you remember what conditions can cause a change in supply.

Changes in Supply

Read each statement below and explain why the situation will cause supply of the product to increase or decrease.

1. A severe frost destroys this year's crop of oranges. Will the supply of oranges increase or decrease? _____

   Why?_____

2. Entrepreneurs learn that the market for a new digital camera looks good, and many producers plan to get into this market. Will the supply of digital cameras increase or decrease? _____

   Why?_____

3. You and your friends learn that five new fast-food restaurants will be opening in your town, and they will pay their employees $12.00 per hour. Will the labor supply increase or decrease? _____

   Why?_____

Summary

The additional costs of producing additional goods and services are known as marginal costs, the change in cost for an additional output. Marginal costs usually go up as a business increases production. This situation occurs because a business uses more costly resources and methods to increase its rate of production.

A decision to produce goods and services, at whatever level, involves opportunity costs. Marginal costs are the opportunity costs of changing production levels. Marginal costs usually rise at higher rates of production. Businesses produce and sell larger quantities only at higher prices that offset these higher costs. As a result, the amount a business supplies depends on the price it receives.

In economics, supply is the various quantities of a product that producers are willing and able to sell at different prices at a particular time. Producers want to sell more of their products at higher prices than they do at lower prices. Prices serve as an incentive for producers to provide consumers with goods and services. This influence of market prices on the amount supplied is the price effect. The Law of Supply is a positive relationship between price and the quantity supplied.

When sellers offer goods and services in the market, their individual supplies are combined into market supply. Market supply also demonstrates the price effect. As a group, all producers in a market produce more as prices increase and less as prices decrease.

The size of the price effect is referred to as the price elasticity of supply. When the percentage change in price is less than the percentage change in the amount produced, supply is elastic; when the percentage change in price is greater than the percentage change in amount produced, supply is inelastic. Supply tends to be more elastic when resources can be easily and quickly shifted into or out of production. The price elasticity of supply also depends on the amount of time that producers have to increase or decrease production when a price changes. The longer producers have to make these adjustments, the more elastic supply tends to be.

The price effect refers to changes in the amount producers want to sell at different prices while supply remains unchanged. A change in supply means that producers are willing and able to sell different amounts at all possible prices. Graphically, a change in supply is a shift of a supply curve to the right or left. In contrast, the price effect (which is not a change in supply) means movement up or down an existing supply curve. Some of the factors that can change (shift) supply are a change in the marginal cost of production, an increase or decrease in the number of sellers, and a change in producer expectations.

Will the supply of digital cameras increase or decrease as more producers enter the market?

Looking Ahead

In the next chapter, "Market-Clearing Price," you will combine demand and supply to see how voluntary exchange creates market prices. You also will learn about the important roles of prices in a market economy.

Notes

Market-Clearing Price

Read to Find Out

As you read this chapter, look for answers to the following questions:

How do competitive markets "clear" the amount buyers want to purchase with the amount sellers want to sell?

What are shortages and surpluses, and how does market competition eliminate them?

How do market-clearing prices send signals to buyers and sellers?

How do market-clearing prices ration goods and services?

How do market-clearing prices motivate people to produce goods and services?

How do changes in demand and supply bring about changes in market-clearing prices?

Mark to Remember

* *This is important.*

? *I have a question about this.*

! *This is a surprise.*

Why It Matters

A market economy always undergoes changes and adjustments. If this were not so, we would not have the rich economy we have in the United States. As our economy changes, markets function to allocate scarce resources. Prices serve to help the economy change and adjust. To understand how prices adjust to accommodate changes in the economy, you must understand the interaction of supply and demand. It is important to notice why price changes take place, and, most important, how to anticipate these changes. Understanding the interaction of supply and demand will help you become a better consumer and, ultimately, a better producer.

Market-Clearing Price

Building On What You Know

You participate in markets every day when you buy products and services. Sometimes you notice that the price of a product you regularly buy goes up. Sometimes that product goes "on sale," and its price is less. What makes prices go up and down? It's not magic, as you will learn.

"Next up is Milk Dud. Raised at Long Valley Ranch, this fine two-year-old Black Angus is being shown today by her proud owner, Shawna." You might hear this statement at a stock show cattle auction.

Across the United States, from large cities to small towns, stock shows attract sellers and buyers of livestock. Livestock is sold at auction. Auctions are markets. Markets occur anywhere and anytime people make exchanges with one another. Wherever markets occur, they give rise to a market price, such as $7,800 for the Grand Champion Junior Market Steer at the 2000 Arizona National Stock Show. In turn, each market price plays a role in guiding buyers' choices in a market economy. How do prices do this? How do markets create prices? By combining the concepts of demand and supply from the previous two chapters, you will be able to better understand market behavior.

Demand and Supply Together

As you learned in Chapter 3, "Demand," market demand shows that consumers buy less gasoline if its price goes up. This is the price effect as it applies to demand.

In Chapter 4, "Supply," you learned that oil companies want to sell more gasoline if its price goes up. This is the price effect as it relates to supply. Notice a potential problem. While a higher price makes sellers want to sell more gasoline, it makes buyers want to buy less! It might seem, then, that buyers and sellers won't agree on the amounts of gasoline they want to buy and sell. In reality there is one price at which sellers want to sell as much as buyers want to buy. This is the price at which quantity supplied equals the quantity demanded.

Some people incorrectly state that supply equals demand at a market price. Why is such a statement incorrect? From what you learned earlier, you should recognize three problems. First, for supply to equal demand, consumers would want to buy as much as sellers would want to sell at every possible price. Second, on a graph, supply and demand would be drawn with the same line at all prices and amounts. Third, it would also mean that the law of demand and the law of supply would have the same definition. Of course, they do not.

How a Market Clears

Look carefully at the graph in Figure 5-1. Notice at $3.00 per gallon, businesses want to sell and consumers want to buy 19 million gallons per week, as shown on the horizontal axis. Economists call this point the **market-clearing price**, as shown on the vertical axis. The market-clearing price is the price at which the amount supplied is equal to the amount demanded. This is the only price that balances or "clears" the market.

Does this price leave everyone in the market satisfied? No! Everyone who wants to buy more gas at lower prices is not satisfied. Any producer who wants to sell gasoline at a higher price is not satisfied. On the other hand, the market has found a level of activity that allows it to continue.

Do markets always operate at the market-clearing price? Sometimes prices are lower than the market-clearing price. At other times, the prices are higher. However, the prices tend to be close to or moving toward the market-clearing price at all times. Let's examine more carefully how a market clears.

Figure 5-1: Market-Clearing Price

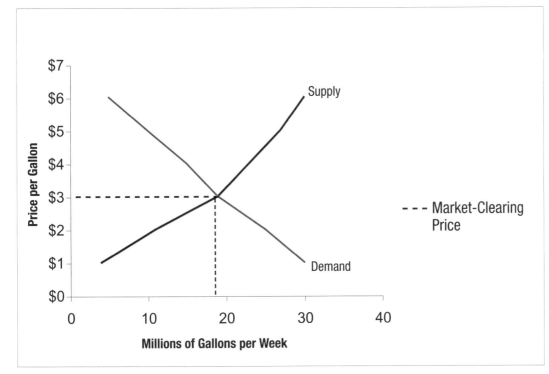

Show Your Understanding

Underline in the text the three reasons why it is incorrect to say that supply equals demand at a market price.

Check Your Understanding

Write in your own words a definition of market-clearing price.

_____

_____

_____

Show Your Understanding

On Figure 5-1, trace the supply line with a broken line (_ _ _ _). Trace the demand line with dots (. . .). Circle the point at which the supply and demand lines intersect. What is this point called?

_____

At $4.00 per gallon, how many million gallons of gas will be demanded?

_____

At $4.00 per gallon, how many gallons of gasoline will be supplied?

_____

Market-Clearing Prices

In the next few days, observe and write down the price of regular gasoline at several gas stations or outlets in your community.

**Price of
Regular Gasoline**   **Gas Station or Outlet**

_____   _____

_____   _____

_____   _____

_____   _____

Analyze the information you collected. Is there a market-clearing price for regular gasoline in your community? _____

If the prices per gallon vary slightly, what does that mean? _____
_____

Market Shortage

Market competition tends to move prices toward market-clearing levels. Study the graph in Figure 5-2. At $1.00, buyers want to buy 30 million gallons of gasoline, but producers want to sell only 4 million gallons. The difference between these two amounts, 26 million gallons, is a *shortage*. In economics, a **shortage** is the difference between the amount supplied and the amount demanded when the asking price is less than a market-clearing price.

Figure 5-2: A Shortage of Gasoline

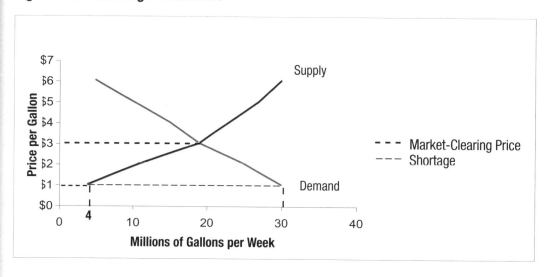

Check Your Understanding

What is the gasoline shortage at a price of $2.00, as shown in Figure 5-2?

_____

2. shortage

A shortage causes buyers to compete more intensely for the amount available. Since all buyers can't buy the gasoline they demand at $1.00 per gallon, many voluntarily (but unhappily) pay more money for gasoline. As they do so, two things happen. First, many buyers reduce the amount of gasoline they want to buy. At $2.00 per gallon, for example, the graph shows that they want to buy 25 million gallons instead of 30 million gallons. Second, many producers increase the amount of gasoline they want to sell. At $2.00 per gallon, they will offer for sale 11 million gallons per week instead of the 4 million gallons they offered at $1.00.

As long as the price is less than its market-clearing level, buyers compete more intensely for the product and push the price still higher. As the price rises, the amount demanded falls, and the amount supplied rises. Figure 5-2 shows these changes as movement up the demand and supply curves. When the price reaches its market-clearing level, the amounts demanded and the amounts supplied are equal. The shortage is eliminated, so buyers don't bid the price higher. Every buyer willing and able to buy gas at this price or higher prices can purchase their gasoline. Every buyer who wants to buy gasoline only at a lower price has to go without it. The suppliers are in a similar situation. Any seller willing and able to sell gasoline at $3.00 a gallon or lower can sell their gasoline. If they wish to sell at a higher price, they will be unsuccessful.

Market Surplus
What if the price is above its market-clearing level? In this case, sellers want to sell more than buyers want to buy. The graph in Figure 5-3 shows that at $5.00 per gallon, producers want to sell 27 million gallons of gasoline per week, but buyers as a whole want to buy only 10 million gallons. The difference between these two amounts, 17 million gallons, is a *surplus*. In economics, a **surplus** is the difference between the amount supplied and the amount demanded when the asking price is greater than a market-clearing price.

Figure 5-3: A Surplus of Gasoline

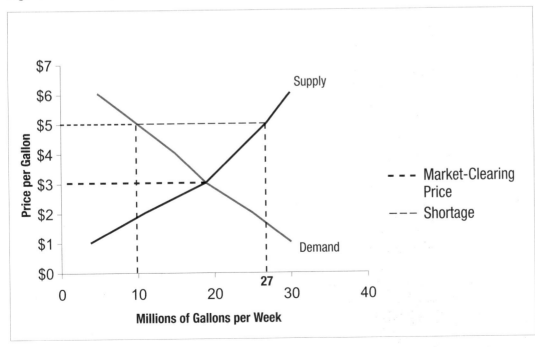

Think Critically

You've heard the expression "Prices are going through the roof." Although prices do sometimes seem high, what keeps prices from going up indefinitely?

_____

_____

Check Your Understanding

What is the gasoline surplus at a price of $4.00, as shown in Figure 5-3?

_____

When a surplus exists, sellers begin competing more intensely against one another for consumers' money. For example, they may offer their gasoline at lower prices. However, as the price begins to fall, two things happen. First, many sellers reduce the amount of gasoline they want to sell. At $4.00 per gallon, for instance, they want to sell 23 million gallons instead of the 27 million gallons they offered when the price was $5.00. Second, some buyers increase the amount of gasoline they want to buy. At $4.00 per gallon, buyers as a group want to buy 15 million gallons per week instead of the 10 million gallons they wanted at $5.00.

A Surplus or Something Scarce?

Can there be a surplus of scarce products? That statement sounds like a contradiction, doesn't it? This is another example of the use of words in economics that may differ from their use in everyday conversation. In everyday conversation, the word *surplus* might mean that sellers are offering more of something than people want. To economists, however, the word means something very different and precise. It means that people don't want to buy all the product that sellers want to sell at the existing price.

The difference between the two meanings is a distinction between wants and demands. Demands are wants backed by a willingness and ability to pay for their satisfaction. We demand less than we want because we must pay a price to satisfy our wants. As the price rises, we then demand smaller and smaller quantities, leaving more of our wants unsatisfied. At prices above the market-clearing level, we not only buy less than we want, but we also buy less than sellers want to sell. The result is a surplus, even of a scarce item, like oil.

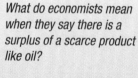

Surplus, Shortage, or Market-Clearing Price

Read the following statements. Indicate whether the markets described are in surplus, in shortage, or in a market-clearing price status.

1. A rock concert will take place in six months. Tickets are $120 per person. The concert has been sold out for a month, and people are trying to buy tickets on eBay. Some eBay tickets are selling for $500.

   _____

2. A major league baseball team is selling tickets for $50 per seat, per game. You can buy a ticket on the day of the game without waiting in line. Of the 60,000 seats in the stadium, only 20,000 people are attending the game.

   _____

3. Cola has been selling at $3.00 per six-pack for the past eight months at the local grocery store. You can buy a six-pack any time you enter the store, and the store never runs out before the next shipment from the supplier.

   _____

Alfred Marshall

Alfred Marshall was born in 1842 into a middle-class family in Clapham, a London suburb. His father was a cashier with the Bank of England and supervised his son's classical education with the ultimate goal of Marshall's ordination in the Anglican church. However, Marshall chose to attend St. John's in Cambridge, where he studied mathematics and became one of the outstanding mathematics students of his time.

Upon graduation, Marshall received a fellowship to pursue his work in mathematics. At Cambridge he became influenced by philosophers who were concerned with the many social problems in England. Marshall realized that poverty in England was a social evil. This led him to the study of economics.

Marshall is best known for his *Principles of Economics*, published in 1890. The influence of the book was significant—so significant that many have called the first quarter of the 20th century in economic thought "the age of Marshall."

Marshall brought mathematics to bear on economic analysis. He did not view mathematics as the core of economic science. To him, mathematical statements should be only footnotes. He believed that mathematical statements could only help explain big ideas in economics and that economic analysis could be applied to social ills.

Marshall's definition of economics, "the study of man in the ordinary business of life," underscores his concern that the discipline should focus on the real world around us. He introduced what economists call comparative statistics. That is, to stop the economy at a point in time and examine it.

Comparative statistics led to Marshall defining demand and the concept of diminishing marginal utility that stands behind a downward sloping demand curve. He extended his thinking to the operation of markets, including supply with demand analysis, and the introduction of market price.

iStockphoto '07

The Functions of Prices in a Market System

Anna wants to buy a new dress for her mother. She visits a nearby shopping mall and compares prices of different dresses. Anna finds a department store that offers dresses for $60, $80, and $120. Anna considers her mother's tastes and her own income, buys the middle-priced dress for $80, and hopes her mother will like it.

When she gets home, Anna browses some mail-order catalogs. She is surprised to find a dress identical to the one she bought. It is on sale for $10 less than the one she bought, and shipping is included. Anna decides to buy the dress online with her credit card, and then she returns the dress to the mall department store.

Anna's story demonstrates the importance of prices in a market economy. The process of buying a gift for a relative would be much more difficult and would take more time without a price system.

Prices serve three main functions in a market system. They send signals to both buyers and sellers. They limit or ration the number of buyers who are willing and able to buy or sell a product in a market. Prices, depending on whether they are high or low, motivate sellers to offer more or less product for sale in a market. They also motivate buyers to buy more or less product.

Prices Send Signals

A market price is like a police officer directing traffic at a busy intersection. If the officer signals you as a seller to "go," the market price is high. As a seller, you know you can produce more and make more sales at high prices. If the officer tells you to "stop," this is a signal that the market price is low. The signal to you as a seller is to cut back on production and offer less of your product for sale.

Apply Your
Understanding

*Merchants often send buyers
signals of favorable prices on
products. What are signals
you might see in a store?*

_____

_____

For buyers, the police officer's signals result in the opposite behavior. At a high market price—a "go" signal for sellers—buyers will buy less of a product. To buyers, this is a "stop" signal. At a low market price—a "go" price for buyers—consumers are encouraged to buy more of the product. Sellers, however, may interpret the signal as a "stop."

Prices send information—signals—to both buyers and sellers in a market. Careful buyers and profit-seeking sellers use prices to make their own thoughtful buying and selling decisions.

Prices Ration

Think Critically

*Do you think it is fair to
ration products so that
only the people who are
willing and able to pay
for the products can get
the products?*

_____

_____

A second function of prices is to ration scarce goods among people who want more goods than are available. **Rationing** means distributing or allocating a product by a price system. The product is rationed to the person who is willing and able to pay the market-clearing price.

Auctions are a good illustration of rationing. You read about cattle auctions earlier. The United States government also has auctions, but when the government holds an auction, it sells U.S. Treasury bills (T-bills), which are also known as government bonds. Selling Treasury bills is the government's way of borrowing money because every Treasury bill is an IOU (I Owe You) in which the government promises to repay the person who buys the bonds within a certain time period.

In August 2006, the U.S. Treasury Department held an auction in which it offered $17 billion worth of $1,000, three-month Treasury bills to the highest bidders. Buyers, who can be individuals or financial institutions, placed bids on the Treasury bills. As with most auctions, bidders started with low bids, but as the auction progressed, more and higher bids were made until the number of bids equaled all the Treasury bills for sale that day. The market-clearing price was $950.20. No Treasury bills were allocated to bidders whose offers were less than $950.20. For those who bought the Treasury bills at $950.20, the government promised to repay them $1,000 in three months.

Every day, we depend on market prices to ration goods and services. In reality, though, we pay little, if any, attention to prices as they perform this necessary task. When using market prices to ration goods and services, we are making one of the three basic choices that people everywhere must make. We are deciding who gets the goods and services the economy produces. The market-clearing price keeps people who will pay less for the product from buying that product. The market-clearing price also prevents sellers from selling their product for more than that price. Look at our analysis of gasoline prices again.

Figures 5-1, 5-2, and 5-3 show that consumers want to buy 19 million gallons of gasoline if the price is $3.00 per gallon. The buyers want more than 19 million gallons per week, but they buy less than they want because they have to pay for each gallon. When the price rises to $3.00 per gallon, they stop using gasoline for purposes they value less than this amount. In this way, the market-clearing price of $3.00 rations the scarce supply of gasoline.

Figure 5-4: Increase in World Price of Oil

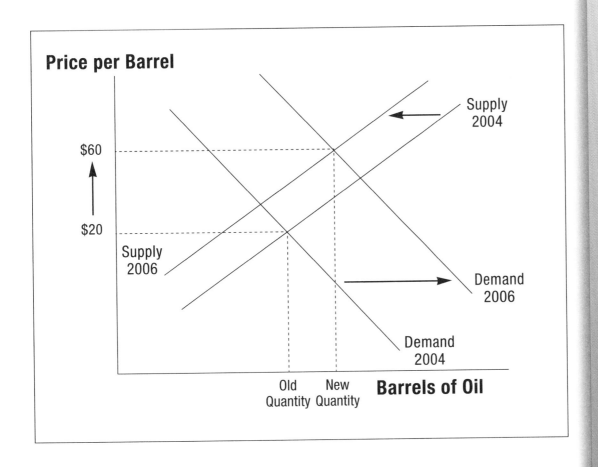

Show Your Understanding

1. On Figure 5-4, draw a line with an arrow between the 2004 and 2006 supply lines to show the direction of the shift or change in supply.

2. Draw a line with an arrow between the 2004 and 2006 demand lines to show the direction of the shift or change in demand.

3. In a market for any product, if supply decreases and demand increases, what happens to price?

Anything scarce must be rationed because there is not enough to satisfy all of everyone's wants. Market-clearing prices are one, but only one, method of doing so. If market prices do not ration, then some other means of rationing may occur. For example, during the 1970s and early 1980s, countries belonging to the Organization of the Petroleum Exporting Countries (OPEC) reduced the amount of oil they were placing on the world market. The world price of oil, and subsequently gasoline, quickly moved higher. The U.S. government passed a law keeping the price of gasoline to consumers below its market-clearing level. As a result, consumers waited in long lines at gasoline stations. Instead of competing in the market by paying a higher price for gasoline, consumers competed by waiting in line. This is a classic case of a market shortage.

During 2006 gasoline prices increased dramatically as a result of the war in Iraq and the increased demand for gasoline by China and India when these countries experienced strong economic growth. In this case, the price was allowed to move to new market-clearing levels. No one had to wait in line for their gasoline, but everyone paid more per gallon. Soon people began to drive less and use more fuel-efficient cars so they could minimize their gasoline consumption.

In Figure 5-4, the graph demonstrates a change that took place in the oil market in 2005–2006. War in the Middle East made it difficult to increase or maintain international oil supplies. Oil companies in the United States did not have time to expand their production, so there was a decline in oil supply. The oil supply line shifted to the left. Meanwhile, positive economic growth in India, China, and the United States contributed to an increased demand for oil, shifting the demand line to the right. The result was a dramatic increase in the price of oil in a short time.

In freely competitive markets, the market-clearing price rations. At this price, sellers have no surplus and buyers experience no shortage.

Prices Motivate

A third function of prices is to provide incentives for people to produce goods and services. In fact, the method used to ration goods and services can have a big effect on the willingness to produce them in the first place. Consider again what happens when gasoline is rationed by waiting in line. In this case, consumers bear an opportunity cost when they sacrifice their time by waiting in line. However, their time isn't a cost they pay to producers, so producers have no motivation to offer more gasoline for sale.

In contrast, when market-clearing prices are determined by the rationing method, consumers still pay an opportunity cost for the gasoline, but the cost is a monetary cost, not a time cost. By paying money to producers, consumers provide the necessary motivation to producers to increase gasoline production. Of course, there would be no gasoline without crude oil to make it, and there would be no crude oil without market incentives to produce it. As Chapter 4, "Supply," explained, companies produce more oil at higher prices and less oil at lower prices. They are responding to market incentives—to prices that motivate oil production.

Examine the graphs in Figure 5-5. The top graph shows U.S. average per barrel oil prices, and the second graph shows U.S. oil production in thousands of barrels per day. During the period 1980 to 1999, crude oil prices in the United States declined. As might be expected in an oil supply situation, the production of oil also declined during the same period. This example demonstrates that suppliers will produce less of a product when the market price declines.

Think Critically

Which method of dealing with a gasoline shortage do you think is preferable: the methods used in the 1970s and 1980s or the one used in 2006?

_____

Why? _____

_____

_____

Think Critically

Sometimes producers decide to put their product into the market at a price below the market-clearing price. Why?

_____

_____

_____

Figure 5-5a: Average Prices of Crude Oil in the United States During 5-Year Periods

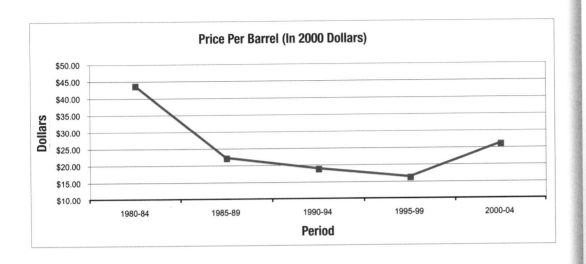

Price Per Barrel (In 2000 Dollars)

Figure 5-5b: Average Daily Production of Crude Oil in the United States During 5-Year Periods

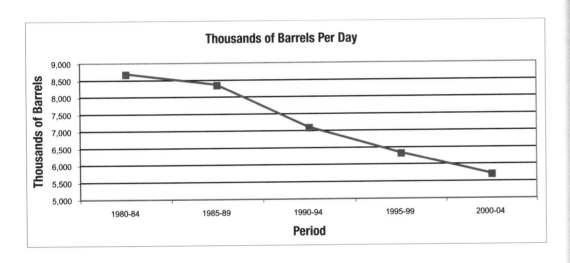

Thousands of Barrels Per Day

Source: U.S. Energy Information Administration, *Annual Energy Review 2004*.
Website: www.eia.gov

Prices of Crude Oil in Two Time Periods, 1985–1989 and 1990–1994

Check your skill at reading historical line graphs. Study Figure 5-5a and Figure 5-5b, and complete the table below with information from the graphs.

	Price per Barrel	Thousands of Barrels per Day
1985–1989	_____	_____
1990–1994	_____	_____

*Following the descriptions
of price situations below,
indicate whether the price
in each is signaling,
rationing, or motivating.*

*1. You have $8.00 that you
saved to see a movie. When
you arrive at the movie, you
find the price has increased
to $9.00.*

_____

*2. You learn that the couple
next door is willing to pay
$20.00 for you to mow
their lawn. You have the
equipment and the time to
mow a lawn.*

_____

*3. You learn that a sporting
event you want to attend will
offer a 50 percent discount
to the first 200 fans in line to
buy tickets.*

_____

**Pause to
Think**

*Study Figure 5-6 and write
two generalizations about
the changes that occurred
in the top U.S. companies
between 1955 and 2006.*

1. _____

_____

_____

2. _____

_____

_____

During the 1990s and the early part of the 21st century, world producers increased the world supply of oil, which contributed to lower oil prices and discouraged new U.S. production. Meanwhile, car manufacturers began producing cars that used less gasoline, and businesses found ways to produce goods and services with less oil. As a result, the market-clearing price of oil declined throughout the world. As the price fell in the United States, so did the amount of oil produced from U.S. oil wells.

Why did U.S. oil production decline while prices increased from 1995 to 2004 as shown in Figures 5-5a and b? U.S. laws have prevented oil companies from drilling for new oil reserves offshore along the Atlantic, Pacific, and Gulf coasts, as well as in the Alaskan wilderness. These laws, passed to protect environmentally sensitive areas, restrict companies from drilling in potentially high oil-producing areas. If Congress changed the laws, would U.S. oil production increase? Perhaps. Economic theory and historical evidence suggest that a change in incentives, in this case fewer restrictive laws and higher prices, would result in greater production. The concern still remains, however, that the environmental costs caused by increasing oil production may be too great to justify the increased output.

Market-clearing prices provide incentives, or motivations, to producers. This is how market prices are used to make the other two basic choices that people in any economy must make. Besides choosing who gets the goods and services produced (rationing), people must also decide what products to produce and how to produce them. In a market system, people make these choices based on market price.

Changes in Prices and Production

Because a product's demand or supply can change, each market price is likely to rise or fall over time. Some may go up, and others may go down. But as market-clearing prices vary, they change the incentives to produce particular products or provide certain services. The result is that over time we see changes in the kinds and quantities of items and services produced in our economy.

The Fortune 500, a listing of the top 500 companies in the United States, is a good illustration. Since 1954, *Fortune* magazine has published a yearly listing of the largest industrial corporations in the United States. The list includes service-producing companies as well as industrial companies. The listings in Figure 5-6 compare the top 10 companies in the Fortune 500 in the years 1955 and 2006.

Figure 5-6: Top 10 Companies in the Fortune 500

1955	2006
1. General Motors (Motor Vehicles & Parts)	1. ExxonMobil (Petroleum Refining)
2. Standard Oil (Petroleum Refining)	2. Wal-Mart Stores (General Merchandising)
3. U.S. Steel (Steel)	3. General Motors (Motor Vehicles & Parts)
4. General Electric (Aerospace, Engines, Etc.)	4. Chevron (Petroleum Refining)
5. Swift (Food Processing)	5. Ford Motor Company (Motor Vehicles & Parts)
6. Chrysler (Motor Vehicles)	6. ConocoPhillips (Petroleum Refining)
7. Armour (Food Processing)	7. General Electric (Diversified Financials)
8. Gulf Oil (Petroleum Refining)	8. Citigroup (Commercial Bank)
9. Mobil (Petroleum Refining)	9. AIG (Insurance)
10. DuPont (Chemicals, Plastics, Etc.)	10. IBM (Computers & Office Equipment)

Source: http://money.cnn.com/magazines/fortune/fortune500, June 2006

Besides increasing the production of services in our economy, variations in demand and supply have caused particular companies to expand and others to contract. For example, the Fortune 500 of 1955 includes two companies, Armour and Swift, that have since disappeared from the list. Both businesses were meat packing companies near the Chicago stockyards. Since 1954, consumer tastes for red meat have declined; chicken consumption has increased; and new, more efficient meat packing companies have opened facilities elsewhere. As Chapter 3 explained, changes in tastes and availability of substitutes can shift a demand line. In this case, the demand for Armour and Swift products declined, so their product demand lines shifted to the left. Both companies gradually became smaller and were eventually purchased by ConAgra, Inc., a large company that produces many products from agricultural crops.

Other companies also disappeared from the list because they were replaced by faster-growing businesses that joined the Fortune 500. Indeed, of the 500 original companies in 1954, only about 20 percent appeared on the list in 2006. What's more, nearly 90 of the companies on the 2006 list did not even exist in 1954. McDonald's, Nike, FedEx, Apple, Wal-Mart, and Microsoft are a few examples.

Some companies new to the Fortune 500 have prospered because they developed more efficient methods of producing goods and services and lowered prices for consumers. Others have introduced new products. These are the businesses that have survived market competition over the years. Through innovation and greater efficiency, they reduced their marginal costs of production and maintained or increased their profits. As Chapter 4 pointed out, lower production costs increase supply by shifting supply lines to the right. Consumers benefit from the new products and lower prices. Workers benefit from new jobs and higher wages, and the companies' owners benefit from more sales and higher earnings.

Figure 5-7: Decrease in the Market-Clearing Price of Computers

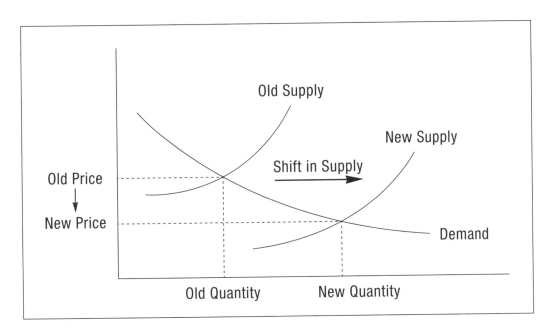

Check Your Understanding

Use Figure 5-7 to answer these questions.

In a market, if supply increases and demand remains the same, what happens to price?

_____

What happens to the amount exchanged?

_____

The graph in Figure 5-7 illustrates a change in market-clearing price for computers. Technological changes enabled businesses to increase the supply of computers. The greater supply then caused the market-clearing price of computers to fall. As the price of computers fell, more people purchased computers for use in their homes and businesses.

Prices play a major role in the products available to us in the marketplace and in how much we pay for these products. Both supply and demand affect prices. Both the actions of producers and consumers affect prices. Next time you see a sign announcing "Price Reduction," think about why the market-clearing price of that product has decreased.

How Shifting Demand and Supply Can Affect Prices

Read the following statement.

When clothes are in season, the prices rise. When the season passes, stores put the clothes on sale. However, when fruits and vegetables are in season, the prices fall. When the season passes, the prices rise.

Explain why price changes for seasonal clothing and seasonal produce seem to be contradictory.

_____

_____

_____

Check Your Understanding

What is the message of this cartoon?

_____

_____

Summary

A market-clearing price exists when the amount of a product that buyers want to buy at that price is the same as the amount that sellers want to sell at that price. At any other price, a shortage or a surplus exists. A shortage occurs at the price at which buyers want to buy more than sellers want to sell. A surplus occurs at the price at which sellers want to sell more than buyers want to buy. Competition among buyers pushes prices up toward their market-clearing levels. Competition among sellers pushes prices down toward market-clearing levels.

Market-clearing prices have important roles in a free enterprise economy. First, they send signals—price information—to buyers and sellers. Second, they ration existing supplies among consumers who want more supplies than an economy's scarce resources can produce. When doing so, market prices enable people to choose who gets the goods and services produced. Third, market-clearing prices also provide incentives or motivations to producers to produce goods and services. Market prices guide decisions about what (and how much) to produce and how to produce these goods and services.

Demand and supply are continually changing, causing some market-clearing prices to rise and some to fall. These higher and lower prices cause some businesses in our economy to expand and others to contract. A comparison of the Fortune 500 list of businesses over the last 50-plus years illustrates dramatic changes in the economy.

Market-clearing prices provide vital information and incentives in free enterprise. They reveal to businesses the kinds and quantities of goods and services that consumers want produced. They also reveal to consumers the cost of producing the various goods and services they want. Both businesses and consumers use this information when deciding what and how much to produce and consume.

Looking Ahead

Consumer demands are a powerful market force that help guide choices in a free enterprise economy. The next chapter focuses on consumer spending. It discusses the role played by consumers in the U.S. economy and how consumers earn their incomes. It also describes how consumers can get more for their money by spending their incomes wisely.

Notes

Consumers, Savers, and Investors

Read to Find Out

As you read this chapter, look for answers to the following questions:

What are the two main sources of household income?

What factors influence wealth accumulation?

How do personal budgets help you make wise choices as a consumer and saver?

What should you consider in making saving and investing decisions?

What are some alternative places to put your savings?

What are the advantages and disadvantages of using credit?

What protects consumer interests in a market economy?

Why It Matters

You have many roles to play in our economy. Right now, you may not think these are very important, but they soon will be. You may now be a worker, earning wages from a part-time job. You may save and soon you might invest. You certainly are a consumer, buying many things. By the time you are an adult, your roles will include worker, saver, investor, and consumer. It is important that you learn as much as you can about these roles and how you can act responsibly in each.

Chapter 6

Consumers, Savers, and Investors

Building On What You Know

Do you know someone who spends all of his or her paycheck? Do you know someone who saves part of each paycheck? Do you know someone who invests in the stock market? Do you know someone who is in credit card trouble? As you have learned, every American has the right to make his or her own financial decisions. Those decisions can lead to a secure financial life or to financial disaster.

Think about the money you spend. According to Teenage Research Unlimited, teens spent $159 billion in 2005. About two-thirds of this amount ($107 billion) was spent on consumer goods and services, including clothes, entertainment, and food. Teens are indeed consumers; they buy goods and services for personal use. Teens also are potential savers and investors. You are no doubt aware that you are a target of advertisers.

Figure 6-1: Consumption as a Percent of Gross Domestic Product, 2004

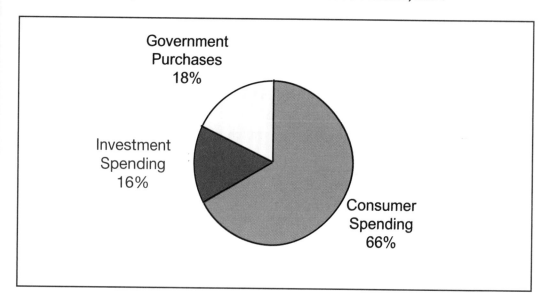

Government Purchases 18%

Investment Spending 16%

Consumer Spending 66%

Source: *Statistical Abstract of the United States: 2006*, Table 650.

Let's look at the overall picture of the United States. The circle graph in Figure 6-1 shows what economists call the *gross domestic product* (GDP) of the United States in 2004. **Gross domestic product** is the final value of all goods and services produced in the country in one year. The U.S. gross domestic product was almost $12 trillion in 2004. Of this amount, 66 percent, or about $8 trillion, was spent on consumer goods and services. When you and other consumers spend your money, you are taking part in markets for goods and services. However, as you learned in studying the Circular Flow of Money, Resources, and Products in Chapter 2, before you can become a consumer, you must have money or earn income.

Sources of Income

Before you can buy the things you want, you need to have money or earn income. In most instances, people earn income from their work. Teenagers receive their income from a variety of sources. According to Teenage Research Unlimited, teens' major sources of income are parents, odd jobs, part-time jobs, and full-time jobs. Gifts also contribute to teen income.

Income from Work

Most of the income you'll earn over your lifetime will come from the work you do for others, or, if you own a business, the work you do for yourself. In return for your labor, you'll receive a *wage* or a *salary*. A **wage** is earnings paid by the hour or unit of production. A **salary** is earnings paid weekly, monthly, or on a yearly basis. How much you earn will depend on the nature of your job, your skills, your education, your performance, your entrepreneurial drive, and other factors. Figure 6-2 is a table that shows the median monthly earnings for a variety of jobs. The median isn't the starting salary or the top income you might receive. The median monthly earnings is the middle amount of earnings in the full range of earnings for a particular job category.

Figure 6-2: Median Monthly Earnings by Job Category, 2004

Pharmacist	$7,263	Auto Mechanic	$2,718
Electrical Engineer	$6,064	Reporter	$2,638
Economist	$6,031	Bus Driver	$2,556
Computer Programmer	$5,248	Photographer	$2,218
Architect	$5,119	Secretary	$2,204
Registered Nurse	$4,470	Bank Teller	$1,763
Accountant	$4,276	Taxi Driver	$1,649
Mail Carrier	$3,823	Janitor	$1,593
Police Officer	$3,800	Retail Sales Worker	$1,566
Plumber	$3,489	Farm Worker	$1,459
Real Estate Agent	$3,079	Cashier	$1,348
Carpenter	$2,928	Waiter/Waitress	$1,174

Source: Bureau of Labor Statistics, *2004 National Occupational Employment and Wage Estimates*
Website: http://www.bls.gov/oes/tables.htm
Calculation: Median annual earnings estimates divided by 12

1. Gross domestic product   2. wage   3. salary

Who Earns What?

Indicate whether the statements below are true (T) or false (F). Use information from Figure 6-2.

1. A janitor makes more money than a bus driver. _____

2. An economist makes more money than an accountant. _____

3. A photographer and a secretary make about the same amount of money. _____

4. The median monthly earnings of a real estate agent are $3,079. _____

Income from Wealth

Wealth is the value of the things you own. Adding together the value of all your tangible possessions, bank accounts, savings, and investments gives you the total amount of your wealth, generally referred to as an individual's *net worth*. **Net worth** refers to an individual's wealth after debts and other obligations have been subtracted. Used in certain ways, wealth can earn income. If you own a lawn mower, for example, you might charge a fee for others to use it. Economists would say that you are using your wealth to earn *rent*. **Rent** is the payment for the use of someone else's property. Wealth in the form of money that is loaned to others or deposited in a savings account will earn *interest*. **Interest** is income earned from allowing someone else to use your financial capital. Rent and interest are two forms of income that can be earned from wealth.

Factors That Influence Wealth Accumulation

Most people want to accumulate wealth. Accumulated wealth is the initial money and/or assets you earn and the money and assets you add to your initial wealth. How can you accumulate wealth? Quite simply, you have to save and invest. By not spending every dollar you earn, you can set aside money and put it to work to make your wealth grow.

According to the U.S. Bureau of Economic Analysis, in 2006 U.S. consumers had a negative average rate of savings of 1½ percent based on their *disposable income*. **Disposable income** is the money you take home after taxes are paid. In 2006, as a whole, people in the United States spent more than their disposable income. This compares with a previous year, such as 2003, when people had a positive average of savings of about 3 percent of disposable income. The amount people save depends on their income, expectations for future income, current rates of interest, and taxation.

Income

As income levels increase, people in a typical household save and invest more. When income levels decrease, people save and invest less. If people in a household are wealthy, they are likely to save and invest more of their current income.

Expectations

Expectations are what people think, or hope, will happen in the future. Expectations can be a powerful force in our economy. When people feel good about their current income situation and their future, they spend more freely. Their rate of savings may fall, but their

4. wealth   5. net worth   6. rent   7. interest   8. disposable income

spending helps boost the economy's growth. However, if job security and incomes are in jeopardy, people tend to save more of their income and spend less. The 1980s and 1990s are prime examples. During the 1980s, when people were more concerned about their economic well-being, the annual savings rate fluctuated between 5 and 10 percent of disposable income. In contrast, when consumer confidence soared during much of the 1990s, the savings rate dipped to an all-time low.

Current Interest Rates

Higher interest rates tend to promote saving—they are incentives to save. For example, if banks paid a 2 percent annual savings rate, interest earned on $10,000 in savings would amount to $200. However, at a savings interest rate of 8 percent, the annual interest earned on $10,000 in savings would be $800. In this case, the 8 percent interest rate would encourage people to save more.

Taxes

Government tax rates can encourage or discourage savings. Higher taxes on income earned from savings and investments discourage people from saving. Cutting taxes on savings and investments encourages people to set money aside for saving and investing.

Banks, insurance companies, and stock brokerages work hard to persuade you to save or invest more of your money. In contrast, U.S. businesses, such as department stores, movie theaters, and cosmetic companies, want you to spend more. Businesses try to encourage more consumer spending through advertising and sales promotions. As a result, not only must you make choices about which things to buy, but you also must choose how much to save and invest.

Think Critically

Of the four factors that influence saving, which do you think most discourages savings?

_____

Why? _____

_____

Deciding Where To Save

Consider the following illustrative scenario. You have $2,000 in a savings account at your bank. You earn 3 percent interest per year on your savings. You can use some of your savings at any time you need extra cash. If you leave your $2,000 in savings for a year, how much interest income will you earn at the end of a year? _____

You know you can earn more interest at another bank, at a credit union, or at a savings and loan institution. If you save at another bank, you can withdraw some money without penalty. At a savings and loan institution, you cannot withdraw any of your savings during the year, even for an emergency, without losing all your interest income. Where will you put your savings? To help you decide, complete the table below.

The interest paid on savings is a factor customers consider when choosing a financial institution.

Savings Institution	Interest Rate	Annual Interest Earned
Bank One	5%	_____
Bank Two	6%	_____
Savings and Loan One	8%	_____
Savings and Loan Two	10%	_____

Where will you put your savings and why? _____

_____

A Budget's Influence on Saving and Investing Choices

To help you with your buying and saving choices, you will want to know how much money you receive (income) and how much you plan to spend. Many people use personal financial plans, or *budgets*. A **budget** summarizes an individual's planned income and spending over a specific time period. Look at the bar graph in Figure 6-3, which shows the budget of the average American consumer in 2003. For our purposes here, the average consumer represents a household. Note that housing costs account for over 30 percent of spending, while spending on reading materials is less than 1 percent.

Think Critically

Review each of the categories of expenditures in Figure 6-3. Identify the three categories in which you think an individual consumer can most readily reduce spending, if necessary.

_____

_____

_____

Why did you select these categories?

_____

_____

Apply Your Understanding

Which of the Figure 6-3 categories describe your personal expenditures? List them all, and then estimate the percent of your total expenditures that each category represents.

_____

_____

_____

_____

Figure 6-3: Budget of Average Consumer in 2003

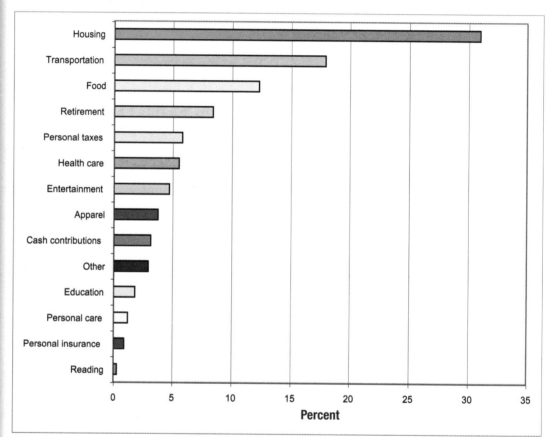

Source: *Statistical Abstract of the United States: 2006*, Table 669.

There are many ways to prepare a budget, but the process usually involves three steps: setting financial goals, estimating income, and planning expenditures.

Setting Financial Goals

Before you can prepare a budget, you need to determine both your income and your expenditure goals. Your income goal might be what you currently earn or are given. However, you may wish to set a financial goal to increase your income, and you may promise yourself that you will work extra time to meet this goal. Setting an aggressive income goal can be motivating, but it is important to be realistic.

9. budget

In setting expenditure goals, you will probably start with your current expenses and add other expenses you know you will be incurring. You may also decide to set a financial goal for saving. Young people often save for expensive purchases that they plan to make sometime in the future, such as college tuition or a car, or they may even save money to start their own businesses. If you have any such financial goals, it is important to clarify them before you start making a budget.

Estimating Income

A critical step in preparing a personal budget is to list your income sources. This may include income from a part-time job, allowances, gifts, or even interest on current savings. If you have a goal of increasing your income, you need to be sure that you can reach this goal. You will need to be honest with yourself in listing your income sources. You should not list income unless you are certain you will receive it.

Planning Expenditures

Finally, you will want to list all the things you are likely to buy or pay for over the time period of your budget, plus what you need to save to meet your longer-term goals. This will enable you to rank the importance of your wants. You can then eliminate the less-important wants that you cannot meet with your limited budget.

A budget can help you learn how to save so that you accumulate wealth for future use. However, there is more than one way to invest your money to get started on becoming wealthy.

Apply Your Understanding

Do you have a personal financial income goal for the next year? _____

If yes, what is it, and how do you plan to meet your goal?

_____

_____

_____

If no, what would be a realistic goal and why?

_____

_____

_____

My Monthly Budget

On a separate sheet of paper, prepare a monthly budget using the format shown below. First, list all your sources of income for a month and total them. Second, list all your planned monthly expenditures, including savings, and total them.

Income		Expenditures	
Source	Amount	Source	Amount
_____	_____	_____	_____
_____	_____	_____	_____
(add lines as needed)			
Total	_____	Total	_____

Now, review your budget. Do you need to cut some planned spending to balance your budget? Have you built savings into your budget?

A budget serves as a plan for managing income and spending over a specific period of time.

Information and Advertising

Advertisements are found in traditional media: television, radio, newspapers, magazines, and direct mail. Outdoor advertisements are found on public benches, buses, billboards, stadium fences, and mall and airport kiosks. Previews in theaters contain advertisements. Finally, the Internet has become the fastest-growing advertisement medium.

Advertising is one of the largest industries in the United States. U.S. businesses spend billions of dollars to advertise their products. Since consumers are the main targets of advertising campaigns, you should know something about how advertisers increase sales through the information they provide.

Benefits of Advertising

Advertising benefits consumers and the economy in several ways.

- Advertising gives consumers information about prices, improvements in goods and services, and the availability of new products.
- Advertising increases competition among sellers. When consumers have more information about available products, sellers are likely to compete more intensely to attract customers.
- Advertising pays most magazine and newspaper costs and all commercial radio and television costs. As a result, advertising subsidizes much of the information available to the public.

Costs of Advertising

Advertising has both obvious, explicit costs and hidden, implicit costs.

- Advertising is costly, and these costs raise prices for consumers. This is an implicit cost because it is not easily known.
- Advertising can lead people to buy things they otherwise would not want. This is an implicit cost because the real effect of advertising is not known.
- Radio, television, and other media supported by advertising may be reluctant to criticize products of advertisers. Therefore, at times, media outlets may fail to be objective. This is an explicit cost because the revenue to the media outlets is known.

Advertising that includes information about prices, product performance, and features is often useful. However, for many expensive items, such as automobiles and appliances, you may want to read about the independent research on these products published in *Consumer Reports* and other sources you will learn about later in this chapter.

Consideration in Making Saving and Investment Decisions

 Just as there are many choices of products and services to buy, there are many saving and investment alternatives. The choices can be confusing. For example, you could invest in a CD (certificate of deposit) or a mutual fund. Or, you could buy a stock or a bond. If you find these terms unfamiliar or puzzling, you are not alone. However, you can become a better investor by learning more about them. One of the first things to learn is that it pays to shop for a place to save or invest. Safety, rate of return, and liquidity are key factors to consider.

Safety

You could hide your savings under your mattress or in a desk drawer, but your money could be stolen or destroyed in a fire. It also would not earn interest. Banks and savings institutions protect your money against fire, theft, and other disasters. Many also offer government-sponsored insurance provided by the Federal Deposit Insurance Corporation (FDIC) that guarantees the safety of any savings account up to $250,000.

Rate of Return

With any savings or investment, keep in mind the concept of the *rate of return*. **Rate of return** refers to the percentage of interest or the amount of dividends paid on savings or on an investment. Typically, the greater the rate of return, the riskier the investment. When you buy **stock**, which is ownership in a corporation, you don't need to worry about fire or theft, but you do need to be concerned with what might happen to the stock's value. The price of a company's stock can fall, and you can lose much of the money you used to buy the stock. This is called **market risk**, the potential decrease in the value of a stock in a stock market. *Inflation* risk is another type of risk. **Inflation** is a general rise in overall prices. With inflation, the purchasing power of your money decreases. Wise investors gather information before they make an investment so that they can minimize their risk.

One of the main reasons to put your savings into a bank is to earn interest. As you know, interest is the income earned by allowing a person or institution, such as a bank, to use your money. Interest is expressed as a percentage of the **principal**, an initial amount of savings. (You will learn later that principal is also an original amount of money borrowed.) The rate of return is expressed as a percentage of the amount on deposit, usually for a period of one year. For example, a deposit of $1,000 in an account paying 5 percent annually would earn a total of $50 in interest over a year. This means the rate of return is 5 percent.

Most savings accounts offer *compound interest*. **Compound interest** is interest calculated on the sum of savings plus the accumulated interest, provided the interest earned is kept in savings. To receive compound interest, you must leave both your initial savings and the interest earned in your account. Suppose you deposit $1,000 today at 5 percent annual interest. At the end of the year, you will have $1,050 in your account. During the second year, you will earn interest on your original $1,000 and on the $50 of interest you earned the first year. At the end of two years, your original $1,000 of savings will have grown—compounded—to $1,102.50.

Pause to Predict

You know what safety is, but what is your understanding of rate of return and liquidity?

Rate of Return _____

_____

_____

Liquidity _____

_____

_____

Think Critically

Here is a statement you might hear a worker make: "My salary increase didn't keep up with inflation." What does the statement mean?

_____

_____

_____

_____

10. rate of return **11. stock** **12. market risk** **13. inflation** **14. principal** **15. compound interest**

Check Your Understanding

Revise or rewrite your predicted definition of rate of return.

_____

_____

_____

The rate of return offered by banks and savings institutions varies with economic conditions and the length of time the banks or institutions hold your money. Generally, the longer you commit to a savings deposit, the higher the rate of return.

At your age, it would be wise for you to think about the long run. Compound interest can make your wealth grow very significantly over the years. Suppose you save $1.00 per day in an account that earns 8 percent interest compounded daily. At the end of 60 years, you will have accumulated $540,000. At a daily compound interest rate of 10 percent, you will accumulate more than $1.4 million at the end of 60 years! The lesson: Saving regularly in an account that provides compound interest pays off.

The Rule of 72

The Rule of 72 illustrates how compound interest works. To apply the rule, divide 72 by the interest rate paid. The answer tells you how many years it will take for savings to double when interest is compounded. For example, if you are paid 8 percent interest, it will take nine years for your savings to double (72 ÷ 8 = 9).

1. If you receive 6 percent compound interest, how many years will it take to double your savings?   _____

2. If you receive 12 percent compound interest, how many years will it take to double your savings?   _____

3. If you receive 5 percent compound interest, how many years will it take to double your savings?   _____

Check Your Understanding

Revise or rewrite your predicted definition of liquidity.

_____

_____

_____

Liquidity

When people put money into a savings account, they generally plan to leave it in the account for a long time. However, sometimes a person might put money into savings knowing that he or she might need to withdraw the money quickly. Banks and savings institutions pay lower rates of interest on accounts that make it easier for you to withdraw your money. **Liquidity** is the ease with which any asset, such as savings or a stock, can be converted to cash. The easier it is to withdraw your funds, the greater your liquidity. However, liquidity usually has a cost. The easier it is for you to withdraw your money from a bank or other savings institution, the lower interest rate you are likely to earn. Why? If a savings institution, which makes loans from money saved, cannot depend on having that money on hand to lend, it will pay a lower rate of interest.

iStockphoto '07

Where People Put Their Savings

 Savers and investors have many alternatives that offer various mixtures of safety, return, and liquidity for their money. The table in Figure 6-4 shows where people in the United States put their savings. In this section, we discuss some of the most common options.

Figure 6-4: U.S. Household Savings
(in billions of dollars)

Assets	Amount in 2000	Amount in 2004	Percent Increase
Deposits at Banks, etc.			
Savings accounts	$ 3,076	$ 4,291	39%
Money market accounts	$ 971	$ 894	-8%
Other financial assets			
Pension funds	$ 8,831	$ 9,638	9%
Corporate stocks	$ 7,806	$ 6,522	-16%
U.S. savings bonds	$ 619	$ 468	-24%
Other government securities	$ 870	$ 1,011	16%
Mutual funds	$ 2,833	$ 3,570	26%
Life insurance reserves	$ 819	$ 1,109	35%
Corporate bonds	$ 645	$ 498	-23%
Total	**$26,470**	**$28,001**	**6%**

Source: *Statistical Abstract of the United States: 2006*, Table 1158.

Savings Deposits

Banks, savings and loan firms, and credit unions offer opportunities to open savings deposits. Known for their safety, bank deposits are insured by the federal government for up to $250,000 per account. This means that if the institution holding your money fails, the government will pay you the amount you have in savings up to a maximum of $250,000. Passbook savings accounts are known for their safety and liquidity. They usually pay a relatively low rate of interest. Minimum balance requirements are usually low, and your savings can be withdrawn at any time, so the liquidity is good. A minimum balance is the minimum amount of money you need to deposit in order to start your account.

A **certificate of deposit** (CD) is a receipt issued by a bank to a person depositing money in an account for a specified period of time at a fixed rate of interest. CDs require savers to leave their money on deposit for a specified period of time, such as six months, a year, or even two years. CDs pay a higher rate of interest than passbook savings. Your money in a CD can be withdrawn early, but you will have to pay a penalty. Your trade-off with a CD is that you give up liquidity for a higher interest rate.

Check Your Understanding

What does the data in Figure 6-4 show to be the top three categories of savings for U.S. citizens?

_____

_____

_____

In the table, put a question mark by any category of savings (assets) that you do not understand. You will learn about each category of savings in the following pages.

Show Your Understanding

Each saving/investment option discussed on the next two pages has advantages and disadvantages. Describe these pros and cons in your own words on the lines provided.

Advantage(s) _____

_____

Disadvantage(s) _____

_____

Advantage(s) _____

_____

Disadvantage(s) _____

_____

Money Market Deposit Accounts

These insured deposits allow the depositor to write a limited number of checks within a defined time period. Your bank will use your money market funds to participate in the "money market." The market consists of short-term loans, usually of one year or less. The bank makes its money on the interest it receives on the loans. The rate of interest the depositor receives on these accounts is higher than a passbook savings account and lower than a CD. These accounts are safe and offer considerable liquidity.

Advantage(s) _____

_____

Disadvantage(s) _____

_____

Pension and Retirement Funds

Investing in these funds provides *tax deferment*. **Tax deferment** is the payment of taxes on interest after the interest is earned, often upon retirement. With retirement funds, you pay taxes on the interest earned usually when you retire from working and your income is lower. However, if you withdraw the pension or retirement funds early, you pay a penalty.

Pension funds are various retirement accounts that people receive through their employers. Depending on the fund, employers and/or employees may pay into the fund. These funds are invested in stocks, bonds, and other alternatives, such as those shown in Figure 6-4. An **individual retirement account** (IRA) is a type of retirement account that an individual can establish with a bank, an insurance company, or a brokerage firm. A *401(k) plan* is another type of retirement plan. Usually, this kind of retirement plan is maintained by an employer. A **401(k) plan** is a for-profit company's retirement plan that allows an employee to save up to a certain amount of income per year and avoid paying taxes on the income until it is withdrawn. Employers will often match a percentage of the employee's 401(k) contribution. An **employee stock ownership plan** (ESOP) is an employer-sponsored retirement plan that allows employees to purchase the employer's stock, often at a reduced stock price.

Advantage(s) _____

_____

Disadvantage(s) _____

_____

Corporate Stocks

A **share of stock** is a share of ownership in a corporation. In effect, stockholders are the owners of the corporation. When the corporation earns a profit, the corporation's managers often decide to distribute a portion of the profits to the stockholders. Profits distributed to stockholders are called **dividends**. However, if the corporation has a loss, the stockholders share the loss, and the value of their stock can decrease. Owning stock can be risky. Stockholders can receive a substantial return on their investment if the corporation does well and earns a profit, but they can lose some or all of their investment if the corporation is not profitable.

Advantage(s) _____

_____

Disadvantage(s) _____

_____

Corporate Bonds

A **bond** is a promise to repay borrowed money to a lender at a fixed rate of interest at a specified time. When a corporation borrows money from people, it issues corporate bonds, called certificates of indebtedness. The certificate, or bond, signifies that the corporation owes a debt to the certificate holder. Corporate bonds are certificates of indebtedness that corporations issue to borrow money. Bondholders receive periodic interest payments on their savings. Like stock prices, bond prices can rise or fall, so investors can gain or lose money.

18. tax deferment   19. individual retirement account   20. 401(k) plan
21. employee stock ownership plan   22. share of stock   23. dividends   24. bond

Mutual Funds

A **mutual fund** is a pool of money used by a company to buy assets, such as stocks or bonds, on behalf of its shareholders. Mutual fund companies are special investment companies in which people "pool" their savings to make a variety of investments. A mutual fund might own stock in 200 different firms. If you invest in a mutual fund, you buy a share in the fund. Indirectly, you become an owner of the different companies whose stock is held by the mutual fund. An advantage of investing in a mutual fund is that the company diversifies its investments, which means that the investment is spread across the stocks the mutual fund owns. Therefore, mutual funds tend to be less risky than individual stocks. Mutual fund companies sometimes have annual management fees. Others charge fees when a share in the fund is bought or sold.

Advantage(s) _____

_____

Disadvantage(s) _____

_____

U.S. Savings Bonds

The United States Treasury issues savings bonds, which are debts of the federal government. U.S. savings bonds are one of the safest investments a person can make. These bonds have face values, which is the amount that will be paid to the bondholder when the bond matures. With face values from $50 to $1,000, the bonds are issued at a discount, which means they are sold at a price below the face value of the bond. When the bond comes due, it is redeemed at its face value.

iStockphoto '07

In 2004, Americans invested $468 billion in U.S. savings bonds.

Advantage(s) _____

_____

Disadvantage(s) _____

_____

Making Investment Decisions

There are risks associated with each type of investment. This means there is a possibility of suffering a loss on any investment. Market risk may cause the investor to lose part or all of his or her investment when the business suffers a loss or fails. Inflation risk relates to the effect of inflation—overall rising prices—on the investment. It is important to seek investments that provide a rate of return that is higher than the inflation rate. Wise investors try to gather good information to make sound decisions in order to minimize risk.

There are many sources of saving and investing information. The Internet and your local library will have publications such as *Fortune*, *Business Week*, and *The Wall Street Journal*. These publications will provide useful information on general business conditions and the status of financial markets. *Value Line* and *Standard & Poor's Stock Guide* provide information about specific companies. Before you risk your money, it is always wise to talk with an expert.

Which Is a Good Investment for You?

Suppose you receive $1,000 as a gift from a relative. You decide to save or invest it. Which saving or investing option will you choose?

Saving/Investment Option _____

Why? _____

_____

Pause to Predict

You have heard of buying on credit. You may even have a credit card. Write your own definition of credit.

_____

_____

_____

Consumer Credit

Many people don't want to wait until they have saved enough money to buy things they want. They also don't want to cut from their budgets items they cannot currently afford. They decide to borrow money—to use *credit*—so they can have what they want now. **Credit** is the ability of a customer to buy goods or services before paying for them, based on an agreement to pay later. People need to be careful about buying on credit. Read this exchange.

What a great sound. It's like being in the front row. But your speakers had to cost a fortune. Where did you get the money?

I have an after-school job, and the people at Discount Appliances gave me a credit card so I could pay in monthly installments.

And meanwhile, the speakers are all yours. So why don't you look happy?

I just got my credit card bill. With interest, the equipment payments are more than I make a month.

iStockphoto '07

Consumer credit enables you to enjoy goods and services before you pay for them in full. It is a way to spend your future income. Charge accounts, credit cards, installment plans, car loans, and home mortgages are some of the best known forms of credit. But there are two important strings attached to every credit purchase. You must repay the principal, the original amount borrowed. You also have to pay the interest, the amount of money charged for borrowing the principal. In most cases, you pay the principal and interest costs in regular, usually monthly, payments.

If you are thinking about borrowing money or buying something on credit, you will want to know how much it will cost (the original price plus interest) and whether you can afford the payments. You need to know the total cost, once you add together the principal plus interest. When you are purchasing on credit, you should shop for the best credit terms, because credit costs vary from one lender to another.

What credit terms should you investigate? First is the **finance charge**, the total amount paid to use credit. It includes interest costs and any other fees, such as a service charge, that the seller or lender may be entitled to add to the loan. The **annual percentage rate** (APR) is the cost of credit calculated as an annual percentage of the principal borrowed. For example, suppose a business is willing to lend you money at "only" 2.5 percent per month. When you calculate the annual percentage rate, you find that you will be paying 30 percent per year for using the money (2.5 percent x 12 months = 30 percent).

Advantages of Credit
Here are five advantages of credit.
- **Immediate possession.** Credit enables people to enjoy goods and services immediately. Otherwise, they would have to postpone their purchases or do without them.
- **Flexibility.** Credit allows people to time their purchases to take advantage of sale items or other bargains, even when their funds are low.
- **Safety.** Credit cards and charge accounts provide a safe and convenient means for people to carry their purchasing power while shopping or traveling. Otherwise people would have to carry cash, which could be lost or stolen.
- **Emergency funds.** Credit gives people a cushion in emergencies, such as the money you need to get back on the road if your car breaks down.
- **Character reference.** The pattern of a person's payment of bills is recorded, and this record, called a credit history, can be used as a character reference.

Disadvantages of Credit
Here are three disadvantages of credit everyone needs to know.
- **Overspending.** Sometimes credit cards and charge accounts make it too easy to spend money. Then, as debt mounts, it is often difficult to make the needed monthly payments.
- **Higher cost.** Stores that accept credit cards pay the credit card companies a fee. Also, handling the paperwork associated with credit purchases can be expensive for merchants. As a result, stores that accept credit cards typically charge higher prices than those that sell their products only for cash.
- **Impulse buying.** Credit shoppers often ignore sales and special prices because they can buy on credit whenever they want to. This situation can lead to impulse buying, meaning a person may buy something on a whim that they really don't need.

Check Your Understanding

When you borrow money or pay on credit, what do you have to repay? Check all the answers that apply.

Stock options _____
Principal _____
Taxes _____
Rate of return _____
Interest _____
Finance charges _____

Apply Your Understanding

When you apply for credit in the future, what are three questions you will ask?

1._____
_____

2._____
_____

3._____
_____

27. finance charge   28. annual percentage rate

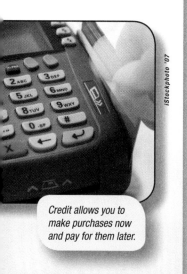

Credit allows you to make purchases now and pay for them later.

What Kinds of Credit Are Available?

Consumer credit is either loan credit or sales credit. Loan credit enables you to borrow money to finance a purchase. Sales credit enables you to buy goods and services now and pay for them later. Here are some examples of each.

Home Mortgages. Home mortgages are long-term loans to purchase a house or condominium. Banks and savings and loan companies, sometimes called mortgage lenders, are common sources of mortgage money. Home mortgages are repaid with interest in equal monthly installments over the life of the loan. Mortgage loans are commonly made for 15 or 30 years.

Auto and Consumer Loans. Loans for specific items, such as automobiles, are available from banks, savings and loans, and credit unions. People usually repay such loans in equal monthly installments, typically from three to five years.

Charge Accounts. Charge accounts are specific to certain stores, often department stores. They enable buyers to make purchases without paying cash. There is usually no charge for the use of the account if the monthly balance is paid in full. Interest is charged on unpaid balances.

Credit Cards. A credit card is a type of charge account that entitles the credit card holder to shop at different places. MasterCard, Visa, American Express, Discover, and Diners Club are the five most widely used credit cards. Credit card companies send a bill to cardholders for their purchases. As with charge accounts, these companies usually do not charge cardholders interest if they pay the account in full each month. However, many credit card companies charge an annual fee to the cardholder.

If you plan to pay off your credit card bill each month, look for a card with a low annual fee or no annual fee. If you plan to carry a credit balance from month to month, choose a card with a low interest rate.

Obtaining and Using Credit

It is a simple fact of financial life that lenders expect to be repaid along with interest and other fees for allowing you the use of their money. Lenders do indeed check the credit history of the person applying for a loan to determine whether the person is worthy of being given credit.

In judging a person's credit worthiness, lenders look at character, capacity, and capital.

- Character refers to your personal qualities—your honesty and willingness to repay debts. If your record shows you have paid your bills on time, lenders will assume you will continue to do so in the future.
- Capacity, sometimes referred to as capability, is a measure of your ability to repay debts. Creditors will want to know about your income sources, how much you earn, and your other financial obligations. If you do not have the capability of repaying a debt, lenders will not give you credit.
- Capital refers to what people own—money in the bank or tangible property, such as a house. Generally, the more you own, the easier it is to repay debts. Lenders also may ask that some capital be used as backup for a loan. Capital used for security is called *collateral*. **Collateral** is capital acceptable to a lender for a loan. For example, an automobile is the collateral for an auto loan. If the loan is not repaid, the collateral can be taken by the lender and sold to pay off the loan.

Young people frequently have difficulty establishing credit, mostly because they have no credit history. There are some steps you can take. You can open a savings account to demonstrate that you are building up some capital. With a savings account, you may be able to apply for a credit card through your bank. You can have a telephone placed in your name and pay the monthly charges. This will demonstrate that you can be trusted to pay your debts. Another option is to establish your credit history with a co-signer. A **co-signer** is a person who has a good credit rating and who guarantees to pay off your loan if you cannot. When you pay off the loan, even if you have a co-signer, you demonstrate that you are a responsible borrower.

Apply Your Understanding

Assume you have a legitimate need to borrow $200. You decide to apply for a loan at the local bank. Describe three reasons you would give the banker to convince him or her that you are a good credit risk.

1. _____

_____

2. _____

_____

3. _____

_____

The Cost of a Credit Card

Young people are often offered credit cards. Here are the conditions you might see on the credit card application: (1) 90 days interest-free credit, (2) no annual fee, (3) only 1.5 percent interest per month on the unpaid balance, (4) no payments required for six months.

Suppose you apply for and are granted a credit card with these conditions. During the first 90 days, you charge $500 to the card, but you make no payments on it. At the end of 120 days, you receive a credit card bill for $507.50. You can't make a payment, but you aren't worried because you have another two months before a payment is required. At the end of 150 days, you receive a bill for $515.11.

What is happening? _____

_____

29. collateral   30. co-signer

Consumer Protection

 A market economy has built-in protection for consumers. Sellers compete against one another to satisfy consumer wants. Sellers also try to satisfy those wants efficiently by providing the variety and quality of goods and services that consumers prefer at a price they are willing to pay. Good consumer choice making means looking for quality products at the lowest possible prices.

No one forces consumers to spend money on any particular item. You have learned that this is the meaning of voluntary trade. You are free to make choices for yourself. The fact that you can choose from many sellers helps protect your interests. There are even consumer publications like *Consumer Reports* and *Consumers' Research* that people buy or read at a local library to get more information about particular goods and services.

Government and Consumers

The market's protection of consumers is far from perfect. Consequently, federal and state governments have made various efforts to help protect consumer rights. In 1962, President John F. Kennedy sent a message to Congress in which he identified a "bill of rights" for consumers. These were the right to safety, the right to be informed, the right to choose, and the right to be heard.

- *The right to safety.* Consumers have the right to be protected from unsafe products. Accordingly, in 1972 Congress created the Consumer Product Safety Commission. Its purpose is to "protect the public from unreasonable risks of injury from consumer products."
- *The right to be informed.* This has been interpreted to mean that consumers have a right to know (1) exactly what they are buying, (2) the terms of the sale and any guarantees accompanying it, and (3) the kinds of risks that might be involved in the use of a product.
- *The right to choose.* Competition is the backbone of free enterprise, so the federal and state governments have enacted legislation making it illegal to restrict market competition.
- *The right to be heard.* Both business and government recognize the need to learn what consumers are thinking. Most large firms have special departments that receive and respond to consumer inquiries and complaints. Many firms provide toll-free numbers or website addresses to make contacting them easier.

Business Self-Regulation

Most businesses know that satisfied consumers are the key to financial success, so they pay attention to consumer satisfaction, try to avoid complaints, and respond quickly when customers point out problems. In addition, many firms have joined forces to provide a measure of self-regulation. Best known for these efforts is the Better Business Bureau (BBB), an international organization that sets standards for business ethics. Local businesses that join the BBB agree to maintain fair business practices. Consumers who feel they have been treated unfairly can call their local BBB to help them resolve their differences with businesses. Chambers of Commerce in local communities also set ethical standards for business.

Think Critically

In a voluntary exchange, do you think it is important to have consumer protection laws? Why or why not?

_____

_____

_____

Apply Your Understanding

Suppose you buy a product but find it is defective when you get it home. You return with the product to the store where you bought it, but the store's manager refuses to talk to you. Which of the consumer rights can you exercise?

_____

_____

Summary

People earn most of their income at jobs. They also earn some of it by putting their wealth to work. Wealth is the money and tangible property people own. Over time, people increase their wealth by saving and investing. It pays for you to be familiar with the options available to investors and to shop for investments that offer the return, safety, and liquidity you desire.

A spending plan, or budget, can help people get the most from their incomes. The steps involved in budgeting include setting goals, estimating income, and planning expenditures and savings. Careful shopping also helps consumers make wise use of their money. It is helpful for consumers to become familiar with the kinds of strategies advertisers use to try to sell their products.

Credit enables people to purchase things now and pay for them over a specified period of time. Credit can be useful, but it does require good character, capital, and the capacity to repay loans. Credit can be expensive. Two of the most important things to look for when shopping for a loan are the finance charge and the annual percentage rate (APR) of interest.

A competitive market is a vital source of consumer protection because it is in the best interest of producers to serve customers. Government agencies and private-sector organizations such as the Better Business Bureau and local Chambers of Commerce also have responsibilities for protecting consumers.

Looking Ahead

In the next chapter, you will explore ways in which businesses organize to produce their goods and services. You will also look at the role of small business in the U.S. economy and the special part played by entrepreneurs.

Notes

The Business of Free Enterprise

Read to Find Out

As you read this chapter, look for answers to the following questions:

What are characteristics of entrepreneurs?

What are some paths successful entrepreneurs have followed?

What is the role of small business in the U.S. economy?

What information can be helpful in starting a small business?

What are the advantages and disadvantages of sole proprietorships, partnerships, and corporations?

What are other types of business organizations?

How are large corporations organized?

Mark to Remember

* *This is important.*

? *I have a question about this.*

! *This is a surprise.*

Why It Matters

In 1776, the year the U.S. Declaration of Independence was signed, a little-known Scottish professor, Adam Smith, wrote a book titled *An Inquiry into the Nature and Causes of the Wealth of Nations*. Commonly called *The Wealth of Nations*, the book became the foundation for the study of the social science we now call economics. In *The Wealth of Nations*, Smith stated that if individuals were allowed to pursue their own self-interests, they would be led by an "invisible hand" of market competition to serve the national interest. Smith went on in *The Wealth of Nations* to describe what we now call a free enterprise economy—one in which the forces of supply and demand would prevail. You live in a free enterprise economy. It is important for you, as a participant in this kind of economy, to understand its characteristics.

The Business of Free Enterprise

Building On What You Know

Do you know someone who owns a business or perhaps someone who is a business partner? Have you met a stockholder? Do you know someone who owns and manages a franchise, such as McDonald's or Subway? Have you met an entrepreneur who had an idea and started his or her own business? A business owner, a stockholder, a franchise owner, and an entrepreneur all have one thing in common: They are risk takers. They have been willing to risk their money and time to participate in our free enterprise system.

An *enterprise* is considered a business undertaking that involves risk. **Enterprise** is a term for a business organization. Free enterprise is a business undertaking in which the business owner is free to produce, buy, and sell in markets. There is no outside agency, such as a government, that becomes involved in free enterprise, as long as the business owner operates within the law and holds to a high standard of ethics. Free enterprise encourages entrepreneurship. Entrepreneurs see opportunities to introduce new or better goods and services into markets. Not all people in business are entrepreneurs. Many people in business—whether the business is a proprietorship, a partnership, or a corporation—are very thoughtful and knowledgeable. They know how to run a business. They are very aware of the markets in which they do business. They often manage several workers. They all have a similar goal—to make a profit in our free enterprise economy.

Becoming an Entrepreneur

Bill Gates and his partner, Paul Allen, realized that easy-to-use software was the key to making the personal computer industry successful. In 1975, Microsoft Corporation was founded, and its Disk Operating System (DOS) became the industry standard. Today, Microsoft is the world's largest software company producing a wide array of software applications. Allen left Microsoft, and one of his current business interests is Charter Communications, a telecommunications company promoting cable TV, the Internet, and other services.

Pause to Predict

Entrepreneurs are often in the news. Name two entrepreneurs with whom you are familiar.

_____

_____

Why do you think the people you named are well known?

_____

1. enterprise

Other entrepreneurs have been an important part of our economic history.

- Ray Kroc took a small hamburger restaurant in San Bernardino, California, and developed a new way to organize food production to guarantee fast, friendly service and uniform quality. Today, McDonald's is a worldwide operation selling billions of hamburgers each year.
- Henry Ford revolutionized car production in the early 20th century with the first assembly line.
- Clarence Birdseye made frozen foods available.
- Debbi Fields introduced gourmet cookies to stores and shopping malls.
- Liz Claiborne, Donna Karan, and Mary Kay Ash found ready markets for clothing and cosmetics among an increasing number of working women.
- Veronica Moreno was a co-founder of Olé Mexican Foods, one of the largest tortilla manufacturers and food distributors in the United States.

Entrepreneurs are creative and individualistic. They are critical thinkers who take their ideas and transform them into goods and services. Here are some characteristics of well-known entrepreneurs.

Start at an Early Age

People often become entrepreneurs at an early age. In junior high school, Bud Hadfield ran a print shop in his basement called The Family News. Going door-to-door, he sold business cards, printing, and stationery. He founded Kwik Kopy in 1967 and became the chairman of the world's largest international alliance of printing and copying franchises. He died in 2011. Cory Spotts of Phoenix, Arizona, started a record label to distribute his band's music. He does the design, printing, and distribution for BLUElight Audio/Media and learned his business skills participating in Junior Achievement. In 1999 Spotts was chosen Young Entrepreneur of the Year by Ernst and Young, a nationwide accounting firm. Junior Achievement students of St. Paul School in St. Paul Island, Alaska, a remote Bering Sea island, showed great entrepreneurial spirit in 1999 when they organized a community movie night for their business activity. The students flew in pizza from Anchorage and made the night a huge hit with the tiny island's residents.

Develop and Sell Ordinary Products

Many entrepreneurs have developed products people can use every day. Ed Lowe thought about a new use for the clay granules that are used to absorb grease and oil at gas stations. He packaged the granules as "Kitty Litter" and started a company that earns millions of dollars each year. Using a $500 investment and working in his garage, high school teacher Ron Rice developed the coconut oil-based Hawaiian Tropic Tanning Oil.

Find New Ways to Sell

Lane Nemeth found that educational toys were not always available at typical toy stores. She couldn't raise the funds to open her own store, so she found a unique way to promote and sell educational toys: through home "toy parties" hosted by friends. Nemeth's firm, Discovery Toys, now has a national sales force that uses this selling strategy. Similarly, the lifelong business partnership between Richard M. DeVos and Jay Van Andel created the Amway Corporation, which revolutionized the direct-selling industry. Today, the company markets hundreds of personal care, nutrition and wellness, home care, home tech, and commercial products that it develops and manufactures. Michael Dell, of Dell Computer, was the first to offer computer hardware for sale on the Internet.

iStockphoto '07

McDonald's has established uniform quality standards for its products as one way to promote its business worldwide.

Spot New Markets and Develop New Products

The six Yee sisters realized how difficult it was for Asian women to find cosmetics that matched their skin tones, and they saw a potential new market. They started Zhen Cosmetics. As a college student in the 1970s, Paul Orfalea spotted a commercial opportunity in the library's photocopy machine. After he leased a copier and an old hamburger stand, Orfalea started selling copy services to college students. His company, Kinko's, was bought by FedEx Corp. in 2004 for $2.4 billion.

Work to Perfect Their Own Ideas

As a college student, Fred Smith had an idea. He believed that an air freight business could successfully operate independently of the major air carriers. He identified a market for overnight letter and small package delivery and used his energy and vision to buy airplanes and organize Federal Express, now called FedEx.

Work within an Existing Business

Sometimes, creativity is fostered within existing businesses. The 3M Company (Minnesota Mining and Manufacturing) encourages its researchers to be creative, allowing them to spend 15 percent of their time on any project that interests them. Art Fry, a scientist at 3M, worked with a colleague who was trying to develop a strong adhesive. However, the adhesive was not good enough to sell. Fry took the poor adhesive and coated small pieces of paper with it. He used the sticky paper as bookmarks and for writing notes. The resulting product, called Post-it Notes, has become one of the world's most recognized brands.

The list of successful entrepreneurs goes on and on, and the men and women, whether business owners or employees, have much in common. Entrepreneurs most often are people who own or operate a business in hopes of earning a profit. To earn a profit, they must combine resources in innovative, creative ways. They must conceive of useful goods and services or develop more efficient ways of production. Often this means having a maverick spirit and willingness to pursue an idea that is unpopular. "Every truly great idea starts out as a minority of one," observed Dee Ward Hock, founder of the Visa credit card company. Success also depends on a willingness to work hard, to persevere, and to take risks. After all, if their plans fail, entrepreneurs can lose a lot of money. Entrepreneurs are not always successful in their first business venture. They often fail, but they rebound time and time again to find success.

Think Critically

The Yee sisters and Lane Nemeth started their businesses to meet personal needs—but needs that they believed were shared by others. Describe another entrepreneur mentioned in the Becoming an Entrepreneur section who originally developed a product or service to meet a personal need.

Person _____

Unmet need for a product or service

_____

Planning to Sell Smoothies

You and a friend think you have a good idea to sell smoothies at your school. As you know, starting a business takes planning. Before you approach the school principal about your idea, make a list of the questions you think the principal might ask about your business. Then describe how you will find the answers to the questions.

Question   How to Find the Answer

_____   _____

_____   _____

_____   _____

(Use additional paper to complete your questions and answers.)

Biography—Oprah Winfrey

Oprah Gail Winfrey was born in Kosciusko, Mississippi, on January 29, 1954. Winfrey has said that because it was difficult to pronounce her given name Orpah. The letters r and p were reversed. Winfrey spent her first six years living in rural poverty with her Grandma Hattie Mae. Winfrey's grandmother taught her to read before the age of three and took her to the local church, where she was nicknamed "The Preacher" for her ability to read Bible verses. At age six, Winfrey moved to a Milwaukee, Wisconsin, ghetto with her mother. At age 14 she was sent to live with her father in Nashville, Tennessee. She excelled as a student. After joining the high school speech team, she placed second in the nation in dramatic interpretation. She won an oratory contest that earned her a full scholarship to Tennessee State University where she studied communications.

Oprah Winfrey
Vince Bucci/Getty Images

Early in her career, Winfrey worked in local television stations in Nashville and Baltimore, Maryland. In 1983, she relocated to Chicago, Illinois, to host WLS-TV's low-rated, half-hour morning talk show, *AM-Chicago*. Within months after Winfrey took over, the show went from last place in the ratings to the highest-rated talk show in Chicago, overtaking the very popular *Phil Donahue Show*. Her show was renamed *The Oprah Winfrey Show*. Broadcast nationally for a full hour, the show became the number one daytime talk show in the United States. TV columnist Howard Rosenberg said this about Oprah's show: "She's a roundhouse, a full-course meal, big, brassy, loud, aggressive, hyper, laughable, lovable, soulful, tender, low-down, earthy, and hungry."

Winfrey has hosted and appeared on numerous television shows. She co-founded the women's cable television network Oxygen. She is president of Harpo Productions (Oprah spelled backward). She has starred in several films, including *The Color Purple*, which earned her a nomination for an Academy Award as Best Supporting Actress. She publishes two magazines and has her own website, www.Oprah.com.

With a net worth of $32 billion in 2015, Winfrey is believed to have been the richest African American woman of the 20th century. Forbes currently lists Winfrey as the world's only African American billionaire. In 2005, she became the first African American listed by *Business Week* as one of America's top 50 most generous philanthropists, having given an estimated $250 million to various charities. She continues her philanthropy, supporting the plight of children in South Africa and raising funds through Oprah's Angel Network for poverty-stricken and AIDS-affected children in Africa. Winfrey has been called "arguably the world's most powerful woman" by CNN and *Time Magazine*.

As a successful entrepreneur, Oprah Winfrey is often quoted. Here are three quotes that give some insight into her character.

- "Become the change you want to see—those are words I live by."
- "The big secret in life is that there is no big secret. Whatever your goal, you can get there if you're willing to work."
- "Think like a queen. A queen is not afraid to fail. Failure is another stepping-stone to greatness."

Apply Your Understanding

As you read each of the paragraphs in this section, think of one more example of an entrepreneur who fits into the category being described. Write the person's name and his/her product or service on the lines provided. You may need to do some research.

Name _____

Product/Service

_____

Name _____

Product/Service

_____

Name _____

Product/Service

_____

Name _____

Product/Service

_____

Name _____

Product/Service

_____

Strategies Used by Entrepreneurs

Many people regard entrepreneurs as lucky people with creative ideas. While they certainly have clever ideas and many have good luck, successful entrepreneurs often follow one or more of these paths.

Capitalizing on Unexpected Opportunities

A major producer of animal medicines got started in the 1950s when companies producing antibiotics for humans wouldn't sell their products to veterinarians. Another unexpected opportunity was the invention of the portable computer. This invention opened up markets for home computers and provided an opportunity for Adam Osborne to publish best-selling books about home computer and software use.

Responding to Changing Market Conditions

Concern about personal health created market opportunities for health spas, exercise equipment, exercise apparel, and the herbal and vitamin industry. Similarly, as more households bought personal computers, companies like CompuServe, America Online, Netscape Communications, and Comcast developed services or software to bring the Internet and other online services to homes. Small businesses that cater to our busy lives have prospered, too—businesses such as mobile car repair and professional shopping services.

Improving a Product or Process

Early cameras required cumbersome and fragile glass plates. In 1884, George Eastman of Eastman-Kodak developed an inexpensive and light, but rugged, cellulose film that completely changed photography. Today, we have further innovations with camcorders and digital photography, which ironically require no film.

Providing an Alternative Good or Service

Tylenol and other aspirin substitutes were developed originally for the small number of people who could not tolerate aspirin. Today, these alternatives dominate the headache relief market. FedEx and others in the air freight business (UPS, DHL) have provided a service once overlooked by the U.S. Postal Service—overnight delivery of packages.

Identifying Population Trends

Changing population trends provide many opportunities. The growth in the number of working mothers created a demand for more child care facilities. Franchise operations like KinderCare and others are a visible example. Similarly, as the population ages, people with good retirement incomes are willing to spend disposable income on health care facilities, housing, travel, entertainment, and leisure activities. Media advertising for these goods and services is directed to senior citizens.

A Home-Based Business

In recent years, many people have started home-based businesses. The business might involve making a product, such as jewelry or websites, or providing a service, such as creating advertising or making telephone calls for another business.

1. Describe a product or service you might provide from your home.

   _____

2. On additional paper, list the equipment you will need to start your business and estimate its cost.

3. Make some notes on how you plan to start the business. Who will you contact as potential customers? How will you advertise your business? How much will you personally work on the business? If you need financing (money) to start the business, how will you get it? How much will you pay yourself from the business revenue?

Electronic Commerce

Electronic commerce, or e-commerce, consists primarily of distributing, buying, selling, marketing, and servicing products or services over electronic systems such as the Internet and other computer networks. E-commerce encourages consumers to shop "electronically" from home or work. The Internet is changing the way some businesses operate, and many entrepreneurs have made e-commerce successful businesses.

Businesspeople from a variety of industries now take orders electronically, handle payments online, and give customers faster, more responsive service. Entrepreneurs are making a mark. Their imagination and energy have resulted in a flurry of new online businesses that started in the late 1990s. The growth in the use of home computers and Internet connections have contributed significantly to the growth of e-commerce. As reported by Internet Retailer, e-commerce generated sales worth $341.7 billion in 2015, compared to $91 billion in 2005.

What do people buy online? Recent surveys find the top-selling items are books, computer software, music, travel, computer hardware, clothing, electronics, and sports equipment. E-commerce is just one area of the economy where enterprising individuals are taking risks and putting their creativity to work. Small businesses are particularly well suited to this model because start-up costs are low.

Here are just a few current e-commerce companies: Amazon.com (retail), eBay (new and used consumer products), Adobe Systems (computer storage software), EarthLink (Internet computer linkage), Dell Computer (computer hardware), and Charles Schwab (stock and mutual fund sales and support).

Technological advances leading to e-commerce have created new opportunities for business.

The Economic Role of Small Business

The businesses that entrepreneurs start are usually small. A federal government agency called the Small Business Administration (SBA) defines a small business as "one that is independently owned and operated and is not dominant in its field of operation." The Small Business Act, a federal law, states that in determining what constitutes a small business, the definition varies from industry to *industry*. An **industry** is a group of one or more firms that produce identical or similar products. For example, the school textbook industry has four major firms that account for over 80 percent of the market and several small firms that account for the rest. A small publishing firm that sells laminated maps to schools and has just a few employees meets the definition of a small business. Business analysts predict that small businesses and entrepreneurs will continue to fuel the economy during the 21st century.

Figure 7-1 is a bar graph that shows the percentage of total employment by the size of the company. Small businesses, which usually have fewer than 100 employees, account for almost 55 percent of the total number of employees working in business.

Figure 7-1: Percentage of Total Employment by Size of Company, 2002

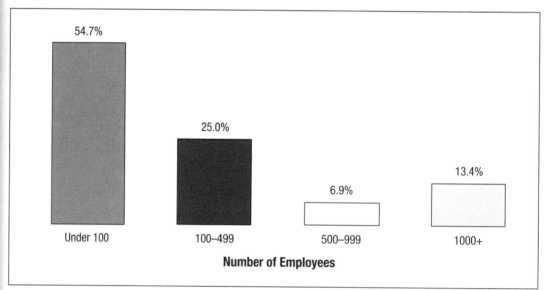

Source: *Statistical Abstract of the United States: 2006*, Table 739.

Reading a Bar Graph

Study the bar graph in Figure 7-1 and answer the questions below.

1. What percentage of companies have more than 1,000 employees? _____

2. What percentage of companies have between 100 and 499 employees? _____

3. What percentage of companies have between 500 and 999 employees? _____

4. What percentage of companies have more than 100 employees? _____

Think Critically

The Small Business Administration (SBA) is an agency of the federal government. Describe two responsibilities you think the SBA has.

1. _____

_____

2. _____

_____

Advantages of Small Businesses

Small businesses are better able than large businesses to quickly add or discontinue merchandise lines, change hours of operation, and alter pricing strategies. In other words, small businesses are flexible in meeting market needs.

While big firms often need large markets to profitably sell their products, small businesses can profit in small, limited markets. For example, small businesses are ideally suited to time-stressed consumers looking for personal services like housecleaning and shopping. Small businesses that appeal to a specific demographic group, like African Americans or Hispanics, can offer ethnic products and services. *Latina* magazine founder Christy Haubegger had been predicting a Latin explosion for years. The success of Latin artists such as Ricky Martin and the annual spending increases by Latino teens have proved this prediction to be true. The beginning of the 21st century saw a surge in consumerism. Teens with Internet access, credit cards, and a willingness to spend are now a targeted market by both small and large businesses. The U.S. Census Bureau estimates that in 2012, the teen population had grown to about 41.8 million, and the average teen will spend about $9,600 per year.

Pause to Predict

What challenges do you imagine that small businesses face? Name two.

1._____

_____

2._____

_____

Challenges Facing Small Businesses

Every year hundreds of thousands of new businesses are formed. Most, however, fail. Small businesses have a higher failure rate than large firms for three reasons: poor management, inadequate financing, and inability to hire highly qualified workers.

It's fairly easy to start a small business, so many people who go into business hope to learn the ins and outs of business management "on the job." Most experts, however, advise people to learn as much as they can about business management before getting started. Peter Drucker, a famous author and an authority on business management, said that most businesses don't fail because the business is risky. They fail because the owners don't know what they are doing. Further, he said that managers need to see workers not as a cost but as a resource. Good managers are successful if they direct people toward desired goals—their own and those of the business.

Check Your Understanding

In your own words, describe what Peter Drucker meant when he said that managers need to see workers not as a cost but as a resource.

_____

_____

_____

Even the smallest businesses have expenses that must be paid, so money is a problem for many small businesses. The National Federation of Independent Business (NFIB) reported that the top three financial problems facing small businesses are insufficient capital, slow sales, and heavy debt. All too often, small business owners find themselves unable to meet expenses when business slows.

Hiring and retaining workers is a third challenge. Small businesses have difficulty finding highly qualified workers because they often can't afford to provide salary or benefits that compare to those offered by larger firms. Another problem can be anticipating future hiring needs. Large firms often engage in large-scale recruiting efforts at college and university campuses. Small businesses, especially start-ups, have difficulty projecting their hiring needs, and they don't have the resources for recruiting. Hiring seasonal workers and retaining them from season to season can also be a problem for a small business. For example, many resorts hire and train new staff each summer because most previous employees have moved on to new jobs. This adds to the training costs and time.

Think Critically

As the text explains, some small businesses meet the challenge of hiring good employees by offering options like flexible work hours or working from home. What do you think are the advantages and disadvantages of flexible work arrangements for small business owners?

Advantages _____

_____

_____

Disadvantages _____

_____

_____

Some businesses avoid the new hire and training problem by offering workers arrangements that may not be offered at a larger firm, such as working from home or flexible work schedules. Some small business owners routinely hire summer interns. Internet-based businesses have been the exception to most small businesses' inability to hire highly qualified workers. In the late 1990s and early 2000s, many highly qualified workers left larger firms in favor of Internet start-ups. Despite the fact that salaries and benefits were lower, these workers were attracted by the entrepreneurial risk and innovative management of these new ventures.

What Would You Ask a Small Business Owner?

You have learned about the advantages and challenges facing small businesses. Imagine you are a reporter for your school newspaper and are assigned to write an article about a small business in your community.

Write five questions you would ask the small business owner to prepare for your article.

1. _____

2. _____

3. _____

4. _____

5. _____

Starting a Small Business

People give many reasons for wanting to own a business. Among them are personal independence, unlimited profit potential, and the opportunity to work at something that they like at hours they can choose. Many business leaders start their careers as entrepreneurs after four years of college or even graduate school. Others become accomplished in business without special training; still others start their own business after working in a large corporation. In any case, advisers urge would-be entrepreneurs to get all the information they can before starting a business. Many people obtain such information by hiring professional consultants, but there are many other sources, such as publications from the Small Business Administration or business development experts associated with local Chambers of Commerce.

Entrepreneurial Programs

Many colleges offer programs to teach students how to start and operate a business. The programs often combine basic information with hands-on experience and the advice of successful business consultants. These programs help students evaluate their business ideas and learn how to follow through with them. Some colleges also offer "incubator" programs, which are special programs to aid students who are trying to start small businesses.

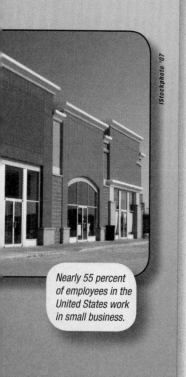

iStockphoto '07

Nearly 55 percent of employees in the United States work in small business.

On-the-Job Training

A common way to learn about a business—and the opportunities for starting a similar one—is to learn while working for someone else. Several of the entrepreneurs mentioned in this chapter did just that. Sam Walton, founder of Wal-Mart, worked for JCPenney before he ventured out on his own.

The Family

Research shows that people who come from families whose members are in business are more likely to start their own companies. Apparently, it doesn't matter whether the business was successful, as there are lessons to be learned from businesses that fail. Relatives can be role models for operating a business and enjoying the fruits of their labor.

Small Business Administration

One source of information for entrepreneurs is the Small Business Administration, established by the federal government in 1953. Its network of offices in cities throughout the country provides business counseling services. Its website provides information on starting and running a business, regulatory information, tutorials, and links to other sites. The SBA website address is www.sba.gov.

Resources on the Internet

An Internet search can yield thousands of web pages that provide information about starting a business. To search the Internet for information, start by typing in: *small business planning* or *entrepreneur's guide to small business information*.

Using the Internet to Plan a Small Business

Below are three Internet activities that can provide important information if you are interested in starting a small business or becoming an entrepreneur. Choose one of the activities to complete. Be prepared to share your results with the class.

1. Go to the Small Business Administration website, www.sba.gov. Once there, click on "Starting a Business" on the upper left of the home page. Read the page and write down the core questions you need to answer before you start your own business.

2. Go to the website www.liraz.com/webquiz.htm. At this site you will find *The Entrepreneur Quiz*. Take the test and determine your score. If other students take the test, compare your results. Be sure to read the interpretation section at the end of the test to find out how you did.

3. Do an open search of the Internet using some of the terms related to small businesses that you have learned. Examples might be *small business planning* or *entrepreneurship*. When you have found two items that interest you, make notes on what you have learned.

Apply Your Understanding

What kinds of information do you think you could learn from an owner whose business had failed?

_____

_____

_____

_____

iStockphoto '07

The Internet provides a wealth of information about how to plan a business.

Forms of Business Organization

In our economy, businesses are organized in three main ways: *sole proprietorships*, *partnerships*, and *corporations*. Many entrepreneurs start small businesses as sole proprietorships or partnerships. If the business prospers, the owner may later need to look for additional funds to finance the company's growth. In that case, the owner may decide to incorporate the business. In this section, you will examine the nature of sole proprietorships, partnerships, and corporations. These three forms of business organization are the major alternative forms of business ownership, and each has advantages and disadvantages.

Sole Proprietorship

A **sole proprietorship** is a business owned by one person. This form of business is the easiest and typically the least costly to start, and it gives the owner full control over operations. Sole proprietorships are the most common type of business organization, but most are very small.

Advantages. The sole proprietorship has several advantages.
- **Organization.** Sole proprietorships are easy to start; there are few restrictions and few forms to complete. Sole proprietors are their own bosses and are free to make all the decisions.
- **Profits.** Sole proprietors gain all the profits of their businesses.
- **Taxes.** Sole proprietorships have few legal restrictions. There is no separate tax return since sole proprietorships are not taxed like corporations.
- **Flexibility.** A sole proprietor is the business manager and can react quickly to problems.
- **Personal achievement.** Sole proprietors have the opportunity to achieve success and recognition through their individual efforts.

Disadvantages. While the advantages of the sole proprietorship seem attractive, there are several serious disadvantages.
- **Unlimited liability.** All business debts and obligations are the responsibility of the sole proprietor. If the business fails, this liability may be covered by the owner's personal assets, including property such as cars, homes, and savings.
- **Limited funds.** The money a sole proprietor can raise is limited by the amount of his or her personal savings and the ability to borrow from other sources.
- **Limited potential.** Lack of opportunities for employees, limitations of size and growth, and lack of management resources are other disadvantages of sole proprietorships.
- **Fragile business existence.** The market for a proprietorship can decline or a competitor can take away a large part of the business. If the sole proprietor becomes physically incapacitated or mentally impaired, the business could fail. If he or she dies, the business ends.

Partnership

A **partnership** is a business organization owned by two or more people who share ownership and control over the business. Like the sole proprietorship, a partnership also has advantages and disadvantages.

Check Your Understanding

What does proprietor *mean?*

_____

_____

What does sole proprietor *mean?*

_____

_____

Think Critically

Think about this statement. Owning your own business is great because you can work half time—any 12 hours out of the day that you choose.

Why is this an ironic statement? Remember that an ironic statement is one that is opposite of what is true.

_____

_____

_____

3. sole proprietorship 4. partnership

Advantages. Experts often cite three major advantages of partnerships.

- **Organization.** Like sole proprietorships, partnerships are relatively easy to form and are not subject to special taxes. A legally binding partnership agreement among all of the partners can clarify the amount of time and energy spent by each partner in the business. Sometimes the partners are unequal in some way. A "silent partner" is inactive and generally just contributes funds in anticipation of a high rate of return. A "limited partner" risks only his or her investment in the business.
- **Potential growth.** Partners bring more money to a business, which increases its opportunities to grow and succeed.
- **Abilities.** Partners often stimulate fresh ideas in each other and benefit from varied talents.

Disadvantages. The disadvantages of partnerships are very similar to the sole proprietorship.

- **Unlimited liability.** In many cases, each of the partners has unlimited liability. Partners are individually responsible for all business debts. If the business fails, creditors (those to whom money is owed) could recover the debt from any, or all, of the partners. In this case, the partner's assets may need to be used to satisfy the obligation.
- **Limited life.** If any partner dies or decides to leave the partnership, the partnership is legally terminated. A new partnership agreement is necessary for the business to continue.
- **Limited funds.** The amount of money a partnership can raise is limited; it depends on the partners' wealth and ability to borrow.
- **Organization.** Each partner acts on behalf of the business; if partners disagree, management conflicts may arise. All partners can be held responsible for the business activities, decisions, and commitments of any partner.

Check Your Understanding

What are two major differences between a sole proprietorship and a partnership?

1. _____

_____

2. _____

_____

Choosing a Partner

Imagine you are planning a business and decide that you need a partner. On a scale of 1 to 5, rate each of the characteristics you value in a partner on the scales below. Number 1 is "not important," and number 5 is "very important." Circle the number that represents your beliefs.

Partner Characteristics	How Important?				
Personal compatibility	1	2	3	4	5
Knowledge of the business	1	2	3	4	5
Work ethic	1	2	3	4	5
Similar financial goals	1	2	3	4	5
Financial commitment	1	2	3	4	5
Honesty/ethics	1	2	3	4	5

In a partnership, two or more people share ownership of the business.

Corporation

A **corporation** is a business organization managed on behalf of its owners, who provide the funds. The law requires a corporation to obtain a state charter to operate. Ownership of a corporation is represented by shares of stock. Stockholders become the corporation's owners. Some corporations are privately held; all stock is owned by a small group or a family.

The stock of publicly held corporations is traded or "brokered" through organizations called *stock exchanges*. A **stock exchange** is a market in which the public buys and sells shares of stock. Courts of law treat a corporation as a "person," a separate entity from those who own it. A corporation can sue, be sued, and enter into contractual agreements. It must pay taxes. Although sole proprietorships outnumber corporations by almost four to one, corporations dominate U.S. business with 83 percent of total sales.

Advantages. Corporations have four major advantages.

- **Limited liability.** Shareholders can be held responsible only for debts up to their investment in the company or what they paid for their shares of stock. In many English-speaking countries, corporations add "limited" (Ltd.) to their company name to make this important distinction. In fact, it is the limited liability feature of corporations that makes it possible for them to raise large amounts of capital. Without this legal protection, it is doubtful whether many people would take the risk of buying stock in large corporations.
- **Ease of transfer.** Stockholders can enter or leave a corporation at will by buying or selling shares of stock.
- **Unlimited life.** When a stockholder dies, the corporation does not dissolve. Corporations are said to live in perpetuity, meaning they can last indefinitely.
- **Ability to raise funds.** Corporations can raise money by selling stock or borrow money by issuing bonds. You will learn more about stocks and bonds in Chapter 8.

Disadvantages. Three disadvantages stand out with respect to corporations.

- **Expense.** Organizing a corporation is more complicated and costly than other forms of business and typically requires legal help.
- **Taxation.** The government taxes a corporation's earnings twice. A corporation is taxed on its profits, and stockholders individually pay taxes on any dividends (corporate profits) distributed to them.
- **Regulations.** Corporations that sell stock to the public give up much privacy. The law requires publicly held or "open" corporations to disclose information about their finances and operations to any interested person. The purpose is to provide information about the firm to both current and prospective investors. But information that helps investors may also help competitors. This is the reason some firms remain private or "closed" and do not trade their stock.

Think Critically

Underline the last sentence in the paragraph to the right, that begins, "Although sole proprietorships ..."

Explain why corporations dominate U.S. business when there are four times more sole proprietorships than corporations.

_____

_____

_____

Check Your Understanding

Listed below are five advantages or disadvantages of various forms of business. On the line below each description, indicate whether it applies to:
- *a sole proprietorship*
- *a partnership*
- *a proprietorship and a partnership*
- *a corporation*

Earnings taxed twice

_____

Unlimited life

_____

Unlimited liability

_____

Easy to start

_____

Subject to regulation

_____

iStockphoto '07

A majority of America's businesses are organized in three main ways: sole proprietorships, partnerships, and corporations.

6. stock exchange

Figures 7-2a and 7-2b are circle graphs that show the number of proprietorships, partnerships, and corporations along with their revenues in 2002.

Figure 7-2a: Number of Business Firms in 2002
(in thousands)

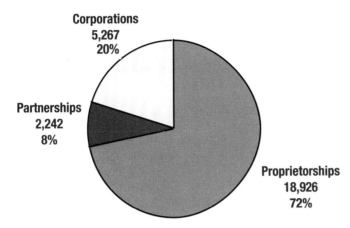

Corporations
5,267
20%

Partnerships
2,242
8%

Proprietorships
18,926
72%

Figure 7-2b: Revenues of Business Firms in 2002
(in billions)

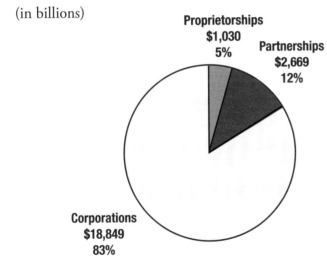

Proprietorships
$1,030
5%

Partnerships
$2,669
12%

Corporations
$18,849
83%

Source: *Statistical Abstract of the United States: 2006*, Table 725.

Check Your Understanding

The information in the two graphs in Figures 7-2a and 7-2b is closely related. Describe how the information goes together to help us understand business in our country.

_____

_____

_____

Proprietorships, Partnerships, and Corporations

Use Figures 7-2a and 7-2b to answer true (T) or false (F) to the statements below.

1. Proprietorships account for the largest percentage of U.S. business firms. _____
2. The United States has more corporations than partnerships. _____
3. Proprietorships account for 72 percent of the firms in the United States. _____
4. Corporations account for 12 percent of the revenue from U.S. businesses. _____
5. Corporations account for 20 percent of the firms in the United States. _____

Entrepreneurship on the Rise

Jeff Whiting has a lot of dough. He's the owner of Aspen Mills Bread Company in Palm Springs, California, which he opened in 1995 at age 29. Aspen Mills would never have come into existence without his desire to be his own boss and his willingness to take a risk. Whiting studied economics in college. He predicted a growing market for nutritious breads, yet he was not a baker, so he visited bakeries and asked questions. "It all came together when I met a bread chemist," he explains. With the chemist's skills and recipes, he was willing to risk his money baking bread.

Risk and Resources

Whiting found a suitable location, signed a lease, and began remodeling the building he chose. He bought a huge, expensive oven and a stone grinder to make fresh flour every morning. The first mixer he bought was a mistake. But he adds, "The key is to learn from your mistakes so you don't make them again."

Competition

Who are his competitors? Whiting believes his products are too different to have close competitors in town. Comparing his breads to those in the grocery store, he says, "is like comparing a Range Rover and a Toyota pickup." How does he price his products? "It's basically demand and supply," he answers. He checked prices of different breads in town and used this as a starting point in determining his prices. Now he adjusts his prices in response to sales. When he sells out of certain products, he raises prices.

Rising Sales

Urged by others who have tasted and enjoyed Aspen Mill's products, Whiting has opened franchises in other cities. Today, he has a staff at the Palm Springs store as well as at two nearby offices. He sometimes wonders if he'd take the risk of business ownership again, but he obviously wouldn't settle for less than a full loaf of entrepreneurship.

Special Types of Business Organization

Not all business organizations fall neatly into the three categories described in this chapter so far. There are six other types of business organization that exist but are less common than sole proprietorships, partnerships, and corporations.

S Corporations

A small business can enjoy many of the advantages of a corporation without having to pay corporate income taxes if it organizes as an S Corporation. The term *S Corporation* is taken from a part of the federal tax laws known as Subchapter S. The stockholders pay personal income taxes based on the dividends they receive. This allows the business to avoid the double taxation that regular corporations are subject to. An S Corporation may not have more than 35 stockholders and may not own 80 percent or more of another corporation. As with regular corporations, organizing an S Corporation usually requires a lawyer's help.

Limited Liability Companies

A limited liability company (LLC) combines the advantages of a corporation and a partnership. LLCs are more complicated to organize than typical partnerships, but they are becoming a popular form of organization for new small businesses, especially among Internet start-ups. Today, all 50 states have passed laws regarding LLCs. An LLC must have two or more members, who own interest in the LLC and who function as partners or shareholders. Each member's liability is limited, as it is in a corporation, but the members are taxed as partners are taxed in a partnership. Unlike a partnership, an LLC may acquire and hold property in the name of the LLC rather than in the names of its members. An LLC can sue or be sued in its own name.

One advantage of an LLC is its ability to limit liability. If the business is sued, the owner's personal assets are not at risk. The disadvantages include various state regulations and strict tax rules. Another disadvantage is that an LLC has a limited life.

Not-for-Profit Corporations

As the name suggests, not-for-profits don't try to earn a profit. Rather, they serve particular educational, social, charitable, or religious purposes. For example, the Student Conservation Association is a nonprofit group with a 59-year record of helping young people preserve the nation's wilderness while teaching them conservation skills. Its sources of income include money from private foundations, government funding, and individual donations.

Since not-for-profit corporations earn no profits, they are not subject to income taxes. However, like other corporations, their income must be great enough to cover operating expenses, including employee wages and benefits. Therefore, the government allows them to hold in reserve a certain percentage of their income to use for day-to-day operations. Some not-for-profit corporations you may recognize are the American Red Cross, the Urban League, Inc., the March of Dimes, and, of course, Junior Achievement USA. These and other not-for-profit corporations rely on the efforts of volunteers, but they also employ paid professional staffs.

Government-Owned Corporations

Federal, state, and local governments also can own and operate corporations. This action is generally undertaken when the market doesn't adequately supply a needed good or service. The U.S. Postal Service, some metropolitan rapid transit services, and publicly owned electric utilities are examples of government-owned corporations.

Cooperatives

Cooperatives (or co-ops) are associations of individuals or companies that perform functions for the members. Here are three common types of cooperatives.
- Housing co-ops are multiple dwelling units owned by their tenants.
- Consumer co-ops are retail businesses owned by people who share in the profits and/or purchase goods and services at lower cost.
- Producer co-ops are companies that manufacture and market products on behalf of their members. One of the largest of these is Ocean Spray Cranberries, Inc. This cooperative includes nearly 2,000 cranberry and citrus growers around the country.

Check Your Understanding

Indicate whether each statement is true (T) or false (F).

1. Employees of not-for-profit corporations cannot be paid a salary.

_____

2. Not-for-profit firms are businesses that are poorly run.

_____

3. Not-for-profit corporations can keep some surplus money in reserve.

_____

4. Not-for-profit corporations do not have to pay taxes.

_____

Think Critically

Do you think it is good for consumers to have both government and private corporations in the same business, such as mail delivery? _____

Why? _____

_____

Check Your Understanding

What is the difference between a not-for-profit corporation and a cooperative?

_____

_____

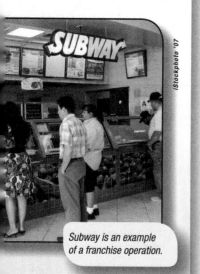

Subway is an example
of a franchise operation.

Think Critically

*Many consumers prefer to
eat in franchise restaurants
rather than independently
owned restaurants. Why do
franchises like McDonald's
and Subway appeal
to many people?*

_____

_____

Franchises

Franchising is a method of distributing products or services that is governed by a contract. A **franchise** is a license that entitles its holder to operate his or her individually owned business as if it were part of a large chain of stores. Isaac Singer started one of the first franchises in 1858 when he came up with the idea of selling the rights to sell his sewing machines. Fees earned from the license rights helped to fund his manufacturing costs. Coca-Cola has used franchising to expand throughout the United States by shifting the burden of manufacturing, storing, and distributing its product to local businesspeople who acquired bottling rights. In the 1950s, Ray Kroc saw the potential in franchising McDonald's. Today many clothing, real estate, fast-food, and motel chains are franchise operations.

Franchises have many advantages. For the franchiser—the corporation that sells its franchises to others—the revenue from selling franchises enables the company to expand operations at little cost to itself. Franchisers also benefit because franchisees, as business owners, have an incentive to increase efficiency, sales, and profits. Those who buy franchises (franchisees) benefit as well. Many franchisers provide training programs, financial assistance, and other kinds of help in operating and managing the business. Advertising campaigns, name recognition, and reputation bring increased sales to franchisees as well.

Franchises do have some disadvantages. Franchisers retain control over their franchisees. They may dictate employee dress or how to operate or decorate the business. In addition, many franchisers require their franchisees to purchase their wholesale products from specified businesses. There is also the possibility that a mistake by one franchisee will result in bad publicity that reflects on all the franchise operations.

Here are several franchises you will probably recognize:

Franchise	Product
Subway	Sandwiches
Mail Boxes Etc.	Postal and business service
Dairy Queen	Frozen desserts
RadioShack	Electronic products
Jazzercise, Inc.	Fitness centers

Which Type of Business Interests You?

In this chapter, you have learned about three major and six special types of business organizations. List them below.

**Major Forms of
Business Organization**   **Special Types of Business Organization**

_____   _____ _____

_____   _____ _____

_____   _____ _____

Think about the various types of businesses you might wish to join when you start a career. Which type most appeals to you, and why?

_____

_____

How Large Corporations Are Organized

State governments require people who want to start a corporation to obtain a state *charter*. A **charter** is a document that states the nature of the business, the initial owners of the stock, and the types of stocks to be sold. It also gives the corporation permission to do business in that state. Rules and policies approved by the issuing states are called corporate bylaws.

Stockholders

Corporations fund initial start-up or expansion projects by selling stock. Stockholders, also referred to as shareholders, are the owners of the corporation. If you own shares of stock in The Walt Disney Company or Apple Computer, for example, then you are a part owner of the business. Each share is a small fraction of total ownership of the corporation's assets and earnings. The number of stockholders of a corporation can vary from just a few to millions.

Board of Directors

With potentially thousands of stockholders or owners, corporations need some way to operate efficiently. To accomplish these goals, the stockholders elect a board of directors as the corporation's policymakers. Each share of stock represents one vote, and elections generally occur at an annual meeting. Stockholders unable to attend can submit a written authorization, called a proxy, to instruct others how to vote. The elected board of directors meets regularly to assess operations. The directors are also responsible for appointing the officers of the corporation to manage the business on a daily basis. With this arrangement, those who run the company are responsible to the directors who hired them, and the directors are ultimately responsible to those who own the firm's stock.

In addition to their proxy vote, individual stockholders can influence management daily by buying and selling the company's stock. If stockholders disapprove of management's decisions, for instance, they may sell shares. This can reduce the value of the company's stock, and a lower stock price can pressure managers to change their policies. On the other hand, if people generally approve of management's decisions, they are likely to buy more shares of stock. A higher stock price encourages managers to continue their policies.

Annual Corporation Report

Once a year, the directors of an open or public corporation issue a report for its stockholders containing information about the financial status of the corporation. The Securities and Exchange Commission (a federal agency) requires publication of this annual report. Today, many firms publish their annual reports on their websites. Most annual reports contain the following information:

- Financial highlights
- Letter to the stockholders from the chairman of the board
- Report on the divisions or departments of the company
- Panorama of products, services, and employees
- Financial statements including report of management, report of independent auditor, statement of earnings, statement of financial position, statement of cash flow, statement of stockholders' equity, and notes to the financial statements
- Listing of the board of directors and the officers of the corporation
- Stockholder information such as stock symbol and investor information addresses

Apply Your Understanding

Imagine that you are elected to serve on the board of directors of a large corporation. What three questions would you ask the company executives at a board of directors' meeting? Remember, your job as a director is to make sure that the company's executives run the company profitably, efficiently, and ethically.

1._____

_____

2._____

_____

3._____

_____

8. charter

Organization of a Corporation

 People in large corporations perform many important and varied jobs. The president and Chief Executive Officer (CEO) is the top person in a large corporation. Usually, the corporation lawyer, called the general counsel, reports directly to the president and CEO and does not report to anyone else in the corporation. Vice presidents report to the president and CEO. Vice presidents might include: Vice President of Research and Development, Vice President of Finance, Vice President of Marketing and Sales, Vice President of Production, and Vice President of Human Resources. Reporting to each vice president is one or more directors. Directors might include: Director of Product Research, Director of Accounting, Director of Advertising, Director of Quality Control, and Director of Employee Benefits.

On a separate sheet of paper, create an organizational chart. Show the president and CEO at the top of the chart. Then show whom each of the other positions reports to. Use the positions named in the above paragraph.

Summary

Enterprising individuals who put their creative talent to work in both large and small companies drive innovation in the U.S. economy. They are entrepreneurs, developing ways to make more efficient use of resources. They see opportunities and take risks in hopes of earning profits. Entrepreneurs use many different strategies to achieve their goals. Small businesses in the United States are major contributors to the market because of their flexibility to meet market demands. Adding to the efforts of entrepreneurs in recent years has been the birth of e-commerce, which is rapidly changing the way businesses operate.

Small businesses are flexible in meeting small market needs, while big firms need larger markets to profitably sell their products. Unfortunately, small businesses often fail because of insufficient capital, slow sales, and heavy debt. Also, small businesses have difficulty finding highly qualified workers because they often can't afford to provide the salary or benefits offered by larger firms. Small businesses, however, do have a bright future with the availability of college entrepreneurial programs, opportunities for on-the-job training, family business backgrounds, the Small Business Administration, and Internet resources.

Most business firms are organized as sole proprietorships, partnerships, or corporations. Sole proprietorships and partnerships outnumber corporations by almost four to one. They have been a major source of new ideas and jobs in the economy, but corporations continue to generate more revenue than sole proprietorships and partnerships. Corporations have the advantage of unlimited life and limited liability. This enables them to raise sums of money well beyond the limits of partnerships and proprietorships. The organization of large corporations enables them to run efficiently despite having thousands of owners called stockholders. Management and ownership are separated through the use of devices such as boards of directors, proxy voting, and annual reports to the stockholders. Stockholders can influence management decisions through the buying and selling of a company's stock. Other forms of business organization also make significant contributions to the economy.

Looking Ahead

In the next chapter, you'll explore ways in which businesses finance their operations. You will see how corporations sell stocks and bonds to raise money, and the opportunities these sales offer to savers who have money to invest. Finally, you'll learn something about the kinds of accounting records that firms maintain to track their progress.

Financing a Business

Read to Find Out

As you read this chapter, look for answers to the following questions:

How do financial markets help businesses obtain capital resources?

How do businesses borrow?

What is equity, and how is it used to finance business growth?

How do businesses save?

How can small businesses get a start?

What is the stock market, and why is it important?

What are a balance sheet and an income statement?

Mark to Remember

* *This is important.*

? *I have a question about this.*

! *This is a surprise.*

Why It Matters

Each business day, Monday through Friday, newspapers and television news programs report information about business finance. Here are some examples: "Interest rates are unchanged." "The Dow Industrials rally." "Investors are optimistic about the bond market." "Oil dividends reach an all-time high." "New business starts are slow." These examples reflect the language of business finance. You may become a businessperson someday. If this is the case, you need to know about the language of business finance and what it means to you. As an informed citizen in any field of work, it is important for you to become familiar with how businesses are financed and why finance matters in a free enterprise economy.

Financing a Business

Building On What You Know

If you want to buy something expensive and you don't have enough money to make the purchase, what do you do? You may choose to save money from your earnings or allowance until you have enough to make the purchase. Another option would be to borrow the money, make the purchase, and pay back the money you borrowed, with interest. Like you, people in business have to figure out how to meet their business needs. Also like you, business owners have options in how to finance those needs.

Starting a business is kind of like baking a cake. Mix eggs, flour, sugar, milk, and baking powder in the correct proportions, and you will get a good result. To start and run a business, an entrepreneur must combine human resources, natural resources, and capital resources. In this chapter, we will focus on capital resources like the buildings, tools, and machines used to produce goods and services. General Motors uses robots for welding and painting its cars and trucks. Domino's Pizza uses ovens and delivery vehicles, and a grocery store in your hometown uses shelves and freezer cases. Most businesses use telephones and computers. Every business, large and small, uses some type of capital resource. When businesses start or expand, they invest in capital resources. Investment money to purchase capital resources has to come from some source. That source is savings—the business owner's savings or other people's savings.

Sixteen-year-old Leticia can tell you about investment needs. Leticia has turned her kitchen into a home bakery business. She wants a new mixer with more power to handle the amount of baking she's doing, but the mixer will cost about $200. She doesn't have enough money, so she must save some of her earnings to buy it. When Leticia saves, she gives up something else she might want to buy, such as a new business telephone or a new pair of shoes. She uses her business earnings, reduces her personal consumption, or borrows money so that she can invest in some capital resources now to improve her business.

From Saving to Investing

In our economy, the money we save personally by giving up current consumption flows to the business community as investment dollars. Many Americans put some of their savings into a bank account or an investment to earn a return in the form of interest or dividends. When they do so, they take part in financial markets, where savers exchange funds with borrowers and others who are willing to pay for the use of the money.

Financial markets are a vital part of a free enterprise economy. They are an extension of the circular flow diagram you studied in Chapter 2. In Figure 8-1 below, the diagram shows how savers give funds to a financial institution that, in turn, gives them a return of interest or dividends. Financial institutions lend funds to businesses like the Mom and Pop Shoppe. The Shoppe's investment in capital and other resources will allow for greater profit, some of which will pay for new equipment. The Shoppe will repay the money it borrows with interest. In this way, the dollars businesses use to increase production bring a return on investment to savers that, in turn, builds their wealth.

Figure 8-1 Flow of Savings and Investment

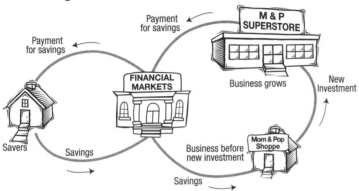

There are two sides to the financial market. On one side are the savers and investors like yourself, looking for the best return. On the other side are the businesses that want to buy capital resources. How do businesses use financial markets to obtain money? They borrow the money, they sell new shares of ownership in the form of stock, or they save the money themselves.

There are risks associated with each option for both the investor and the business. This is because there is a relationship between risk and return. As the risk of an investment increases, the return that investors require also increases. Businesses aren't always successful. Investing in the market with the risk of losing part or all of your money is called market risk. Businesses risk the high rates of return that they must pay investors. Inflation risk is another type of risk. This is the effect of rising prices. If prices are rising, the purchasing power of an investment decreases. For example, at an annual inflation rate of 10 percent, the purchasing power of a $1,000 investment would decrease to $900 in a year.

When Businesses Borrow

Businesses often finance investment in new capital resources with long-term loans. The principal (the amount borrowed) is repaid, usually at the end of the loan period. Interest is paid at intervals during the life of the loan. These long-term loans are called bonds; borrowers get the cash they need, while lenders earn interest. Governments also issue bonds. Federal, state, and local governments have a need to finance long-term spending for roads, bridges, schools, and recreation centers. Bonds are issued by governments at each level and work in ways similar to corporate-issued bonds. The public buys the government bonds with various maturity dates, and the government pays the principal and interest at maturity. The 30-year U.S. Treasury bond is the benchmark by which all other bonds are measured. Government-issued bonds are thought to be less risky than other bonds because the U.S. government guarantees repayment of the bonds.

Check Your Understanding

Describe in your own words what the diagram in Figure 8-1 illustrates.

_____

_____

_____

Show Your Understanding

1. Underline a sentence in the text that describes a risk an investor takes when investing money.
2. Double underline a sentence that describes a risk a business takes when borrowing money.

Check Your Understanding

Generally, which has the greater risk, a government-issued bond or a business-issued bond?

_____

Why? _____

_____

People who invest their savings in bonds rather than stocks assume a lower risk in most cases. The bond investor is considered a creditor, the one to whom the bond debt is owed. Creditors are paid before dividends can be distributed to shareholders.

Standard and Poor's and Moody's Investors Service are two firms that rate bonds for risk. Both services rate the best bonds in terms of financing condition and potential for profit. Triple A (AAA, Aaa) is the highest rating, with AA or Aa, A, BBB, or Baa next, and so on down the alphabet. These ratings influence the rates paid: A low rating on a bond will cost the issuing company or government more in interest over the term of the bond. Investors seek a higher interest rate return because there is greater risk that the issuing company may default on repayment.

The Long of It

Corporations issue bonds to raise funds to purchase new technology, expand operations, or finance corporate takeovers or mergers. When corporations want to issue a new bond, they ask investment banks to sell the bond issue. An investment bank is in the business of selling bonds to and buying bonds from the public. Suppose an investment banker announces its intent to sell $200 million in bonds of ABC Corporation. The bonds will mature and payment will be required in five years, so the bonds represent a five-year loan. Each bond has a face value of $1,000, the most common face value of bonds. It pays the bond buyer (bondholder) a fixed yearly interest amount of $95. The corporation pays bondholders annual interest. At the end of the five-year term, the corporation pays the bondholder the principal, the original amount of the bond's face value. If you had bought one of these bonds for $1,000, the annual rate of return on your investment would have been 9.5 percent ($95 / $1,000 = 9.5%). In business finance, a five-year bond would be considered a long-term investment.

The Short of It

Sometimes a business's income does not exactly match its expenses on a weekly or monthly basis. More money goes out than comes in, and cash is temporarily unavailable to pay current bills. This situation is often referred to as a "cash flow" problem. Short-term borrowing is the answer to this common problem. These loans are usually repaid within the year and generally are not used to finance investments in new buildings, equipment, or other capital resources. Short-term loans are used to finance the everyday costs of doing business, such as employee payrolls and purchases of raw materials and merchandise. The most common forms of short-term financing are trade credit, loans from financial institutions, and loans from other companies.

Apply Your Understanding

Individuals, as well as businesses, can have a "cash flow" problem. Describe in your own words what a cash flow problem is and how an individual can solve this problem.

_____

_____

_____

Trade credit works like a charge account. The buyer purchases supplies or goods from a seller on account (credit) for payment at a later date. Trade credit may be a simple delay in payment for purchases (30, 60, or 90 days), sales on consignment, equipment loans, or a variety of different options to assist buyers in financing purchases. Trade credit usually comes at a high interest rate.

Loans from financial institutions, such as banks and finance companies, are another source of short-term credit. A new business will often open a *line of credit* with a bank. A **line of credit** is an agreement a business makes, usually with a bank, to borrow up to a certain amount of money for ongoing cash needs. Long-standing corporations often use this method, too. Most lenders will want to examine the borrower's credit history, the company's cash flow history, profit projections for the business, the type of collateral that is available to secure the loan, and the character of the borrower. Lenders will closely examine loan documentation, including business and personal financial statements, income tax returns, and, frequently, a business plan. The interest rate on a business loan often depends on its size and risk and on the ability of the borrower to repay.

Loans from other companies are common among the nation's largest businesses. For example, if ABC Corporation needed a $10 million loan for a short time to finance its payroll, it could borrow directly from other companies that have cash available to invest for financial gain.

Choosing a Borrowing Option

The matrix below lists eight purposes a business might have for borrowing money. Five borrowing options are shown across the top of the matrix. Use an X to indicate which borrowing option you think would be best for each borrowing purpose.

Purpose	Five-Year Bond	One-Year Loan	Trade Credit	Line of Credit	Loan from Another Company
1. To purchase a new software system					
2. To make up a cash flow shortage					
3. To meet overtime payroll needs					
4. To remodel the current office building					
5. To purchase another company's inventory					
6. To meet current payroll needs					
7. To buy new office furniture					
8. To buy a new fleet of delivery trucks					

When Businesses Issue New Equity

Equity means ownership, often stock ownership or business ownership. If you have equity in a business, you own at least part of it. Your equity might be a percentage of the business or it could be ownership of stock in a company. A sole proprietor can "sell" part ownership in his or her business to form a partnership and gain additional funding. A partnership can add new partners or incorporate (become a corporation) by selling shares of stock. Newly formed or existing corporations may issue new shares of stock in what is called an *initial public offering*. An **initial public offering** (IPO) is a company's first sale of stock to the public. Unlike bondholders, who are creditors, stockholders are owners. For example, if a corporation has 70 million shares of stock and you own one share, then you own 1/70,000,000 of the company. However, while bondholders must receive their interest payments, stockholders receive their share of a corporation's profits only if the corporation's board of directors votes to distribute them as dividends.

Common or Preferred

Most corporations issue *common stock*. **Common stock** is a claim to a share of the profits of a company after all expenses and taxes are paid. Common stockholders vote for the board of directors of the corporation and can vote directly on many policies. Many corporations also issue **preferred stock**, ownership shares issued as nonvoting stock. The advantage is that preferred stockholders receive preferential treatment and are paid first if the corporation issues dividends. If a firm has a period of poor performance, the preferred stockholders may get paid a dividend while the common shareholders receive nothing. Further, if the corporation becomes bankrupt and goes out of business, preferred stockholders receive their share of the assets ahead of the common stockholders.

Apply Your Understanding

Suppose you learn that a fast-growing energy drink company in your community is issuing an IPO. If you had money to invest, would you be interested in buying shares of the IPO stock?

_____ *Why or why not?*

_____

_____

What are two questions you would ask about the company before buying the stock?

1. _____

_____

_____

2. _____

_____

_____

2. equity   3. initial public offering   4. common stock   5. preferred stock

What does this statement mean? A new car depreciates the minute you drive it off the lot.

_____

_____

_____

Check Your Understanding

Study Figure 8-2 and reread the paragraph above it. The percentages shown in the graph are a compilation of all U.S. businesses in 2004. Do you think the percentages shown in the graph reflect the way most small, fast-growing businesses would be likely to distribute their profits?

_____

Why or why not?

_____

_____

When Businesses Save

Businesses save money in a couple of ways. A big part of business saving is called depreciation. Depreciation occurs as tools, machines, and other capital resources wear out or become obsolete. The cost of depreciation is included in the price of products businesses sell. By saving this money, businesses can reinvest in capital resources to replace worn-out equipment. After allowing for depreciation and deducting other expenses from their income, businesses determine how to use their profits.

As the graph in Figure 8-2 shows, corporations use their profits in three ways. First, they pay income taxes to state and federal governments. Second, corporations distribute some of their profits to stockholders as dividends. Finally, they set aside a portion of their profits to be used to purchase new capital resources. These funds are called undistributed profits or retained earnings. As a source of financing, retained earnings are very important to new, small, and rapidly growing businesses. Typically, these businesses do not pay dividends to their shareholders. Instead, they keep the profits and invest them in the company's growth.

Figure 8-2: Uses of Corporate Profits, 2004
(Profit = $1,161 billion)

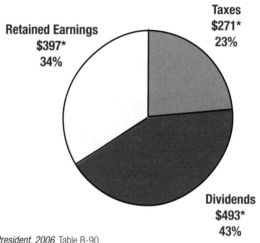

Source: *Economic Report of the President, 2006*, Table B-90.   * In millions

What Businesses Do with Their Profits

Use the circle graph in Figure 8-2 to answer the following questions.

1. What were the total U.S. corporate profits before taxes in 2004? _____

2. Undistributed profits are called *retained earnings*. In 2004, what amount of corporate profits were allocated to retained earnings? _____

3. In 2004, what percentage of corporate profits were paid in taxes? _____

4. Businesses distribute their profits to pay taxes, to pay dividends, and to reinvest. Of the three, which category does a company have the least flexibility in how much money is allotted to it? _____

Small Business Start-Up Financing

In Chapter 7, you learned that entrepreneurs who start businesses are often responsible for new products, services, and jobs in the economy. These start-up businesses must have finances. How are they financed?

One way startups are financed is through the personal savings of the entrepreneur founder. While personal savings are often limited, they are necessary, especially if a business owner is asking other people to invest. Another way startups are financed is through loans from family and friends, although this kind of financing can strain personal relationships if the business is not profitable within a reasonable length of time.

Startup business owners can form partnerships. Sharing ownership may better fulfill capital needs, but it will also lessen control since decision making and profits must be shared. Incorporating and selling stock is a common form of financing a startup business. Incorporation offers limited liability to stockholders and easy transfer of ownership, but the costs to incorporate are high and profits must be shared.

Some startup owners seek commercial bank loans to start their businesses. To qualify for a bank loan, a startup is often required to prove that its owners are worthy of credit. In many cases, a bank will require that a comprehensive business plan be prepared to show the bank that the start-up owners know how they will operate the business.

The Small Business Administration, an agency of the U.S. government, provides loans and loan guarantees to small and minority-owned businesses. It may be possible for a start-up business to attract funds from **venture capitalists**, investors who make loans to new companies. Venture capitalists have extensive financial resources and are often willing to loan funds to start-ups. However, these funds come at a price: Venture capitalists seek high rates of return.

Pause to Predict

Name two ways you think new, small businesses can get start-up money.

1. _____

_____

2. _____

_____

When you finish reading this section, check your answers.

Getting Start-Up Money for a New Business

Imagine that you are trying to start a new company. To get the company up and running, you need $10,000 to buy equipment. In the section above, five sources of start-up financing are described. List each source and explain why you think that source would or would not be a good choice of financing for your business.

Financing Source   **Why It Would or Would Not Be a Good Source**

1. _____   _____

2. _____   _____

3. _____   _____

4. _____   _____

5. _____   _____

6. venture capitalists

The Stock Market

Every day throughout the world, billions of shares of stock are bought and sold. However, there is more than one kind of market for stocks. When a corporation first issues shares of stock, it is said to "go public." The corporation generally works with an investment banking firm that agrees to sell the stock issue. When a firm agrees to sell a stock issue, it buys all the stock at an agreed price and then resells it to the public through an initial public offering (IPO). This is referred to as the new issues market or primary market.

After a stock has been initially sold, people buy and sell the shares apart from the issuing company. Secondary buying and selling of stock shares is done in what is commonly called a *stock market*. A **stock market** is a market in which the public is able to buy or sell stock. In a stock market, money spent to buy and sell shares goes to other people who are buying and selling stock shares; the money does not go to the businesses. It might seem, then, that the stock market is unimportant to businesses that want to raise money in the financial markets. However, the stock market still plays a crucial role for businesses. Without a secondary market, few people would buy new issues in the primary market, and businesses would have difficulty raising money to finance the capital resources they require.

Stocks

The stock market has many parts. One part consists of organized exchanges like the New York Stock Exchange (NYSE), the American Stock Exchange (AMEX), and smaller, regional exchanges in Los Angeles, Chicago, Boston, Cincinnati, and Philadelphia. The NYSE lists nearly 3,000 large and mid-size companies worth more than $16 trillion, including nearly 400 non-U.S. companies. The NYSE is the world's largest equity market. The AMEX lists more than 700 common stocks. It concentrates on mid-size companies with strong growth potential.

Another part of the stock market consists of over-the-counter (OTC) trading. The term originated when people actually bought and sold shares of stock from merchants who sold food or other supplies "over the counter." Today, this market is a decentralized, electronic trading system. It is comprised of various dealers, the largest being the National Association of Securities Dealers Automated Quotation system (NASDAQ). Currently listing more than 3,100 mostly small and new companies, NASDAQ is also home to some of the nation's best-known companies, especially in the technology arena. Microsoft, Apple, and Yahoo are all listed on NASDAQ.

Check Your Understanding

Indicate whether the following statements are true (T) or false (F).

1. There is one stock market in the world.

_____

2. A stock market is open only to private investors.

_____

3. A stock market is a secondary market.

_____

4. In a stock market, stock is both bought and sold.

_____

5. Only issuing companies can sell their stock in a stock market.

_____

Apply Your Understanding

What do the following sets of initials stand for?

NYSE

_____

AMEX

_____

NASDAQ

_____

7. stock market

Take a Bow, Mr. Dow

Each day, more and more Americans carefully watch the activities of the stock and bond markets.

This is not surprising since more Americans than ever before have some of their savings invested in these markets. Some people have invested through their employer's pension funds, while others use large investment houses to buy and sell stocks, bonds, and mutual funds. Some people do their own research and make their own trades in the market. Today, there are many indexes that measure the movement of the stock market. The Dow Jones Industrial Average (DJIA) is the *index* most widely reported and watched. An **index** is a combination of different numerical data, such as prices, into one measure that is reported over time. An index begins with a base year, combines prices and usually averages them, and then multiplies the result by 100. Indexes are often called averages.

In 1882, Charles H. Dow and his partner Edward Jones worked with Charles Bergstresser for funding to start the Dow Jones Company. In an office next to the New York Stock Exchange, Dow and Jones began publishing the Customer's Afternoon Letter, which later became *The Wall Street Journal*.

In 1884, Dow compiled his first stock average, which consisted of nine railroads and two manufacturing firms. Twelve years later, in 1896, the paper began publishing the Dow Jones Industrial Average, known today as "the Dow." The new average consisted of 12 manufacturing companies. The average was determined by adding the stock prices and dividing by 12.

By 1928, the Dow consisted of 30 stocks, and that number remains to this day. However, from that first list in 1896, only General Electric remains on the list. The companies in the Dow have changed over the years to reflect the evolution of our economy. For example, some have merged while others have failed. Others have been dropped in favor of companies thought to be more representative of the market, especially the growing importance of service-producing companies in our economy.

While the Dow was at 11,260.28 on June 1, 2006, you cannot calculate the number by just adding the stock price of the 30 companies and dividing by 30. Instead, you have to divide by a special number called the divisor, which was .12493117 on June 1, 2006. To maintain the historical continuity of the average, the divisor is recalculated for stock splits, when a company divides one share of stock at $100 into two shares for $50 each, for example. The divisor is also recalculated to account for changes in the structure and components of the companies. Consequently, the Dow isn't a true average today. If the Dow weren't adjusted to reflect changes, it would suddenly move up or down and give false information about stock prices in the market.

Understanding a Stock Table

Each day, *The Wall Street Journal* publishes the results of stock transactions that occurred the previous day in stock markets. It is helpful to understand how to read a stock table, which is shown below as Figure 8-3. The selection of stocks in Figure 8-3 appeared in *The Wall Street Journal* on June 21, 2006.

Figure 8-3: Reading a Stock Table
New York Stock Exchange Composite Transactions

Tuesday, June 20, 2006

| 52-WEEK | | | YLD | | VOL | | NET |
HI	LO	STOCK (DIV)	%	PE	100s	CLOSE	CHG
63.22	49.90	Allstate 1.40	2.6	17	20025	53.14	-0.16
↑40.57	23.05	AnnTaylor	…	28	12363	40.60	0.89
↓19.45	17.05	BurgerKing n	…	…	15096	17.06	-0.22
31.03	22.89	Disney .27f	0.9	22	134671	29.23	0.16
43.98	36.04	HomeDpt .60	1.6	13	118082	36.42	-0.44
3.49	2.25	LucentTch	…	14	362625	2.35	-0.03
36.75	27.36	McDonalds .67f	2.0	17	35471	32.96	0.11
36.65	25.50	③Merck 1.52	4.4	16	92102	34.92	0.46

↑ = New 52-week high.
↓ = New 52-week low.
HI = Highest price at which shares sold in the last 52 weeks.
LO = Lowest price at which shares sold in the last 52 weeks.
③ = Annual report available.
STOCK (DIV) = Stock name and quarterly dividend.
n = Newly issued stock in the past 52 weeks.
f = Annual rate, increased on latest declaration.
YLD% = Stock yield is the dividend per year as a percent of the share's current price.
PE = Price/earnings ratio; the closing price of a share divided by the per share earnings for the latest four quarters.
VOL100s = Total number of shares traded on this day in hundreds of shares.
CLOSE = The last trading price for this day.
NETCHG = The difference between today's closing price and the previous trading day's closing price.

Source: *The Wall Street Journal*, June 21, 2006, pp. C7, C8.

What Can You Learn from a Stock Table?

Study the table in Figure 8-3, and answer the questions below.

1. How many Allstate shares were traded on June 20? _____

2. What was the stock closing price for Ann Taylor on June 20? _____

3. What was the decline in stock price for Burger King between June 19 and 20? _____

4. On June 20, what was the price/earnings ratio of Disney stock? _____

5. What was the yield of Home Depot stock on June 20? _____

6. What was the 52-week high in the price of Lucent Technology stock? _____

7. What company's annual report is available? _____

Figure 8-4: Trail of a Stock Transaction

The use of computers and satellite communication systems has reduced the number of people and time needed to buy or sell stock on the New York Stock Exchange.

1. Customer calls a local broker to buy or sell stock.

iStockphoto '07

2. The local broker records the order and sends it by satellite to a "floor broker" in New York. The floor broker matches it with other orders and confirms the transaction electronically while the original customer is still on the phone with his or her broker.

iStockphoto 07

4. Within 7 days, the stock is officially transferred to the new owner. Stock certificates are mailed.

iStockphoto '07

3. The brokerage firm asks Stock Clearing Corp. to transfer the stock certificate to the new owner's name.

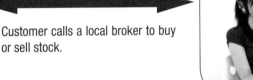

Bull and Bear Markets

As stock prices change, the Dow Jones Industrial Average rises and falls. These movements are called changes in "the market." At the beginning of the 1950s, the Dow stood at 200. It reached 1,000 in 1983, 5,000 in 1996, and was over 11,000 in 2006 and topped 17,000 in 2016.

When "the market" rises for months on end, people refer to the trend as a "bull market." In contrast, they call it a "bear market" when the Dow continually drops. The "bulls" are people who buy stocks because they expect the stock prices to rise. "Bears" are people who sell stock shares because they expect stock prices to fall.

No one can predict accurately the up and down movements in the stock market. You need to know there are risks to stock investments, but knowledge and research by investors will aid you in making good stock purchasing decisions. Despite risks from year to year, the stock market has generally risen over time. Figure 8-4a is a table showing the Dow Jones Industrial Average from 1950 to 2005. Figure 8-4b is a graph showing the same data.

Think Critically

Why do you think bull *is used to describe a rising market and* bear *to describe a falling market?*

_____

_____

_____

Figure 8-4a: Dow Jones Industrial Average (1950–2005)

Year	DJIA	Year	DJIA	Year	DJIA	Year	DJIA
1950	216.31	1964	834.05	1978	820.23	1992	3,284.29
1951	257.64	1965	910.88	1979	844.40	1993	3,522.06
1952	270.76	1966	873.60	1980	891.41	1994	3,793.77
1953	275.97	1967	879.12	1981	932.92	1995	4,493.76
1954	333.94	1968	906.00	1982	884.36	1996	5,742.89
1955	442.72	1969	876.72	1983	1,190.34	1997	7,441.15
1956	493.01	1970	753.19	1984	1,178.48	1998	8,625.52
1957	475.71	1971	884.76	1985	1,328.23	1999	10,464.88
1958	491.66	1972	950.71	1986	1,792.76	2000	10,734.90
1959	632.12	1973	923.88	1987	2,275.99	2001	10,189.13
1960	618.04	1974	759.37	1988	2,060.82	2002	9,226.43
1961	691.55	1975	802.49	1989	2,508.91	2003	8,993.59
1962	639.76	1976	974.92	1990	2,678.94	2004	10,317.39
1963	714.81	1977	894.63	1991	2,929.33	2005	10,547.67

Figure 8-4b: Dow Jones Industrial Average (1950–2005)

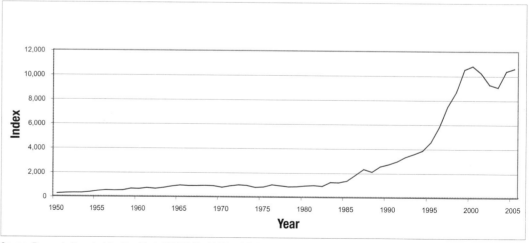

Source: *Economic Report of the President, 2006*, Tables B-95 and B-96. Averages of daily closing prices.

Bull or Bear Market?

Study the table in Figure 8-4a. Indicate whether the years below were bull or bear years.

1956–1957 _____   1963–1964 _____

1976–1977 _____   1996–1997 _____

Now examine the line graph in Figure 8-4b. Write a one-sentence statement that describes the Dow Jones Industrial Average between 1997 and 2000.

_____

Bonds

The secondary market that allows people to trade stock also enables them to exchange corporate and government bonds. A bond's interest rate is fixed when it is sold, but market rate changes can cause the bond to become more or less valuable. Paying more or less than the face value of the bond in this market affects the *yield*. **Yield** is the percentage return actually earned over time on a bond investment and is figured by dividing the annual interest in dollars by the price paid. For example, a bond with a face value of $1,000, paying 6% interest ($60 per year) is sold for $980. The yield then is 6.12% ($60 ÷ $980 = 6.12%).

Paying a lower price (less than face value) for a bond raises the yield. Paying a higher price for a bond (more than face value) lowers the yield. Government-issued bonds like U.S. Treasury notes and municipal bonds are traded in the secondary market after initial issue. The Federal Reserve System handles transactions for new sales of Treasury bills and bonds. The Federal Reserve System (called The Fed) is the nation's central banking system. The Fed is often referred to as the commercial bankers' bank. Municipal bonds (bonds issued by cities and states) are sold through investment banks.

Market rate changes impact the yield that is paid on bonds.

What Is the Yield?

A bond has a face value of $2,000. It pays 8% interest. It sells in the bond market for $2,200. What is the bond's annual yield?

First calculate the bond's annual interest. _____

Using the bond's annual interest, calculate the bond's yield. _____

Think Critically

What is insider trading?

_____

_____

What is the danger of insider trading?

_____

_____

Pause to Predict

List two reasons why businesses need to keep accurate financial records.

1._____

_____

2._____

_____

Apply Your Understanding

Why does a businessperson need to know what the assets and liabilities of his or her business are?

_____

_____

_____

The Securities and Exchange Commission

The Securities and Exchange Commission (SEC), an agency of the federal government, is responsible for protecting investors in the sale of stocks and bonds. Its basic objectives are to prevent fraud, deceit, and misrepresentation. The SEC requires corporations to provide the public with a prospectus containing financial information, including risk factors involved. The SEC also enforces the Securities Exchange Act of 1934, which prohibits insider trading. Insider trading occurs when confidential information about securities, unavailable to the general public, is misused by people who work at a company.

Business Accounting

All businesses must keep business records in some orderly way. Business accounting includes standards and rules that businesses follow so that interested parties, like investors and loan officers, can understand a basic set of facts about the operations of the business. All businesses periodically issue financial statements, especially a balance sheet and an income statement.

Financial statements are like two different types of pictures. Imagine you could take a snapshot of a business on a specific date. If you had a video camera, you could also make a movie of the business as it operates day by day. Accounting practices provide both types of pictures. Like a snapshot, a **balance sheet** is a report of a company's, or individual's, *assets*, *liabilities*, and net worth on a specified date. An **asset** is anything of monetary value owned by an individual or company. A **liability** is anything of monetary value owed by an individual or company. As you learned previously, net worth is the difference between assets and liabilities of an individual or company.

The income statement shows how much revenue a company brings into the business by providing goods and services to its customers. It also shows the costs and expenses associated with earning that revenue. Usually an income statement reports revenue and costs during a year. However, with advanced computer accounting programs, income statements can be calculated for any time period. The net income (or loss) is often called the "bottom line" because it is usually at the bottom of the statement and shows how much a company made in profits or losses. Accounting systems can vary, but the examples that follow are typical.

The Balance Sheet

For every business, the difference between what it owns (assets) and what it owes (liabilities) is equal to its net worth or owner's equity. The fundamental accounting equation can be stated two ways:

(1) Assets = Liabilities + Net Worth. This equation tells you that a balance sheet must balance.

(2) Assets – Liabilities = Net Worth. This equation identifies the value of the company in terms of its net worth.

The balance sheet shown in Figure 8-5 is that of The Walt Disney Company on October 1, 2005.

10. balance sheet   11. asset   12. liability

Figure 8-5: The Walt Disney Company Balance Sheet
(As of October 1, 2005; millions of dollars)

Assets		Liabilities	
Cash and Cash Equivalents	$1,723	Accounts Payable	$5,339
Receivables	$5,334	Long-Term Debt	$10,157
Inventory	$1,136	Other Liabilities	$11,452
Investments	$1,226		
Property, Plant and Equipment	$16,968	Total Liabilities	$26,948
Other Assets	$26,771		
		Net Worth	$53,158
		Common Stock	$13,288
		Retained Earnings	$17,775
		Treasury Stock	($4,281)
		Other Stockholder Equity	($572)
		Total Net Worth	$26,210
Total Assets	**$53,158**	**Total Liabilities + Net Worth**	**$53,158**

Source: Yahoo! Finance Website:
http://finance.yahoo.com/q/bs?s=DIS&annual
(Accessed on June 8, 2006)

Assets
- Disney has cash and other cash equivalents, such as certificates of deposit.
- Receivables are short-term obligations that buyers of Disney products owe.
- Inventory includes films and other merchandise the company has available for sale.
- Investments are short-term securities that earn interest for Disney.
- Property, plant, and equipment represent the value of all the land, tools, and buildings.
- Other assets might include projects in progress or prepaid income tax.

Liabilities
- Accounts payable include income taxes payable and the short-term debt of Disney. Accounts payable are amounts owed to sellers for work performed or materials purchased. A portion of income taxes payable are taxes withheld from employees' paychecks and held until sent to the government.
- Long-term debt consists of bonds and other long-term loans Disney has issued to raise funds to purchase capital resources.
- Other liabilities may include deferred income tax and unearned royalties.

Net Worth
- Disney's net worth of $26,210 billion includes the common stock with a value of more than $13 billion. The **retained earnings**, the amount of money that has been saved over the year for reinvestment, is nearly $18 billion. Treasury stock is negative because this is the value of stock that Disney has repurchased and withheld from public sale.
- Net worth is the amount of remaining assets after liabilities are met. Sometimes net worth is called owner's equity, which measures the owner's value in the firm.

Check Your Understanding

What are the three major categories of information in a balance sheet?

_____

_____

_____

How is net worth calculated?

_____

_____

13. retained earnings

The Income Statement

An **income statement**, a statement of earnings or a profit-and-loss statement, shows how much income a business has made or lost over a period of time, usually a year. Figure 8-6 shows the Disney income statement dated October 1, 2005.

Figure 8-6: The Walt Disney Company Income Statement
(Year ending October 1, 2005; millions of dollars)

Total Revenue	$31,944
Operating Expense	-$27,837
Extraordinary Income/Expense	$485
Earnings Before Interest and Taxes	$4,592
Interest Expense	-$605
Income Before Tax	$3,987
Income Tax Expense	-$1,241
Other Adjustments	-$213
Net Income	$2,533

Source: Yahoo! Finance Website:
http://finance.yahoo.com/q/is?s=DIS&annual
(Accessed on June 10, 2006)

- The income statement (Figure 8-6) shows that Disney sold $31,944 billion of entertainment products and services around the world during the year ending October 1, 2005. The cost of goods sold and other expenses of $27,837 billion combines the cost of labor, materials, and other resources used to generate that revenue.
- This left Disney with a pre-tax profit of $3,987 billion. Income taxes to be withheld and other deductions produced a net income of $2,533 billion.

Standard business accounting uses two tools to keep track of and to report business activity—the balance sheet and the income statement. The balance sheet shows assets, liabilities, and net worth as of a specified date. The income statement shows revenue or income, costs, and profit or loss, usually over a year.

Create Your Own Balance Sheet

 You have learned that a balance sheet states what a business or person owns (assets) and what the business or person owes (liabilities) on the same date. You have also learned that assets minus liabilities equal net worth.

You can create your own balance sheet because you have both assets and liabilities. Complete a balance sheet for yourself on this date.

Assets	Liabilities
Cash _____	What you owe others _____
Savings _____	Other debts you owe _____
Loans owed to you _____	
Property value _____	
Other assets _____	
Total Assets _____	**Total Liabilities** _____
Your Net Worth	_____
Date	_____

iStockphoto '07

Business accounting helps both owners and investors understand the finances of a business. The balance sheet describes the financial status of a business at a point in time by identifying assets, liabilities, and net worth. The income statement identifies income, expenses, and profit or loss over a period of time. Without these tools, the decisions owners and investors make could not be as wise or as timely.

Summary

Financial markets play an important role in a free enterprise economy by channeling money from savers to businesses that use it to invest in new capital resources. Businesses use the financial markets as a source for capital investment funds by borrowing, selling new shares of ownership, and by saving the money themselves. To borrow money, corporations and government often sell long-term debts called bonds. Bondholders lend money and are called creditors. They receive interest payments during the term of the bond and are paid the face value of the bond at maturity.

Businesses can also borrow for short periods of time by using trade credit, loans from financial institutions, and direct loans from other companies. Small start-up businesses have unique financing options including savings from family and friends, loans from banks and the Small Business Administration, and venture capital.

Corporations sell stock or equity ownership to raise funds in the financial markets. The stockholders gain ownership rights when they buy common and preferred stock. All corporations issue common stock with dividends paid at the discretion of the board of directors. Businesses can also gain funding for new capital resources by retaining some of their earnings for reinvestment. Newly established firms often use their retained earnings to increase the company's future earnings potential.

New issues of stocks are called initial public offerings (IPOs) and are financed in the primary market. After buying the shares, investors can trade them in the secondary market, which is called the stock market. The stock market has organized exchanges like the New York Stock Exchange and the American Stock Exchange and electronic trading markets like NASDAQ. An agency of the federal government, the Securities and Exchange Commission, oversees the market for stocks, bonds, and other securities.

Investors and others interested in the financial condition of a firm can learn much from its balance sheet and income statement. The balance sheet is like a snapshot describing a firm's assets and its liabilities. The difference between these is the firm's net worth. The income statement shows revenue and expenses for a period of time. The difference between revenue and expenses is net income or profit.

Looking Ahead

Many factors determine the quantity and quality of goods and services that a business produces. Among these are the skills of its employees, the efficiency of its machines and equipment, and the ability of its managers to continually improve the organization. Production involves creating goods and services, while productivity is a measure of efficiency. As you read Chapter 9, you will learn more about each of these concepts and the effects they have on our incomes.

Production and Productivity

Read to Find Out

As you read this chapter, look for answers to the following questions:

What is gross domestic product (GDP), and how is it measured?

How is real GDP calculated, and what does it mean?

How do changes in real GDP affect living standards?

What is real per capita GDP?

What is productivity, and what are the main determinants of productivity over the years?

How have business managers improved productivity?

Why do production costs change as output changes?

What is the law of diminishing marginal returns, and how does it affect production costs?

At what point do managers decide what to produce?

What are the benefits of economies of scale?

Mark to Remember

* *This is important.*

? *I have a question about this.*

! *This is a surprise.*

Why It Matters

Increased production of goods and services allows people to enjoy improved living standards. Measuring production levels provides citizens with information about production increases and decreases so people can monitor changes in their living standards. Productivity increases allow business managers to increase production while minimizing the use of costly resources. Learning to be more productive enhances work opportunities for young people.

Production and Productivity

Building On What You Know

You already know what production is in your daily life. You may have duties at home that require you to take out the trash, do the dishes, or clean up your living quarters. When you perform these duties, you are producing services. You may be required to produce homework for your school classes. Homework is a type of good or product. In our market economy, we produce goods and services. We measure the value of production. And we value productivity, especially the productivity of labor.

Do you have a favorite kind of pie? Whether you prefer chocolate cream, apple, blueberry, sweet potato, or some other kind, all pies have one thing in common: Someone has to produce them, or you can't eat them.

An economy is similar. People must produce goods and services so that consumer wants can be satisfied. How does a nation determine how much of the economy's production each member receives? We sell our personal resource, mostly our labor, to help produce the "economic pie" in exchange for income. With our incomes, we can buy our share of slices of the economy's economic pie. Production is important because it provides real goods and services to satisfy human wants. The amount produced in an economy determines total income, and total income determines how much consumers enjoy of the economy's production.

Gross Domestic Product

How is the production of the U.S. economy measured? The most common measurement is the *gross domestic product* (GDP). **Gross domestic product (GDP)** is the final value of all goods and services produced within a country in a year. The U.S. Department of Commerce measures GDP by adding together the value of the purchases of final goods and services produced during a year. GDP is calculated using today's current prices. GDP reported in current prices is called **nominal GDP**.

Think Critically

You produce various services and probably some goods. List several of them below.

_____

_____

_____

_____

_____

Now star those services or goods that you think will be most valuable to you when you enter the labor force as an adult.

1. gross domestic product   2. nominal GDP

GDP does not include items produced and sold to businesses that use them to produce final goods or services. For example, the final price of the jeans you buy is counted in the GDP. However, GDP does not include the cost of denim, zippers, thread, or labor that go into making the jeans. Their value is already counted in the final price of the jeans.

The table in Figure 9-1 shows GDP and its spending components from 1960 through 2005. Total GDP in 2005 was $12,479.4 trillion. Consumption (C) accounts for 70 percent of GDP in 2005 and includes spending for such things as clothes, refrigerators, dental care, and fast food. Business investment (I) accounts for 16.8 percent of GDP in 2005 and includes spending for such things as delivery trucks, manufacturing equipment, and business computers. All government spending (G) accounts for 18.9 percent of GDP in 2005 and includes spending for such things as national defense, fire protection, welfare, and education. Net exports (NX) were negative for 2005 and account for a minus 5.7 percent of GDP. This means that U.S. consumers and businesses bought more goods and services from other countries than businesses and consumers in other countries bought from the United States.

Figure 9-1: Gross Domestic Product, 1960–2005

Year	GDP	C	I	G	NX
1960	526.4	331.7	78.9	111.6	4.2
1965	719.1	443.8	118.2	151.5	5.6
1970	1,038.5	648.5	152.4	233.8	4.0
1975	1,638.3	1034.4	230.2	357.7	16.0
1980	2,789.5	1757.1	479.3	566.2	-13.1
1985	4,220.3	2720.3	736.2	879.0	-115.2
1990	5,803.1	3839.9	861.0	1,180.2	-78.0
1995	7,397.7	4975.8	1,144.0	1,369.2	-91.4
2000	9,817.0	6739.4	1,735.5	1,721.6	-379.5
2005	12,479.4	8745.9	2,099.5	2,359.7	-725.7
Percents		**70.0**	**16.8**	**18.9**	**-5.7**

GDP = Gross domestic product, billions of dollars
C = Personal consumption expenditures, billions of dollars
I = Gross private domestic investment, billions of dollars
G = Government consumption expenditures and gross investment, billions of dollars
NX = Net exports of goods and services, billions of dollars

Source: *Economic Report of the President, 2006*, Table B-1.

Calculating a Small Country's GDP

Imagine a small country with only three products: bicycles that sell for $100 each, oranges priced at $1 each, and airplanes priced at $1 million each. Producers sell 10 each of these products every year. What is the country's GDP?

Value of :
Bicycles $_____
Oranges $_____
Airplanes $_____   GDP $_____

Apply Your Understanding

Gross domestic product is commonly mentioned in news reports. Find an example of such a report in a newspaper or magazine or on the Internet. Tape a copy of the report to this page.

Check Your Understanding

Indicate whether the statements below are true (T) or false (F).

1. GDP in the United States has gone up and down since 1970.

_____

2. Investments were under $2,000 billion in 1995.

_____

3. If the trend of the last 45 years continues, GDP will be greater in 2010.

_____

Show Your
Understanding

*Underline the sentences in
each of the three paragraphs
in this section that most
helps you understand that
paragraph's main idea.
Use the sentences you
underline to answer the
following question.*

*Why is a GDP deflator
important to having accurate
knowledge of growth or
decline in GDP?*

_____

_____

_____

Real Gross Domestic Product

Real GDP is GDP adjusted for inflation. As you have learned, inflation is an overall rise in prices. When the U.S. Department of Commerce accountants gather statistics to calculate GDP, the prices reported are current prices. The accountants are calculating nominal GDP—GDP in current prices. The accountants do not know whether any increase in GDP is the result of an increase in the quantity of goods and services sold or an increase in prices. They solve the problem by adjusting nominal GDP for price changes. To adjust nominal GDP for price changes, a *GDP deflator* is used.

The **GDP deflator** is a price index that reduces current prices into prices of a base year. The most direct way to reduce nominal GDP into base year prices is to divide nominal GDP by the price index and to state the index in decimal form. The base year used is 2000, and the price index for that year is set at 100. As shown in Figure 9-1, nominal GDP for the year 2005 was $12,479 billion. The price index used for 2005 was 111. Stated as a decimal, the index becomes 1.11. To find real GDP for 2005, divide $12,479 by 1.11. The result equals a real GDP of $11,233 billion ($12,479 billion ÷ 1.11 = $11,233 billion). This means that the 2005 GDP, stated in 2000 prices, was $11,233 billion. Real GDP is a more accurate measure of production changes because it excludes the influence of rising prices.

You may wonder, why not just use GDP as a measure of the economy's production? You may think it is too complicated to use real GDP. A serious shortcoming of GDP is the inability to accurately measure production from year to year. For example, GDP increased from $526 billion in 1960 to $12,479 billion in 2005. This is an increase of more than 23 times! Does this mean that there were 23 times more goods and services produced in 2005 than in 1960? No, a large part of the increase was the result of inflation. After adjusting for inflation, real GDP more than quadrupled, from $2,502 billion in 2000 prices in 1960 to $11,233 billion in 2000 prices in 2005. This is much less than the increase of 23 times that would be reported using nominal GDP.

Production Increases and Prices Double

In the activity on the previous page, you imagined a small, three-product country. Now imagine that it is Year 2 in the country, and each producer increases production from 10 to 12 units. They also double the prices for their products. What is the country's Year 2 GDP?

Value of:

Bicycles $_____ Oranges $_____ Airplanes $_____

GDP $_____

The Year 2 GDP is a 140 percent increase from Year 1, but most of the increase is because of increases in prices of the products. To find the real change in production, multiply the production by the first-year prices.

Value of:

Bicycles $_____ Oranges $_____ Airplanes $_____

GDP in Year 1 prices $_____

What is the real dollar production increase in GDP from Year 1 to Year 2? _____

By using Year 1 as the base year, what happened in Year 2 when you measured production at Year 1 prices? _____

Real Per Capita GDP

Another way to measure how the level of production has changed in the economy is to use a measure called *real per capita GDP*. Per capita means per person. **Real per capita GDP** is the real gross domestic product divided by the country's population. The change in real per capita GDP is a good indicator of a change in a nation's standard of living. It is a measure of the amount of goods and services available to a nation's citizens.

The table in Figure 9-2 shows the real per capita GDP of the United States from 1960 to 2005. Note that real per capita GDP more than doubled between 1960 and 1990, from $13,840 to $28,429.

Figure 9-2: Real Per Capita GDP, 1960–2005

iStockphoto '07

Year	PCGDP	PCCon
1960	13,840	8,837
1965	16,420	10,331
1970	18,391	11,955
1975	19,961	13,320
1980	22,666	14,816
1985	25,382	17,040
1990	28,429	19,067
1995	30,128	20,382
2000	34,759	23,862
2005	37,504	26,476

PCGDP = Per capita gross domestic product in year 2000 dollars
PCCon = Per capita personal consumption expenditures in 2000 dollars

Source: *Economic Report of the President, 2006*, Table B-31.

Shortcomings of GDP

GDP is a very good indicator of the size of production in an economy. But GDP is not a perfect measure of the well-being of people in an economy. GDP does not measure most of the goods and services that people produce but do not sell, such as the contributions of volunteer time to churches and other not-for-profit organizations. GDP does not measure the many services that households produce and consume themselves, such as child care, meals, and lawn maintenance. Similarly, GDP does not measure the value of leisure time. Nor does GDP include the value of illegal activities (for example, making and selling drugs) in the underground economy, because illegal activities do not contribute to a nation's overall well-being.

Overall production in our economy is measured as a total dollar amount of goods and services sold. Gross domestic product is the measure used to calculate this dollar amount. In the next section, we examine a related idea—productivity.

Productivity

Productivity is the output of goods and services measured per unit of input by labor, capital, or land. The input may be workers, capital resources, or the amount of work space used. When productivity goes up, more or better products are produced with the same amount of resources.

Check Your Understanding

Why does population growth or decline matter in calculating per capita GDP?

_____

_____

_____

Per capita GDP increases only when the production of goods and services grows faster than the population. If per capita GDP increases by 5 percent and the population increases by 2 percent, then per capita GDP has had a net 3 percent increase. This means that more goods and services are available to the entire population.

Labor productivity is a common measure in our economy. **Labor productivity** is the amount of goods and services the workforce can produce during a given time period—an hour, a week, a month, or a year. Increasing labor productivity is the main force behind growing real per capita GDP. For example, the graph in Figure 9-3 shows that the real value of goods and services produced per employed person increased from $38,034 in 1960 to $78,537 in 2005, an increase of nearly 105 percent. Despite the increase, labor productivity has not grown as much in recent years as in the past. This is why the line on the chart becomes less steep after the early 1970s. However, early indications in 2000 had economists predicting that labor productivity was increasing more rapidly again

Figure 9-3: GDP per Employed Person, 1960–2005 (in 2000 dollars)

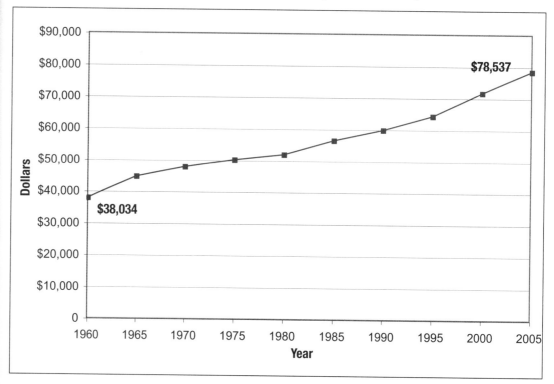

iStockphoto '07

6. productivity   7. labor productivity

Trend in GDP per Employed Persons

Use the graph in Figure 9-3 to answer the following questions.

1. What was the GDP per employed person in 1975, to the nearest thousand dollars? _____

2. What was the GDP per employed person in 1990? _____

3. Write a statement to describe the trend in GDP per employed person between 1960 and 2005.

_____

_____

Pause to Predict

What actions do you predict can improve productivity over time?

_____

_____

_____

What makes productivity improve over the years? Some of the most important factors are changes in the quality of human resources and management, increases in the quantity and quality of capital resources, and technological change.

The Quality of Human Resources

The education, training, and attitudes of workers have a significant impact on productivity. Well-educated and skilled workers can usually produce more than those who are not as knowledgeable and skilled. Workers' enthusiasm for their jobs also contributes to their productivity. Those who like their jobs and gain dignity and respect from their work are likely to produce more than those who lack motivation to do their best.

It's not surprising, then, that increases in the quantity and quality of education and job training can raise productivity. Historically, productivity of labor has been studied extensively. For example, *Economic Report of the President* for 1995 reported that changes in the amount of education and job experience between 1963 and 1992 accounted for about 10 percent of the yearly growth of productivity.

Education has played a critical role in the U.S. economy's shift from goods-producing industries to service industries and to a more technology-intensive workplace. While workers with all levels of education benefited from a strong labor market in recent years, the service and technology industries that require highly skilled workers are the industries that are projected to grow well into the 21st century.

The Quality of Management

Henry Ford installed an assembly line as a new method of organizing production in 1913. Before Ford introduced his Model T, workers and their tools moved from station to station to build each automobile. One slow worker slowed down everyone else. Ford introduced an assembly line that brought the car to the worker on a conveyor belt. As a result, each worker had to finish a task before the car passed the workstation. If a worker could not finish in time, the task was modified or the worker was retrained.

Ford's first line was used to assemble generators. One worker had been putting together 25 to 30 generators in a nine-hour day or one generator every 20 minutes. But the new

Think Critically

In the past, workers who performed primarily physical work were called blue-collar workers. Those who performed primarily mental work were called white-collar workers. Today, those distinctions are less often used. Why do you think this is true?

_____

_____

_____

line broke the operation into 29 steps performed by individual workers. The new process reduced assembly time to an average of 13 minutes per generator. One year later, more experimentation divided production into 84 steps and reduced assembly time to 5 minutes per generator.

Assembly-line methods brought automobile prices within reach of millions of American families. As a result, automobile sales jumped from 944,000 in 1912 to 2.5 million in 1915 and to 20 million by 1925. Ford reorganized production and greatly increased workers' productivity. He created mass-produced products of uniform quality. Ford's innovative production strategies had a revolutionary impact on American industry and living standards. Innovative management can be the difference between a prosperous, productive business and a business that falters or fails. Managerial decisions can affect the quality of human resources at work, increase the amount of capital resources, and spark innovations—all of which have an impact on the productivity of labor.

Check Your Understanding

How did the use of assembly-line production by Henry Ford lower the price of Model Ts?

_____

_____

_____

Sometimes a manager's decisions may seem insignificant, yet still yield big increases in productivity. For example, a cafeteria-style restaurant had been serving its customers on plates divided into sections. As customers moved along the serving line, they would receive black-eyed peas in one section, potatoes in another, and so forth. This made serving slow. When the restaurant's managers replaced the old plates with separate bowls and dishes, attendants could fill each dish and hand it quickly to a customer. Because of this seemingly small change, restaurant workers could move customers along a serving line much faster. The restaurant went from serving about 300 customers per hour to 400 per hour. This increase represents a one-third productivity increase! This situation is an excellent example of why economists and business managers focus on marginal changes. A small change can yield large returns.

United States businesses are raising their productivity by putting into practice new management ideas. These include emphases on customer satisfaction, high-quality work, employee involvement in decision making, and shared vision.

Apply Your Understanding

As you participate in the economy as a worker or consumer, you have probably observed inefficiencies in getting jobs done or in satisfying customers. Describe one of these situations and explain how you think the situation could be made more efficient. Use additional paper, if needed.

_____

_____

_____

- **Customer satisfaction.** Companies know that their success depends on delivering to customers what they want and expect. This might involve conducting research before a sale or a survey following a sale to assess customer satisfaction.

- **High-quality work.** Today's consumers recognize and demand high quality. Most companies set clear quality standards and provide training and equipment to guarantee that these standards are met.

- **Employee involvement.** To improve worker productivity and increase product quality, managers need to listen to their employees. Sometimes called "empowerment," this basic idea of involving employees in making decisions has revolutionized production processes at many companies.

- **Shared vision.** Sharing a vision means nurturing employees' commitment to the company and its goals. Shared vision can be cultivated through mission statements, company slogans, or even internal reward systems to recognize employee contributions to company goals.

142

The Quantity and Quality of Capital Resources

As businesses invest in new capital resources, workers become more productive. Over the years, businesses have made many such investments. As a result, today's workers have many more tools, equipment, and buildings to use than they did in the past. The graph in Figure 9-4 shows how the real (inflation-adjusted) value of equipment per worker has grown from $2,130 in 1960 to $9,085 in 2005. This is an increase of 427 percent and was an important contributor to the 64 percent increase in real GDP produced per worker during the same period.

Figure 9-4: Capital Expenditure per Employed Person, 1960–2006 (in 2000 dollars)

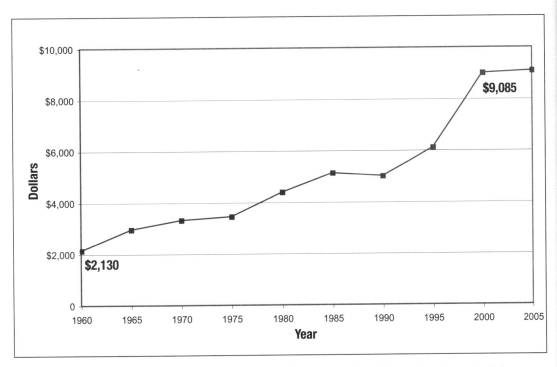

Source: Calculated from data in the *Economic Report of the President, 2006*, Tables B-2, B-6, and B-36. Capital is the nonresidential component of gross private domestic investment.

These changes occur because a free enterprise system gives entrepreneurs and business owners incentives to risk their retained earnings to develop new ideas, start new businesses, and expand existing ones. At the same time, free enterprise provides incentives to individuals to save and invest in their own human resources through education and training. Just as successful investments in equipment can yield profits, successful investment in human resources can yield higher earnings. More and better resources go hand in hand in raising productivity.

Technological Change

The quality of human resources, management, and capital resources don't tell the whole story. Technological change is another contributor to the growth of productivity. From the development of plows to the invention of computers, history offers many examples of technologies that have increased productivity. New products, new methods of production, new ways of organizing production or of marketing products, and new methods of communication can each demonstrate how productivity increases. Consider again the example of Henry Ford and his assembly line.

Today, consumers still demand the quantity of goods that assembly lines can produce. However, consumers want variety. More recent improvements in technology now allow flexible "batch production," which combines the efficiency of assembly lines and the flexibility and quality of smaller, custom operations. For example, a batch in car production might be a certain number of cars all of one color. A batch in computer production might be a specific number of computers all with a specified amount of software.

Improved technology can impact productivity rapidly, but sometimes the impact is gradual. In fact, the introduction of computer technology into offices in the United States did not improve productivity for several years. However, according to the 2003 *Economic Report of the President*, computer technology was a major contributor to increased productivity between 1995 and 2002.

The four sources of productivity growth discussed in this chapter are interrelated. For example, innovative U.S. businesses like Google and Oracle have developed new ideas for communicating and doing business using the Internet. To implement these new ideas (technological change), other businesses (management) buy new computers and software (investment in new capital resources). Their workers must be sufficiently educated and trained, so they know how to use the new equipment and methods (quality of human resources). As a result, improvements in the quality of human resources and management, increases in the quantity and quality of capital resources, and technological change join hands to increase productivity.

Improving Worker Productivity

The Best Food grocery store is planning to buy self-checkout equipment. Accountants say the equipment will increase worker productivity because customers will check out their own groceries while workers do other tasks. Company owners are planning for the changes needed to successfully implement this new system. What managerial, capital equipment, and technology challenges should they expect in meeting their goal to increase worker productivity?

Managerial challenges _____

_____

Capital equipment _____

_____

Technological challenges _____

_____

Production and Cost Changes

Since managers search for ways to make products efficiently, they pay close attention to production costs. They find that costs usually vary when the level or speed of production changes. To see how and why, we will examine two kinds of production costs.

Fixed Costs Plus Variable Costs Equal Total Cost

Producing computer chips can be expensive and risky. Doing so can mean building a specially equipped fabricating plant. Such a plant can cost hundreds of millions of dollars to build. Yet because of rapid advances in chip technology, the plant may be out-of-date in a few years.

Suppose a company called Microductor builds a fabricating plant with *fixed costs* (or overhead) of $200 million a year. **Fixed costs** are costs that remain the same regardless of the amount of product a firm produces. These costs include depreciation, engineering costs, real estate taxes, managers' salaries, and interest on loans.

Unlike fixed costs, **variable costs** are costs that change with changing amounts of production. Examples are hourly wages, electrical power, chemicals, and other raw materials used in production.

Microductor plans to run the plant seven days a week to produce and sell a large volume of chips in a short time. If sales slow unexpectedly, Microductor can reduce production and lay off some workers, shut down some of its complex equipment, and buy fewer materials and supplies. When business picks up, those expenses will go up again.

While designing the new plant and new chip, managers ask the company's financial analysts and economists what the average cost of a chip is likely to be in the first year of operation.

"It all depends on how many chips we make," the analysts answer. "However, there is a more important question to ask. A study we just completed explains why all costs are important but marginal costs are most noteworthy."

Then the financial analysts show the managers the numbers in Figure 9-5.

iStockphoto '07

Check Your Understanding

Answer the following questions.

1. Do accountants who create business budgets start with fixed costs or variable costs?

_____

Why? _____

_____

2. Why are variable costs not the same from year to year?

_____

_____

3. If you were employed by a company, would you rather have your salary be in the company's fixed costs or variable costs?

_____

Why? _____

_____

8. fixed costs   9. variable costs

Figure 9-5: Microductor's Costs of Producing Computer Chips
(m = million)

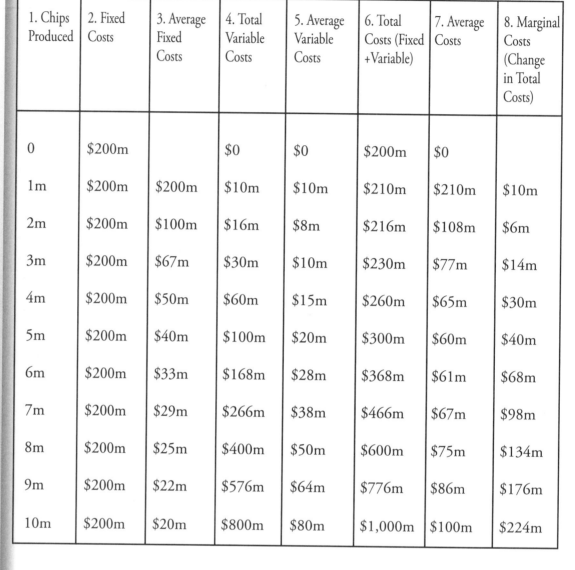

1. Chips Produced	2. Fixed Costs	3. Average Fixed Costs	4. Total Variable Costs	5. Average Variable Costs	6. Total Costs (Fixed +Variable)	7. Average Costs	8. Marginal Costs (Change in Total Costs)
0	$200m		$0	$0	$200m	$0	
1m	$200m	$200m	$10m	$10m	$210m	$210m	$10m
2m	$200m	$100m	$16m	$8m	$216m	$108m	$6m
3m	$200m	$67m	$30m	$10m	$230m	$77m	$14m
4m	$200m	$50m	$60m	$15m	$260m	$65m	$30m
5m	$200m	$40m	$100m	$20m	$300m	$60m	$40m
6m	$200m	$33m	$168m	$28m	$368m	$61m	$68m
7m	$200m	$29m	$266m	$38m	$466m	$67m	$98m
8m	$200m	$25m	$400m	$50m	$600m	$75m	$134m
9m	$200m	$22m	$576m	$64m	$776m	$86m	$176m
10m	$200m	$20m	$800m	$80m	$1,000m	$100m	$224m

Check Your Understanding

Study Figure 9-5 to answer the following questions.

Why do average fixed costs fall as production increases?

_____

_____

_____

What happens to total variable costs as production increases?

_____

_____

_____

The table includes costs for 10 different rates of production. Production rates, measured in millions of chips, are shown in Column 1, Chips Produced. Columns 2 and 3 list fixed costs. Total fixed costs remain the same at every production rate. As production increases, these fixed costs are spread over a larger quantity. As a result, Column 3 shows that *average fixed costs* drop as production goes up. **Average fixed costs** are total fixed costs divided by quantity produced. This column is calculated by dividing total fixed costs (Column 2) by the number of chips produced (Column 1). For example, the average fixed cost per chip would be $40 if the plant produces 5 million chips per year ($200 million / 5 million chips = $40 per chip).

iStockphoto '07

10. average fixed costs

Total variable costs listed in Column 4 increase with the rate of production. **Average variable costs** are total variable costs divided by quantity produced. Average variable costs (Column 5) are calculated by dividing total variable costs in Column 4 by the number of chips produced in Column 1. **Total costs** are the sum of total fixed costs and total variable costs. The total costs listed in Column 6 are the sum of total fixed and total variable costs. Average total cost is the sum of average fixed and average variable cost. **Average total costs** in Column 7 are the sum of average fixed and average variable costs. Notice that as planned production increases, average total cost declines at first.

As production increases still further, so does the cost of each million chips produced. Note that the average costs start to rise as production goes from 5 million to 6 million chips. This is because of the *law of diminishing marginal returns*, which is discussed below. The information in Column 8 provides very useful cost data about the results of expanding production levels. The *marginal cost* of each expansion is shown in Column 8. **Marginal cost** is the additional cost of increasing one unit of production. The marginal cost of the first million chips is $10 million. The marginal cost of the second million chips is $6 million—$4 million less than the first million chips. After the second million chips, marginal costs increase—to $14 million for the third million chips, $30 million for the fourth million chips, and so on. The marginal cost of increasing production from 9 million chips to 10 million ships is a whopping $224 million.

Think Critically

Figure 9-5 provides a lot of data about costs of producing computer chips. Can the Microductor managers make a decision about how many computer chips to produce based on the data in the table? Why or why not?

_____

_____

_____

Determining Marginal Costs

Look at the total costs column in the table in Figure 9-5. What happens to total cost as chip production increases?

_____

Study the total costs column again. By how much do total costs change as production increases from:

0m to 1m chips?   _____

1m to 2m chips?   _____

4m to 5m chips?   _____

7m to 8m chips?   _____

Now, look at the marginal cost column. You just calculated four marginal cost amounts!

The Law of Diminishing Marginal Returns

Economists define the **law of diminishing marginal returns** in this way: an economic principle which holds that as more and more variable resources (such as workers or materials) are added to a fixed amount of other resources (such as buildings and equipment), the additional (marginal) amount produced eventually decreases. The decreasing amount produced leads to increasing costs. As production is expanded, each additional chip batch costs more than the previous batch. This production situation occurs because increasing amounts of variable resources eventually crowd out the fixed quantities of other resources.

**11. average variable costs   12. total costs   13. average total costs
14. marginal cost   15. law of diminishing marginal returns**

Check Your Understanding

Explain the meaning of the law of diminishing marginal returns *in your own words.*

____

____

____

____

If it weren't for the problem of diminishing marginal returns, for example, you could grow all the world's corn in a flowerpot by adding progressively more water. Thus, if Microductor crowds its fixed resources by adding progressively more labor and other variable resources to its fixed plant, it will experience diminishing marginal returns. The cost of producing an additional batch of chips will be greater than the cost of producing the prior batch.

How Much to Produce?

Although Microductor's cost situation is well-known to its managers, they still must decide how many chips to produce. As good managers, they know they have studied only the cost side of their business. Businesses don't exist just to focus on costs. They have a different goal, which is to maximize profits. How many chips should be made to receive the best return for their production? To make this decision, the managers need information from the analysts about demand for their chips.

Check Your Understanding

In Figure 9-6, columns 1, 2, and 7 are easy to understand. Make sure you also understand the other columns by describing what they show.

Marginal Revenue

____

____

Total Revenue

____

____

Total Cost

____

____

Marginal Cost

____

____

Figure 9-6: Demand for Chips and Marginal Analysis

(m = million)

1. Number of Chips Sold	2. Price	3. Marginal Revenue	4. Total Revenue	5. Total Cost	6. Marginal Cost	7. Profit
1m	$100	$100m	$100m	$210m	$10m	–$110m
2m	$100	$100m	$200m	$216m	$6m	–$16m
3m	$100	$100m	$300m	$230m	$14m	$70m
4m	$100	$100m	$400m	$260m	$30m	$140m
5m	$100	$100m	$500m	$300m	$40m	$200m
6m	$100	$100m	$600m	$368m	$68m	$232m
7m	$100	$100m	$700m	$466m	$98m	$232m
8m	$100	$100m	$800m	$600m	$132m	$200m
9m	$100	$100m	$900m	$776m	$176m	$124m
10m	$100	$100m	$1,000m	$1,000m	$224m	$0

The demand information is in Figure 9-6. It indicates that Microductor can sell the chips at $100. This is considered a very competitive market. If the company raise its prices, buyers will buy from other sellers. There is no need to drop price because it can sell all the chips it can produce at $100. That means **marginal revenue**, the additional

16. marginal revenue

revenue generated from the sale of an additional quantity of product, is also $100. Every time Microductor sells a batch of chips, it receives an additional $100 from the sale of each chip.

Column 4 identified the *total revenue* received from the sale of chips. **Total revenue** is a calculation of revenue that is determined by price times quantity sold. At a production level of 3 million chips, total revenue is equal to $300 million. Column 6 contains the same total cost figures found in Figure 9-5. Column 7 contains the same marginal cost information from Figure 9-5. Column 8 lists very important information regarding the company's profit.

The primary goal of most firms—after being good stewards to their owners, workers, and community—is to make the largest possible profit, or to maximize profits. Pursuing lower profits is inefficient and wasteful. In its quest for profits, managers must determine a level of production based on the criteria of profit maximization.

To understand a firm's reasoning, look at how Microductor determines its profits. As in any other business, Microductor's total profit is the difference between revenue received from selling its product, or total revenue, and the amount it pays to produce that product, or total cost. (Total Revenue – Total Cost = Total Profit)

However, there are different combinations of prices and production levels from which the company can choose. Each of these combinations provides a different level of profit. Some may even result in a loss. So managers must try to find the combination of price and production that will earn the largest profit for the company's owners.

Show Your Understanding

Use Figure 9-6 to complete the following items.

1. Circle the greatest total revenue.

2. Circle the highest total cost.

3. Circle the highest total marginal cost.

4. Circle the greatest profit.

5. Why isn't the greatest profit found in the same year that the greatest revenue is found?

_____

_____

_____

Deciding How Much to Produce

The table below shows the revenue and cost data for XYZ Widget Corporation. Complete the blank spaces using the information provided, and then answer the questions that follow.

Price	Number Sold	Total Revenue	Total Cost	Profit
$10	12	$120	$130	$ –10
11	11	121	120	____
12	10	____	110	____
13	9	____	100	____
14	8	____	90	____
15	7	____	85	20
16	6	96	80	16

Can XYZ Widget Corporation make a profit with these cost and revenue figures? _____

What will be its profit at this price? _____

What is the profit at a price of $13? _____

What is the profit at a price of $15? _____

Businesses set their level of production to maximize profits.

Marginal Analysis

How can Microductor's managers find the best combination of price and production? One way is through trial and error. Managers can experiment with different prices and production levels and find the best combination. However, this method is time-consuming and costly. A better way is to use what economists call *marginal analysis*. **Marginal analysis** is decision making that involves comparing marginal (additional) benefits and marginal costs.

As long as the additional benefit (marginal revenue) of producing another chip is greater than its additional cost (marginal cost), the company can increase its profit by raising production. In this example, marginal revenue remains the same regardless of the production level set by the firm managers. On the other hand, marginal cost eventually increases as the law of diminishing marginal returns sets in when Microductor attempts to squeeze still more production from its facilities.

As production increases, therefore, marginal revenue remains the same and marginal cost rises toward marginal revenue. At some point, marginal cost will be greater than marginal revenue. Just before reaching this point, a company will want to stop expanding its production. This is the point where marginal revenue and marginal cost are as close to equal as possible. This is the point where profit is maximized.

The Search for Maximum Profit

Figure 9-6 relates this information to Microductor. As the company begins increasing production from 1 million to 7 million chips per year, its marginal revenue is above its marginal cost. This means that each chip is adding extra profit to the firm's total profit. In these situations, raising production increases profits. As long as marginal revenue exceeds marginal cost, profits go up when the company expands production.

iStockphoto '07

However, each time production goes up, marginal cost rises while marginal revenue remains the same. At some point, such as at a production level of 8 million, marginal cost ($134m) is greater than marginal revenue ($100m) If Microductor operated at that level, it would still make a profit but less profit than its maximum because the last batch of chips cost $34m more than the price for which they were sold. A good manager would recognize that even though the company is making a profit at 8 million chips, the company should shift back to a 7 million production level. At that point, the company has total revenue of $700 million, total costs of $466 million, and maximized profit of $234 million.

Microductor managers could also operate at 6 million chips and receive the same profit. The 7 million chip production level allows the managers to employ more resources (workers) with no loss of profits.

Show Your Understanding

With a highlighter pen, highlight the Marginal Revenue and the Marginal Cost columns in Figure 9-6. Circle the points at which marginal revenue exceeds marginal cost. Box the points at which marginal costs exceed marginal revenue.

Think Critically

Would managers ever choose to produce more products beyond the amount at which profits are maximized?

_____

Why?

_____

_____

Economies of Scale

How large must a firm be before it pays to use large-scale methods like Microductor? The answer to this question varies depending on the product. When a firm reaches the size to employ large-scale methods, economists say that it begins to enjoy **economies of scale**— reductions in cost resulting from large-scale production. For example, an eye clinic might serve 10 people per day with total costs of $500 per day. If they could expand to 100 patients a day, the total costs would also go up, possibly to $1,000 a day, but the cost per patient has decreased from $50 to $10. If the patients continued to pay the same fee of $40, then the clinic would change from losing money to being a very profitable enterprise. Here are the calculations: Total Revenue ($4,000) = 100 patients x $40 per patient. Total Cost ($1,000) = 100 patients x $10 per patient. $4,000 – $1,000 = $3,000—a nice profit indeed.

As new technologies are introduced, allowing for more flexibility and speed in producing different products, the price benefits of economies of scale become available to smaller companies as well.

Firms enjoy economies of scale for the following reasons:

- They can provide more opportunity for dividing labor into specialized tasks.

- They can buy raw materials and supplies in larger quantities that entitle them to discounts.

- They can use specialized machinery and equipment to reduce unit costs.

- They can invest in research and development programs that enable the company to reduce production costs and produce new and improved products.

Business managers usually know their business costs. However, they are not always certain how much revenue the business will receive. To maximize profits, managers need to look for the level of production that provides the greatest difference between total revenue and total cost. This is the same as looking for the production point at which marginal cost equals marginal revenue.

Achieving Economies of Scale

Two natural juice companies of approximately the same size and located in the same city have decided to merge. List at least four areas in which the merged company might achieve economies of scale.

_____

_____

_____

_____

Explain in your own words economies of scale.

_____

_____

_____

Think Critically

Sometimes competitive businesses merge to achieve economies of scale. One savings in a merger can be reducing the total number of employees. What is one plus and one minus of this economy of scale?

Plus _____

_____

Minus _____

_____

Economies of Scale and Saving the Eyesight of Many People

What do Model T's, Burger King, and McDonald's have in common with eye care procedures in India that save poor people from the blindness caused by cataracts? Need a hint? Economies of scale and assembly-line techniques help reduce the cost of these items so that even the very poor can benefit from this production.

In India, many people who cannot afford health care suffer from blindness caused by cataracts, a cloudiness of the lens of the eye. About 20 million people suffer from blindness in that country, and about 80 percent is due to cataracts, which are easily treatable.

Dr. Govindappa Venkataswamy (Dr. V) was an ophthalmologist who created one of the largest eye-care systems in the world, catering largely to the poor in Tamil Nadu, a state in southern India. He became known as the man who saved 2.4 million eyes.

His business began when he was inspired by the assembly-line model of McDonald's founder Ray Kroc. Dr. V learned this model when he visited Hamburger University in Oak Brook, Illinois. In 1976, he opened the Aravind Eye Hospital in Madurai, in Tamil Nadu, to serve rich and poor alike. All patients were asked to pay for procedures. The basic price was $40 but the poor were asked to pay whatever they could. If they could not pay, the procedure was free. It was Dr. V's judgment that with an assembly-line procedure, he could reduce costs to a level at which any amount paid by the poor, if there were enough patients, would allow him to cover his costs and continue operating.

The Aravind system offers services that range from a simple pair of eyeglasses to eye surgery. The bulk of surgeries are to treat cataracts—removing the cataract and replacing it with an artificial lens.

The operating room at the clinic is a good example of assembly-line procedures and economies of scale. Each surgeon works two tables, one with a patient undergoing treatment and one table with a patient being prepped for treatment. They use state-of-the-art equipment like microscopes that swivel between tables. Surgeons usually work 12-hour days and perform up to 100 surgeries a day. They perform about 2,000 surgeries a year, which is 10 times the production of an average surgeon in India.

Starting with an 11-bed clinic in 1976, the Aravind Eye Care System has grown to a five-hospital system. This model is the subject of a Harvard Business School study and is being copied elsewhere in Southeast Asia. The inexpensive, high-quality implantable lenses manufactured by the system are exported to more than 80 countries.

Govindappa Venkataswamy died on July 7, 2006, but his eye care system continues to provide eye care to patients in India.

Source: Stephen Miller, *The Wall Street Journal*, August 5-6, 2006, p. A6.

Summary

Production of goods and services is important because it determines people's incomes and their consumption of goods and services. An economy's total production is measured by gross domestic product (GDP). GDP is the value of all final goods and services in a country during a year. It consists of spending by consumers (consumption), by businesses (investment), and by government (government spending). It also includes net exports, which is the total of goods and services produced and exported, minus the value of those imported.

Comparing GDP for different years requires adjustments for price level changes, usually for inflation. The result is real GDP, which is an important measurement because it measures production changes. Real GDP can be further adjusted to account for the size of a population in a country. The result is real per capita GDP. Changes in this measure over time indicate changes in the standard of living. Improved living standards require increases in real per capita GDP over time.

Raising living standards over the years requires increases in labor productivity—the amount of goods and services that workers can produce in a given time period. Productivity is increased by improvements in the quality of human resources through greater education and training and through improvements in the quality and innovation of management. It also is increased through business investment that provides more and better capital resources for each worker. Also vital to increased productivity is technological change through innovation, or the development of new ideas.

Total production costs consist of fixed and variable costs. Fixed costs remain constant as the rate of production changes, while variable costs change as production changes. Unit costs contain both fixed and variable costs. Fixed costs per unit always decrease as output increases. Variable costs per unit can decline at first, but as output increases still further, they increase because of the law of diminishing marginal returns. Because various measures of cost depend on the rate of production, a business must search for a production rate that maximizes its profit by finding the level at which marginal revenue is equal to its marginal cost.

iStockphoto '07

Large firms often achieve greater productivity than small firms because of economies of scale. Through these efficiencies, unit costs fall to levels that smaller firms often can't match. Smaller businesses have to find ways to compensate for their lack of economies of scale, by increasing their efficiency or establishing positions in niche markets.

Looking Ahead

In Chapter 10, you will study the United States labor force in depth. You will examine labor productivity, the growth of wages, changes in the labor force, and labor-management relations.

Notes

The U.S. Labor Force

Read to Find Out

As you read this chapter, look for answers to the following questions:

How has the growth of labor productivity enabled businesses and workers to earn more over time, while also providing consumers with better and lower-priced products?

What is the relationship between product demand and the demand for labor?

What major changes in the U.S. labor force have occurred over the past 100 years?

What accounts for differences in wages and salaries?

What nonmarket forces have affected the labor force, and what are some of the consequences of these forces?

How did unions arise in the United States, and how was their growth influenced by labor legislation?

What are the basic aspects of labor-management relations?

Mark to Remember

* *This is important.*

? *I have a question about this.*

! *This is a surprise.*

Why It Matters

Today, about 70 percent of men and slightly over 60 percent of women are in the labor force. Most men and woman will be in the labor force for at least 40 years. Unless you are independently wealthy and don't need to work, you will likely be in the labor force for a long time. You are now at an age when you will need to make some significant and very important decisions about your life, particularly your work life. What kind of career interests you? What level of education will this career require? If you decide on this career, what is likely to be your income?

Chapter 10

The U.S. Labor Force

Building On What You Know

A hundred and fifty years ago, most American workers engaged in some aspect of farming. Today, only about 2 percent of workers are in farming. Close to 70 percent are in service businesses, meaning that chances are good that you will be in a service business. What do people today do when they work? Why do they get paid the amount they do? You may already know that you won't get paid much unless you perform on the job. There is more to work than just performing, however. For an employee to get paid, people must demand the product the employer wants to sell. If there is no demand for a product, the resource called labor does not get paid.

Imagine cooking without a stove, storing milk or juice without a refrigerator, or even washing dishes without running water from the tap. Your kitchen most likely includes appliances that increase the productivity of food preparation and cleanup. Kitchens have many conveniences that we take for granted. Consider the benefits of having a dishwasher, a garbage disposal, or a microwave oven. Think of the convenience of frozen foods, peanut butter, cereal, and other ready-to-eat foods. All of these things and others enable you to make more good things to eat in less time than it used to take. As a result, you are more productive in the kitchen.

Increasing U.S. Labor Force Productivity

Capital resources such as hand tools, computers, and modern buildings contribute to increased productivity. Investments that society, businesses, and individuals make in acquiring skills and expanding knowledge also add to productivity, as do innovations, inventions, and technological change. Together, these investments and advances enable us to produce much more.

In this sense, taking part in our economy is like fixing something to eat in our kitchens. We don't think about all of the things our productivity depends on, but we still use them to produce meals in our kitchens or goods and services in our economy.

Because our economy provides strong incentives for people to create capital resources, develop new ideas, and cultivate skills, our productivity has generally increased over the years. The increased productivity, in turn, has pushed up workers' wages. The table in Figure 10-1 shows annual, inflation-adjusted (real) earnings of nonfarm employees each decade between 1920 and 1960, a time period when economists were just beginning to measure labor productivity and earnings.

Think Critically

If better tools and equipment help employees to be more productive, why don't employees' earnings stay the same rather than increase?

Figure 10-1: Annual Earnings of Employees

Year	Earnings
1920	$ 6,180
1930	$ 7,228
1940	$ 7,514
1950	$12,295
1960	$16,149

Source: *Historical Abstract of the United States*, Series D

As the table in Figure 10-1 shows, real earnings increased almost three times in the 40-year period between 1920 and 1960. This increase in earnings is remarkable, especially given the growing labor force during these years. In 1920, for example, there were 23 million workers on nonfarm payrolls. By l960, that number had more than doubled to 54 million. Over this period, the real earnings of U.S. workers rose significantly, despite the fact that the number of workers soared. This tells us that U.S. workers during the 40-year period were very productive.

Productivity Since 1960

What about the years since l960? Economists have much better information about wages and productivity over the next 45 years. The graph in Figure 10-2 shows an index of inflation-adjusted hourly labor compensation (wages plus fringe benefits) and hourly productivity (output per hour) for 1960 to 2005. This index allows you to compare compensation and productivity over different years. You should note that the two measures closely parallel each another.

Apply Your Understanding

Why is the fact that the number of workers more than doubled during the period from 1920 to 1960 important to understanding the remarkable growth of real earnings during the same period?

_____

_____

_____

Figure 10-2: Indices of Real Hourly Labor Compensation and Productivity, 1960–2005

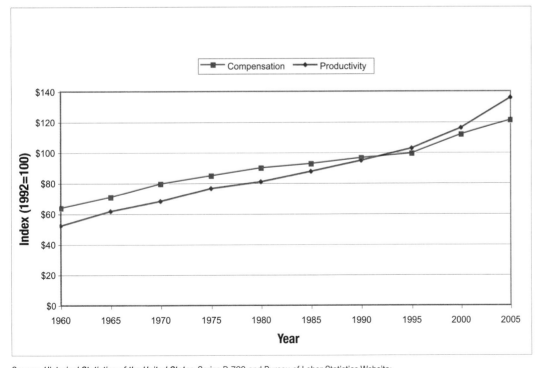

Source: *Historical Statistics of the United States*, Series D 723 and Bureau of Labor Statistics Website:
    http://data.bls.gov/PDQ/servlet/SurveyOutputServlet (Accessed on June 6, 2006)

Check Your Understanding

Using the graph in Figure 10-2, indicate if the following statements are true (T) or false (F).

The graph reports indices of real hourly compensation.

_____

Between 1960 and 1990, productivity exceeded compensation.

_____

In about 1993, compensation and productivity were equal.

_____

In 2005, productivity was about 15 index points greater than compensation.

_____

This relationship doesn't surprise economists because the key to rising wage rates over time is increasing labor productivity. Increasing labor productivity means that businesses can pay workers higher real hourly wages without increasing production costs. In fact, rising productivity can mean lower prices for consumers, higher earnings for business owners, and higher wages for workers—all at the same time!

Think of it this way. Rising productivity means that everyone working together can produce a larger "economic pie." With a larger pie, everyone earns a larger slice when helping to produce it. Workers are paid more, consumers benefit from lower prices and better products, and business owners receive higher earnings. As a result, real wages have increased along with business profits.

How Do Productivity Increases Benefit Everyone?

A factory that produces widgets has 50 workers. One year, the workers produced 100,000 widgets. The next year, with the addition of one new piece of equipment and a production line reorganization, the same 50 workers produced 120,000 widgets. How might this productivity increase benefit

the business owners? _____

the workers? _____

widget consumers? _____

iStockphoto '07

The productivity of the American workforce increased steadily from 1960 to 2005.

158

The Demand for Labor

As you have learned, labor is a productive resource. When combined with capital and land, labor becomes a key resource in producing goods and services. A resource such as labor does not directly satisfy consumer wants. Labor indirectly satisfies consumer wants because it is the significant resource that produces goods and services.

The demand for labor depends on the demand for the goods and services that labor produces. Economists say that the demand for labor is *derived demand*. **Derived demand** is demand for a resource (such as labor) based on the demand for the goods and services that the resource produces. No one wants the labor services of a farmer, for example, but people want farmer-produced products, such as corn or beef.

Here are three real-world examples of derived demand. Computer games have increased in popularity. As a result, there has been an increase in the derived demand for computer game software designers. People have also increased their demand for movie DVDs. Consequently, more labor has been hired to manufacture DVD players. In 2006, there was a decline in the demand for American-produced automobiles. As a result, this triggered a decline in the derived demand for U.S. automobile workers.

Between 1920 and 1960, earnings of U.S. labor almost tripled, indicating increasing productivity of labor. Between 1960 and 2005, inflation-adjusted labor compensation rose significantly, also indicating increasing labor productivity. One caution is in order, however. The demand for labor is a derived demand. If there is no demand for a product that labor produces, there is no demand for labor for that product.

Check Your Understanding

Explain in your own words the meaning of derived demand.

_____

_____

_____

Apply Your Understanding

Name a product that was once popular and is now purchased by only a few consumers.

_____

What do you imagine happened to the labor force that produced the product?

_____

_____

Derived Demand

Read each of the events below. Then indicate whether the event would cause the derived demand for labor to increase or decrease.

Event	Increase/Decrease in Derived Demand
A tainted spinach scare	Effect on spinach field worker _____
Opening of a new movie complex	Effect on movie projectionists _____
A large decrease in the price of gasoline	Effect on hotel/motel workers _____
A large energy company goes bankrupt	Effect on oil field workers _____

Changes in the Labor Force

Think Critically

Do you think that not counting discouraged workers in the unemployment figures distorts the number of unemployed workers?

_____

Why or why not?

_____

_____

_____

In the United States, the Bureau of Labor Statistics within the U.S. Department of Labor defines the **labor force** as all people not in prison or the military who are 16 years of age or older and who are currently employed or who are unemployed and looking for work. People are considered employed if they worked at least one hour for pay during the past week; they worked 15 or more hours without pay in a family business, such as a family grocery; or they held a job but did not work due to illness, vacation, a labor dispute, or bad weather.

People are considered unemployed if they are temporarily laid off from their jobs; they will be reporting to new jobs within 30 days; or they are not working but have looked for jobs within the last four weeks. People who do not have jobs and are not looking for them, such as students, are not considered unemployed. People who have looked for work but are no longer looking for work are not considered unemployed; these people are known as discouraged workers.

Figure 10-3: Total, Women, and Teenage Employment, 1960–2006

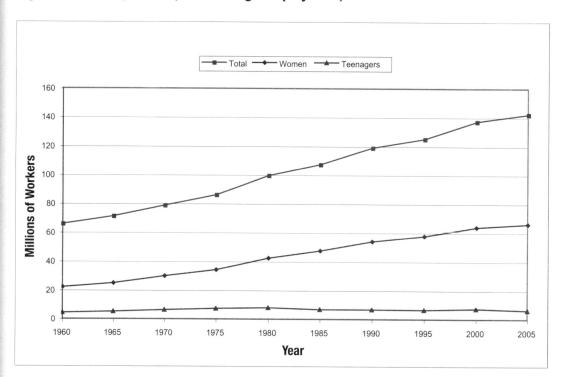

Study the graph in Figure 10-3. In 2005, almost 142 million men and women 16 years of age and over constituted the labor force in the United States. Of this amount, about 66 million were female. About 6 million members of the labor force were in their teens, ages 16 through 19.

One of the biggest changes in the labor force over the years has been the shift of employment from one sector to another. To simplify, think of our economy as having three basic sectors. One is agriculture; another is the production of other physical goods through manufacturing and construction; and the third consists of services, such as retailing, insurance, entertainment, and health care.

2. labor force

Labor Force Trends

The graph in Figure 10-4 shows that more than 100 years ago, employment began shifting from agriculture to industries producing goods and services. From about 40 percent of all employment in 1900, agricultural jobs declined to about 2 percent in 2000. This huge change occurred as the demand for nonagricultural workers increased and as growing productivity in U.S. agriculture required fewer workers to feed the nation's growing population. Instead of impoverishing or starving America with lack of food production, the loss of farm jobs over the years has been a source of its rising prosperity.

While jobs were lost in agriculture, new jobs opened up in both the goods and services sectors. By moving from agriculture to these new jobs, people shifted their work to more productive uses. As painful as this transition was for farm families, it occurred because people wanted to produce and earn more. The key to their doing this was to become more productive.

Figure 10-4: Percent of Workers Employed in Goods, Service, and Farm Industries, 1900–2000

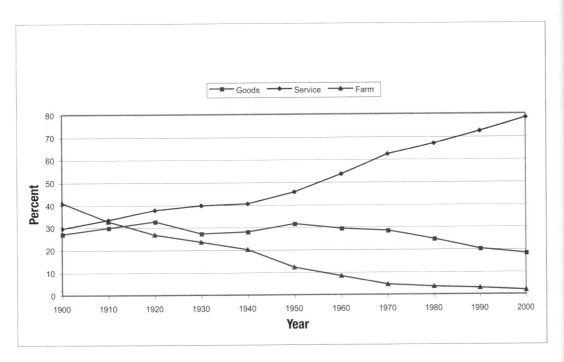

The graph in Figure 10-4 holds another economic lesson for us. Early in the 20th century, the percentage of workers in manufacturing and other goods-producing industries rose very slowly. It fell, then rose, between 1920 and 1950. After 1950, it fell steadily. Like the earlier decline in farm employment, the drop in the percentage of all workers producing goods can be attributed to increases in productivity. Simultaneously, workers found they could use their labor more productively in service-producing jobs.

Like the past shift of work from farms to factories, the shift of employment from factories to services has produced much discomfort. Workers typically must learn new skills, they may need additional education, and they and their families may have to relocate to be near sources of employment. Like past change from agriculture to manufacturing, the transition to services promised to make workers more productive and our nation more prosperous.

Check Your Understanding

From 1900 to 1950, the number of farmworkers declined while manufacturing jobs increased. Do you think the number of food products that were available to consumers increased or decreased?

_____

Why? _____

_____

Think Critically

Do you think the service industry will ever decline in the way that agriculture and manufacturing have?

_____

Why or why not?

_____

_____

Employment of Workers in Goods, Service, and Farm Industries

 Based on your reading and study of the graph in Figure 10-4, indicate whether the following statements are true (T) or false (F).

____ Service workers accounted for 40 percent of employed workers in 1940.

____ Employment in farming has consistently declined since 1900.

____ The change to a service economy has been welcomed by workers.

____ By 2000, service employment accounted for about 10 percent of total employment.

____ Work in goods industries has declined each decade since 1900.

Think Critically

Why are there fewer teens in the labor force now than in the past? Give two possible reasons.

1. _____

_____

2. _____

_____

Women in the Labor Force

Another big change in our economy's labor markets has been the increase in the number of female workers. The number of women workers has increased faster than total employment, and their percentage of total employment has risen from about 29 percent of the labor force in 1960 to more than 60 percent in 2000. In contrast, the number of teenage workers had not risen as fast as total employment. As a result, the percentage of teens in the labor force declined. The population of teenagers began growing faster than the overall population. In the years ahead, employment in this age range should rise as a percentage of total employment.

Productivity and Market Changes

Increases in productivity also enable people to devote fewer hours to work, if they choose, and still earn adequate income. Many U.S. workers in the 19th century had to work six days a week, often from sunrise to sunset and beyond, to survive. In the 20th century, according to the U.S. Department of Labor, average hours worked declined steadily from 38.7 per week in 1965 to 34.6 in 2000.

Besides producing changes in employment patterns, shifts in the demand for and supply of labor affect particular jobs. Many of these changes occur because of technological change and the introduction of new ideas and products. For example, many years ago people were employed in the candle-making industry, but today many more people are employed by utilities that produce electricity. Similarly, automobile manufacturing jobs replaced buggy-making jobs, and jobs in computer technologies replaced many of those in other areas, such as the typewriter industry.

These are only a few examples of the continual changes occurring in our economy and in its labor markets. Existing businesses, industries, and jobs are constantly changing or declining, while others are growing. To benefit from these changes, workers must have the skills and knowledge that will enable them to take part in the nation's economic growth. As technology allows change to occur more rapidly, businesses are constantly demanding workers with new sets of skills. In fact, it is far more common today to hear of workers not only changing jobs but changing careers to adapt to workplace demands. One labor expert estimated that today's workers will change jobs as many as eight times and will change careers up to three times.

Cooperating in the workplace helps increase productivity.

Finding an Occupation That Interests You

Soon you will need to make an initial career choice. The lists of jobs/occupations and their forecasted growth in Figures 10-5a and 10-5b on the next page can help you in making that choice.

Select two or three occupations that interest you. When you have access to the Internet, log on to www.bls.gov. This is the website for the United States Department of Labor, Bureau of Labor Statistics. The website has extensive information on these occupations. Explore the site to see what information is available about the occupations of interest to you. Be sure to look at the Occupational Outlook Handbook at the site. This handbook will give you details on specific occupations.

Prepare a short report on what you learn from the website.

Apply Your Understanding

Identify an older worker who has changed jobs or careers in his or her work experience. Ask the person the following questions and more of your own:

1. What jobs/careers have you had?

2. Why did you change jobs/careers?

3. Was it difficult to change jobs/careers?

4. Do you think your job/career change was positive in the long run?

Write the results of your interview on a separate sheet of paper.

Put a checkmark beside all
of the occupations listed in
Figure 10-5a that are not
familiar to you. Research the
jobs, and then write a short
description of them beside
their listings.

**Check Your
Understanding**

Use the list in Figure 10-5a
to answer the following
questions.

How is occupation growth
rate measured?

What occupation has
the highest projected
growth rate?

What is the growth rate for
postsecondary teachers?

Review the entire table. What
general occupational area
has the most entries?

Use the list in Figure 10-5b
to answer the following
questions.

How is the occupation
growth rate measured?

Teachers, preschool and
K-12, are projected to
increase by how many jobs?

What occupation has the
lowest projected increase?

Why do you think food
and beverage serving and
workers jobs show the
highest increase?

Projected Job Growth

Just as business owners invest in their businesses, workers invest in their skills and knowledge. Indeed, upgrading skills has never been more important because knowledge, ideas, and "brainpower" contribute to increased value of goods and services produced in our economy. The lists in Figure 10-5a and Figure 10-5b illustrate this change. They show the fastest-growing occupations and occupations with the most new jobs for the time period 2004 to 2014.

Figure 10-5a: Projected Growth of Occupations in U.S. Economy, 2004–2014

Fastest-Growing Occupations	Growth Rate*
Medical assistants	52%
Physician assistants	50%
Computer software engineers	46%
Dental assistants	43%
Dental hygienists	43%
Personal and home care aids	41%
Computer scientists and database administrators	40%
Physical therapist assistants and aids	40%
Physical therapists	37%
Diagnostic medical sonographers	35%
Veterinary technologists and technicians	35%
Medical scientists	34%
Occupational therapists	34%
Cardiovascular technologists and technicians	33%
Occupational therapist assistants and aids	33%
Nursing, psychiatric, and home health aids	32%
Teachers, postsecondary	32%
Computer systems analysts	31%
Hazardous materials removal workers	31%
Paralegals and legal assistants	30%
Social and human service assistants	30%
Surgical technologists	30%
Athletic trainers	29%
Medical records and health information technicians	29%
Pharmacy technicians	29%
Registered nurses	29%
Computer support specialists and systems administrators	28%
Instructional coordinators	28%
Emergency medical technicians and paramedics	27%
Fitness workers	27%

*Projected percent change in employment over the 2004–14 decade.
Source: *Occupational Outlook Quarterly*, Spring 2006.

Figure 10-5b: Projected Growth of Occupations in U.S. Economy, 2004–2014

Occupations with Most New Jobs	Thousands**
Food and beverage serving and related workers	1,117
Retail salespersons	736
Registered nurses	703
Teachers, preschool through K-12	689
Nursing, psychiatric, and home health aids	676
Building cleaning workers	653
Teachers, postsecondary	524
Customer service representatives	471
Chefs, cooks, and food preparation workers	468
Truck drivers and driver/sales workers	449
Material moving occupations	419
Top executives	374
Computer software engineers	369
Personal and home care aids	287
Grounds maintenance workers	282
Accountants and auditors	264
Office clerks, general	264
Secretaries and administrative assistants	255
Receptionists and information clerks	246
Sales representatives, wholesale and manufacturing	244
Computer support specialists and systems administrators	226
Medical assistants	202
Computer scientists and database administrators	200

**Projected increase in number of jobs, in thousands, over the 2004–14 decade.
Source: *Occupational Outlook Quarterly*, Spring 2006.

Differences in Wages and Salaries

Because of supply and demand for products and consequently for labor, it should be no surprise that there are different wages and salaries for different jobs. Medical doctors and some lawyers tend to earn more than teachers. Teachers generally earn more than store clerks. Star athletes and performers in the arts and entertainment industry earn more than many doctors and lawyers. In fact, there are several reasons why workers earn different amounts.

- **Differences in ability.** Some people type faster than others, some have an aptitude for math, and others are exceptional public speakers. Some people are good at organizing complex ideas, while others are good at selling.
- **Differences in effort and jobs.** Some people work harder or longer hours than others, so it should be no surprise that they earn larger incomes than others in the same occupation. Also, some jobs are more difficult or dangerous than others. Steelworkers who specialize in building skyscrapers and spend their days on girders 50 stories above the ground earn more than typical construction workers.
- **Experience.** Workers with more experience tend to earn more than inexperienced workers doing similar work. Experienced workers are presumed to have skills and knowledge that make them more productive.
- **Education and training.** Workers with more education or special training tend to earn more than those with less education.
- **Good timing.** Some workers happen to be at the right place at the right time. An entry-level worker may have joined a company just as the company became very successful and gave all its workers stock options.

More Learning Is Higher Earning

Here is an economic fact of life: The more education you have, the more money you are likely to earn during your lifetime. Those extra earnings are more than simple pocket change. Over a lifetime of earning, they amount to a significant amount of money.

The chart below shows income data prepared by the U.S. Bureau of Labor Statistics. The chart shows estimated median annual and lifetime earnings for full-time workers age 25 or older in 2005.

Education Level	Median Annual Income	Lifetime Income
No High School Diploma	$21,500	$900,000
High School Diploma	$30,500	$1,300,000
Bachelor's Degree	$49,000	$2,000 000
Master's Degree	$59,000	$2,400,000
Doctoral Degree	$74,000	$3,000,000

Here are some observations about the earning data. You are welcome to make your own observations as well.

- If you drop out of high school, you are not likely to earn more than $1 million during your working lifetime.
- If you only get a high school diploma, you will earn about half the annual income as someone with a master's degree.
- A person with a doctoral degree will earn more than three times the amount a person without a high school diploma will earn during a working lifetime.
- A bachelor's degree is worth $700,000 more during a lifetime than a high school diploma.

Diplomas and degrees are not the only routes to higher income. Apprenticeships and other types of long-term, on-the-job training also increase earnings. Many occupations that require long-term training, such as machinists and electricians, also have median earnings comparable with those of college graduates.

Check Your Understanding

You have read that workers without a high school diploma can expect to earn $900,000 over a lifetime. That might seem like a lot of money, but how much is it per year over a 40-year working life?

_____

Compare that yearly amount with the $2,000,000 a college graduate can expect to make over 40 years. How much will the college graduate earn yearly?

_____

_____

Wage and Salary Differences

You may have a part-time job. If so, other employees in your workplace are probably paid more or less than you. List your job and the jobs of other employees. Then, considering the five reasons listed on the previous page for differences in earnings, explain why you think other employees make more or less money than you. Write your explanation on another sheet of paper.

If you do not have a job, interview a friend who works, in order to do this task.

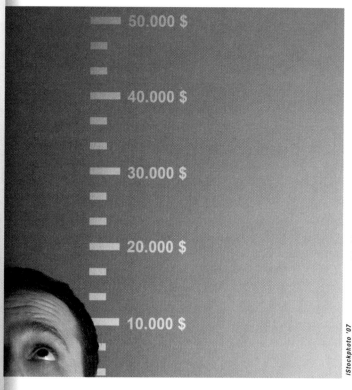

50.000 $

40.000 $

30.000 $

20.000 $

10.000 $

iStockphoto '07

The more education you have, the more money you are likely to earn during your lifetime.

Nonmarket Forces

Knowledge, skills, education, experience, and even timing all affect demand and supply in product markets and, consequently, in labor markets. As a result, some wage rates go up, while others go down. In this way, a market economy provides workers with valuable information and incentives. Based on these wage-rate price signals, more workers enter growing industries and occupations, while others leave those industries that are falling behind. Workers also tend to invest more in the skills, education, and experience when they know the labor market will reward their efforts.

People Like to Stay Where They Are

Market considerations, of course, don't mean that earning the highest wage is the only, or even the most important, goal of every worker. For example, wages differ from one part of the country to another. Look at the table in Figure 10-6, which shows median family income by United States region in 2003. That year, families in the Northeast earned $12,552 or 26.5 percent more than those living in the South. Some of this difference reflects higher

166

costs of living in the Northeast. Despite the earnings difference, some people prefer to stay where they are. Perhaps they want to stay close to family and friends, they enjoy their existing climate or location, or they don't want to pay the cost of moving. Whatever the reasons, they willingly forego a higher wage elsewhere to stay where they are.

Figure 10-6: Median Family Income by Region, 2003

Region	Income
Northeast	$59,874
Midwest	$55,613
South	$47,322
West	$55,095

Source: *Statistical Abstract of the United States: 2006*, Table 681

Job Discrimination

Job discrimination is the practice of favoring one person over another for reasons that have nothing to do with ability to perform a job. Determining the extent of job discrimination and its actual costs is very difficult. The table in Figure 10-7 provides an initial clue about some level of discrimination. The table shows that black and Hispanic workers earn much less than both white and Asian workers. The table also shows that blacks and Hispanics have much higher poverty rates than whites and Asians.

Figure 10-7: Median Family Income and Incidence of Poverty, 1980–2003

Year	Median Income (2003 Dollars)				Percent Below Poverty Level			
	White	Black	Asian	Hispanic	White	Black	Asian	Hispanic
1980	$21,904	$12,674	--	$14,716	8.0	28.9	--	23.2
1985	$29,152	$16,786	--	$19,027	9.7	32.3	--	25.9
1990	$36,915	$21,423	$42,246	$23,431	8.1	29.3	11.0	25.0
1995	$42,646	$25,970	$46,356	$24,570	8.5	26.4	12.4	27.0
2000	$53,029	$33,676	$62,617	$34,442	7.1	19.3	7.8	19.2
2003	$55,768	$34,369	$63,251	$34,272	8.1	22.3	10.2	20.8

Source: *Statistical Abstract of the United States: 2006*, Tables 679 and 698

The reasons for these differences, however, are complex. They may be related to education or access to education and training; community or regional wage differences; past discrimination and levels of experience; or other factors. Nevertheless, most people agree that some degree of continuing job discrimination is present in our society.

Discrimination also is present with respect to gender. A September 2004 report on women's earnings in 2003, published by the U.S. Bureau of Labor Statistics, stated that median weekly earnings for women who were full-time wage and salary workers equaled 80 percent of men's median weekly earnings. This percentage was up

Apply Your Understanding

Figure 10-6 shows that workers in the Northeast region of the United States earn the highest median income. If you don't live in the Northeast, would you consider moving there to earn more money? _____

What information would you want to gather before making your decision?

_____

_____

_____

If you currently live in the Northeast, what factors might make you consider moving to another region?

_____

_____

_____

Think Critically

Study the table in Figure 10-7. Write two sentences to explain how the table provides evidence of discrimination.

_____

_____

_____

_____

from 78 percent in 2002. In 1979, the first year that comparable earnings for men and women were reported, women earned 63 percent of what men earned.

Among middle-aged and older workers, ages 45 to 54, women earned 73 percent as much as men in 2003. In comparison, among 16-to-24-year-olds, women earned 93 percent as much as men.

Between 1979 and 2003, the gender earnings gap between women and men narrowed for most major age groups. For the same time period, inflation-adjusted earnings for white women grew fairly steadily, rising by 31 percent. Earnings growth over the period was 24 percent among black women and 11 percent among Hispanic women. In contrast, real earnings for white and black men rose only slightly, while those for Hispanic men fell by 10 percent.

It is fair to say that we are still experiencing gender discrimination in terms of women's earnings, but that the gap has narrowed slowly over the past three decades.

According to some economists, a market economy may penalize businesses that discriminate because discrimination raises their costs of production. This occurs because it reduces the total supply of labor by blocking the employment of equally productive workers. Wages then rise for the favored workers, and those higher wages push up the costs of doing business. Discrimination doesn't increase profits; it reduces them.

Businesses that do not discriminate can reduce their costs and raise their profits. Over time, these firms will be more competitive and prosperous than their rivals who discriminate. What's more, discrimination shrinks the overall productivity of the economy and keeps living standards lower. Everyone is poorer as a result. Of course, this doesn't mean that a market economy by itself will eliminate all discrimination, any more than it will motivate all workers to move from lower-wage to higher-wage areas. However, in either case, a free enterprise economy has stiff market penalties for those who engage in these behaviors.

Apply Your Understanding

From your reading, you know that in 2003 women earned 80 percent of what men earned. If a man in 2003 earned $40,000 a year, how much would a woman have earned?

_____

If a man earned $100,000 a year, how much would a woman have earned?

_____

What factors do you think will cause the earnings gap to continue to close?

_____

_____

Why Discrimination Doesn't Pay

Explain in your own words why in a free enterprise economy, discrimination does not increase profits.

_____

_____

_____

Government Legislation

The federal and many state governments have passed minimum wage laws that establish the lowest legal wage that an employer can pay. Other laws address issues such as overtime pay, hours of work, and child labor. They also have a direct effect on labor costs. Other laws establish workplace safety standards. These laws are examples of nonmarket forces that influence wages.

Economic Analysis of Income Inequality: The Lorenz Curve

 The distribution of income can tell us about inequality in a particular country. In 1905, Max Otto Lorenz, a U.S. statistician, developed a statistical technique to analyze the distribution of income in a country. Called the Lorenz curve, this technique can show the relative equality or inequality of income in a country at different time periods. A Lorenz curve that compares income distribution for 1980 and 2003 is shown in the graph in Figure 10-8.

Figure 10-8: Lorenz Curve: Distribution of Income, 1980 and 2003

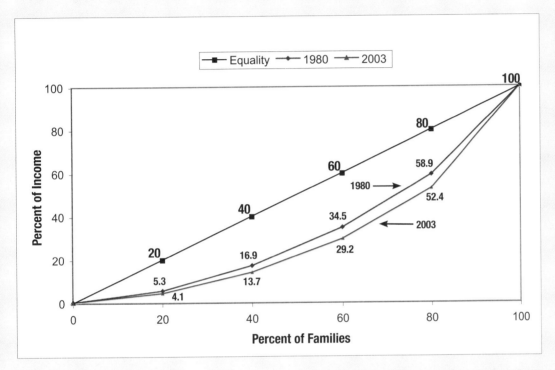

In the graph, the diagonal straight line running from the lower left corner in the box to the upper right corner shows what income distribution would look like if income distribution were perfectly equal. Notice that the vertical axis of the graph shows the percent of total income earned. The horizontal axis of the graph shows the percent of families receiving the income. On this diagonal straight line of equal income distribution, 20 percent of families would earn 20 percent of income, 60 percent of families would earn 60 percent of income, and so on. To read the graph, begin at the horizontal axis (percent of families) and read up to the income line. Then read left to the percent of income axis to determine what percent of families received what percent of income.

The question is, what do actual percentages of income data tell us about the distribution of income? The Lorenz curve shows income distributions for 1980 and 2003. In 1980, 40 percent of families earned 16.9 percent of income. In 2003, however, 40 percent of families earned only 13.7 percent of income. This difference represents a decrease of slightly more than 3 percent of income over the 23-year period. In 1980, 60 percent of families earned 34.5 percent of income, while in 2003, 60 percent of families earned 29.2 percent of income, more than a 5 percent decrease during the 23-year period. Clearly, income was more equally distributed in 1980 than in 2003. Also, the income data show a trend indicating that income inequality was considerably greater in 2003 than it was in 1980.

Labor Unions

You learned in the first section of this chapter that most of us do not produce goods and services by ourselves. Our labor must be combined with capital and land. Although we own our own labor, production of goods and services requires the labor of many others. Very few of us are employers who own businesses and hire labor. Most of us are employees who work for a business or a government agency. As individual employees, we don't have much control over the conditions of our work, such as hours of work, wages, or safety in the workplace. Historically, American workers have joined together to bring their concerns to the attention of employers or management. We have formed *labor unions*.

A **labor union** is an association of workers that seeks to improve its members' wages, working conditions, and benefits. Wages in unionized industries and shops are often determined by *collective bargaining*. **Collective bargaining** is a process in which union and company representatives meet to negotiate a new labor contract. Collective bargaining is often another nonmarket influence on wages. In this section, our focus will be on the role of labor unions in the economy.

Unions and the Labor Market

As the labor market has changed over the years, so have labor unions. Unlike European unions, American labor does not sponsor its own political parties, but it has influenced labor legislation over the years. Unions have various methods of altering labor markets to accomplish their objectives. One is to restrict the supply of labor through membership requirements or lengthy apprenticeship programs. With a smaller supply of labor, market competition pushes up the wage rate of union members. Another method is collective bargaining. If a union and management cannot agree on wages, benefits, or working conditions through collective bargaining, the union may *strike*. A **strike** is a withholding of labor services by a union.

Collective bargaining and restrictions on labor supply may result in a higher wage rate, but they may also result in less labor demanded by businesses—fewer available jobs. This means that unions must often cope with conflicting objectives and trade one objective for the other.

Although union activity dates back to the days of George Washington, unions didn't play an important role in the U.S. economy before the Civil War. One reason was that most people worked on farms or for small businesses; they were not interested in joining unions. Another reason was that the courts initially rejected union efforts to organize labor.

Many labor unions were founded during the period of industrial growth after the Civil War. The most successful of the early unions was the Knights of Labor. Organized in 1869, the Knights had more than 700,000 members by 1886. However, internal conflict and public suspicion that the organization used violence led to its rapid decline. By 1917, the Knights of Labor had disappeared.

4. labor union   5. collective bargaining   6. strike

Collective Bargaining

Generally, both employees and employers want their company to succeed. Yet there is often a need for collective bargaining when workers and owners are trying to agree on a new labor contract. List below the different goals you believe employers and employees might have in a collective bargaining session over a new labor contract.

Employer Goals

_____

_____

_____

_____

Employee Goals

_____

_____

_____

_____

Union and company representatives negotiate contracts through the collective bargaining process.

The Rise of the AFL and the CIO

In 1886, a new labor organization that represented labor unions, the American Federation of Labor (AFL), was formed under the leadership of Samuel Gompers. Gompers introduced a policy of business unionism that concentrated union efforts on obtaining higher wages and better working conditions rather than on asserting political influence. Except for one short period, Gompers ran the AFL until his death in 1924.

Unlike the Knights of Labor, which attempted to recruit both skilled and unskilled workers, the AFL united several local and national craft unions. A craft union consists of skilled workers in a particular trade. Membership in the AFL rose rapidly, reaching 800,000 in 1900 and more than 4 million in 1920.

By the 1930s, many AFL members wanted to include unskilled workers. In 1938, the United Mine Workers of America, led by John L. Lewis, broke away from the AFL and formed a rival organization. Known as the Congress of Industrial Organizations (CIO), this organization joined ranks with workers from the steel, automobile, rubber, textile, and meat packing industries, giving rise to the term *industrial union*. An industrial union is made up of both skilled and unskilled workers in a particular plant or industry.

Immediately before and during World War II (1939–1945), union membership continued its rapid growth. At the war's end, however, unions had difficulty to recruiting members. A series of strikes and the Taft-Hartley Act of 1947, which forbade workers from engaging in certain "unfair labor practices," were the principal culprits. Many union leaders also blamed competition between the AFL and the CIO for the problem. Efforts to end the rivalry finally succeeded when, in 1955, the two came together to form the AFL-CIO.

Check Your Understanding

In the 1940s, there were two major labor unions. Write their full names and the main difference in their members.

_____

_____

_____

_____

What is the current status of the two unions?

_____

171

**Show Your
Understanding**

*Beside each bulleted section
are writing lines. On the
lines, write a phrase or short
sentence to remind you of
the importance of the
law that is described.*

Labor Legislation and the Growth of Unions

Before World War I, federal court decisions usually supported the rights of employers to fire or discipline workers for union activity. Many judges felt that workers banding together "restrained trade" in the same way that business monopolies operating together disrupted the marketplace.

In 1914, the Clayton Antitrust Act was passed to define a variety of illegal business practices. Part of the law, however, made labor unions "exempt" from antitrust rules and regulations. Nevertheless, the courts continued to support the rights of employers over those of workers. The 1930s and the Great Depression brought many changes to American life. Production fell to record lows, and unemployment reached record highs. In an effort to revive the economy, Congress passed laws whose effects are still being felt. Among them were several laws that helped the growth of labor unions. The most important of these were the following:

* *The Norris-LaGuardia Act of 1932.* This law limited the ability of the courts to use injunctions—orders issued by a judge—in labor disputes. Injunctions were used mainly to stop workers from striking. Failure to obey an injunction resulted in a fine or imprisonment. The act also ended the use of "yellow-dog contracts," which required workers to promise that they would not join a union.

* *The National Labor Relations Act of 1935.* Also known as the Wagner Act, the measure guaranteed the right of workers to join unions and engage in collective bargaining. It also prohibited employers from engaging in certain "unfair labor practices" and created a National Labor Relations Board (NLRB) to carry out the provisions of the act.

* *The Fair Labor Standards Act of 1938.* This law provided a minimum wage of 25 cents per hour and time-and-a-half for overtime beyond 40 hours per week. The federal minimum wage has been periodically increased. On July 24, 2009, it was increased to $7.25 per hour. However, one of the exceptions in the law is that the minimum wage is $4.25 per hour for persons under 20 years of age, limited to the first 90 calendar days of employment.

By the end of World War II, there was a feeling that federal legislation had given labor so much power that business managers were at a disadvantage. In an effort to restore the balance, Congress enacted the following laws:

* *The Labor-Management Relations (Taft-Hartley) Act of 1947.* The Taft-Hartley Act prevented labor unions from engaging in "unfair labor practices." It also outlawed the closed shop—one in which a worker had to belong to a union to be hired. It did not outlaw the union shop, which allows nonunion workers to be hired on condition that they must then join the union. However, the law does allow states to pass legislation to outlaw the union shop arrangement. Such "right-to-work" laws have been passed in 25 states, creating the open shop by making it illegal to require a worker to join a union. Another provision of the act enables the U.S. president to obtain an injunction that delays for 80 days a strike that threatens "national health or safety."

* *The Labor-Management Reporting and Disclosure Act of 1959.* Also known as the Landrum-Griffin Act, this law sought to improve democratic procedures and reduce corruption within unions. The law requires that regularly scheduled elections of union officers be

held and that the voting be carried out by secret ballot. Union officials are prohibited from borrowing large sums of money from the union, and the embezzlement of union funds is a federal offense.

About 16 million workers belonged to unions in 2006, slightly more than 11 percent of the nation's total employment. This was a huge decline from nearly 32 percent of all workers at the peak of the unions' popularity in 1945. As the graph in Figure 10-9 shows, union membership skyrocketed during the 1930s and 1940s, but then began falling as a percentage of all workers in later years. Yet, while the percentage continued to fall, the actual number of union members was increasing. Union membership among employees of private businesses dropped in total numbers as well as a percentage of the workforce. In contrast, union membership grew among public sector workers. Still, the fastest-growing parts of the labor force (women, service providers, and college-educated employees) have been traditionally the most reluctant to join unions.

Figure 10-9: Union Membership as a Percent of Nonfarm Employment (1900–2005)

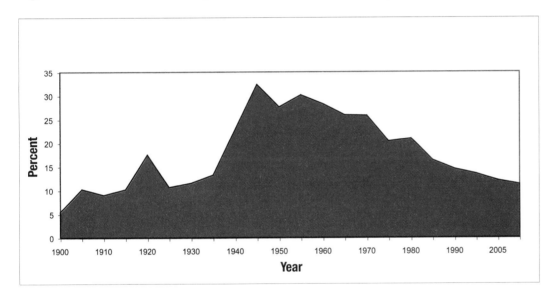

Think Critically

Why do you think the minimum wage law allows a lower starting wage for teens than for people over 20 years old? Give two reasons.

1. _____

_____

2. _____

_____

Think Critically

List some examples of public sector workers.

_____

_____

_____

_____

Why do you think public sector workers are joining unions?

_____

_____

Labor Legislation Matchup

Match the act named on the left with its major provision listed on the right.

_____ Clayton Act   A. outlawed the closed shop

_____ Norris-LaGuardia Act   B. limited injunction

_____ Wagner Act   C. minimum wage law

_____ Fair Labor Standards Act   D. guaranteed workers the right to join unions

_____ Taft-Hartley Act   E. made unions exempt from antitrust regulation

173

Union Membership Over Time

 Using information from the graph in Figure 10-9, write a two- or three-sentence explanation of labor union history in the United States from 1900 to 2005.

_____

_____

_____

Do you think the downward trend in union membership will continue?

Why or why not? _____

_____

AFL-CIO

John J. Sweeney
Paul J. Richards/Getty Images

 John J. Sweeney became president of the AFL-CIO in 1995 and retired in 2009. Beginning in 1980, Sweeney headed the Service Employees International Union (SEIU). During his term, SEIU's membership nearly doubled, a remarkable feat at a time of shrinking union membership in private U.S. businesses. A big reason for the growth was rising membership among government workers. Today, more than half of the members of SEIU are public service employees.

In his efforts to build membership in the AFL-CIO, Sweeney emphasized government workers. He wanted to establish a new "social contract" between labor and business to raise members' wages and increase their job security. While technological change, deregulation, and foreign producers have magnified market competition for businesses and workers throughout the United States and consequently harmed unions, most government workers don't directly compete with workers in other countries who provide similar goods or services. Nor must their employers typically deal with the same competitive pressures as profit-seeking businesses. For these reasons, unions may find it easier to raise wages for government employees than for those in private businesses.

Still, unions face stiff obstacles when trying to raise wages for government workers. Not only have taxpayers become more reluctant to finance higher wages of public employees, but more citizens today express interest in restraining the growth and size of government.

Union-Management Relations in Action

 One of the first objectives of any union is to achieve recognition as the bargaining agent for the workers in the organization. This is achieved when workers vote, through an election supervised by the NLRB, on whether they want a union and, if so, which one. Once a union is selected, it is, by law, the sole bargaining agent for the workers it represents. When a union is recognized, collective bargaining can begin.

The union can negotiate with management to prepare a labor contract. Labor contracts typically spell out the terms and conditions of employment. They provide for "bread-and-butter" issues (wages and hours) and supplemental benefits. These supplemental benefits may include health insurance, vacations, and retirement plans.

Other parts of the contract may outline *grievance* procedures and define the privileges of seniority. A **grievance** is a formal complaint made by a union if it feels that one member or a class of its members have been treated inappropriately under the terms of a contract. Most contracts spell out a procedure for the parties to follow to enable them to resolve the grievance quickly and peacefully without disrupting the flow of work.

When it comes to questions of raises, promotions, and layoffs, most union contracts consider *seniority*. **Seniority** is a worker's length of service with an employer. For example, if a plant were about to lay off several assembly-line workers, under the rules of seniority those with the least amount of service would be laid off first.

Settling Labor-Management Disputes

In most instances, collective bargaining is successful, and labor and management agree on a new contract. In fact, the number of "work stoppages" and time lost as a result of labor conflicts have declined steadily in recent decades. When negotiations fail, however, impartial third parties often are brought in to help settle the dispute. This process may involve conciliation, mediation, or arbitration. Trained independent professionals work with both parties to help them reach mutually acceptable settlements.

Conciliation means that a third party will try to bring labor and management together to work out their disagreements on their own, without the third party's help. Mediation requires greater involvement by the third party, who will listen to both sides and make suggestions for settling the dispute. The suggestions, however, usually will not be binding on either labor or management.

Under arbitration, a third party (an arbitrator) will listen to both sides and hand down a decision that is final and binding. Some arbitration cases result in compromises, but in other cases the arbitrators rule for one side or the other. In recent years, many professional baseball players have taken their salary disputes to arbitration.

When Discussions Break Down

When business negotiators or union leaders believe that neither collective bargaining nor third-party intervention will succeed, they may turn to other means to achieve their goals. Historically, these sometimes included intimidation and violence by either side. Sometimes state militias or federal troops were needed to control such situations. Other, more peaceful, actions are now used.

7. grievance   8. seniority

iStockphoto '07

On the employer side, *lockouts* have been used. A **lockout** is the closing down of a business to pressure a union into accepting employment conditions. An *injunction* may be used by an employer. An **injunction** is a court order to keep a union from striking and picketing.

On the union side, the strike is the most common action taken when discussions break down. A strike may be accompanied by *picketing*. **Picketing** is the act of employees carrying signs that call attention to a labor strike with the goal of arousing public sympathy. Unions often want to establish a *union shop* as part of the bargaining agreement. In a **union shop**, nonunion members can be hired by the factory, business, or agency but only on the condition that they join the union after they are hired.

Strikes or lockouts are serious actions to take in trying to resolve union-management issues. Both actions are costly to both parties. In some industries, management and the union have agreed to involve employees more in work-related decision making. Some actions that may prevent strikes or lockouts include peer review panels in which workers' colleagues become involved in assessing worker performance, and the development of flextime that will enable workers with young children to arrange their work schedules to meet their children's needs. These and other efforts to resolve conflicts may change the relationship between union and management in the future.

iStockphoto '07

If a union and management cannot agree on wages, benefits, or working conditions through collective bargaining, the union may strike. A strike is a withholding of labor services by a union.

SUMMARY

Rising productivity is the key to an economy's growth over time. It is also the key to higher wages and increasing profits. This is true because work that is more productive is more valuable to businesses and the consumers they serve. However, it is important to understand that labor demand is a derived demand.

Higher wages supported by higher productivity do not increase the cost of producing goods and services. Instead, workers share the gains of producing a bigger "economic pie" by receiving higher real wages. Consumers also obtain new and better products at lower prices, and business owners earn higher returns on their invested savings. Because rising wages generally come from higher productivity, wages and profits have generally risen over time.

The U.S. labor force has changed over the years. Beginning in the 19th century, the percentage of all workers in agriculture began to drop while the percentage of workers in goods-producing and service-producing industries rose. The percentage of workers in service-producing industries has continued to rise, but the percentage in manufacturing and other goods-producing industries has fallen. Meanwhile, recent years have seen a huge increase in the number of female employees in the labor force. Teen-age workers declined as a percentage of total employment but should begin to rise as the percentage of teens in the nation's population rises in future years.

Changes in wages and the labor force are the result of changes in the demand and supply of workers. Wage rates have increased over the years because labor productivity has increased. When workers become more productive, businesses bid wages up as they compete against one another for the more valuable workers.

Supply and demand also are influenced by certain nonmarket forces. These include differences in regional economies, government legislation, labor unions, and discrimination. Discrimination lowers productivity and raises costs.

Labor unions arose in the early years of America's Industrial Revolution. The growth of unions is related directly to the desire of workers to improve their wages and working conditions and indirectly to legislation that has helped to promote them. More recent legislation, however, curbed what Congress perceived as an imbalance of power in favor of labor unions. After peaking in the 1940s, membership in labor unions declined to slightly more than 11 percent of total employment in 2006. This decline masked an increase in labor unions in the public sector.

Although most collective bargaining between labor unions and management results in mutual agreement, third parties are sometimes needed to settle disputes through conciliation, mediation, or arbitration. At other times, failure to settle differences has led to more serious results, such as lockouts, strikes, and picketing.

LOOKING AHEAD

The next chapter examines how businesses compete against one another to sell their products to consumers.

Notes

Competition Among Businesses

Read to Find Out
As you read this chapter, look for answers to the following questions:

How is a business like a sports team when competing in a market?

What are the four characteristics used to identify a market structure?

How do market structures of perfect competition, monopolistic competition, oligopoly, and monopoly affect business production and pricing decisions?

What are the kinds of business mergers, and why do business firms merge?

How does marketing help businesses compete?

What do the 4 P's of marketing mean?

Mark to Remember

* *This is important.*

? *I have a question about this.*

! *This is a surprise.*

Why It Matters

Business competition influences the price, quality, and quantity of all the retail products you purchase in the marketplace. It is no accident that video game producers introduce their new game consoles in the same week or that many new models of televisions or home computers are introduced just before a holiday season when consumers are in a buying mode. The number of firms in the market and their size determine the prices you pay as a consumer and the quality of the products you are provided. The ways in which firms market their products also influence the decisions you make as a consumer. This chapter will help you understand how competition among businesses is important in a free enterprise economy.

Competition Among Businesses

Building On What You Know

Think about a major business street in your community. Within several blocks, how many fast-food restaurants or drugstores are there? How many food markets, dry cleaners, or banks? Why do so many businesses choose to go head-to-head with similar businesses along the same street? How do you decide which business you will patronize when you have choices? Business competition is an important fact of commerce in our economy.

Team sports can produce very exciting entertainment involving the joy of winning or the sorrow of losing. What you may not notice in watching sports is how each game in a team sport depends on coordination among players. Individual athletes who make difficult moves with ease and grace must coordinate their behavior with their teammates to win. Competition requires individuals to play at a high personal level and teams to play at a high team level. It is also true that a lack of serious competition in an athletic event will often result in players not performing at their personal best or not coordinating their actions well with their teammates.

Our economy is much the same. The ability to compete depends on successful coordination. How people compete makes a big difference in the outcome. In a free enterprise economy, competition is market competition. People try to get ahead by producing goods and services that others want to buy. By doing so, they earn money in exchange for these goods and services. To compete successfully, individuals within a business willingly work together so their coordinated actions enable them to produce more of what consumers want.

Market Structure

The outcome of market competition is more and better products at lower prices, more jobs, more efficient use of resources, often higher business earnings, and higher wages. Business owners seek to innovate in order to earn higher returns on their investments. In fact, market competition is similar to sports competition. In sports, every win by one team means the other team must lose, but the spectator (the consumer) gains by experiencing good entertainment. In business, there are also winners and losers. Unsuccessful businesses fail while successful businesses grow, but the consumer wins by receiving more, better, and less-expensive products.

Think Critically

In your own words, explain why people who work for a business should cooperate in doing their assigned jobs.

_____

_____

_____

_____

There are many ways for businesses to compete in the marketplace. An obvious competitive strategy is to keep business costs and product prices low relative to other businesses. However, as you read a magazine, watch television, surf the Internet, or stroll through a mall, you can find businesses using a variety of other methods to compete in the marketplace. For example, some companies compete by advertising particular features of their products. Others focus on special services they provide. Still others emphasize that the better materials and production methods used to produce their products result in higher-quality products than those of their competitors. Many businesses make more than one kind of appeal. Just as a champion basketball coach works hard to develop the team's competitive edge with many innovative plays, entrepreneurs and business managers search for strategies to compete successfully within the marketplace. Unlike coaches, business owners and managers must recognize that they do business within a *market structure*.

Businesses use a variety of methods to compete in the marketplace.

What Competitive Strategy Appeals to You?

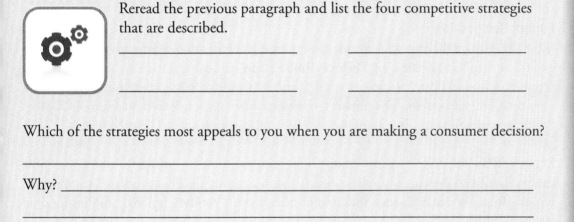

Reread the previous paragraph and list the four competitive strategies that are described.

_____   _____

_____   _____

Which of the strategies most appeals to you when you are making a consumer decision?

_____

Why? _____

_____

The table in Figure 11-1 shows the characteristics of *market structures*. A **market structure** is a set of conditions that describes the characteristics of a market in which a business firm competes. Economists use four major characteristics to describe a market structure: the number of firms, ability of a business to set product price, product differentiation, and ease of entry into a market. Economists have identified four major market structures: perfect competition, monopolistic competition, oligopoly, and monopoly. Competition expresses itself in different ways in each type of market structure.

Figure 11-1: Characteristics of Market Structures

Characteristic	Perfect Competition	Monopolistic Competition	Oligopoly	Pure Monopoly
Number of Firms	Many businesses	Many businesses	A few large businesses	A single large business
Ability to Set Its Price	None; market determines price, and businesses accept it	Have limited ability to set prices because of the ability of substitutes	Have considerable ability to price their products	One company determines product price
Product Differentiation	None; products are identical	Products and services are differentiated to meet the demands of specific markets	It is significant for some products like cars, but less for standardized products like gasoline	None
Ease of Entry	Relatively easy to start new businesses	Relatively easy to start new businesses	Can be difficult	Very difficult

Apply Your Understanding

Suppose you want to open a teen clothing store in your neighborhood. How would you differentiate your store from similar stores in your community?

_____

_____

_____

_____

1. market structure

iStockphoto '07

Apply Your Understanding

Bottled water has become a very popular product. Which of the four conditions of perfect competition does the selling of bottled water fit?

Answer yes or no, and explain why.

Many sellers _____

_____

_____

Identical goods _____

_____

_____

Complete information exists

_____

_____

Free entry _____

_____

_____

Do you think bottled water represents a perfect competition market structure? _____

Why or why not?

_____

_____

Perfect Competition

Most economists believe that demand and supply work most efficiently in conditions described as *perfect competition*. **Perfect competition** is a market structure in which a large number of firms all produce an identical product. This market structure rarely exists in its pure form, but it serves as a standard to measure how efficiently producers are behaving. Perfect competition requires all of the following four conditions to be present.

Many sellers. In perfect competition, hundreds or more businesses produce the same product, and each business supplies only a small fraction of the entire market's production. No one business can influence the market price for the product by changing production levels, because there are so many sellers. In agriculture, corn, whether it is grown in Kansas or Iowa, is basically the same product. In fishing, salmon or cod fish are the same products. Regardless of the broker that sells a company's stock, a share of stock is the same product.

Identical goods or services. One producer's product is indistinguishable from another's, so a consumer has no reason, other than price differences, to buy one product rather than another. For example, king salmon in the Seattle fish market is basically the same product regardless of who sells it. Exxon stock is the same stock, whether it is sold by a Chicago broker or a New York broker.

Complete information exists. Buyers and sellers know all there is to know about the product and its price. They also know about the competitors' products. There are no industry secrets, no special sauces on the food or secret recipes in the cola, so the product's price guides the buyer's decision to purchase.

Free entry. Sellers can enter or leave the market whenever they wish with relatively small costs. While it does cost to obtain fishing or broker's permits to buy a fishing boat or to set up an office, compared to other businesses, these costs are relatively low.

The characteristics of perfect competition are illustrated in the graphs in Figure 11-2. The graph on the right shows the market demand. The graph on the left shows a firm, or business, in the market. Study the graphs.

Figure 11-2: Perfect Competition

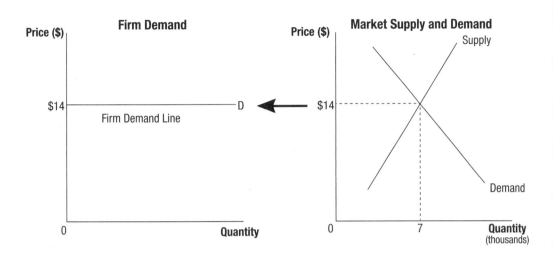

On the right side of Figure 11-2, you see the market demand in thousands of units of a product. The total quantity sold in this market is 7,000 units, and the market price is $14.00. When these conditions are in effect, no seller has any influence over the price it receives. Follow the arrow from the graph on the right to the graph on the left, which shows one firm in a perfectly competitive market. The price of $14.00 is given to the firm. The firm has to take the market price as given; it cannot influence this price. In effect, the firm has a flat, horizontal demand line. If a business charges more than the market price, it will eventually sell nothing because customers will switch to other businesses offering identical products at the lower market price. Under perfect competition, a business has no reason to lower its price because the business is such a small part of the market that it can sell all it wants at the market price.

For these reasons, businesses in perfectly competitive markets must take, or accept, the price determined by the market and decide how much to produce at that price. Successful competitors in perfect competition are businesses that can profitably produce and sell at the market price.

Few markets have all these characteristics. Some markets, like the farming and fishing industries, have many characteristics of perfect competition. With products like grain, fruit, beef, catfish, or shrimp, one seller's product is virtually identical to another's. Similar market structures may occur with iron ore, copper, and salt.

Decision Making When the Price Is Set

Imagine that you own a business in which the market price is set. You cannot influence the price. In what kind of market structure are you operating?

_____

Given this market structure, what is the major business decision you have to make?

_____

Check Your Understanding

Use the information in Figure 11-2 to answer these questions.

1. Can the firm illustrated in the graphs sell its product at $15.00?

_____

Why? _____

_____

_____

2. Can the firm sell its product at $13.00?

_____

Why? _____

_____

_____

183

Monopoly

Monopoly is the opposite of a perfectly competitive market. A **pure monopoly** is a market structure with only one seller in the market. Pure monopolies have the following characteristics:

A single seller. By definition, a monopoly has only one seller. An example might be a business that sells electrical power in a community.

No close substitutes. No other firm in the market offers a similar product. Unless some other business offers electrical power, which is unlikely, the electric power company sells a product that has no close substitutes.

Barriers to entry. Potential rivals are unable to enter a market because of legal restrictions or high investment costs. Electric power companies operate under legal authority of the state or a community. Usually, only one company is legally allowed to operate. Also, the investment costs of generating power and delivering it to homes and businesses are very high.

Legal Monopolies

Like perfectly competitive markets, pure monopolies are rare. In fact, when economists talk about monopolies, they often refer to companies that are more accurately described as near monopolies. However, there are situations in which monopolies are efficient and supported by law. These legal monopolies include natural monopolies, government licenses, patents, copyrights, and trademarks.

Natural monopolies. Traditionally, economists have thought of telephone, electric, and water companies as natural monopolies. Often called public utilities, they are markets regulated by government in which economies of large-scale production are so great that costs are minimized by concentrating production in one large company. Government supervision determines the services the utilities provide and how much they are permitted to charge.

Mass transit systems are other examples of natural monopolies. After all, some economists have argued that it doesn't make sense for more than one transit system to lay track to the same transit stop to pick up passengers. Consequently, without competition driving costs and prices down, output under monopolies tends to be less and prices tend to be higher than they would be under perfect competition.

However, new technologies have changed the way some services are provided. This has altered economic thinking about natural monopolies. Consider the example of cellular phones. Offered by various companies, these phones have substantially reduced the effects of a natural monopoly in the telecommunications industry, formerly known as the phone company. Cable companies have been competing with phone companies, too. Several states have passed legislation to deregulate electric power companies. Consumers have been given a choice of companies from which they might purchase electric power to their homes. While natural monopolies continue to exist in some markets, this market structure is undergoing change.

Government licenses. Another type of legal monopoly is a government license that grants a particular business the right to operate without direct competition. Consider the fictional Taystee Dog Company, which has the exclusive right to sell hot dogs at a local sports arena. Taystee Dog Company would not normally be considered a monopoly because there

iStockphoto '07

Pause to Predict

You have probably heard of patents, copyrights, and trademarks. Describe in general what you understand about these terms.

_____

_____

_____

Read to find out why these are considered legal monopolies.

3. pure monopoly

are many hot dog vendors, but it does have a monopoly in the city arena. In most cases, companies like Taystee Dog compete with similar businesses by bidding for the right to have a monopoly. If they fail to serve their customers well, another company will replace them. Various industries and occupations require such licenses for people to enter the market.

Patents as monopolies. Would you like to think of a new idea for a product or service that could make you wealthy? To encourage you, the federal government grants patents to cover new products and processes. In a sense, a patent is a monopoly. It gives the inventor the private property right to a new product or idea for 14 or 20 years, depending upon what is being patented. You may sell or give away your "intellectual property right," as it is called, because it is yours to do with as you wish. Eventually, someone will develop a product or service that will be an acceptable alternative to yours. It, too, might qualify for a patent and perhaps compete with your idea.

The products of certain industries, such as pharmaceuticals, chemicals, and electronics, are protected by patents. Competing firms cannot enter those industries unless they pay the patent holders for permission to use the process or find a new method of production not covered by existing patents.

Copyrights and trademarks as monopolies. Through the U.S. Copyright Office, the government gives the authors of original writing and artistic work a copyright, which is the exclusive right to sell, reproduce, or distribute their works. That copyright is a special monopoly for the lifetime of the author, plus 50 years. Trademarks are special designs, names, or symbols that identify a product, service, or company. Coke is a trademark of the Coca-Cola Company, for example. Competitors are forbidden from using registered trademarks or ones that look so much like trademarks that consumers will confuse them with the originals.

Enforcement of these monopolies poses a major problem, however, especially outside of the country granting the trademark. For example, you and your friends may find a recording studio, produce an original DVD, and distribute copies for $14.99. Then, on tour in Asia to promote your DVD, you discover a store selling it for $3.99. What can you do? Someone has probably "pirated" a copy of your DVD, duplicated it, and resold it. U.S. copyright laws are difficult to enforce in other countries even though most trade agreements between countries include provisions about respecting patents, copyrights, and trademarks.

Think Critically

What would happen in a free market system if the government did not protect new products and processes with patents?

_____

_____

_____

These symbols protect producers. Can you find out what they mean?

Sources of Monopoly

Each statement below describes a monopoly. Indicate beside each which kind of monopoly the statement describes: a natural monopoly, a monopoly resulting from a government license, a monopoly resulting from a patent, or a monopoly resulting from a copyright.

1. Your plastic model airplane has no competition. _____

2. You own the New York City subway system. _____

3. You write a song that a famous singer wants to perform. _____

4. You are granted permission to be the only seller of nachos at a rock concert. _____

185

Business and Market Power

Most businesses are not perfect competitors, nor are they monopolists. Most companies operate in a market with competitors, and they can also change the price of their product without losing all their customers. These businesses seek the right price to charge for their products. These businesses operate within market structures called *monopolistic competition* and *oligopoly*.

Monopolistic Competition

Monopolistic competition is a market structure with many firms that offer similar but not identical products. Monopolistic competition is also called imperfect competition. In these markets there are many firms, just as there are many firms in perfect competition. However, the products they sell are not exactly the same, so each firm can raise or lower its price to alter its sales.

Differentiated products. In monopolistic competition, businesses that offer similar products often describe their products as "new and improved," "used by professionals," or "the best value for the lowest price." They emphasize distinctive features of their products to differentiate them from competitors' products. For example, Wendy's, McDonald's, Carl's Jr., and Burger King all sell hamburgers, but each company uses special sauces, cooking methods, or added cheese or bacon to differentiate its burgers. Businesses try to attract customers by differentiating their products in many ways.

Customer services. Suppose you approach an intersection that has four gas stations. Each charges the same price for gasoline of similar quality. Why would you choose one station over another? Perhaps one offers a free car wash with each fill-up, while another provides a low price on coffee and a doughnut. These are examples of special services that businesses provide to attract you as a customer.

Warranties and support. People who buy computer software often buy from the company that provides the best technical support. Even toothpaste comes with a "1-800" phone number that people with questions can call. Often a guarantee or warranty will convince you to buy one product rather than another. The reputation of a car dealer's service department can influence the type of car you buy.

Prestige. Many businesses use highly visible labels to differentiate their products. Have you ever purchased a shirt, cap, or purse because it displayed a particular logo or emblem? Companies work hard to develop an image. People who purchase a popular brand of sunglasses are often interested in more than simply protecting their eyes from the sun.

Monopolistic competition, then, occurs in markets with many businesses selling similar goods and services. The clothing and restaurant industries are good examples of monopolistic competition in the United States. It is relatively easy to enter or exit these markets, but competition is intense, and businesses must work hard to create a special demand for their products.

Apply Your Understanding

On the line beside the end of each paragraph describing a competitive strategy, give another example of that strategy used by a business with which you are familiar. Do not repeat an example that is given in the text.

Characteristics of Monopolistic Competition

Indicate whether the statements below are true (T) or false (F).

____ "Our sweatshirts last forever" is an example of customer service.

____ "We service what we sell" is an example of customer service.

____ "If it fails to perform, bring it back for a refund" is an example of a warranty.

____ "This is the only product on the market like this" is an example of product differentiation.

____ "Talented people wear our jeans" is an example of appealing to prestige.

Joan Robinson

Joan Robinson taught economics at England's University of Cambridge for more than 40 years. Her book, *The Economics of Imperfect Competition* (1933), gained her fame as one of the world's foremost economists.

Economists of the 1930s based their theories on the concepts of perfect competition and monopoly. Perfect competition, with a single uniform product and many buyers and sellers, rarely occurred. Neither did pure monopoly, where buyers pay a price selected by the monopolist. What usually happened was something between these extremes. Professor Robinson referred to this kind of trade as *imperfect competition.*

Robinson's concept of imperfect competition described markets in which sellers were able to adjust their prices but were not pure monopolists. Unlike businesses in perfect competition that had to take the price given by the market, these businesses could choose which price to charge. They had this ability because of their market structure, which we know today as monopolistic competition or oligopoly.

Robinson regarded imperfect competition as a major weakness of capitalism. She said that businesses earn high returns by receiving higher prices than they would under perfect competition. Meanwhile, the economy operates at levels under its capacity to employ workers to produce goods and services. Conditions of underproduction and unemployment, she said, lead to periodic recessions and political unrest.

Oligopoly

Competition can be fierce in industries dominated by a few large firms. **Oligopoly** is a market structure in which a few large businesses supply most or all products in a market. Breakfast cereals, major appliances, and carbonated soft drinks are examples of such industries. Compared with monopolistic competition, oligopoly has a high *concentration ratio*. A **concentration ratio** is a percentage of an industry's sales accounted for by its four largest firms; the concentration ratio for an oligopoly is considered to be 60 percent or more. For example, in precollege textbook publishing in the United States (textbooks used in elementary, middle, and high schools), the four largest firms account for about 80 percent of sales.

Oligopoly and Competition

As in monopolistic competition, businesses in an oligopoly compete in various ways. They work to differentiate their products. For example, it is important to Ford Motor Company for consumers to know the difference between a Ford and a Chevrolet, even though both products have the same basic features.

Businesses in an oligopoly are able to adjust their prices. They seek the best combination of price and production quantity. However, because there are only a few companies in the market, each is dependent on what the others do. If one company in an oligopoly reduces its price, the others are likely to reduce prices to keep their customers. As a result, all companies may end up with lower prices and earnings.

Figure 11-3: The Kinked Demand Line for an Oligopoly

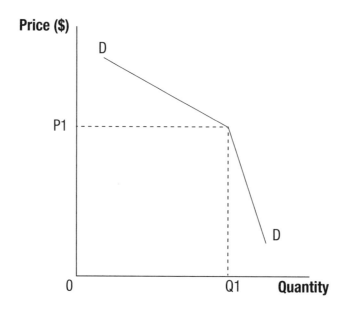

The graph in Figure 11-3 shows what economists call a kinked demand line for an oligopoly. The analysis can be described in this way. The oligopoly firm sets its price at P1 and sells an amount of its product at Q1. At a price above P1, the oligopoly firm will lose a significant amount of sales, because other firms are not likely to raise their prices. At a price below Q1, the oligopoly firm will not gain very many sales, as other firms are likely to follow the price decrease to keep market share. As a result, the oligopoly will tend to keep its price at P1. Note that price P1 is the place that forms the kink in the oligopoly's demand line.

Think Critically

In general, do you think consumers are better off or worse off when they buy from an oligopoly rather than from a business that has many competitors?

_____

Why?

_____

_____

_____

Check Your Understanding

Study Figure 11-3. What will happen if the oligopoly sets its price above P1?

_____

_____

_____

5. oligopoly   6. concentration ratio

Which Market Structure?

Read the descriptions of products below. Indicate which market structure—perfect competition, monopolistic competition, oligopoly, or monopoly—each is likely to be.

1. Sportswear sold at Old Navy   _____

2. Corn produced by a Kansas farmer   _____

3. The only source of electricity in your community   _____

4. The four brands of TV sets sold at an electronics store   _____

5. Towels sold at Kohl's department store   _____

6. The one kind of soft drink sold at a sports event   _____

Restricting Competition

Businesses in an oligopoly have a strong temptation to restrict price competition so they all can earn higher profits. When businesses work together to restrict price competition, their action is called *collusion*, which in many instances is illegal. **Collusion** is an agreement in which companies restrict production to raise prices and profits. It may result from an explicit agreement among companies, or it can occur in unspoken understandings that businesses will behave in certain ways. One form of collusion is **price-fixing** in which all firms in a market agree to charge the same or similar prices. However, a desire to collude is different from the ability to do so. There are very strong obstacles to successful collusion. The obstacles are price, production cuts, law enforcement, and the potential of new companies entering the industry.

Companies in an oligopoly must agree on how much higher the price should be than it would be in a competitive market. Companies with lower production costs may want smaller price increases than those with higher costs.

Oligopoly companies must agree on the amount by which each will reduce production. Keep in mind that cutting back on production reduces sales. Each company wants the others to bear the brunt of cutting back production, leaving one company to sell more at the higher price.

If the first two obstacles are overcome and the market price does go up, each company must still be prohibited, through enforcement of some kind, from breaking the agreement. The higher price gives each a strong incentive to sell more of its own product to increase its earnings. If enough companies do this, the agreement breaks down.

If collusion succeeds in raising the price, the higher price will attract new companies into the industry. If the new companies refuse to collude, their competition will drive the price back down. Without effective barriers to keep new companies out of the market, existing firms may have little desire to collude and increase price in the first place.

Apply Your Understanding

Within the text, number the four obstacles to collusion that are described. Which of the four do you think is most powerful in preventing collusion?

_____

Why? _____

_____

_____

7. collusion   8. price-fixing

Under most circumstances, collusion restrains trade. In the United States, it is against the law—the Sherman Antitrust Act—to restrain trade, so the law presents the greatest obstacle to collusion. Despite these obstacles, collusion sometimes occurs and companies at times succeed in fixing prices.

Whether collusion occurs or not, economists have carefully studied the relationship between profits and oligopolies. What they find is that highly concentrated markets typically are the result of either innovation or of economies of scale that result in lower production costs by successful companies. For example, because airplane and automobile manufacturing is so complex, the industries are limited to a few large businesses today. However, in the early 1900s, dozens of mechanics started small automobile manufacturing businesses. But larger, innovative firms proved to be more efficient producers than the smaller ones. Over the years, only these efficient, larger companies survived the competition. Today, there are few U.S.-owned automobile manufacturers. They compete directly with auto companies from Japan, Germany, Korea, and other countries.

In the automobile industry, only the largest and most efficient companies manage to stay in business.

iStockphoto '07

One Owner to Another

Suppose you overhear the statements below. After each, indicate what illegal act or acts the statement suggests.

"Let's cut back on our production of natural gas this winter. I'm sure with the cold weather the price will go sky high, and we'll get rich."   _____

"Keep the price of your widgets the same for six months, and I'll do the same."   _____

"Let's raise our prices together. No one will find out that we talked."   _____

Business Mergers

Business firms expand in one of two ways—internally or externally. Firms that grow internally expand their activities by adding facilities, equipment, and personnel based on current or predicted demand. Those that grow externally acquire other companies through *mergers*. A **merger** occurs when one business buys another. Another term often used for merger is "buyout." Following a merger, the acquired firm is either dissolved or becomes a division of the new firm.

Mergers take place for various reasons. Some companies buy others to add new products, to gain access to established markets, and/or to diversify their business, thereby "spreading the risk." Some want the benefits of increased size. Some merge to eliminate a competitor. Others think they can manage the absorbed company more efficiently. Still others wish to reduce costs by acquiring assets like marketing or transportation facilities. In 1995, for example, Walt Disney Company bought Capital Cities/ABC, a television network,

9. merger

because it wanted to own a broadcasting system to distribute its films and other forms of entertainment. In January 2000, America Online (AOL) bought Time Warner to increase its multimedia market share. In November 2006, U.S. Airways attempted to buy Delta Airlines to increase the number of flights that U.S. Airways could provide across the country and in other countries. Mergers fall into one of three categories: *vertical*, *horizontal*, or *conglomerate*. Another kind of business arrangement is called a *joint venture*.

Vertical Mergers

A **vertical merger** is a combination of two or more companies involved in different steps of a production process. Disney's merger with Capital Cities/ABC illustrates a vertical merger. Disney was a producer of entertainment content, while Capital Cities/ABC was a distributor.

Horizontal Mergers

The combination of two or more companies engaged in the same business is a **horizontal merger**. In 1999, for example, Wells Fargo and Norwest Banks announced a merger. In 2003, Starbucks Coffee purchased Seattle's Best Coffee to acquire more coffee shops without having to build new ones. Horizontal mergers can increase an industry's concentration ratio by eliminating a competitor.

Conglomerate Mergers

A **conglomerate merger** combines two or more unrelated companies under a single management. Examples of conglomerate mergers include Liggett & Meyers, a cigarette manufacturer, merging with Alpo, the dog food company. General Mills, which markets breakfast cereals and other food products, also owns Izod Lacoste clothing, Lark Luggage, and Parker Brothers. The advantage of a conglomerate merger is that it allows the company to diversify the range of products it sells, so that if one product does not sell well, the entire company will not fail.

Joint Ventures

Instead of merging, some firms in an oligopoly establish joint ventures with other companies. In a **joint venture**, two companies keep their independence while cooperating on a particular project. Toyota and General Motors, for example, teamed up to produce the Pontiac Vibe, a small car. Joint ventures allow companies to combine resources without experiencing many of the problems of mergers.

What Happens in Mergers?

Mergers often result in higher profits for businesses that combine their resources. However, the impact on employees often varies with the kind of merger. Describe what you think might happen to employees in each of the four kinds of mergers.

Vertical merger _____

Horizontal merger _____

Conglomerate merger _____

Joint venture _____

Check Your Understanding

The text describes four kinds of mergers. Indicate which kind of merger is described in the situations below.

An airline company merges with a book publishing company.

_____

A cereal-producing company merges with a box-making company.

_____

A car manufacturer works with a solar battery producer to set up battery charging stations along freeways.

_____

Taco Papas merges with Taco Mamas.

_____

Business Competition and Information

The way in which businesses compete depends on the structure of their markets. At one extreme, perfect competition, businesses compete only by taking the market price as given and then producing products that are identical to those of many other competitors. In these markets, buyers have complete information about prices and products. In most cases, however, information is scarce and costly. If you shop for a car or for clothes, you are bearing a cost to find valuable information about something you want to buy. If you have a used bicycle or car you want to sell, you might spend time and money to find a buyer.

Similarly, a business pays to learn about its customers and their preferences. While each company has a demand line for its good or service, it isn't likely to know just what its entire demand line looks like. Yet, it must have some information about demand so it can decide how much to produce and which of many possible prices to charge. For these reasons, the scarcity of information makes exchanges costly. However, there are many exchange costs besides obtaining and providing information. Finding out about the kinds of products people are likely to want, the product features people desire, and what they might be willing to pay has led to a field of business called marketing.

What Kind of Information Does a Business Need?

Imagine that you want to open a bakery in your neighborhood. You

talk with a banker about borrowing money. She tells you that before she can consider a loan, you need to gather information on competition and on potential customers.

Write three kinds of information you will gather on both competition and on potential customers.

Information on competition

_____

_____

_____

Information on potential customers

_____

_____

_____

Pause to Predict

You have heard the term marketing. *Write a description of what you think it means.*

_____

_____

_____

Marketing

A jeans factory in Durham, North Carolina, produces designer jeans for men and women. These jeans can be purchased in stores throughout the United States from Portland, Oregon, to Miami, Florida. What happens from the time the jeans are produced in North Carolina to the time a shopper in Portland or Miami decides to buy them?

As you have learned, a market is an arrangement in which buyers and sellers make exchanges. To an economist, everything that takes place between production and purchase is considered **marketing**. These are activities that bring buyers and sellers together. In addition to advertising, marketing includes buying and selling, product planning, market research, product packaging, product support, customer service, financing, insuring, and other tasks.

Businesses market their goods and services to people they think will buy them. To accomplish this goal, businesses assign different marketing jobs to different parts of their workforce. A major corporation may have hundreds of people who test new product ideas. Other people will develop and perfect packaging designs. Still others will promote and advertise the products. Further, entire industries have developed to offer specialized marketing support and services to businesses. They help businesses differentiate their products, establish competitive prices, develop effective promotions, and see that products are available when and where consumers want them.

The table in Figure 11-4 provides a good reference to the general aspects of marketing.

Businesses use many approaches to attract customers to purchase their products and services.

Figure 11-4: The Major Marketing Functions

Gathering Data	Business firms collect information about the market to forecast potential sales.
Buying	Before finished goods can be sold by retailers, they must be selected and purchased from a manufacturer or wholesaler.
Transporting	Goods must be shipped to the place where they will be sold.
Selling	Goods must be advertised, promoted, and sold.
Storing	Business firms hold more goods than they can sell in a single day. Inventories must be securely stored and managed until sold.
Financing	Cash or credit must be found to pay for the goods the business intends to sell.
Standardizing	"Standardizing" is establishing uniform specifications for a product or service.
Grading	"Grading" is classifying products by quality and size.
Managing Risk	People in business risk loss if things fail to go as planned. Steps taken to limit these risks fall into this category.

Think Critically

What do you think is the most important marketing function described in Figure 11-4?

_____

Explain your answer.

_____

_____

Figure 11-4 details a number of marketing functions. However, there are four key ideas that everyone in the field of marketing needs to know and act upon. They are called the 4 P's of marketing.

The 4 P's of Marketing: Product, Price, Promotion, Place

Before the 1970s, nearly all babies wore cloth diapers. In the 1960s, however, Procter & Gamble (P&G) introduced paper diapers. As a first step, the company conducted surveys to determine whether parents liked the idea of disposable diapers. They did. The next step was to find a way to manufacture a paper diaper that could profitably be sold at a price that consumers would be willing to pay.

You can guess the end of this tale. Procter & Gamble developed a disposable paper diaper. Pampers and competing brands were so successful that most parents today prefer them to cloth diapers. Disposable diapers successfully applied the 4 P's of marketing to create a total marketing concept.

Product. First, the product must be one that consumers want. It must have the features and quality consumers expect for the price they pay. McDonald's and other national fast-food franchises have been successful because they give consumers exactly what they expect for a reasonable price in Tallahassee, Toledo, or Tel Aviv. Successful businesses like McDonald's and Procter & Gamble pay close attention to what their customers want.

Companies use market research to find out what's on consumers' minds. They might use online, phone, or mail surveys, or they might conduct face-to-face interviews. The product warranty card you return after a purchase provides information about customers, too. The questions researchers ask can identify the product features consumers value most, the quality standards they expect, or the service they want. Researchers also can estimate what products consumers might want in five to 10 years, so that a company can begin developing new products.

Price. Another major part of marketing is determining price. Companies have to search for the price that enables them to earn the most profit. This means the price must cover fixed costs, such as rent and insurance, and variable costs, such as materials and labor. The company then uses these costs to compute its **break-even point**—the point of production at which income from sales equals total fixed and total variable costs. If total fixed and total variable costs are not met, the company will have a loss. If costs are below total fixed and total variable costs, the company makes a profit. Companies must be careful not to overprice their products. If competitors' prices are lower, it probably means that they have information that allows them to produce and market for less or that they are more efficient.

Promotion. Promotion is a key part of marketing and product differentiation. It is the way businesses get their messages to consumers. Advertising, direct mail, and personal contact are a few such ways customers receive marketing messages. If consumers don't know about a product, they won't buy it.

Some critics of American advertising say that money used to inform and promote sales is wasted. Advertisers, on the other hand, say that through market research, businesses discover what American consumers want. Through advertising, businesses tell people what products are available. Advertising even gives customers reasons to buy, especially when there is a discount incentive or some kind of bonus for buying.

Place. The fourth "P" is place. For a product to be useful, it has to be in a place when and where consumers will buy it. A poor location, such as at the back of a strip mall, has caused many businesses to fail. Today, place need not be thought of only as a specific location. More and more products are being advertised and sold on the Internet. Mail-order catalogs are extremely efficient ways to market a variety of products from clothing to kitchen gadgets. Similarly, the success of large retail outlets, such as Target and Wal-Mart, makes it possible for "place" to be shelf space in a national chain of stores.

© McDonald's

Through market research McDonald's has successfully determined what customers want.

Apply Your Understanding

Before you started reading this section, you wrote your understanding of what marketing means. Now that you have read more, revise and add to your definition of marketing.

_____

_____

_____

_____

15. break-even point

The Economics of Advertising

Advertising is controversial in the field of economics. Some economists believe that advertising is wasteful and a poor use of resources. This may certainly be the case with advertising under conditions of perfect competition or monopoly. In perfect competition, there is no difference in the product that businesses sell, so there should be no need to advertise. Similarly, in a monopoly, there is only one seller and that seller should not need to advertise because it has no competition. However, there is extensive advertising in monopolistic competition. The Worldwatch Institute reported that global advertising expenditures amounted to $497.3 billion in 2012. United States advertising expenditures were nearly a third of the global total.

There are two kinds of advertising—informational and persuasive. Informational advertising tells potential customers about product characteristics and prices. It is considered a low-cost means of helping customers make informed decisions about the choices among competing products. It is argued that informational advertising reduces customer search time and reduces their personal costs in comparing product characteristics and prices.

Persuasive advertising has received considerable criticism in economics. Think about advertisements that attempt to persuade you. A soft drink commercial may suggest that you will attract a member of the opposite sex if you buy the "drink that gives you charisma." An aspirin commercial may try to convince you that only a certain seller's product will make you feel better, even though aspirin is much the same drug regardless of the brand name. A jeans commercial may encourage you to buy only a certain brand of jeans, thereby trying to obtain your "brand loyalty." Economists express two concerns about persuasive advertising. One is that this kind of advertising is often based on extravagant claims that confuse potential customers and insult their intelligence. The other is that persuasive advertising tends to reduce competition and limit the number of firms that are able to compete in a market.

To some, marketing might be seen as a waste of resources. To others, it may be valued as useful and informative. In American business, however, marketing will continue to be with us—to determine what buyers want, to inform, or to persuade.

Create an Advertisement

Suppose you work for an advertising agency. You have been assigned to write a proposal for a television commercial advertising Mountain Mocha, a hot coffee drink being marketed for the first time. The product comes in both cans and resealable vacuum-packed bags. According to its manufacturer, the product has a refreshing aftertaste that warms the body and reminds consumers of the Colombian highlands. The manufacturer hopes to sell Mountain Mocha for about 10 percent more than other brands.

The commercial will run for 30 seconds. You may work with a classmate to create the commercial. It will be important to point out how this product is different from other hot coffee drinks.

Write your advertising copy on a separate sheet of paper.

Think Critically

Some critics of advertising argue that certain types of claims or images should not be allowed in television ads. Name two types of claims or images that you would favor forbidding in television advertisements.

1. _____

_____

2. _____

_____

iStockphoto '07

Buy mountain mocha coffee. It will...

195

Summary

In a free enterprise economy, businesses compete by coordinating their efforts with one another to produce things that others value and are willing to pay for. As a result, consumers can get better products at lower prices, workers can get more jobs at higher pay, and company owners can get a higher return on their investments.

The way businesses compete in the marketplace depends on the structure of their markets. The structure of markets ranges from perfect competition, in which businesses produce an identical product for many buyers and sellers, through monopolistic competition and oligopoly, and finally to pure monopoly, in which there is only one seller. Businesses in perfect competition markets must accept the market price as given and then decide how much to produce at that price. In other market structures, businesses can adjust their prices. They can charge different prices, so they can determine a price in order to maximize profits. No business can charge any price it chooses, however. A business is restricted by the level of demand for its product, as well as by its costs.

Most businesses in the United States have some control over the prices they charge. In monopolistic competition, many sellers provide a variety of similar products, each with its own unique characteristics. In an oligopoly, the production of a particular good or service is concentrated in a few large businesses. Because of this concentration, there is a greater incentive and likelihood in these markets for businesses to engage in collusion to restrict production and thereby raise prices and profits. Despite the incentive for collusion, there are substantial obstacles to it. In most cases, successful business innovation and the efficiency of larger scale production are the factors that allow businesses to grow and become more concentrated.

Some businesses grow through mergers. Horizontal mergers unite businesses producing a similar product in the same market. Vertical mergers join businesses operating at different steps in the production process. Conglomerate mergers bring businesses from different industries together.

Although pure monopolies are generally prohibited by law, there are some legal monopolies. These include natural monopolies, as well as businesses protected by trademarks, patents, and copyrights.

In most markets, the costs of information, particularly about the nature of consumer demand, affect what businesses do and the way they compete. Many of these competitive functions are part of marketing. Marketing is everything that takes place between production and purchase—a wide range of activities, including informative and persuasive advertising, that bring buyers and sellers together.

Looking Ahead
Chapter 12 focuses on the role of government in a free enterprise economy.

Government and the United States Economy

Read to Find Out
As you read this chapter, look for answers to the following questions:

What are the four referee roles the federal government fulfills in the economy?

What does the federal government do to manage the economy?

How does the federal government spend and raise its money?

What are the two principles of taxation?

How do proportional, progressive, and regressive taxes differ?

What are justifications for and criticisms of federal deficits and the national debt?

Mark to Remember

* *This is important.*

? *I have a question about this.*

! *This is a surprise.*

Why It Matters

Think about your daily life for a moment. If you read about or listen to the national news, you may learn that Congress is debating a tax policy or increased spending for the military, space exploration, or interstate highway construction. Closer to home, your state or local government officials may raise concerns about higher education funding, the cost of police protection, or public school teachers' salaries. These national, state, and local matters should concern you. They involve government in your life. As a citizen, it is your responsibility to become informed about how government is involved in your life and in our economy.

Government and the United States Economy

Building On What You Know

You most likely are a citizen and a consumer, and you may even be a worker. As a citizen, you have a responsibility to become concerned about how government affects your life. As a worker and consumer, government affects your life directly. If you work for wages at a business, you pay taxes. To which levels of government do you pay taxes? What do you receive in return for your tax payments? If you buy something at a store, chances are you also pay taxes—sales taxes. To which levels of government do your sales taxes go? What are your sales taxes used for? How fair are the taxes you pay? How do you feel about what you receive for the taxes you pay?

Imagine a football game in which the players had the responsibility to enforce the rules. In the heat of competition, who would voluntarily penalize the players for holding, illegal procedure, or committing a personal foul? How would the players assure that the game entertained the fans and that it was played fairly, regardless of the outcome? The intensity of the marketplace is much like a sporting event. Consumers and businesses pursue their own self-interest in an economy. They compete! However, a referee is needed to establish and enforce the rules. Also, a referee is needed to ensure that the economy works toward a good outcome for all. Government has assumed the economic role of referee, as well as the role of manager.

Government's Role in the Economy

What role should government play in the economy? This difficult and controversial question was raised when our nation was founded and the Constitution was written. Not surprisingly, the controversy continues today. In defining what role government should play, the fundamental question is this: Are businesses and individuals better off when decisions are made through voluntary exchange in markets or when government intervenes to make sure the public's best interests are served?

Think Critically

When you were a child, you probably played in a family or neighborhood game for which there was no official "referee" to settle disputes about rules of conduct. What happened in those situations?

_____

_____

_____

Did the outcome satisfy the players? Why or why not?

_____

_____

How Large or Small Should Government's Role Be?

An ongoing question in our society is how large or small should government's role be in our economy. Some people believe businesses can't be trusted to play fair and that government must take a strong hand in settling disputes and managing the economy. Other people believe that the free market is the best referee in our economy and that government should have a limited role. What do you think?

Take a stand on whether you favor a large role or a limited role for government in our economy, and write two reasons for your position.

_____

_____

_____

Think about your position as you read the next two sections of this chapter.

There is no agreement about how large or small government's role in our economy should be.

Each position on the role of government in the economy has its advantages and disadvantages—its costs and benefits. What's more, each is obviously better for certain kinds of choices. For example, we prefer to make our own choices about what clothing to buy. However, we want government to provide for our nation's defense because it is impractical for each individual to purchase such services in the market.

Most economists and elected officials agree that government needs to play some role as referee in the economy—to enforce reasonable rules. The ongoing controversy, during and between elections, is whether the government's role should be smaller or larger. To better understand this debate, the various roles of government need to be considered. In this section, we will examine four important referee roles of government in the economy. These roles are (1) to enforce private property rights, (2) to monitor external costs and benefits, (3) to ensure market competition, and (4) to protect consumers.

Enforce Private Property Rights

Markets don't automatically establish and support the "rules of the game." A neutral party needs to intervene and ensure that the market system functions properly and fairly. For example, without clearly defined and secure property rights, people can't freely make exchanges in markets. If property rights were not protected, individuals would worry that someone might seize their homes, cars, or personal belongings. In a society with no rules, there would be less incentive to care for or invest in capital resources. If contracts could be broken without consequences, no one would enter into a contract. Without this foundation of trust, markets would fail because there would be no coordination between creditors and businesses, or between businesses and labor. In short, property rights are needed for a free market economy to work and grow. Only through government and the courts can people establish necessary rules and regulations and enforce private contracts.

Monitor Externalities

An **externality** is an economic side effect of producing or consuming a good or service that generates benefits or costs to someone other than the person who decides how much to produce or consume. Economists term these costs or benefits "external" because they fall beyond the control of the producer or consumer.

Check Your Understanding

As you read about the four roles of government in our economy, underline one or two sentences about each role that will help you remember its key aspects.

1. externality

An example of an external cost might involve a business that cleans boats in a seaside vacation community. After the boats are cleaned, the water is released into a nearby stream. Although this water contains nothing harmful to humans, it does contain a chemical that prevents the fish from spawning. Hotels, bait shops, and sporting goods stores all begin losing business as the fish population dwindles and tourists choose to vacation elsewhere. The owner of the boat-cleaning shop does not factor the negative economic impact of this chemical into the cost of his or her service. The owner doesn't consider the economic impact because the impact doesn't affect business costs directly. For this reason, customers of the boat shop will not be charged for this expense. Instead, the costs are borne exclusively by those people whose businesses suffer because of the diminishing fish population.

When markets fail to address such costs, the government can take various steps to encourage people to account for the external costs they unintentionally force others to bear. For example, the boat shop could be ordered to eliminate this chemical from its cleaning process. It could also could be ordered to financially compensate the businesses that were hurt. In either instance, the external costs would be shifted back to the boat shop or its customers.

The Environmental Protection Agency (EPA), an agency of the federal government, deals with external costs by setting and enforcing standards for clean air and water. When businesses or individuals use air or water, they must clean those resources to meet EPA standards before returning them to the environment.

External benefits also can fall beyond the decision maker. For example, suppose a medical clinic inoculates people against communicable diseases. The people receiving the shots benefit, but others in the community also gain because of their reduced risk of disease. Since individuals often recognize only the direct benefits they receive (and not the external benefits), the government may require and subsidize the activity. An example of this would be subsidies for polio or flu vaccines.

Apply Your Understanding

Suppose several students leave their lunch trash on the cafeteria floor. No one takes responsibility for the action, so school administrators restrict all students' lunch period to 10 minutes.

What is the external cost of trash being left on the floor?

_____

Who should bear the cost?

_____

External Cost or Benefit?

Indicate on the line beside each statement whether it describes an **external cost** or an **external benefit**.

1. Your neighbor raises beautiful flowers in a garden next to your backyard.   _____

2. A child sitting in the airplane seat next to you coughs frequently.   _____

3. A pig farm next to your rural home emits a horrible odor.   _____

4. From your back deck, you can easily hear great music coming from an outdoor concert that people have paid to attend.   _____

200

Ensure Market Competition

A market economy doesn't always ensure that markets are open to competition. A business or group of businesses in a particular market can restrict competition by controlling a resource or using *predatory pricing*. **Predatory pricing** is selling a product below its cost with the goal to drive competitors out of business. In these instances, existing businesses agree to temporarily drop their prices to force out of the market a competitor who can't match their price.

When competition is restricted, consumers have fewer free market choices and producers don't feel as pressured to reduce costs and eliminate inefficiencies. To ensure market competition in the United States, Congress has enacted antitrust laws. These laws obtained their name from the "trusts" of the late 1800s. A trust is an illegal combination of companies into one company. The best known trust in U.S. history is Standard Oil Company. To form the Standard Oil trust, John D. Rockefeller bought oil companies throughout Ohio and Pennsylvania in the 1870s and 1880s and established one oil monopoly.

There are four key laws that form the basis of antitrust legislation in the United States.

Show Your Understanding

Write a phrase on the line beside each key law that summarizes the law's significance.

- *The Sherman Antitrust Act of 1890* made it illegal to create a monopoly, enter into a conspiracy to create a monopoly, or restrain trade. This includes agreements to fix prices, rig bids, and divide markets.

- *The Clayton Antitrust Act of 1914* prohibits certain business practices, such as giving special rates to certain customers if the practice lessens competition or tends to create a monopoly.

- *The Federal Trade Commission Act of 1914* created the Federal Trade Commission (FTC) to enforce antitrust laws. In 1938, the FTC was given the added responsibility of protecting the public against false or misleading advertising.

- *The Celler-Kefauver Act of 1950* amended the Clayton Act by broadening it to include any merger that lessens competition or tends to create a monopoly.

In some cases, antitrust laws have clearly prevented or reduced price-fixing agreements. In other cases, they have kept businesses from growing to their most efficient size. In still other instances, they have helped businesses restrict competition. To maintain competition, however, antitrust laws need to be enforced. Historically, enforcement of antitrust laws has not always been the case. Some policymakers suggest that we need to review all antitrust laws to assure that they help establish and maintain market competition.

Think Critically

In a free market economy, do you think the government should intervene if a couple of companies want to drop the price of a product below the price being charged by competitors?

Why or why not?

One case in point was the government's legal dispute with Microsoft that occurred in the late 1990s. The company was and is currently the largest distributor of software for personal computers. Supporters of Microsoft said that the company competed fairly in the open market and rightfully won its dominant market share. Others argued that Microsoft created a monopoly, engaged in unfair competition, and violated antitrust laws.

The government sued Microsoft to give other companies the chance to put new software into the market. Microsoft's defenders pointed out that other companies competed with Microsoft and that people bought Microsoft software because they believed it to be the best available. In November 1999, a federal judge ruled that Microsoft was a monopoly and began to take steps to weaken the company.

2. predatory pricing

Congress and the president share responsibility for establishing trade agreements with other countries.

One of government's most important roles to ensure market competition involves international trade, which is discussed in more detail in Chapter 15. Congress and the president share responsibility for establishing trade agreements between the United States and other countries. Once these trade agreements are in place, federal officials assist U.S. companies in conducting business overseas. United States officials may also get involved if they believe our trading partners are engaging in unfair trading practices that inhibit the sale of U.S. products.

Which Law Applies?

Which antitrust law would most likely apply in the following situations?

1. An artificially high price for natural gas is charged by a national energy company to a local community.
   _____

2. An appliance you recently purchased fails to operate when you plug it in, despite its advertising that guarantees it will work.
   _____

3. Two large national oil companies merge and begin to charge outrageously high prices.
   _____

Protect Consumers

Federal agencies such as the Food and Drug Administration and the National Transportation Safety Board are responsible for enforcing laws that protect the general public from faulty products or deceptive advertising. These agencies require that businesses comply with certain standards and rules when producing a good or service. These agencies ensure a level of safety and quality for consumers and prevent businesses from cutting corners to reduce costs.

Government as a Manager

Although markets are generally efficient in allocating resources, the results may produce inequalities, such as large disparities in individuals' incomes that are not desirable in a society. In a study published in 1999, it was reported that the richest 2.7 million people in the United States received as much income after taxes as the poorest 100 million people. In early 2006, many people expressed concern about the seemingly outrageous profits reported by oil companies.

In addition, market economies are subject to volatile movements in prices and unemployment. In both these instances, government may intervene to redirect resources and influence market dynamics. In other words, government, particularly the federal government, serves as a manager of the economy. In this management role, the federal government seeks to (1) stabilize the economy, (2) promote economic security, and (3) provide public goods and services.

Apply Your Understanding

When an outbreak of E. coli bacteria is traced to food served in a particular restaurant, what action should the government take? Check all the responses you think are appropriate.

Alert the public _____
Close the restaurant _____
Fire the managers _____
Write a confidential report _____
Take no action _____

Stabilize the Economy

When prices are stable and employment is high, people generally feel positive about their future. However, when people become discouraged, businesses close, prices fluctuate significantly, and unemployment rises. These were the concerns of the American public at the end of World War II. People feared that after the war, the United States would return to the economic depression that existed before the war.

These concerns led Congress to pass the Employment Act of 1946. The act states that it is the government's intention to promote employment, production, and purchasing power. In the act, the government assumed a new kind of responsibility for people's general welfare by becoming committed to full employment with price stability. Full employment ensures that every person who wants to work should have a job. The act goes on to state that the federal government will "promote maximum … purchasing power." When overall average prices rise significantly, people's purchasing power is reduced. In this case, we no longer have price stability. The federal government under the Employment Act of 1946 is charged with using its economic power to keep prices stable.

Two of the tools used by government to manage the economy are fiscal and monetary policy. **Fiscal policy**, which is discussed in depth in Chapter 14, uses government spending and taxation to stabilize the economy. Both government spending and taxation influence levels of consumer spending and business investment. Fiscal policy is the joint responsibility of Congress and the president.

An independent body known as the Federal Reserve Board controls *monetary policy*. **Monetary policy** involves regulating the money supply to help the economy achieve a full-employment, noninflationary level of total output. Regulating the supply of money influences interest rates in the economy. Interest rates affect how much businesses are likely to invest in capital equipment. They also affect how much consumers are likely to purchase, particularly big ticket items such as cars and appliances, as well as houses. You will learn more about monetary policy in Chapter 13.

Government as Manager

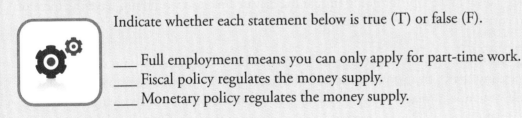

Indicate whether each statement below is true (T) or false (F).

____ Full employment means you can only apply for part-time work.
____ Fiscal policy regulates the money supply.
____ Monetary policy regulates the money supply.

Promote Economic Security

When a market economy exists, the nation pays close attention to the productivity of individuals. Those who own more resources or have resources that are more productive generally earn more because they produce more. This means that a market economy distributes little, if any, income to individuals unable to contribute to the nation's production. As a result, these people end up with little economic security. Not surprisingly, government has a role to play in promoting economic security. Since the 1930s, government has developed various programs to ensure that every citizen is guaranteed a minimum standard of living by providing income supplements, subsidies for food and housing, and access to medical care. Some of these programs assist people who are retired or disabled, while others benefit low-income citizens and try to increase their economic opportunities.

Many of these programs involve government transfers of money from one group to another. For example, today's workers pay Social Security and Medicare taxes on their wages. The government then transfers those taxes to retired and disabled citizens. As you will find later in this chapter, these and similar transfer programs are mainly responsible for the growth of federal spending in recent years, and they account for a significant percentage of the federal budget. Programs to help poor, disabled, and retired people fall into two categories:

- Programs to increase income and the standard of living include Social Security and other retirement programs, welfare payments, Medicare and Medicaid, food stamps, and unemployment insurance.

- Programs to eliminate the causes of poverty and economic disadvantage include enforcement of anti discrimination laws and provide for educational opportunities designed to help people develop skills and increase their labor productivity.

Provide Public Goods and Services

Government is considered the *public sector* of our economy. The **public sector** is the part of our economy that involves the transactions of government. Government in our economy is considered a service provider. As a service provider in the economy, the federal government's major emphasis of government includes management of veterans' hospitals, national security, and business regulation. In a market economy, it is often impractical for the businesses to produce some services. It then becomes necessary for government to provide these.

One example of government-provided services is the interstate highway system. It is generally not feasible for a business to provide this kind of transportation system. It is too costly, and the highways cut across city, county, and state boundary lines. Another example of a federal government service is the Environmental Protection Agency, which monitors and regulates air and water quality throughout the United States. It is unlikely that a business could make a profit doing this, and a private business would not have the force of law to correct air and water pollution problems.

The government also provides some goods, one of which is national defense. A **public good** is something that, once provided, is available to anyone without additional cost. Once a defense system is in place, there is no way to prevent citizens from receiving its benefits. Your use of national defense does not limit or decrease the benefit your neighbor receives. Consequently, government provides most national defense. However, private businesses do provide goods for the United States Department of Defense. You may have heard of large defense contractors such as Boeing and Lockheed Martin. In reality, few goods and services are purely public or private. Most fall somewhere in between.

Where, then, is the line between goods and services that should be provided by the government and those that should be provided by private businesses? There is no simple answer. Some goods and services are supplied by both private businesses and government. For example, local governments typically provide police services, yet many private

Think Critically

In a free market economy, do you think the government should provide aid to people who are unable to work because they are ill, old, poor, or without skills needed to work? Why or why not?

_____

_____

_____

_____

5. public sector   6. public good

businesses also offer security services. In recent years, governments in the United States have shifted away from some services that they once provided. They have done so by selling, or "privatizing," government-owned assets, such as landfills, wastewater treatment plants, and airports.

The answer to the question of who should provide public goods and services will continue to be debated. Those who support private enterprise believe that business can be more efficient than government in providing public goods. Those who think that business should not make a profit on providing public goods by using taxpayers' money advocate that government should be in control.

How Large or Small Should Government's Role Be?

Review your answer to the question in the "How Large or Small Should Government's Role Be" activity at the beginning of this chapter. After having read more about government's role in our economy, how would you change or add to your answer now?

_____

_____

_____

It is necessary for government to provide services to the public when it is impractical for businesses to do so.

Check Your Understanding

Which of the following are public goods? Check them.

__ *Local police providing security at a rock concert.*

__ *A bouncer who provides security at a teen club.*

__ *Your opportunity to attend public school.*

__ *Your opportunity to attend a movie.*

__ *A free bus ride to downtown provided by the city government.*

Federal Government Spending and Taxation

 The table in Figure 12-1 shows a summary of the budget for the federal government for the *fiscal year* 2007. A **fiscal year** is a 12-month period that can begin on any date. For the United States federal government, the fiscal year begins on October 1 and ends on September 30 of the next year. The fiscal year 2007 begins on October 1, 2006, and ends on September 30, 2007.

Figure 12-1: Budget of the Federal Government, 2007 (estimated)

Outlays	Billions of Dollars	Percent of Total
National defense	**$527.4**	**19.0**
Human resources	**$1,787.5**	**64.5**
Education, training, employment, and social services	$87.6	3.2
Health	$280.9	10.1
Medicare	$392.0	14.2
Income security	$367.2	13.3
Social security	$585.9	21.2
Veterans benefits and services	$73.9	2.7
Physical resources	**$147.7**	**5.3**
Energy	$1.0	0.0
Natural resources and environment	$31.0	1.1
Commerce and housing credit	$11.2	0.4
Transportation	$76.3	2.8
Community and regional development	$28.2	1.0
Other functions	**$154.3**	**5.6**
International affairs	$33.3	1.2
General science, space, and technology	$25.4	0.9
Agriculture	$25.7	0.9
Administration of justice	$44.3	1.6
General government and allowances	$25.6	0.9
Net interest	**$247.3**	**8.9**
Undistributed offsetting receipts	$-94.3	-3.4
Total budget outlays	**2,769.9**	**100.0**

Receipts	Billions of Dollars	Percent of Total
Income taxes	**$1,357.0**	**56.2**
Individual income taxes	$1,096.4	45.4
Corporate income taxes	$260.6	10.8
Social insurance and retirement receipts	**$884.1**	**36.6**
Employment and general retirement	$834.5	34.5
Unemployment insurance and other	$49.6	2.1
Excise taxes and trust funds	**$74.6**	**3.1**
Alcohol	$8.2	0.3
Tobacco	$7.6	0.3
Other excise taxes	$5.0	0.2
Highway	$39.7	1.6
Airport and airway	$11.3	0.5
Other trust funds	$2.8	0.1
Other receipts	**$100.2**	**4.1**
Estate and gift taxes	$23.7	1.0
Customs duties and fees	$28.1	1.2
Miscellaneous receipts	$48.4	2.0
Total budget receipts	**$2,415.9**	**100.0**

Source: Budget of the United States Government, Fiscal Year 2007: Historical Tables, Tables 2.1, 2.4, 2.5 and 3.1.

Apply Your Understanding

Analyze the 2007 federal budget in Figure 12-1. Based on your analysis, will the federal government have a budget surplus or a deficit in fiscal year 2007?

_____

How do you know?

_____

_____

7. fiscal year

Note that the top section of the federal budget shows outlays or federal government spending. The bottom section of the budget shows receipts, almost all of which come from taxes. The figures are shown in billions of dollars. To the right of the dollar amounts, the percentages represent either a percent of the total outlays or a percent of total receipts. Look at the bottom line under outlays. The total budget outlays are $2.77 trillion, which account for 100 percent of the total outlays.

Federal Government Spending

Examine the table in Figure 12-1. The first line in the outlays section shows that national defense expenditure for fiscal year 2007 is $527.4 billion. The next item under outlays is human resources. This outlay represents direct benefit payments to individuals. The federal government spends almost two-thirds of its budget (64.5 percent) to transfer money directly to individuals. A transfer payment is a transfer of money by a level of government to a household or business firm for which the payer (government) receives no good or service directly in return. Health care, Medicare, income security, and Social Security account for nearly all of these payments. Human resources payments are the fastest-growing part of the federal budget.

Retired people receive many of the human resources payments. Income security includes retirement benefits for government workers, but most of these payments provide assistance to people with low incomes and to unemployed workers. Social Security payments of $585.9 billion account for 21.2 percent of total outlays. Most of the Social Security payments go to retired people. The $280.9 billion spent in the health category consists mostly of health care for low-income families. It also includes health benefits for federal employees and funds for health research and training.

Federal Government Taxation

The bottom section of the table in Figure 12-1 shows the receipts to the federal government. Almost all of these receipts come from taxes. Income taxes account for 56.2 percent of total receipts. Individual income taxes, the largest source of federal budget receipts, are over $1 trillion and account for 45.4 percent of total receipts. Social insurance and retirement receipts in the amount of $884.1 billion account for 36.6 percent of federal budget receipts. If you receive a paycheck, you will see a deduction on your check labeled *FICA*. **FICA**, which stands for the Federal Insurance Contributions Act, represents the taxes people pay for Social Security and Medicare.

Check Your Understanding

What is the difference between Social Security and income security?

_____

_____

_____

Reading the 2007 Federal Budget

Refer to the 2007 federal budget in Figure 12-1, and record the dollar amounts and the percent of total spending or revenue for each of the following budget categories.

	Dollar Amount	Percent of Total
Medicare	_____	_____
International affairs	_____	_____
Corporate income taxes	_____	_____
Highway taxes	_____	_____

Paul A. Samuelson
Yale Joel/Time & Life Pictures/Getty Images

Milton Friedman
George Rose/Getty Images

Two Views of the Proper Role of Government

Paul Samuelson and Milton Friedman, now deceased, were two of America's most distinguished economists. In recognition of their achievements, Samuelson was awarded the Nobel Prize in Economics in 1970 and Friedman in 1976. Both spent most of their professional lives on the faculty of major universities, Samuelson at the Massachusetts Institute of Technology and Friedman at the University of Chicago. Given their similarities, one would think that the two also would have agreed on economic issues. Nothing could be farther from the truth. Some of their sharpest differences occurred over government's proper role in the economy.

Classical economists like Adam Smith recognized the need for government to provide goods and services such as national defense that would not or could not be provided by private business. However, they urged that government's role be kept small.

Samuelson argued that too many of the problems that the classical economists wanted to leave to the marketplace were external costs and not subject to the laws of supply and demand. He argued that it is up to government to establish goals for the economy and use its powers to solve problems related to issues such as public health, education, and pollution.

Friedman saw things differently. Like classical economists, he regarded supply and demand as the most powerful of economic forces. The best that government could do to help the economy, in Friedman's view, was to keep its hands off business and allow the market to "do its thing."

The minimum wage laws are a case in point. Whereas Samuelson endorsed minimum wage laws to help low-income workers, Friedman said they harm the very people they were designed to help. He argued that, by increasing labor costs, minimum wage laws made it too expensive for many firms to hire low-wage workers. As a result, those who might otherwise be employed are not hired at all.

Samuelson endorsed the concept of government-sponsored programs such as public housing and food stamps to reduce poverty. Friedman, though, preferred giving low-income families additional income and allowing them to use the funds to solve their own problems without government interference. To apply this concept, Friedman suggested a "negative income tax." The graduated income tax would take an increasing amount in taxes as one's income rises. The negative income tax would apply a sliding scale of payments to those whose income from work falls below a stated minimum.

State and Local Government Finances

Budgets of state and local governments have increased dramatically. In 1980, expenditures for all states and localities totaled about $434 billion. In 2007, they had increased more than fivefold to about $2.4 trillion, according to the U.S. Census Bureau. Grants from the federal government accounted for about 20 percent of state and local government revenue. Taxes are the principal source of income for state and local governments. Sales taxes account for about half of all these state tax revenues. You pay sales taxes "a few cents at a time" on most of your purchases.

Most states and communities collect sales taxes of about 4 to 7 percent of the purchase price of most goods and services. These pennies add up to billions of dollars. Individual income taxes are another important source of state revenue. Individuals in most states are required to pay a percentage of their income to the state in taxes. Among local governments, the property tax provides the most revenue. Property taxes are usually based on the value of real estate, land, and buildings.

State and local governments have much different spending priorities than the federal government. These levels of government provide services that are close to their citizens. As you might expect, education accounts for about 30 percent of state and local spending for both higher education and public school K-12 education. Other important categories of state and local spending include funds for highways, hospitals, public welfare, community housing, sewage and waste management, and public safety (police and fire protection).

Adding Government to the Circular Flow

Think back to Chapter 2 for a moment. In that chapter, you were introduced to the diagram called The Circular Flow of Money, Resources, and Products. The diagram in Chapter 2 showed the flow of resources from households to businesses and the return of money from businesses to households as payment for resources. Also, the diagram showed business production of goods and services and household spending for these goods and services.

Now we add government to the Circular Flow of Money, Resources, and Products, shown in the diagram in Figure 12-2. All levels of government—federal, state, and local—play an important role in the U.S. economy. These governments employ thousands of people, such as police officers, firefighters, military personnel, forest rangers, accountants, and clerks. The government buys everything from paper clips to aircraft carriers, and it provides important goods and services, such as highways, airports, police protection, national defense, and scientific research. It also transfers some of the nation's tax revenues to provide individuals with Social Security and other benefits.

Figure 12-2: The Circular Flow of Money, Resources, and Products

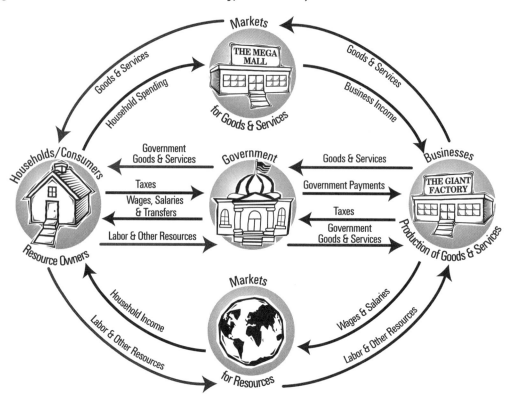

Check Your Understanding

Based on the circular flow diagram in Figure 12-2, what are the government's two sources of revenue?

_____

_____

The flow of money, resources, and products among and between households, businesses, and now government are illustrated in the diagram in Figure 12-2. Businesses and households both pay taxes to government. These taxes are "recycled." First, governments pay households for their resources through wages and salaries, interest on investments or loans, and rent for the use of property. Second, governments send billions of dollars to households in the form of transfer payments—Social Security, Medicare, and unemployment benefits, for example. Governments also purchase goods and services from private businesses, such as medical research, space exploration, highway repair, airplanes, and uniforms for military personnel.

Understanding the Circular Flow

Match the actions in the left column with the letters of the appropriate descriptions in the right column.

___ Purchase of a DVD

___ Unemployment payment to a worker

___ Payment of $500 in wages to a worker by XYZ company

___ A tax payment by XYZ company

___ A personal income tax payment

a. Payment of taxes by a household to government

b. Payment of taxes by business to government

c. Payment to a household by a business

d. A transfer from government to a household

e. Household spending

Tax Policy

In 1789, Benjamin Franklin stated, "In this world nothing can be said to be certain, except death and taxes." Few economic topics are more controversial than taxes. But as Franklin noted long ago, they are a certainty, so we need to understand them.

The principal purpose of taxes is to pay the cost of government. Taxes can discourage activities the government believes to be harmful. For example, taxes on cigarettes and liquor, so-called sin taxes, have been levied to raise money and to discourage people from smoking and drinking.

Taxes have been used to encourage certain activities. In the 1980s, for example, the government wanted businesses to modernize their plants and increase productivity. It offered tax incentives to firms that purchased new machinery and equipment. A tax incentive allows the firm that purchases new machinery and equipment to pay lower taxes as a result of the purchase. The federal government also encourages home ownership by allowing citizens to deduct from their taxable income interest paid on their home mortgages. For most taxpayers, this represents their largest tax deduction.

The federal government can use tax policy to alter the level of economic activity. By increasing or decreasing taxes, government can affect overall spending and production and thereby stabilize the economy. You have learned that use of taxes to stabilize the economy is called fiscal policy.

Principles of Taxation

Tax experts have identified two principles of taxation—the *benefits-received principle* and the *ability-to-pay principle*. Each principle is discussed briefly in this section.

The **benefits-received principle** of taxation states that government should tax people in proportion to the benefits they receive from a government good or service. Gasoline taxes and bridge tolls are two examples. Why? People who drive their automobiles on highways contribute to wearing them out, and government will be responsible for paying for highway repairs. People who use government-owned bridges pay a toll that will be allocated to bridge repair. In both these examples, the principle is that those who benefit from a good or service should pay for its use.

The **ability-to-pay principle** states that the government should tax people in proportion to their ability to pay the tax. For example, someone earning $100,000 a year is better able to pay taxes than someone earning $25,000 a year. Yet the question remains: How much greater is the higher income person's ability to pay? Is it four times greater, 10 times greater, or perhaps only two times greater? Tax experts only make the general statement that the wealthier person has a greater ability to pay. Not surprisingly, people reach different conclusions about the tax rates that best reflect their ability to pay. For example, some people argue that tax rates should be the same for people of all incomes, while others argue that they should be higher for wealthier individuals. Tax rate policy leads to a discussion of the types of taxes people pay.

Think Critically

Reread the quotation by Benjamin Franklin. Rewrite it in your own words to explain Franklin's point.

_____

_____

_____

Apply Your Understanding

Give one example of how the federal government can encourage or discourage economic activity by increasing or decreasing taxes.

_____

_____

_____

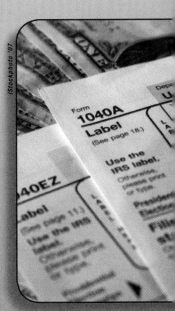

9. benefits-received principle   10. ability-to-pay principle

Principles of Taxation: What's Your View?

Which principle of taxation—benefits-received or ability-to-pay—do you think is the more fair way to tax citizens?

_____

Explain your answer _____

_____

_____

The federal income tax requires people to pay a progressively higher rate as their income increases.

iStockphoto '07

Types of Taxes

There are three types of taxes—*proportional*, *progressive*, and *regressive*.

A **proportional tax** is a tax for which the percentage of income paid in taxes is the same for all income levels. Someone earning $100,000 a year would pay the same tax rate or percentage of income as someone earning $25,000 a year. A proportional rate of 20 percent would require the lower-income person to pay $5,000 (.20 x $25,000 = $5,000) and require the higher-income person to pay $20,000 (.20 x $100,000 = $20,000). In this case, both the income and the tax of the higher income person are four times greater. A proportional tax is also called a *flat tax*. With a flat tax, as a person's income goes up, the person's income tax goes up by the same proportion. Many state income taxes are proportional taxes.

In contrast, a **progressive tax** takes a higher proportion of income from higher income earners than from lower income earners. For example, suppose a person with an annual income of $25,000 pays a tax rate of 20 percent ($25,000 x .20 =$5,000) while someone earning $100,000 a year pays a 40 percent tax rate on their income ($100,000 x .40 = $40,000). In this case, the person with the higher income pays a tax of $40,000, and the person with the lower income pays $5,000. As a result, the individual whose income is four times greater pays a tax that is eight times more. As someone's income goes up, the income tax goes up by a greater proportion.

The federal income tax is considered a progressive tax. In 2002, people earning between $25,000 and $49,999 annually paid 7.0 percent of their income in taxes. In the same year, people earning between $100,000 and $499,999 paid 18.1 percent of their income in taxes.

Check Your Understanding

In most states, citizens must pay a sales tax on some or all items that they buy. Is a sales tax a progressive or a proportional tax?

_____

Explain your answer.

_____

_____

212   **11. proportional tax   12. progressive tax**

Does a higher income person sacrifice less when paying a dollar of tax than someone with a lower income? Economists don't know the answer to this question, because they can't measure each person's subjective value of a dollar. A person's subjective value of money is how highly a person values money. Logic would predict that a person with a low income would place more value on a dollar than a person with a high income because he or she does not have a lot of money and needs to be careful about its use. However, this is not always the case. Some people who are rich are also greedy and want to continue to acquire money because they place a lot of value in merely having money.

Different answers to this question often lead people to disagree about the desirability of a proportional or progressive tax. What's more, people disagree about which type of tax would promote more growth in our economy. Advocates of the ability-to-pay principle would argue that when you tax the poor, you take away necessities because the poor use a greater amount of their income to pay for necessities, while taxing higher income earners may take away only luxuries.

In addition to proportional and progressive taxes, there is also a **regressive tax**. With a regressive tax, the percentage of income paid in taxes decreases as income increases. A regressive tax takes a higher percentage of taxes from low-income persons than from high-income persons. Sales taxes are regressive. For example, consider the situation in which a low-income family and a high-income family each buy a $1,000 refrigerator with a sales tax of 8 percent. They both pay an $80 sales tax, but the $80 represents a higher percentage of the low-income family's total income than it does of the higher-income family's income.

Characteristics of a Good Tax

It is important for both citizens and their elected representatives to understand the characteristics of a good tax, regardless of their general views of taxation. There are five characteristics of a good tax.

- A good tax is efficient to collect. The government should not have to spend too much money to collect the tax.
- Government must provide a good reason for imposing a tax. Taxpayers must know what purpose their taxes will serve.
- A tax must treat taxpayers fairly.
- A tax must be certain. Taxpayers must know when a tax is due, exactly how much it will be, and how to pay it correctly.
- Paying a tax must be simple and convenient for the taxpayer.

Check Your Understanding

Briefly explain the following types of taxes.

Progressive tax

_____

_____

Regressive tax

_____

_____

Proportional tax

_____

_____

Adults' Views on Taxes

Interview three adults to find out their views on the pros and cons of proportional, progressive, and regressive taxes. Be prepared to describe the taxes if adults are unsure of the differences. Record their answers below and on an additional sheet of paper, if needed.

_____

_____

_____

_____

_____

Debt and Deficits

Citizens should be able to debate the proper role of government as budgets are prepared at the federal, state, and local levels. A government budget is a financial plan that summarizes expected income and expenses for an upcoming fiscal year. When anticipated income equals anticipated outlays, the budget is balanced. When budget expenses exceed income, the difference is a deficit. When income is greater than expenses, the difference is a surplus.

For the past 30 years, federal budget deficits have been the rule rather than the exception. The continued economic expansion in the late 1990s did manage to produce consecutive years of budget surpluses. Why are economists and policymakers so concerned about the deficit? What is the relationship between annual budget deficits and the *national debt*?

The **national debt** is the cumulative sum of all federal government borrowing used to finance annual deficits. The debt includes money the government owes U.S. citizens and businesses, foreign lenders, and even itself. In early November 2006, the national debt exceeded $8.6 trillion. In January 2015, it was $10.6 trillion. But this figure does not tell the entire story.

There are two types of national debts. One is the gross debt, which is the total of all the federal government's IOUs. However, some of these obligations are simply owed by the federal government to one of its agencies. For example, suppose the Air Force keeps $1 million of its budget in Treasury bonds. The million dollars will be carried on the government's books as an addition to the national debt. It's somewhat like money that one member of your family might borrow from another. The publicly held debt is the gross debt minus the amount government agencies have invested in government securities. These numbers have renewed an economic debate that has been going on for many years. Some economists argue that a properly managed national debt can benefit the economy. Others maintain that the burdens of the government's debt outweigh any advantages.

The federal budget provides an annual plan for government income and expenses.

14. national debt

Figure 12-3: Gross Federal Debt as a Percent of Gross Domestic Product (GDP) (1940–2005)

Check Your Understanding

Examine the graph in Figure 12-3, and then answer these questions. You may give approximate percentages.

1. The highest percentage of federal debt occurred just after World War II in 1945. What was the approximate federal debt as a percentage of GDP in that year?

_____

2. Federal debt was lowest as a percentage of GDP in 1980. What was the approximate percentage?

_____

3. What was the federal debt as a percentage of GDP in 2005?

_____

Justification for Federal Deficits and the National Debt

Those who defend the government's debt and budget deficits usually make the following two points.

- The national debt is not as large as it seems. To a family on an annual income of $20,000, a $20,000 debt represents an entire year's income. Repaying such a loan might be more than it could handle. To another family, earning $200,000 a year, a $20,000 debt repaid over a period of years is not likely to be much of a burden. When compared to the nation's production, the national debt was less of a burden in the early 2000s than it was during the years immediately following World War II. See the graph in Figure 12-3.
- When our economy is sluggish or declining, the budget deficit might increase total spending in the nation. This can occur if the government borrows and spends dollars that people have saved but that businesses are not investing.

Criticism of Federal Deficits and the National Debt

Many economists worry about deficits for the following reasons.

- Annual interest payments on the national debt have been a large, growing portion of the federal budget. Just to pay the interest on the national debt in the 2007 federal budget, $247.3 billion was needed. Unless budget deficits fall, interest payments will continue to rise in the future.
- Large deficits might lead to higher interest rates. To cover its deficits, the government can borrow money from the same places that businesses borrow: banks, corporations, and foreign lenders. The cost of the loans in the form of interest is a price just like other prices. If government borrowing adds significantly to the demand for available funds, interest rates might increase.
- Deficits may reduce private investment. When government borrows to finance its deficits, it can take funds that businesses could have used to invest in factories and equipment. Less investment in plants and equipment means that fewer new jobs will be created.
- Deficits may trigger inflation. A government may simply print money to finance its deficits or repay its debts. This would increase the amount of money faster than the supplies of goods and services that people spend money on. Inflation would result.

215

- Gross debt as a percent of gross domestic product is not a problem. While those who worry about the debt agree that it doesn't represent as large a percentage of the GDP as it once did, they are concerned about its sharp rise in recent years. Borrowing to finance World War II was justified, they say, but no such crisis exists today. So the government should live within its means.

Individuals are often taught at a young age that debt is not a good thing. We are told to "pay our way" and to stay out of debt. Being debt-free is looked upon as the best fiscal practice. However, the federal government is different. It controls the money supply and can print money if necessary. The federal government can also finance its deficit by selling Treasury bonds. Individuals are not in charge of the money supply, and they certainly cannot finance their debts by selling bonds. It is important to look at the differences between individual debt and government debt when forming an opinion on government deficits and the national debt.

Analyzing Views on Deficits

 Look through newspapers, newsmagazines, or on the Internet for an editorial or opinion column on federal deficits or the national debt. Summarize the author's position below.

_____

_____

_____

Summary

People debate the proper role and size of government in our free market economy. The federal government has assumed a referee role in the economy with respect to establishing and enforcing private property rights and the law, dealing with external costs and benefits, ensuring market competition, and protecting consumers. The federal government also has taken on the management tasks of stabilizing the economy, promoting economic security, and providing public goods and services.

Spending by the federal government has grown along with the economy. The federal government spends money on such items as direct benefits to individuals, national defense, interest on its debt, and grants to states and localities. It receives income from personal income taxes, social insurance taxes, corporate income taxes, and miscellaneous taxes, such as sales taxes.

Taxes can be levied according to the benefits-received or the ability-to-pay principle. Taxes can be proportional, progressive, or regressive, depending on whether the rate of tax remains constant, increases, or decreases as income rises. Federal income taxes are progressive, social insurance taxes are proportional, and sales taxes are regressive. The relative importance of the various federal taxes has changed over the years. While personal income taxes have remained stable as a percent of the federal budget, social insurance taxes, primarily for Social Security and Medicare, have grown rapidly.

For many years, the federal budget experienced deficits. Because of these continual deficits, or borrowing, the federal or national debt increased. The yearly deficits and rising debt worry many people for various reasons, while others offer reasoned defenses of deficits and the debt.

Looking Ahead

This chapter mentioned that governments collect money to finance their spending. What is money, and where does it come from? How do banks create money? What is monetary policy and how does it work? You'll find answers to these and other questions in the next chapter.

Notes

Money and Financial Institutions

Read to Find Out

As you read this chapter, look for answers to the following questions:

What is money? What are the functions of money?

What kinds of money are used in the United States?

What services do banks and other financial institutions provide?

How do banks "create" money?

What are the roles and responsibilities of the Federal Reserve System?

Why does the value of money change?

What is inflation, and how are people affected by it?

Mark to Remember

* *This is important.*

? *I have a question about this.*

! *This is a surprise.*

Why It Matters

It is said that money is the oil that keeps our economic engine running smoothly. Historically, this has not always been the case in the United States. Until the ratification of the U.S. Constitution in 1790, the various states each had their own kind of money. Some bankers were not always honest. We did not have a national central bank until 1913. Today, things are much different. Banks must meet high standards before they can operate. Most of our bank accounts are insured against loss. We have a national central bank, called the Federal Reserve. Today, monetary policy is effective in maintaining economic stability. A knowledgeable citizen has the responsibility to understand how our monetary system functions.

Money and Financial Institutions

Building On What You Know

Money is a favorite topic of discussion among many people. While people don't talk about how much money they have because it seems impolite, they do discuss other money-related matters. They talk about their banks' lending policies. They discuss the interest rates they pay on loans and the interest rates they receive on their savings. Most people are concerned about inflation and its impact. As a consumer and saver, it is important that you become familiar with and understand money and banking in our economy.

When the English colonists first settled in the New World, they brought a few of the pounds, shillings, and pence they had used for money at home. It didn't matter, though, because the American Indians weren't interested in exchanging food or furs for odd pieces of paper or metal. The Indians were, however, willing to swap or barter. As you have learned, barter, the exchange of one good or service for another, can be complicated and inconvenient.

The many problems associated with barter in the Massachusetts Bay Colony led the early colonists to use wampum. Wampum, a form of money used by American Indians in the 1640s and earlier, consisted of certain black or white seashells. Black shells were worth twice as much as the white shells. Colonists and Native Americans both accepted wampum in payment for anything they had to sell. Those who had to have English money could purchase it at the rate of six white shells to the penny.

The Functions of Money

While we might think of seashells as an odd sort of money, wampum was as useful to the people of that time and place as the dollar is in today's economy. Was wampum money? It was. It met the definition you already know. Money is anything that is generally accepted as payment for goods and services, as you learned in Chapter 2.

Some people define money by saying that "money is what money does." This is not a good economic definition, but does suggest that money serves several functions by providing (1) a generally accepted medium of exchange, (2) a measure of value, and (3) a store of value.

Pause to Remember

In Chapter 2, you read about the functions of money. You will learn more in this chapter. Write what you remember about the functions of money on the lines below.

Medium of exchange

_____

_____

Measure of value

_____

_____

Store of value

_____

_____

A Medium of Exchange

Money is a medium of exchange because sellers will part with things in exchange for money knowing that it can be used to purchase other goods and services. When people agree on the value of money, it becomes a medium, a means, of exchange. From earliest times, precious metals such as gold, silver, and copper have been the most popular forms of money. Still, they were not the only forms. Just as certain American Indian tribes used shells, other peoples accepted things like tobacco, fishhooks, and whales' teeth as money.

Almost anything can serve as money. As a practical matter, however, whatever is chosen should have the following qualities:

- **Stability.** The value of money should be nearly the same today as it is tomorrow. People living in societies in which the value of money fluctuates widely save money in hopes that its value will increase, or they spend money immediately thinking it will be worth less tomorrow. Either can be harmful to the economy.
- **Portability.** Money has to be small and light enough for people to carry. Bowling balls, for example, would be impractical as money.
- **Durability.** The material chosen must have a reasonable life expectancy, especially the material for paper money. For that reason, most countries use high-quality paper. U.S. currency actually contains cloth fibers, which is why it doesn't disintegrate if you accidentally put it in the washing machine.
- **Uniformity.** Equal denominations of money should have the same value. People could become confused if some quarters or dollar bills were worth more than others.
- **Divisibility.** One of the principal advantages of money is that it can be divided into parts. In other words, making change for a dollar is easy; making change for a bowling ball is not.
- **Recognizability.** Money should be hard to copy and easy to recognize for what it is. The quality of the paper and intricate engravings make paper money extremely difficult to counterfeit. The designs and stamping process of U.S. coins also make them hard to counterfeit.

A Measure of Value

Money enables us to state the price of something in terms that everyone can understand. One can say that a new pair of jeans sells for $35. This is far simpler than figuring out how much milk, meat, or sweatshirts one could barter for a pair of jeans. Money allows you and your employer to agree on a wage, and it lets you compare the value of a new basketball to a new pair of athletic shoes. Money indicates the relative value of products and resources.

A Store of Value

After accepting a money payment, one can either spend it or set it aside for use at a later time. Most people will put money they do not intend to spend right away in a bank rather than a desk drawer where it could be stolen or destroyed by fire. The function of money as a store of value means that you can keep it to use sometime in the future.

Apply Your Understanding

Why wouldn't soccer balls be a good form of money?

_____

_____

Why might small precious stones be a good form of money?

_____

_____

221

Functions of Money

Which function of money does each action represent?

1. Putting loose change in a piggy bank   _____

2. Buying a hamburger   _____

3. Opening a savings account   _____

4. Learning that the price of a used car you want to buy is $5,000   _____

5. Buying the used car you want   _____

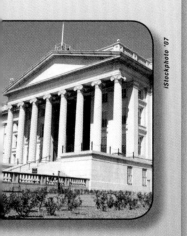

iStockphoto '07

Treasury, Federal Reserve, and Secret Service Issue Report on High Use, Low Counterfeiting of U.S. Currency Abroad

The following is from a press release issued by the Federal Reserve Board on October 25, 2006.

The Treasury Department, the Federal Reserve Board, and the U.S. Secret Service issued their third collaborative report on the use and counterfeiting of U.S. currency abroad. The report revealed that while more than half of the circulated U.S. banknotes are held in other countries, counterfeiting incidents remain low. [A banknote is paper currency.]

"People all over the world look to American currency for safety and security," said U.S. Treasurer Anna Escobedo Cabral. "I am pleased to learn that while counterfeiters may try to undermine the integrity of our money, American vigilance has upheld its reliability."

Residents of countries with unpredictable political and economic conditions have used U.S. currency as a means of reliability for decades. The report estimated that about $450 billion of the $760 billion in circulation as of December 2005 is held abroad.

The international popularity of U.S. currency makes it an obvious target for counterfeiters. But the report estimated that of U.S. notes in circulation abroad and at home, only about one in 10,000 is counterfeit.

Additionally, the introduction of the new currency design starting in 1996 and related educational outreach around the world made counterfeit detection easier.

The Money Supply

The **money supply** is the total amount of money in circulation within a country at some time period. Exactly how much this is depends on how the money supply is defined. If you thought that coins and paper currency were part of the total U.S. money supply, you would be correct. Currency can be used to purchase anything offered for sale, although sales of expensive items like sound systems and dishwashers are more likely to be paid for by check than with cash. Since, in most instances, checks are as acceptable as cash, they are included in the money supply. In the money supply, checking accounts are called *demand deposits.*

The table in Figure 13-1 summarizes the U.S. money supply in December 2005. It is called M1. You can think of M1 as Money 1. M1 consists of currency, traveler's checks, demand deposits, and other checkable deposits—the most liquid forms of money. However, the money supply includes other categories of money as well. These are referred to as M2 and M3. M2 monies are less liquid than MI, and M3 includes the less liquid forms of money.

Figure 13-1: Measuring the Money Supply—M1, M2, M3
(December 2005, billions of dollars)

M1, Total	**1,369.0**
Currency	723.8
Traveler's checks	7.3
Demand deposits	321.0
Other checkable deposits	316.9
M2, Total	**6,680.6**
M1	1,369.0
Small savings deposits	973.7
Passbook and money market savings deposits	3,620.5
Mutual fund money market accounts	717.4
M3, Total	**10,169.4**
M2	6,680.6
Institutional money market accounts	1,136.2
Large savings deposits	1,359.4
Eurodollars	430.2
Other	563.0

Source: *Economic Report of the President, 2006*, Tables B-69 and B-70.

Check Your Understanding

Study Figure 13-1. Which is largest—M1, M2, or M3?

_____

Why is it largest?

_____

_____

In which of the three segments of the money supply do you have money? Check all that apply.

M1 _____

M2 _____

M3 _____

M1

Currency consists of paper money and coins. Currency is legal tender. This means the law requires that it be accepted in payment of a debt. The term *hard currency* refers to paper money that is widely accepted and easily exchanged for the currency of another country. For example, American dollars are considered hard currency, but Russian rubles aren't because the value of the ruble is considered unstable. Currency in the United States consists only of paper money and coins issued by the federal government.

Traveler's checks are sold in a variety of denominations by banks, travel agencies, and other businesses servicing the tourist industry. In addition to the face amount of the check, buyers may be charged a fee for issuing the checks. Traveler's checks are popular with travelers because they can be replaced if lost or stolen.

Demand deposits are checking accounts held by the public at commercial banks. They are called demand deposits because the money in them is available "on demand" by writing a check. The amount of checks that people can write depends on the amount of money on deposit in their checking accounts. Debit cards serve the same function as checks.

Like commercial banks, savings and loan associations, savings banks, and credit unions also provide checking accounts for their depositors. Total deposits in those accounts are classified as "other checkable deposits."

Credit cards are not considered money, even though they are used frequently to make purchases. Credit cards are short-term loans from a bank or financial institution, and these loans must be repaid in a lump sum or in installments with interest.

Economists define **near monies** as assets that can easily be converted into cash, such as savings accounts. Although near monies are not included in M1, they are counted in the two other measures of the money supply, M2 and M3.

M2

M2 consists of M1 plus savings accounts, money market accounts, certificates of deposit, and mutual fund money market accounts. The funds in M2 can be converted to cash relatively easily.

M3

M3 includes everything in M2 (and thereby M1) plus large-denomination ($100,000 and above) savings accounts, certificates of deposit held by private institutions, Eurodollars (money issued by the European Union), and other large financial assets. As of March 23, 2006, the Federal Reserve no longer publishes M3 information.

Money has become more complex and sophisticated than just currency. Today, most money consists of electronic entries in accounts stored on banks' computers. But even "electronic money" is changing as people look for ways to use their computers to exchange with one another. For example, banks and businesses have teamed up to develop computerized payment systems. Known as e-billing, you can receive your bills online, and then pay your bills through online payment services offered by your local bank or other institutions with such services. Through e-billing and electronic payment, no actual currency has exchanged hands, but money has been transferred.

Think Critically

Why would the accuracy of the money supply be distorted if credit card transactions were counted as money?

_____

_____

_____

224

2. currency   3. demand deposits   4. near monies

Such change shows that money is continuing to evolve as people look for better ways to exchange with one another. No matter what form money takes, however, it is always a medium of exchange, a store of value, and a measure of value.

The Money Supply

Indicate whether each of the following is M1, M2, or M3.

Your checking account   _____

Your savings account   _____

Your traveler's checks   _____

Euros you buy for a trip to Italy   _____

Your $20 bill   _____

The Development of Banking

Demand deposits and other checkable deposits account for the largest share of the nation's money supply, and most originate from financial institutions called banks. While there are different kinds of banks—such as commercial banks, savings and loans, credit unions, and savings banks—all banks safeguard funds for people who have no immediate need for the money, pay interest on those funds, and lend them to borrowers.

The Middle Ages

The development of our banking system began in Europe during the Middle Ages. The major forms of early banking did not pay interest, but merely stored money for safekeeping. Gold and silver coins were inconvenient to carry and likely to be stolen. To make business transactions safer and more convenient, people began depositing their coins with local goldsmiths, who gave them written receipts in exchange. People accepted the receipts because they knew they could present them at any time and redeem their deposit. They also discovered that merchants often accepted the goldsmiths' receipts in payment for goods and services. In effect, goldsmiths became the first bankers. As the use of receipts spread, the earliest form of paper money in Western Europe came into being.

Banking Today

In the Middle Ages, merchants had to depend on the honesty of the goldsmiths to safeguard their deposits. Today, the state and federal governments regulate and supervise the banking industry. Federal law defines a **bank** as a financial institution that accepts demand deposits and makes commercial loans. Technically speaking, commercial banks fall within that definition and are, therefore, banks. Savings and loans, savings banks, and credit unions provide financial services to consumers, rather than business firms, and for that reason are

iStockphoto '07

Check Your Understanding

In your own words, explain how paper money originated.

_____

_____

_____

5. bank

Apply Your Understanding

Suppose you were given a gift of $500, and you decide to open a bank account. Write three questions you will ask the banker before you open your account.

1. _____

   _____

2. _____

   _____

3. _____

   _____

Think Critically

What would happen if all customers wanted to withdraw all of the money they had on deposit in banks on the same day?

_____

_____

Do you think fractional reserve banking provides enough security to avoid a collapse of banking should there be a "run on banks" by customers wanting to withdraw their money?

_____

Why or why not?

_____

_____

_____

_____

classified as thrift institutions—institutions where "thrifty" folks deposit their money. As a practical matter, however, most people today say "bank" when they speak of any financial institution that provides the following services:

- **Accepting and holding deposits.** People deposit their savings in banks and thrifts because they know their money will be returned when they want it. In addition to the physical protection against fire and theft, banks and thrifts offer deposit insurance, which guarantees savings or checking accounts up to a value of $250,000 per account.
- **Making loans.** A main function of banks and thrifts is to act as financial intermediaries, or a market to coordinate lenders and borrowers. They do this by transferring money from depositors (those wishing to save money for future use) to borrowers (those wanting money to spend now). Banks and thrifts do this by making loans to businesses and consumers. This vital financial service also earns money. Interest from loans is one of the principal sources of income for banks and thrifts. In turn, such loans help businesses meet current bills and finance expansion. Loans also help consumers enjoy goods and services immediately while paying for them with future earnings.
- **Collecting and transferring funds.** Managing checking accounts for their customers is a major responsibility of most banks and a great convenience for businesses and individuals alike.

Fractional Reserve Banking

Originally, a goldsmith's receipts were fully backed by gold. That is, the receipts represented a specific amount of gold in storage. In time, however, goldsmiths noticed that on most days, the gold that people withdrew was less than the amount deposited. Secure in the knowledge that depositors were not likely to ask for all their gold at the same time, the goldsmiths began to lend portions of their deposits to borrowers for a fee called interest. As you learned in Chapter 6, interest is income earned from allowing someone else to use your financial capital. Simply stated, interest is the price of borrowing money. Goldsmiths lending portions of their deposits was the beginning of what we now call *fractional reserve banking*. **Fractional reserve banking** means that banks withhold a percentage, or fraction, of their depositors' money and are able to lend the remainder of the deposits. Since goldsmiths' receipts were a form of paper money, goldsmiths' loans had the effect of increasing the money supply.

Banks Create Money

Like the medieval goldsmiths, modern banks make loans and create money. Let's examine how this happens.

Banks cannot lend all the money entrusted to them because depositors have the right to withdraw their funds at any time. However, experience has shown that on most banking days, deposits are greater than withdrawals. For this reason, banks can lend a substantial portion of their deposits and still meet withdrawal demands. As an added measure of safety, however, banks keep a portion of their deposits on hand. These funds are known as the bank's reserves.

The amount of reserves that banks are required to keep is their *reserve ratio*. The **reserve ratio** is the percentage of total deposits held in reserve by a bank. The higher the reserve ratio, the less a bank can lend, and vice versa. For example, with $1 million in deposits, and a reserve ratio of 15 percent, a bank would be required to hold $150,000 in reserve. The remaining $850,000 would be available for loans. If the reserve ratio were 25 percent, then $250,000 would have to be held in reserve, and the bank's lending ability would be reduced to $750,000.

Required Reserves

A bank receives a deposit of $1,000. How much of the deposit will the bank have to keep in reserves at each reserve ratio?

Reserve Ratio	Required Reserves
10%	_____
20%	_____
30%	_____

If the reserve ratio becomes 35%, what size loan can the bank make on a new deposit of $2,000?

_____

Loans Increase the Money Supply

In most instances when a bank makes a loan, the money is credited to the borrower's checking account. For example, Dean's Jeans, Inc. does its banking with the Fourth National Bank. Last week, Dean's Jeans borrowed $30,000. At the time of the loan, Dean, the owner, received no currency. The $30,000 was simply credited to the store's checking account at the bank.

Checking accounts are included in the money supply. When Dean's Jeans received its $30,000 credit, the nation's money supply was increased by that amount. Where did the $30,000 come from? It came from the bank loan. While individual banks can add to the nation's money supply, the consequences of their individual actions are magnified many times by the banking system as a whole.

iStockphoto '07

Banks and credit unions provide people with a safe place to deposit their savings and to obtain loans to finance large purchases.

Pause to Predict

Loans are transactions in which people borrow money. How does borrowing increase the money supply?

_____

_____

_____

227

How Loans Become Additions to the Money Supply

As you read this description, follow along in the diagram in Figure 13-2. Uncle Walt deposited his tax refund of $10,000 into a new checking account at First National Bank. This represents an addition to the money supply. With a reserve ratio of 20 percent, the bank could lend as much as 80 percent, or $8,000, of Uncle Walt's deposit. That day, Wendy Wilcox borrowed the $8,000. The sum was credited to her checking account, while the remaining $2,000 of Uncle Walt's deposit was added to the bank's reserves.

For her part, Wilcox used the $8,000 to buy a car from the Gonow Auto Company. Gonow Auto deposited the $8,000 in its account at the Second National Bank. Second National loaned $6,400 of that amount (80 percent of $8,000) to the Sports Shop. The $6,400 was credited to the Sports Shop's account, and the balance of $1,600 was added to the bank's reserves.

The Sports Shop used the $6,400 to buy computers from Commendable Computers, which deposited this amount in its account at the Third National Bank. Let's freeze the action here and summarize what has happened.

Figure 13-2: How Loans Become Additions to the Money Supply

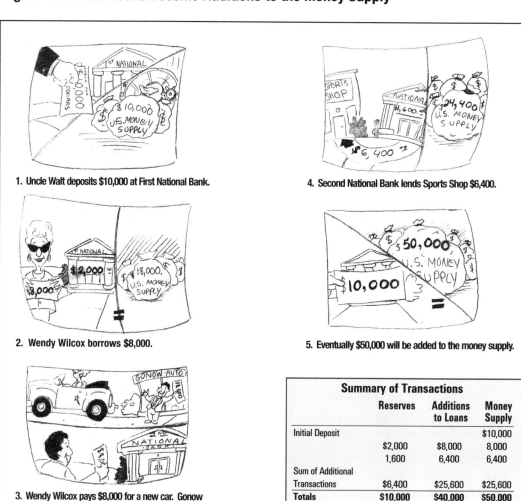

1. Uncle Walt deposits $10,000 at First National Bank.

2. Wendy Wilcox borrows $8,000.

3. Wendy Wilcox pays $8,000 for a new car. Gonow Auto deposits the money in Second National Bank.

4. Second National Bank lends Sports Shop $6,400.

5. Eventually $50,000 will be added to the money supply.

Summary of Transactions			
	Reserves	Additions to Loans	Money Supply
Initial Deposit			$10,000
	$2,000	$8,000	8,000
	1,600	6,400	6,400
Sum of Additional Transactions	$6,400	$25,600	$25,600
Totals	$10,000	$40,000	$50,000

As a result of the first deposit of $10,000 in the First National Bank, additional demand deposits of $8,000 and $6,400 were made in the Second National Bank and Third National Bank for a total of $24,400. Each new demand deposit added to the money supply. However, as you can see, the story is not likely to end there because successive deposits and loans of smaller and smaller amounts could continue until nothing was left to lend. Meanwhile, the money supply would have expanded even further.

We can calculate the total possible increase in the money supply, resulting from an initial increase in deposits by applying the *deposit multiplier*. The **deposit multiplier** is the total possible increase in the money supply calculated by dividing 100 by the reserve ratio (100/ reserve ratio = deposit multiplier). With a reserve ratio of 20 percent, the deposit multiplier is five (100 divided by 20 = 5).

By applying the deposit multiplier to Uncle Walt's $10,000 tax refund, we find that his deposit could lead to an expansion of $50,000 in the money supply. Had the reserve ratio been 10 percent, the deposit could have expanded the money supply by $100,000. Of course, loans need to be repaid, and as they are, the money supply is reduced in much the same way as it was expanded.

For example, suppose your Aunt Matilda withdrew $10,000 from her checking account. Her withdrawal reduced her bank's available reserves by that amount. Since the reserve ratio at the time Aunt Matilda made her withdrawal was 20 percent, the bank's lending ability was reduced by $8,000.

As a practical matter, people are making deposits and withdrawals constantly. Most of these activities cancel out one another, but gradual trends can and do develop. The money supply tends to grow when businesses are optimistic about the future and borrow to finance their growth. The money supply tends to shrink when businesses are cautious about the future and reduce their borrowing and spending.

Check Your Understanding

Define deposit multiplier *in your own words.*

_____

_____

_____

Now show deposit multiplier as an equation.

_____

The Deposit Multiplier

 Start by looking at the reserve ratios in the far left column. For each of those ratios, calculate the deposit multiplier in the second column. In the third column, indicate the potential expansion in the banking system money supply on an initial new loan of $2,500.

Reserve Ratio	Deposit Multiplier	Money Supply Expansion
5%	____	_____
10%	____	_____
25%	____	_____

The Federal Reserve System

Following a series of painful economic downturns between 1873 and 1907, a United States National Monetary Commission was established to recommend ways to improve the banking system. Its proposals led to the Federal Reserve Act of 1913 and the creation of the *Federal Reserve System.*

The Twelve Federal Reserve Districts

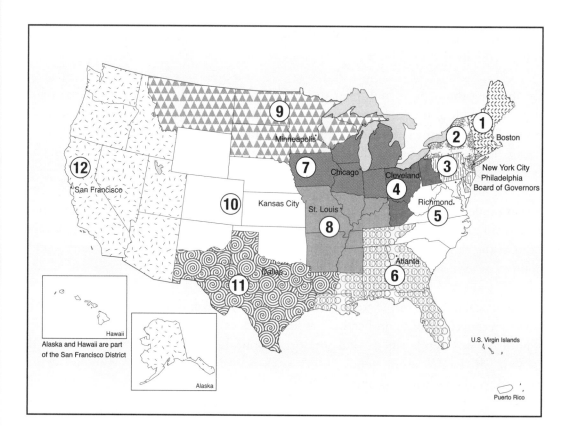

Show Your Understanding

On the map, trace the boundaries of the Federal Reserve District that serves you.

In what city is your Federal Reserve Bank located?

Structure of the Federal Reserve System

The **Federal Reserve System** is the nation's central bank. It is often referred to as the "Fed." It is responsible for issuing paper currency, collecting and clearing checks, holding the banking system's reserves, regulating the money supply, and, along with other agencies, supervising and regulating the nation's banking institutions.

The Federal Reserve System consists of 12 *Federal Reserve Banks* and their 25 branches, a Board of Governors, the Federal Open Market Committee, and three advisory committees.

- **Federal Reserve Banks.** The Federal Reserve System is built around 12 geographic districts, each of which is headed by a Federal Reserve Bank. Federal Reserve Banks (1) hold the reserve balances for the depository institutions (e.g., commercial banks, savings banks, and savings and loans) in their district, (2) furnish currency as needed by the districts' financial institutions, (3) collect and clear checks, and (4) provide banking services to the U.S. government.

9. Federal Reserve System

- **Board of Governors.** The Board of Governors establishes policies for the system. It consists of seven persons appointed for 14-year terms by the president of the United States and confirmed by the U.S. Senate. After serving a full term, a board member may not be reappointed. One of the governors is appointed to a four-year term as chair. Today's chairman is Janet Yellen, a faculty memeber at the University of California at Berkeley since 1980. Yellen succeeded long-time chairman Ben Bernanke. Governors have a great deal of independence because their terms of office are long, and they are not easily removed from office.
- **Federal Open Market Committee (FOMC).** The FOMC includes the seven members of the Board of Governors and the presidents of five of the Federal Reserve Banks. The committee's primary responsibility is to regulate the nation's money supply. It does this by increasing or decreasing the amount of reserves available to the banking system, as well as by setting interest rates. In the next chapter, we will describe how the FOMC employs open market operations to achieve these goals.
- **Advisory Committees.** Three committees provide special advice and assistance to the Board of Governors: (1) the Federal Advisory Council, composed of one commercial banker from each of the 12 Federal Reserve Districts, which offers advice on economic and banking matters; (2) the Consumer Advisory Council which advises the Board on matters concerning consumers and consumer credit; and (3) the Thrift Institutions Advisory Council—made up of representatives of savings and loan associations, savings banks, and credit unions—meets periodically to advise the Board.

Think Critically

Economists believe that it is important for the Federal Reserve System's Board of Governors to not be a part of, or show favoritism toward, any political party. What are two conditions of their appointment that help to assure that the governors remain nonpolitical?

1. _____

2. _____

The Fed in Your Own Words

Write a paragraph to explain the Federal Reserve System in your own words. Within the paragraph, answer these questions. (1) What is the purpose of the Federal Reserve System? (2) Where is the Fed located? (3) Who runs the Fed? (4) How are the Fed Governors appointed? (5) Why is the Fed important in your life?

_____

_____

_____

_____

_____

The Federal Reserve System is the central bank of the United States.

MISSION OF THE FEDERAL RESERVE SYSTEM

The Federal Reserve System is the central bank of the United States. It was founded by Congress in 1913 to provide the nation with a safer, more flexible, and more stable monetary and financial system. Over the years, its role in banking and the economy has expanded.

Today, the Federal Reserve's duties fall into four general areas:

- Conducting the nation's monetary policy by influencing the monetary and credit conditions in the economy to try to achieve maximum employment, stable prices, and moderate long-term interest rates
- Supervising and regulating banking institutions to ensure the safety and soundness of the nation's banking and financial system and to protect the credit rights of consumers
- Maintaining the stability of the financial system and limiting systemic risk that may arise in financial markets
- Providing financial services to depository institutions, the U.S. government, and foreign official institutions, including playing a major role in operating the nation's payment system

Source: The Federal Reserve Board (www.federalreserve.gov/generalinfo/mission/default.htm)

How the Federal Reserve System Functions

The Federal Reserve System performs the following functions.

- **Supplies the economy with cash.** The Fed sees to it that enough paper money and coins are in circulation to meet the public's demand. Just as you would go to your bank to withdraw or deposit cash, banks draw and deposit currency from their accounts with their District Reserve Bank. The process provides the economy with an *elastic currency*. An **elastic currency** is the supply of currency that expands and contracts with the needs of business. If you look closely at a piece of currency, you will find a letter and number designating the Reserve Bank that put it into circulation.

- **Processes checks and electronic transfer of funds.** When individuals, business firms, and others receive checks, they usually deposit them in their banks. There, the checks are credited to the depositors' accounts and passed along for collection from the institution on which they were drawn. Most checks drawn on banks other than the one in which they were deposited are presented to the District Banks for collection. Federal Reserve Banks process more than 25 billion checks each year. Electronic funds transfer (EFT) is a faster and safer method of making payments than cash or check. This service of the Fed transfers funds electronically from one person's or firm's account to another.

- **Holds reserves for depository institution.** All depository institutions (commercial banks, savings banks, savings and loan associations, and credit unions) must retain a percentage of their deposits as reserves. The reserves are held, along with other funds, in their accounts at the District Federal Reserve Bank.

Show Your Understanding

Underline the key sentence in each description of a Federal Reserve System function.

10. elastic currency

- **Serves as banker to the federal government.** The Federal Reserve Banks are the federal government's bankers. They receive payments from taxpayers, maintain the Treasury Department's "checking account," and issue and redeem government bonds and other securities.

- **Supervises and regulates banking institutions.** The Fed ensures the safety and soundness of the nation's banking and financial system, and it protects the credit rights of consumers. In addition, it sets limits on the amount of money that stockbrokers and banks may lend customers. It does this by setting minimum down payments that buyers need to pay toward the purchase of stock.

- **Regulates the money supply.** The Fed's most important responsibility is to regulate the nation's money supply. The next chapter describes how the Fed uses these powers to promote full employment and stable prices.

The Federal Reserve System is one of the most important economic institutions serving our market system. It is the banker for the federal government. In many ways, it is also the banker for commercial banks. Perhaps most importantly, the Fed controls the money supply of the United States with the goal of preventing both inflation and deflation.

About the Federal Reserve System

Indicate whether the statements about the Federal Reserve System below are true (T) or false (F).

___ The Federal Reserve System is the nation's central bank.
___ Federal Reserve Banks are located in 12 geographical areas of the United States.
___ Members of the Fed Board of Governors are elected officials.
___ The Federal Open Market Committee regulates the nation's money supply.
___ The Federal Reserve is the U.S. government's bank.
___ You can deposit your money in a Federal Reserve bank.
___ The Federal Reserve System processes checks.
___ The Federal Reserve System makes commercial loans.

The Changing Value of Money

You may have heard something like this statement before:

"When I was your age, money could buy a lot more than it can these days. Hot dogs, candy bars, and soft drinks all cost a nickel. Seems like you can't buy anything for a nickel anymore. As for quarters, well, you could see a movie or buy a loaf of bread or a gallon of gas for a quarter back then. Those were the good old days."

In fact, the dollar was worth more "in the good old days," and prices for most goods were a lot lower than they are today.

Check Your Understanding

According to the text, what are the three Fed functions that make it one of the most important economic institutions in our economy?

1._____

2._____

3._____

Purchasing Power of Money

Economists use the term *purchasing power* to describe the quantity and quality of goods and services people can buy with their money. Simply defined, **purchasing power** is the value of money to purchase goods and services. When prices increase, money cannot buy as much as in some previous time period. In this case, money's purchasing power has declined. When prices fall, the opposite occurs. Put another way, when prices rise, the value of money falls; when prices fall, its value rises. Since the 1970s, the United States has witnessed periods of purchasing power decline and has experienced some serious times of inflation. As you have learned, inflation is a general rise in overall prices. It is inflation and the accompanying decline in purchasing power of money that most concerns policymakers at the Federal Reserve.

The purchasing power of the dollar has been shrinking over the past century. This is illustrated in the table in Figure 13-3. In the table, positive price changes indicate that the purchasing power of money has decreased; when price changes are negative, the purchasing power of money has increased. As you can see, inflation was present in eight of the 10 decades in the 20th century. For example, prices rose 6.7 percent in the 1910–1919 decade. They rose 5.6 percent in the 1940-1949 decade. They rose significantly by 7.1 percent in the 1970–1979 decade. They rose only 2.7 percent in the five-year period from 2000 to 2005. You can also see that despite the general shrinkage in the value of the dollar, there were two decades of deflation in which the dollar's purchasing power increased: 1920–1929 and 1930–1939.

iStockphoto '07

The purchasing power of the U.S. dollar has been shrinking during the past century.

Apply Your Understanding

How does the information in Figure 13-3 explain that a dollar was worth a lot more in the good old days than it is now?

_____

_____

_____

_____

Figure 13-3: A Century of Inflation and Deflation

Decade	Change in Prices (Percent)
1900-09	0.8
1910-19	6.7
1920-29	-0.1
1930-39	-2.1
1940-49	5.6
1950-59	2.0
1960-69	2.3
1970-79	7.1
1980-89	5.5
1990-99	3.0
2000-05	2.7

Average annual rate of change in the year-to-year CPI.

Sources: *Historical Statistics of the United States,* Series E135 and *Economic Report of the President, 2006,* Table B-63.

11. purchasing power

Calculating the Effects of Inflation

 Below in the left column are three annual inflation rates. Indicate in the right column how much purchasing power will be lost in a year on the $300 you have hidden under your mattress.

Inflation Rate	Loss of Purchasing Power
5%	_____
7%	_____
8%	_____

Types and Causes of Inflation

Economists have identified two major types of inflation—*demand-pull* and *cost-push*.

Demand-pull inflation. A situation in which rising prices cause too much money "to chase" too few goods is called demand-pull inflation. When demand for goods and services increases faster than industry's ability to satisfy that demand, prices increase. During the Vietnam War in the late 1960s and early 1970s, for example, factories that might have been producing consumer goods turned instead to the production of goods for use in the war. Government spending for military goods increased the purchasing power of many Americans. The result was an increase in the demand for consumer goods and services at the very time industry's ability to satisfy that demand was being redirected to military goods. Since it was impossible to increase output to satisfy demand, prices rose.

Cost-push inflation. A situation of rising prices resulting from increases in the cost of production is called cost-push inflation. Cost-push inflation can be caused by one or more of the following: costs, wages, and monopoly power.

- *Increases in the cost of raw materials.* In 1974 and 1980, the Organization of Petroleum Exporting Countries (OPEC) restricted oil production. Gasoline shortages resulted, and prices of fuel, oil, and other energy sources rose. The United States also experienced significant natural gas and gasoline price increases in 2005 and 2006.

- *The wage-price spiral.* When labor unions win wage increases that outpace increases in productivity, management will often raise prices in order to maintain profits. With prices rising, other unions may ask for wage increases to keep up with the cost of living and so on in an inflationary spiral.

- *The price-wage spiral.* Business firms that have no fear of competition may increase prices. This, in turn, will trigger demands for wage increases to keep up with living costs, and industry will initiate another round of price hikes as it seeks to keep up with rising labor costs.

Effects of Inflation

Inflation affects people differently—some suffer, others benefit. Those most likely to suffer are people living on relatively fixed incomes, savers, lenders, and businesses.

iStockphoto '07

- **People living on relatively fixed incomes.** During periods of inflation, the cost of living increases. Therefore, it is necessary to earn more just to maintain your present living standard. How much of an increase is necessary? At least as much as the rate of inflation—the increase in the cost of living. In other words, if the cost of living increased by 10 percent in 2006, a person with a $40,000-a-year income in 2006 would have to earn $44,000 ($40,000 + 10 percent) in 2007 just to maintain the same purchasing power. Certain groups, such as those living on fixed retirement pensions, cannot increase their incomes enough to offset the effects of inflation. When this happens, their standard of living declines. To protect some people on fixed incomes, Social Security benefits are adjusted for inflation.

- **Savers.** Some people put their money into savings accounts or bonds that guarantee a fixed rate of return—interest. Unless the rate of return is at least as high as the inflation rate, the money returned to savers will purchase less than the sum in savings.

- **Lenders.** Those who lend money are in the same position as those who save. If inflation increases during the term of a loan, then the money paid when the loan comes due will be worth less than the original loan. An exception would be if the interest rate on the loan was greater than the inflation rate.

- **Business firms.** Business firms are hurt by inflation because it causes uncertainty and makes it hard for managers to predict future costs. It also raises production costs.

Those who benefit from inflation are those who can easily increase their incomes, borrowers, and government. Here are some reasons why.

- **Those who can increase their incomes.** Certain professions, industries, and labor groups find it easier to increase prices and wages during periods of inflation than at other times. If the increases are greater than the inflation rate, these people will be better off than before the run-up in prices. A case in point is the retail jewelry trade. During periods of inflation, the price of jewelry has generally increased faster than the cost of living. The result has been higher profit margins for jewelers.

- **Borrowers.** Individuals and firms that borrow during a period of inflation will be repaying money that is worth less at the end of the loan period than it was at the beginning. If the interest charged on the loan is less than the inflation rate, those who borrowed will benefit from the difference.

- **Government.** The federal government and several state governments collect graduated income taxes. This means the tax rate increases as one's income increases. During inflation, people tend to earn higher incomes, putting more taxpayers into higher tax brackets. In this way, people with significant increases in income may find their income taxes increase by a higher percentage.

Think Critically

Explain why this statement is true or false. "Inflation hurts everyone."

_____

_____

_____

_____

236

While the United States has experienced deflation, this has not been the case during the past 65 years. Inflation, particularly high inflation, has been the major concern of economists and policymakers. Inflation hurts more people than it benefits, and it makes economic decision making uncertain. There is ample uncertainty in a market economy. This is why policymakers, particularly at the Federal Reserve, maintain an ongoing concern about inflation.

Just because you have money does not mean that it will hold its value over time, although policymakers try to assure that it will. As you read or listen to the news, you will hear reports about prospective inflation. This kind of news is important; you can be assured that policymakers will be concerned about it and that the Fed will pay attention to it.

What Policy Would You Recommend?

Imagine that you have been appointed to the Federal Reserve's Board of Governors. You are informed that the economy is likely to experience significant inflation during the next year. What kind of policy would you consider and why?

_____

_____

_____

Compared to other items, jewelry may hold or increase its monetary value better over time.

iStockphoto '07

Summary

Money can be anything that is generally accepted as final payment for goods or services. It functions as a medium of exchange, a store of value, and a measure of value. Principal forms of money are currency, demand deposits (checking accounts), and other checkable deposits.

Financial institutions such as commercial banks, savings and loan associations, and savings banks are essential to the smooth operation of the U.S. economic system because demand deposits and other checkable deposits held by banks and thrifts make up the largest part of the money supply. These institutions also provide a safe place for the deposit of funds and serve as a source of loans and other financial services.

Because loans are typically added to demand deposits, the lending ability of banks serves to create money. How much money the commercial banks can create is limited by the reserve ratio, which determines the amount of money that a bank can lend at any particular point in time.

The Federal Reserve System is the nation's central bank. It provides banking services for financial institutions, supervises their activities, and regulates the money supply. It also acts as a bank for the federal government.

The "value of money" is really its purchasing power or the amount of goods and services it can buy. The purchasing power of money can increase, as it does during periods of deflation, and it can decrease, as it does during periods of inflation.

The causes of inflation are generally described as either demand-pull or cost-push. Demand-pull inflation is brought on by an excess of purchasing power that serves to drive up prices ("too much money chasing too few goods"). Cost-push inflation is brought about by rising production costs that feed upon one another. Although certain groups within the economy may benefit from the increasing prices associated with inflation, more people and the economy as a whole are likely to suffer.

Looking Ahead

In good times, jobs are plentiful and business profits are high. In bad times, quite the opposite happens. Jobs are difficult to come by, and business is slack. Chapter 14 focuses on these "ups and downs" in the economy and tells what government can do to promote the nation's economic health.

Economic Stability

Read to Find Out

As you read this chapter, look for answers to the following questions:

What major indicators do economists use to measure the health of the economy?

What are the characteristics of the gross domestic product?

What is unemployment, and what are the types of unemployment?

What are the tools of fiscal policy?

What are the tools of monetary policy?

What are the advantages and disadvantages of fiscal and monetary policies?

Mark to Remember

* *This is important.*

? *I have a question about this.*

! *This is a surprise.*

Why It Matters

People want to live in an economy that is stable with low unemployment and prices that do not change very much. Unemployment is devastating for individuals and families. People do not want to feel uncertain about their source of income. Stable prices allow people to plan their spending, from buying a house to saving for their children's education. We have excellent information about the performance of the economy in the United States. Economic indicators tell us what has happened and what is likely to happen. Policymakers pay close attention to levels of employment, potential inflation, and economic growth. The federal government, and particularly the Board of Governors of the Federal Reserve System, stand ready to make policy changes to assure the stability of our economy. The decisions made by policymakers affect every American citizen.

Chapter 14

Economic Stability

Building On What You Know

 You may have had the experience of your parent being laid off from a job because his or her company closed or downsized. During the time your parent was unemployed, your family probably had to give up buying things other than necessities because there was not enough income to afford extras. Yet news on television reported that the American economy was doing well, with the stock market going higher each week and inflation holding steady. How could the economy be strong while your family was suffering?

In Colorado, four farmers drink coffee together and quietly discuss how much longer they can survive financially. The drought has continued, and crop prices have slumped for the second straight year. Farm losses continue to mount. To have enough money to pay the mortgage on their land, each of these farmers is working a second job.

Meanwhile in California, three young owners of a technology firm are told by their accountant that the business they started three years ago is now worth more than half a billion dollars. The growth in Internet use and e-commerce has made these women

Figure 14-1: U.S. Business Cycle in the 20th Century

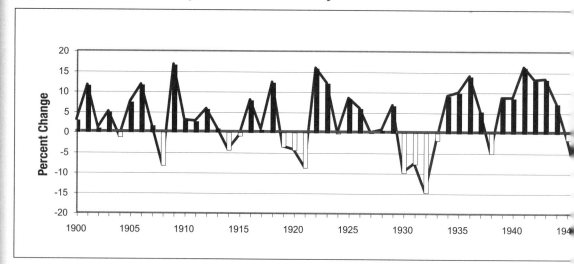

Percent change over previous year in real gross national product.
Source: Calculated from *Historical Statistics of the United States*, Series F-3, and *Economic Report of the President, 2003*, Table B-2

multimillionaires. They sip cappuccino and discuss whether they should retire immediately or wait until they are 40. Is the United States economy strong or weak? The answer to that question will always depend on individual circumstances, the region of the country, and a specific segment of the economy, such as farming.

Measuring Changes in the United States Economy

 The United States economy is in a constant state of change. Economists and business analysts study the U.S. economy very carefully. They look at **economic indicators**, measures of different parts of the economy that are used to determine what has happened and what is likely to happen in the economy. One indicator is the **business cycle**, a measure of recurring ups and downs in the level of economic activity in the economy over time. You'll study the business cycle next. Then you will examine four other indicators of economic performance: durable goods purchases, housing starts, jobless claims, and the index of leading economic indicators. Finally, you will learn about an indicator called the consumer price index (CPI). There are many other indicators that could be studied, but the business cycle, the four performance indicators, and the CPI will give you a good idea of what analysts study.

The Business Cycle

The graph in Figure 14-1, the U.S. Business Cycle in the 20th Century, shows the business cycle of the United States for the 100-year period 1900–2000. The business cycle provides a big-picture look at the economy over time. The business cycle measures the annual percentage changes in Real gross national product. *Gross national product* is somewhat different from *Gross domestic product,* which you studied previously. The term *real* means that the effects of inflation have been removed from the calculations.

Gross national product is the total market value of all final goods and services produced annually by American residents, whether these residents are located in the United States or in a foreign country. You may recall that gross domestic product measures the total market value of all goods and services produced within the boundaries of the United States. Gross national product includes income received by U.S. citizens who may be working in other countries. For example, a computer technician who is a U.S. citizen earning all her income in Germany would have her income counted in the GNP but not in the GDP.

Think Critically

Does it make sense to you that our national economy can be considered strong even if large groups of workers, such as auto workers or computer programmers, have been laid off and are not finding new jobs.

Why or why not?

_____

_____

_____

_____

Check Your Understanding

Look at the ups and downs of the business cycle over the 100 years shown in Figure 14-1. Write a one-sentence generalization about the business cycle over the time period.

_____

_____

_____

| 50 | 1955 | 1960 | 1965 | 1970 | 1975 | 1980 | 1985 | 1990 | 1995 | 2000 |

Year

1. economic indicators 2. business cycle 3. gross national product

241

Let's examine the business cycle more carefully. In Figure 14-1, you see ups and downs—cycles—in the percentage changes over time. The graph in Figure 14-2 shows the phases of a business cycle. It represents a very small section of the business cycle—a snapshot—from Figure 14-1. The graph in Figure 14-2 may be a two-year, three-year, or even five-year period. The level of business activity is measured on the vertical axis, with time shown on the horizontal axis. Through the middle of the cycle is an upward sloping line showing the growth trend of the economy. Basically, business activity cycles, fluctuates, around the growth trend line.

Figure 14-2: The Business Cycle

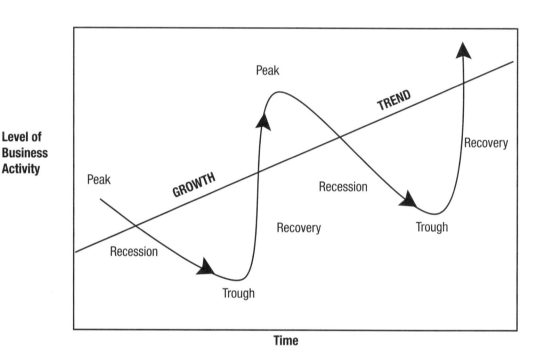

Show Your Understanding

Using a highlighter pen, trace the growth trend line. Draw a box around the peaks shown on the business cycle phase line. Circle the troughs on the phase line.

What is the period between a peak and a trough called?

_____

What is the period between a trough and a peak called?

_____

On the top side of the business cycle, you see the term *peak*. During a **peak** phase in the business cycle, business activity is at a temporary maximum, and the economy is close to full employment. Following a peak in the cycle, the economy often goes into what is called a *recession*. A **recession** is a period of time, six months or longer, during which total GNP output declines. Following a recession, the business cycle reaches a **trough**, the point at which output and employment reach their lowest level in the cycle. The trough phase in the cycle can be short or can last a long time. Following the trough, the economy experiences a *recovery* phase. During a **recovery**, output and employment expand toward full employment. Keep in mind that as a recovery continues, prices may begin to rise and inflation may set in.

Look at Figure 14-1 again for a moment. Note that there have been many ups and downs (cycles) of business activity during the hundred years shown in the figure.

4. peak   5. recession   6. trough   7. recovery

Studying the Business Cycle

Use information from Figures 14-1 and 14-2 to respond to the questions below.

1. Between 1900 and 1950, how many major troughs with percentage changes of -5 or more occurred? _____

2. Between 1950 and 2000, how many major troughs with percentage changes of -5 or more have occurred? _____

3. Look at the period 1929 to 1934. Describe this period in your own words.

_____

_____

4. Describe the period from 1939 to 1945. _____

_____

5. What happened to economic activity after 1945 and the end of World War II?

_____

_____

6. Contrast the changes in economic activity from 1900 to 1950 with the

period from 1950 to 2000. _____

_____

_____

7. Describe what happened in the economy between about 1990 and 2000.

_____

_____

Four Important Indicators

Economists and business analysts are like medical doctors. Just as medical doctors monitor the health of a person in different ways, these analysts monitor the health of the economy. They know there are multiple causes of strength or weakness in an economy, and they want to learn what is happening. Here are four important indicators that analysts study and that are often reported in business news reports in the media.

Durable goods orders. A **durable good** is a consumer good that is expected to last three years or more. Durable goods include household appliances, automobiles, and recreational vehicles. The index of durable goods orders looks at the backlog of orders. A backlog signals that demand for durable goods is strong and that the economy is likely to continue expanding.

Show Your Understanding

For each of the economic indicators described in this section, underline the sentence that will best help you remember the significance of the indicator.

8. durable good

Housing starts. A house is usually the most expensive purchase a consumer makes. A measure of the economy's health is the number of housing permits being issued, because that number indicates how many new houses are being built. If the economy is strong and growing, there is usually an increasing demand for new housing.

Jobless claims. People who become unemployed file claims to receive unemployment insurance in their states. These are called jobless claims. If jobless claims are declining, there is low unemployment. Decreasing jobless claims is a sign the economy is growing. If jobless claims are increasing, unemployment is increasing. This is a sign the economy could be moving toward recession. The graph in Figure 14-3 shows the unemployment rate in the United States between 1960 and 2005.

Figure 14-3: Unemployment Rate, 1960–2005

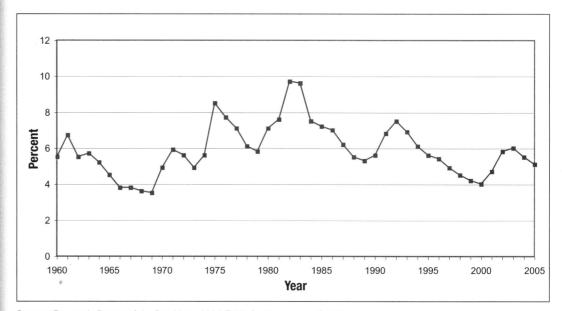

Source: *Economic Report of the President, 2006,* Table B-42; percent of civilian labor force.

Check Your Understanding

Explain in your own words why economic indicators help economists determine the health of the economy.

Durable goods

_____

_____

Housing starts

_____

_____

Jobless claims

_____

_____

Unemployment Since 1960

Study Figure 14-3 to answer the questions below.

1. During what year was the unemployment rate the lowest?

_____

2. During what year was the unemployment rate the highest? _____

3. Describe the unemployment rate between 2000 and 2005.

_____

_____

Index of leading economic indicators. The Conference Board, a private business organization, has created the index of leading economic indicators, which looks at the economy's overall health. Three consecutive monthly increases in this index signal that the economy is growing. Three consecutive monthly decreases in the index are a sign of economic decline and a potential recession.

The Consumer Price Index

In Chapter 9, you learned that the GDP price deflator reduces current, or nominal GDP, into the GDP of a base year. When applied to the gross domestic product, the deflator changes GDP to real gross domestic product—GDP with the effect of inflation removed. Another index, called the *consumer price index*, functions somewhat like the GDP because it also has a built-in deflator. However, the **consumer price index** (CPI) is a separate index that measures the prices of a "market basket" of 300 specific goods that typical consumers purchase. The CPI has a current base period of 1982–1984 when it was 100. In 2004, the CPI was 188.9; in 2005 it was 195.3. This is a percentage change from 2004 to 2005 of 3.4 percent, a relatively low inflation rate (195.3 − 188.9 = 6.4 points; 6.4 ÷ 188.9 = 3.4 percent). According to the Bureau of Labor Statistics, as of the end of September 2006, the CPI was 1.3%, also a low inflation rate.

The CPI is considered a good measure of inflation in the economy because it is tied directly to common, everyday products people buy. The CPI affects many people. Federal government Social Security payments to retired persons are tied to the CPI. These payments increase when the CPI increases. Similarly, millions of unionized workers have cost-of-living adjustments in their collective bargaining contracts that are also tied to the CPI.

Now we turn to probably the most well-known, most talked about, and most useful economic indicator in our economy. It is the gross domestic product, which was introduced in Chapter 9.

The Gross Domestic Product

You learned previously that the gross domestic product (GDP) is the final value of all goods and services produced within the United States in a year. The GDP reveals much about the nation's economic health. If the U.S. GDP increases, Americans are producing more goods and services. If the GDP decreases, they are producing less. Economists, as well as government officials, news reporters, and business decision makers pay attention to the GDP. Because the GDP is mentioned so frequently in the news, it is important to know what it includes and what it omits.

Characteristics of the GDP

The GDP includes only final goods and services. To avoid overstating the GDP by counting the same item two or more times, only final goods are included. Suppose a bicycle manufacturer pays $300 for the parts and labor used in making a mountain bike. The manufacturer sells the bike to a bicycle shop for $400. The bike store sells the bike for $750. How much did the production of a single mountain bike add to the GDP? Since only final goods are counted, the answer is $750. The $300 paid to the parts suppliers and the $400 paid to the manufacturer were not added to the final price because the $750 includes these costs.

The GDP includes production only within our borders. The GDP does not include goods and services produced overseas, even by companies owned by U.S. citizens or firms. However, products produced in the United States by foreign firms are counted. So while a Hewlett-Packard computer assembled in Mexico is not counted in the GDP, a Honda produced in Ohio is included.

Inflation can distort the significance of growth in the GDP. When prices are rising, as occurs during periods of inflation, the GDP may increase even when the production of goods is unchanged. This is because the GDP is measured in terms of current prices. You learned that this is called nominal GDP.

To avoid these problems, economists adjust the GDP for changes in the price level. Note the two columns of GDP in the table in Figure 14-4. When an adjustment for inflation is made, the result is real GDP, or the GDP expressed in *constant dollars*. **Constant dollars** is the term used to reflect the changes in the purchasing power of the dollar from a base year. The base year is 2000 in Figure 14-4. Economists use constant dollars when comparing the nation's gross domestic product in different years.

Figure 14-4: Gross Domestic Product

Year	GDPC1	GDPR1
1960	$526.4	$2,501.8
1965	$719.1	$3,191.1
1970	$1,038.5	$3,771.9
1975	$1,638.3	$4,311.2
1980	$2,789.5	$5,161.7
1985	$4,220.3	$6,053.7
1990	$5,803.1	$7,112.5
1995	$7,397.7	$8,031.7
2000	$9,817.0	$9,817.0
2005	$12,479.4	$11,131.1

GDPC1 = Gross domestic product, billions of current dollars
GDPR1 = Gross domestic product, billions of 2,000 dollars
             (real gross domestic product)

Source: *Economic Report of the President, 2006*, Tables B-1 and B-2.
      Preliminary data for 2005.

10. constant dollars

GDP Since 1960—How Much Better Off?

The table in Figure 14-4 shows gross domestic product in current (nominal) prices and gross domestic product in 2000 (real) prices between 1960 and 2005.

1. By how many times did GDP increase in current (nominal) prices between 1960 and 2005? _____

2. By how many times did GDP increase in real (year 2000) prices between 1960 and 2005? _____

3. Which is a better measure of the growth of GDP since 1960? Explain.

_____

_____

_____

GDP does not account for population changes. The GDP is like a huge pie that contains everything produced in a year. The portion of that pie available to every American depends on the size of the GDP and the population that intends to consume that pie. Should the pie (GDP) grow by 5 percent, and the number of consumers increase by 10 percent, the amount of pie available to each person would decrease, if it were shared equally. Although the output of all goods and services (GDP) may increase in a given year, the income and output available per person may drop. Economists find it useful to use per capita GDP (GDP divided by the total population) to account for population changes.

Quality changes are not considered in GDP. Suppose you paid $500 for a bicycle last year, and the price of a similar bike was $500 again this year. The price is unchanged. However, the manufacturer may have lowered the bike's quality. The GDP does not always show these changes in quality because only price is taken into account. The opposite can be true, too, especially with products that use technology. A computer you buy today for $2,000 may have more power and be of higher quality than a computer purchased last year for $2,500.

Used goods are not included in the GDP. If you sold your old bike for $250, how much was added to the GDP? Zero. Only new goods are counted; used goods add nothing to the nation's current wealth. Used goods were accounted for when they were first sold as new products.

Unfortunately, harmful goods and services are included in the GDP. We cannot assume that the GDP is an agreed-upon measure of the nation's well-being. Some goods and services included may be useless or even harmful. For example, cigarettes cause lung cancer and other serious ailments, but they are added to the GDP along with fresh vegetables, medicine, and other beneficial items. Also, in producing the GDP, Americans pollute the air, water, and land. The costs of these harmful externalities are omitted from GDP. Money spent on illegally produced and sold goods like illegal drugs is also omitted.

Apply Your Understanding

The nominal GDP of the mythical nation of Xania is $2,500,000. Xania has a population of 5,000. What is the per capita GDP of Xania?

_____

Show the equation you used to calculate the per capita GDP.

_____

While the cost of a product may stay the same from one year to the next, the quality may not.

GDP does not include nonmarket production. If you mow a lawn and receive payment, your wages are included in the GDP, and your service is recognized as being part of the nation's product. If you mow your own lawn, however, your work is not recognized by the GDP figures. The same is true for the family that decides to care for preschool children at home rather than paying a day care provider. However, payments to a day care provider are included in GDP.

What's In, What's Out of the GDP?

Review the "Characteristics of the GDP" section to list three products or types of products that are included in the GDP and three that are not.

Included in the GDP

_____

_____

_____

Not Included in the GDP

_____

_____

_____

Think Critically

Is the household labor of a stay-at-home parent counted in the GDP?

_____

Do you think that household labor should or should not be counted in the GDP?

_____

Why?

_____

_____

_____

Despite its shortcomings, GDP is still the best indicator of what the United States economy produces each year, as well as an indicator of the economy's growth. How is such a huge, complex statistic calculated? Two approaches are used to calculate GDP: the expenditure approach and the income approach.

Calculating GDP: The Expenditure Approach

The GDP is calculated by a process called national income accounting. The largest and most difficult accounting job in the world, national income accounting, is done under the direction of the United States Department of Commerce.

The most common approach to determining GDP is called the expenditure approach. This approach adds together all final spending in the economy for a year. Here is the equation that shows the approach: **GDP = C + I + G + NX.**

Where: GDP = **Gross domestic product**
C = Consumption expenditures by household
I = Gross private domestic investment (spending for new capital goods, such as machinery, tools, and buildings)
G = Government purchases of goods and services
NX = Net exports (goods made in the United States and sold abroad minus goods made abroad and sold in the United States; i.e., exports minus imports)

Think back to the Circular Flow of Money, Resources, and Products in Chapter 12 for a moment. In that diagram, the three major spending groups in the economy were shown—households, businesses, and government. The table in Figure 14-5 shows the expenditure of the three spending groups in 2005, as well as net exports, which were negative. They were negative because people in the United States bought more goods from abroad than people in other countries bought from the United States.

Figure 14-5: GDP by Expenditure, 2005
(Billions of Dollars)

Consumer Spending	$ 8,745.7
Investment (Business Spending)	$ 2,105.0
Government Spending	$ 2,362.9
Net Exports	$ -726.5
Gross Domestic Product (GDP)	**$12,487.1**

Source: *Survey of Current Business, June 2006,* Table 1.1.5.
Bureau of Economic Analysis website.

Calculating GDP: The Income Approach

You learned from the Circular Flow diagram that spending results in income. Consumer spending results in income for businesses. Businesses, in turn, pay wages to households. Also, businesses use income to pay rent on property they occupy, and they pay interest on loans to financial institutions for money they borrow. As you know, businesses want to make profits. Profits are income to businesses. The equation for the income approach to calculating GDP is: **GDP = Wages + Rents + Interest + Profits.**

> Where: **GDP** = **Gross domestic product**
> Wages = Payments to employees, including benefits
> Rents = Payments for the use of property resources
> Interest = Payments for the use of capital
> Profits = Payments to owners of businesses

Simply stated, the income approach to calculating GDP shows the returns received by the four factors of production—land, labor, capital, and management. The return to land is rent. The return to labor is wages. The return to capital is interest. The return to management is profits.

Check Your Understanding

Study Figure 14-5. Imagine that in 2005, people in other countries bought $726.5 billion more in goods from the United States than Americans bought from other countries.

Change the Net Exports in the table to reflect this change. Then calculate the new total.

What would the new GDP total be?

In the income approach, wages paid to labor in households accounted for the largest percentage of GDP. According to the U.S. Department of Commerce, wages accounted for $7,119 billion, or 57 percent of income paid in 2005. As you know, consumer spending by households is the largest percentage of GDP when using the expenditure approach. If people become unemployed, they spend less and consumption spending decreases.

The expenditure approach to calculating GDP is more commonly used than the income approach. It is often favored because the accounting procedures to measure expenditures are more accurate than the procedures used to calculate the income approach.

Calculating Gross Domestic Product

Expenditure and income components of gross domestic product are listed below for a hypothetical year. Identify those that are expenditures and those that are income.

		Expenditure or Income?
Consumption expenditures by households	$ 8.500 trillion	_____
Wages	$ 9.100 trillion	_____
Gross private domestic investment	$ 2.100 trillion	_____
Rents	$ 1.600 trillion	_____
Government purchases of goods and services	$ 2.500 trillion	_____
Interest	$ 700 billion	_____
Net exports	$ -600 billion	_____
Profits	$ 1.100 trillion	_____

Using the above expenditures and incomes, show how GDP is calculated by the expenditure approach.

_____

Using the same information, show how GDP is calculated by the income approach.

_____

Unemployment

Becoming unemployed can be a troubling experience, as you learned at the beginning of this chapter. We are reminded of this statement with respect to unemployment: "When your neighbor loses his job, it's a recession; when you lose your job, it's a depression."

We noted that jobless claims are an important indicator in the economy. If people are jobless, they are unemployed. The **unemployment rate** is the number of people looking for work divided by the number of people in the labor force. The United States Department of Labor gathers unemployment information nationwide and gives it to its Bureau of Labor Statistics (BLS). The BLS then calculates the unemployment rate—the percentage of those in the labor force, over the age of 16, actively seeking work but unable to find jobs. Look back to the graph in Figure 14-3 for a moment. You will note that the unemployment rate in 2005 was close to 5 percent. This means that 5 percent of the labor force over the age of 16 (about 7 million people) was actively seeking work but unable to find it.

Some economists criticize the government's method of calculating unemployment because it fails to include "discouraged workers" in its data. Discouraged workers are those who have been without work for so long that they have simply stopped looking for work. For this reason, critics say, real unemployment may be far more serious than government statistics show. Others believe that the unemployment rate overstates unemployment because it includes individuals who say they are unemployed but who are not really motivated to find a job.

Occasionally, government statistics will show a large increase in total employment, but the unemployment rate will increase at the same time. How can that be? Remember that the unemployment rate is calculated by dividing unemployed workers by the total labor force. Even though employment has increased, the pool of available labor may have increased more substantially. Often, during a time of business expansion, discouraged workers will reenter the labor force, resulting in a temporary increase in the unemployment rate.

Types of Unemployment

The reasons people are unemployed vary depending on their motivations, their employment skills, their length of time in the labor force, available employment, and the general strength of the economy. Economists have identified four types of unemployment.

- **Frictional unemployment.** Temporary, unavoidable unemployment is described as frictional unemployment. There are always some people who are out of work for completely unavoidable reasons. For example, it takes time for workers to find a new job after they have left their previous employer. Until they actually start working again, they will be counted in government data as "unemployed." People entering the labor force for the first time, such as recent high school and college graduates, are considered to be unemployed until they find their first job.

Explain in your own words what this means: "When your neighbor loses his job, it's a recession; when you lose your job, it's a depression."

_____

_____

_____

iStockphoto '07

Unemployment may be far more serious than government statistics indicate due to the number of discouraged workers.

Show Your Understanding

In the paragraphs that describe the four types of unemployment, underline the sentence that will best help you remember the importance of each type.

- **Seasonal unemployment.** Seasonal employees are another category of workers. They spend a part of the year in voluntary unemployment. Waiters who earn their living at summer and winter resorts, for example, add to the unemployment statistics during the fall and spring months.

- **Structural unemployment.** When structural unemployment exists, there are jobs available, but individuals may not have the skills to fill those jobs. This mismatch between available jobs and existing skills results from technological and other changes in the economy. Beginning in the 1980s, overseas competition and innovations in technology changed the structure of large manufacturing. Factories substituted technology for labor and often were able to reduce the number of employees needed while maintaining or increasing output. The result was unemployment among skilled blue-collar workers. High-paying, computer-related jobs were available in other parts of the economy, but these workers were not trained to fill those positions.

Changing technology is not the only cause of structural unemployment. Long-term changes in consumer preferences or movement of jobs from one region or country to another can cause structural unemployment, even among skilled workers. Failure to acquire needed skills also keeps many on the unemployment rolls. Young high school dropouts make up a large portion of today's structurally unemployed.

- **Cyclical unemployment.** A downturn in the economy will cause cyclical unemployment, which is characterized by an economy-wide shortage of jobs. The recession phase of the business cycle is caused by declining demand for goods and services. That results in rising unemployment. Increases in business activity will eventually result in increasing employment.

Full Employment

Full employment does not mean the total elimination of unemployment. Frictional and structural unemployment are expected, and economists combine these two rates to derive what is described as the natural rate of unemployment, which is explained below.

When the actual rate of unemployment equals the natural rate, the economy is said to be at full employment. Some economists believe that the natural rate of unemployment represents the highest rate of employment that can be sustained without inflation.

In the past, the natural rate of unemployment was estimated at 5 to 6 percent of the labor force. However, in January 2000, unemployment dropped to about 4 percent, without significant inflation. Economists had to rethink their long-held assumptions about how low the natural rate of unemployment could drop. The combination of record-low unemployment and low inflation was generally attributed to increases in productivity throughout the economy, resulting largely from the introduction of new technology.

As you learned in Chapter 12, a management role of the federal government is to stabilize the economy. A major goal of policymakers is to achieve full employment without inflation. The Employment Act of 1946 states that the role of the federal government is "to foster and promote free competitive enterprise and the general welfare, conditions under which there will be afforded useful employment opportunities for those able, willing, and seeking to work, and to promote maximum employment, production, and purchasing power." To achieve these goals, the federal government relies on fiscal policy and monetary policy.

Apply Your Understanding

Describe the type of employment being experienced by the following persons.

1. A former steelworker whose job has been moved overseas does not pass a skills test for a computer programming job.

2. A summer camp counselor is looking for work in October.

3. A snowmobile salesman loses his job when an economic recession reduces the number of people shopping for snowmobiles.

4. A waitress who quit her job when she finished college is looking for a job as an accountant.

Fiscal Policy

 The Congress and the president of the United States are responsible for managing the nation's financial affairs. The president submits a budget to Congress for approval, and Congress authorizes spending. Congress also passes laws establishing taxes. Through *fiscal policy*—the use of government spending and taxation to stabilize the economy—the government can do more than provide basic services. It can also influence economic activity.

Suppose the economy is in a recession. This means consumers are spending less, and businesses are not investing in new facilities and equipment. In fact, businesses may even be laying off workers. As a result, GDP may be falling or growing too slowly to sustain full employment without inflation. If spending by consumers, businesses, and governments were to increase, GDP would increase.

Government can stimulate economic activity or increase demand for goods and services. What do the president and Congress use to stimulate the growth of GDP? They can lower taxes and continue to spend the same amount on government programs. They can increase government spending while keeping taxes about the same, or they can simultaneously increase government spending and reduce taxation. Increased government spending and/or tax reduction is referred to as expansionary fiscal policy.

When taxes are cut, individuals and businesses have more income to spend. As business and consumer spending (and therefore GDP) begin to increase, the economy will enter an expansion phase. Similarly, if the president and Congress increase government spending, the GDP increases.

A flow chart of expansionary fiscal policy is shown below.

Figure 14-6: Effects of Expansionary Fiscal Policy

Government Buys More Goods and Services

Business Earns More Profit and Hires More Workers

Businesses and Labor Have More Money to Spend

Business and Worker Spending Results in Business Hiring More Workers

This Leads to More Jobs and More Output (Increased GDP)

Pause to Predict

The president and Congress can "speed up" the economy by lowering taxes and spending more on government projects. How might they "slow down" the economy when inflation becomes a problem?

_____

_____

_____

253

Fiscal tools also can be used to slow the economy. For example, in a very strong economic recovery, prices may begin to increase at an alarming rate. To end inflation, the president and Congress can decide to use their fiscal powers. They can increase taxes, reduce government spending, or both. If they increase taxes, consumers and businesses would have less to spend. This reduces the total demand for goods and services and reduces the rate of inflation. Reducing government spending and/or increasing taxes is referred to as *contractionary fiscal policy.*

Flow Chart of Contractionary Fiscal Policy

Figure 14-6 is a flow chart of expansionary fiscal policy. On a separate sheet of paper, create a flow chart of contractionary fiscal policy. The first block of your chart should read, "Government Reduces Spending on Goods and Services." Save your chart.

iStockphoto '07

Close cooperation between the president and Congress is necessary to establish and carry out effective fiscal policies.

Show Your Understanding

In this section, "Criticism of Fiscal Policy," circle the statements that make an argument for fiscal policy. Underline the statements that make an argument against fiscal policy.

Criticism of Fiscal Policy

Many economists believe that fiscal policies, when properly applied, provide effective weapons for fighting recession and inflation. Others believe that fiscal policies have several serious flaws.

If government reduces taxes to correct a recession, government revenues decrease. Government must then borrow money to cover expenditures, creating a budget deficit. Consequently, the national debt increases. Further, since government borrows from the public to offset a tax reduction, it can crowd out private borrowers by reducing the supply of available funds. This can cause an increase in interest rates, making it more difficult for individuals and businesses to borrow. Consequently, a tax reduction offset by borrowing can actually make a recession worse by discouraging business investment and growth.

The federal government can also finance its debts by printing money. When it does this, the money supply increases, and so does consumer and business spending. Unfortunately, such increases in the money supply fuel inflation by pushing up prices even higher. For this reason, many economists are opposed to this strategy.

254

The political problems associated with fiscal policies often make them difficult to carry out. Fiscal policy can call for a tax increase or a reduction in government spending during periods of inflation, but neither the president nor Congress likes to increase taxes, least of all during an election year. Who, for example, would want to run on a campaign slogan that says, "Vote for me, and I will guarantee an increase in your taxes"?

Similarly, efforts to reduce spending are frequently opposed by those who benefit from the programs that Congress wishes to cut. Consequently, members of Congress, who are often reluctant to risk defeat at election time, give their support to spending cuts. In years when continued large deficits become a political issue, politicians know it is unpopular to reduce taxes or increase government spending, because either policy would add to the deficit. As a result, politicians take no action. Such inaction causes critics to believe that fiscal policy is not a completely effective tool for managing the economy today.

Supporters of using fiscal policies to control the economy admit that the success of government intervention depends heavily on timing. Fiscal policies must be applied at the right moment. Economic problems must be quickly diagnosed, and legislation passed in a very timely manner. This requires the close cooperation of the president and Congress. All too often, the delay in passing necessary legislation prevents effective action to address an overheated or depressed economy. Even if legislation is quickly passed, it still takes time for tax cuts or spending to take effect.

Views of Fiscal Policy

What do you think is the strongest argument in favor of fiscal policy?

_____

_____

What do you think is the strongest argument against fiscal policy?

_____

_____

John Maynard Keynes
Walter Stoneman/Getty Images

John Maynard Keynes: Theorist Who Brought Economics into the 20th Century

 John Maynard Keynes stands with Adam Smith as one of history's most influential economists. The son of a British economist, Keynes earned a fortune by trading stocks and commodities. He served the British government as a financial adviser and treasury official, and he was a key participant in the negotiations with Germany after World Wars I and II. He was a keen observer of both inflation and depression.

Although Adam Smith wrote *The Wealth of Nations* in 1776, mainstream economic thinking had changed little by the 1930s. Most policymakers agreed with Smith that the best thing government could do to help the economy was to keep its hands off. They reasoned that as long as the economy operated without interference, the forces of supply and demand would balance. With supply and demand in equilibrium, everyone looking for work could find a job at the prevailing wage, and every firm could sell its products in the marketplace.

The Great Depression occurred in the 1930s. Despite the assurances of classical economists who supported Smith's views, the fact was that unemployment and business failures had reached record proportions in the United States and the rest of the industrialized world. In 1936, Keynes published *The General Theory of Employment, Interest, and Money*. This book transformed economic thinking in the 20th century in much the same way that *The Wealth of Nations* had in the 18th century.

Keynes demonstrated that it was possible for total supply and demand to be at equilibrium at a point well under full employment. Moreover, he showed that unemployment could persist indefinitely unless someone stepped in to increase total demand.

The "someone" Keynes had in mind was government. He reasoned that if government spent money on public works, the income received by formerly idle workers would lead to increased demand, a resurgence of business activity, and the restoration of full employment.

The suggestion that government abandon its commitment to the market in favor of an active role in economic stabilization was regarded as revolutionary in the 1930s. Since then, the ideas advanced by the "Keynesian Revolution" have become part of the conventional wisdom. Now, whenever a nation appears to be entering into a period of recession or inflation, economists and others who support Keynes' ideas—Keynesians—immediately think of steps the government might take to reverse the trend.

Monetary Policy

There is a direct relationship between the money supply and the level of business activity. Without available funds, consumers are not able to spend, and businesses cannot invest. Recall that banks create money when they make a loan to a consumer or business. When interest rates are low, businesses are more likely to borrow money for investments. It follows that in times of recession, policies that make credit less expensive may help bring about economic recovery. On the other hand, when prices are rising, policies that make credit more expensive may help reduce inflation.

Government policy that affects interest rates and the quantity of money in circulation is called *monetary policy*. It is the Federal Reserve's responsibility to set monetary policy to reduce the effects of recession or of a too-rapid expansion of the economy. As you have learned, monetary policy set by the Federal Reserve regulates the money supply to help the economy achieve a full-employment, noninflationary level of total output.

The Federal Reserve and the Money Supply

The Federal Reserve System has several tools it can use to influence interest rates and to regulate the money supply. The most important of these are listed below.

- **Open-market operations. Open-market operations** is the purchase and sale of government securities (bonds issued by the U.S. Treasury) by the Federal Open Market Committee (FOMC). As you learned in Chapter 13, the FOMC is composed of the seven members of the Board of Governors of the Federal Reserve System and five of the 12 Reserve Bank presidents. When the Open Market Committee directs the Federal Reserve to buy government securities from banks and other investors, it injects money into the economy by increasing bank reserves. The money from the sale of these securities is deposited by securities sellers into their checking accounts. Banks try to lend as much of the new deposits as possible; this lending adds to the money supply. As these new loans move through the banking system, the total money supply is increased further by the deposit multiplier, which you learned about in Chapter 13.

  When the FOMC sells government securities, it takes money out of the economy. Bank reserves are reduced, as those who purchased the securities pay the government by writing checks. The reduction in reserves also reduces the ability of banks to lend money, which slows the growth of the money supply.

- **The discount rate.** Just as business firms look to their banks when they need to borrow, banks look to their Federal Reserve Bank when they are in need of funds. Like other borrowers, the banks are charged interest on their loans by the Fed. The **discount rate** is the interest rate charged by the Federal Reserve on its loans to banks and other financial institutions. When the Board of Governors raises the discount rate, banks increase the interest rates they charge their customers. Similarly, when the discount rate is reduced, banks drop their loan interest rates. Higher interest rates tend to discourage borrowing, so the money supply falls. Lower rates have the opposite effect. As you know, when loans are increased, the money supply grows.

Check Your Understanding

Explain in your own words the difference between fiscal policy and monetary policy.

_____

_____

_____

_____

12. open-market operations   13. discount rate

• **The reserve ratio.** As you learned in the previous chapter, banks are required to keep a percentage of their deposits in reserve. The percentage of deposits held in reserve is the reserve ratio. A portion of bank reserves is deposited at the bank's district Federal Reserve Bank. The remainder is available for loans to bank customers. When the Board of Governors increases the reserve ratio, it reduces the amount of money banks are able to lend. When the reserve ratio is reduced, commercial banks are free to lend a larger portion of their deposits, thereby increasing the money supply.

Think Critically

Review the three tools that the Federal Reserve can use to regulate the money supply. What institutions does the Fed work through to regulate the money supply?

The flow chart below summarizes contractionary monetary policy.

Figure 14-7: Effects of Contractionary Monetary Policy

The Fed Raises the Interest Rate

This Discourages Consumers and Businesses from Borrowing Money

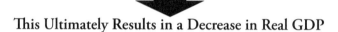

This Results in a Decrease in the Money Supply

This Ultimately Results in a Decrease in Real GDP

Flow Chart of Expansionary Monetary Policy

Figure 14-7 is a flow chart of contractionary monetary policy. On a separate sheet of paper, create a flow chart of expansionary monetary policy. In the first block of your chart, enter "The Fed Reduces the Interest Rate."

Compare your expansionary monetary policy flow chart with the contractionary fiscal policy flow chart you did after studying Figure 14-6.

How are the flow charts alike? _____

How are the flow charts different? _____

Limitations of Monetary Policy

Monetary policy is least effective at the extremes of the business cycle. During periods of rapid expansion, when optimism among buyers and sellers is running high and prices are rising, the Fed may try to hold down spending (and prices) by increasing interest rates. Because the business outlook is so bright and prospects for profits are so high, many firms continue to borrow, despite the high cost of loans. They expect that their interest expenses will be more than offset by higher prices and greater sales revenue. Higher interest rates increase the cost of doing business and can even add to inflationary pressure.

Recent changes in the U.S. economy have also limited the effect of monetary policy. Until the 1980s, the interest rate that banks could pay their depositors was limited by law. In those days, the Fed could reduce the money supply by increasing the interest paid on government securities. As interest rates rose above those paid by banks, money flowed out of deposits and into Treasury securities. This, in turn, reduced bank reserves and the money supply. Today, this is less likely to happen, since banks are free to raise interest rates and the public has a wider variety of places to invest its savings.

Monetary vs. Fiscal Policy

During the 1960s and 1970s, economists frequently debated the question, "Which is more effective in controlling changes in business activity, monetary or fiscal policy?" Although there seems to be a consensus emerging that monetary policy is more effective, two schools of thought still exist. Those favoring the monetary side of the argument are known as monetarists; those arguing the fiscal case describe themselves as Keynesians.

Monetarists believe that competitive markets provide the economy with a high degree of economic stability. They are much less inclined to support government intervention in the economy. When intervention is necessary, monetarists favor monetary policy through changing the money supply, but not necessarily attempting to control interest rates. Keynesians believe that instability is inherent in a free market system and that no mechanism exists to automatically stabilize the economy. They support government being actively involved in managing the economy, primarily through the use of fiscal policy.

More recently, economists have begun to see that both fiscal and monetary policies are effective tools to stimulate the growth of the economy and to reduce the effects of inflation. In general, fiscal policies are more difficult to implement because of the time necessary to navigate the political process. However, once agreed upon, the impact of a new fiscal policy can be felt quickly. Monetary policies, on the other hand, can be changed or adjusted quickly. The effects of higher or lower interest rates or changes in the money supply are more subtle, and such measures often take longer to have an impact.

Check Your Understanding

Compare the beliefs of monetarists with those of Keynesians.

_____

_____

_____

_____

What Would You Recommend?

Imagine that you are a member of the Federal Reserve's Board of Governors. For two consecutive months, the Consumer Price Index has shown an increase of over 6 percent, at an annual rate. Durable goods orders are up, jobless claims are down, and housing starts are up. You know the federal government is experiencing an annual federal deficit because of recent hurricanes that have devastated three cities in the southeastern United States.

In the space below, write an analysis of the current state of the economy. Then recommend a monetary policy that you think will deal with the current economic situation. Use additional paper if needed.

_____

_____

_____

_____

AUTOMATIC STABILIZERS

The fiscal policies described in this chapter are, for the most part, discretionary. They are applied when the policymakers decide to use them. One principal drawback of discretionary fiscal policies is that unless they are properly timed, they may be implemented too late to do any good. This is not true, however, of fiscal tools called automatic stabilizers.

Automatic stabilizers are automatic because they go into effect without action by the president, Congress, or their representatives. They are stabilizers because during recessions, they increase government spending, reduce taxes, or some combination of the two. In times of expansion, when personal income and prices are rising, the automatic stabilizers follow an opposite course. They reduce government spending and increase taxes.

One such automatic stabilizer is the personal income tax. During times of recession, people earn less and, therefore, are taxed at a lower rate. In this way, the personal income tax provides the public with exactly what is called for during recession—a tax cut. In boom times, inflation pushes wages and salaries to higher and higher levels. As this happens, people pay higher income taxes. Once again, tax policy automatically meets fiscal goals by increasing taxes during inflationary times.

Two other automatic stabilizers increase or reduce government spending, when needed, to combat recession or inflation. These are the nation's unemployment and welfare benefits. In times of recession, government spending automatically increases as the number of those eligible to receive unemployment insurance and welfare benefits increases. When the economy improves, unemployment declines, and government spending for these programs is automatically reduced. During periods of prosperity and high employment, unemployment contributions automatically rise, putting money into the unemployment insurance fund. This helps reduce spending at a time when inflation is a threat, and it makes funds available when a recession appears.

Summary

iStockphoto '07

United States economic activity is monitored very carefully by government officials, members of the business community, and economists. A variety of statistical measurements—economic indicators—are used to assess the economy's health. The business cycle provides a big picture of the economy's ups and downs over time. Other indicators, such as durable goods orders, housing starts, jobless claims, and the index of leading economic indicators, provide additional information on the economy's performance. The consumer price index, reported monthly, is considered a good measure of inflation.

Perhaps the most monitored indicator is the gross domestic product (GDP). It is the final value of all goods and services produced in the country in a year. The GDP does not account for population changes or for changes in the quality of products, and it is true that harmful goods are included in the GDP. Despite these shortcomings, GDP is a very important economic indicator.

In its efforts to stabilize the economy and achieve the goals set forth in the Employment Act of 1946, the federal government relies on the tools of fiscal and monetary policy. Fiscal policies seek to adjust total demand through the appropriate use of the government's powers to tax and spend. Fiscal policy is in the hands of the president and Congress. Monetary policies seek to achieve similar goals by regulating the money supply. Monetary policies are determined by the Board of Governors of the Federal Reserve System.

In times of recession, fiscal policies call for some combination of tax reductions and increases in government spending. During economic slowdowns, monetary policies seek to increase the money supply by increasing purchases of government securities, lowering the discount rate, and reducing the reserve ratio. In times of inflation, fiscal and monetary policies follow opposite courses.

Looking Ahead

Although most of the goods and services produced and consumed by U.S. citizens are made in the United States, many come from other countries. Economic conditions in the United States and other countries affect each other. The next chapter will describe what many economists call the international marketplace.

Notes

International Trade

Read to Find Out

As you read this chapter, look for answers to the following questions:

Why is international trade considered a two-way street?
How do imports and exports depend on one another?
How do absolute advantage and comparative advantage differ?
Why is productivity important in international trade?
What are the arguments for and against barriers to trade?
What is the overall purpose of international trade organizations?
What are exchange rates, and why do they often rise and fall?
Why does a nation's balance of payments always balance?

Why It Matters

International trade influences the United States economy more every year. In 1970, imports represented only about 7 percent of the United States' real gross domestic product. More recently, imports are closer to 16 percent of real GDP. Half of all automobiles driven in the United States today are foreign-produced. In 1970, most mechanics did not know how to repair foreign-produced autos. Now, a mechanic may have trouble finding work if he or she cannot repair Volvos, Toyotas, and BMWs. Over 80 percent of all the consumer electronics (computers, televisions, cell phones, DVD players) that United States consumers buy are produced abroad. Increased trade is good for the United States economy because international trade allows businesses in our economy to specialize in the production of goods and services. Yet, many people in the United States express concerns about the value and importance of international trade.

International Trade

Building On What You Know

Have you watched television in the last day or so? Have you used a calculator or played a DVD recently? Perhaps you bought a new sweatshirt or athletic shoes this month. Look at the labels on these and many other products you use. The labels tell you where the products were made. Much of the clothing we wear and many of the electronic products we use were made outside the United States. This means that we have traded for these and many other products we consume. Why do countries trade? Are there benefits to trade? Is international trade a good thing? These and many other questions will be answered in this chapter.

If you were an economist, how would you approach learning about international trade? Think about the concepts and skills you have learned so far in this book. Recall that we have talked about the benefits of voluntary trade. To an economist, voluntary trade is mutually beneficial to the trading partners.

This proposition is true if the trading partners are located within one country or if they reside in different countries. For example, the next time you buy running shoes made in China, use your economics knowledge to consider your decision to buy the shoes rather than making them for yourself. At this point in your economics course, the answer may seem obvious. Making running shoes can take a lot of time, and time is valuable. So, instead, most people buy shoes, often those made in China, and use their valuable resources and time for more important activities.

Where Were Products Made?

Make a list of up to five items in your household that were made in another country. Look at labels on clothing, electronic items, and household appliances. List the items by name and the country in which they were made.

_____   _____

_____   _____

In groups of four or five students, compile your lists into one. Be prepared to share your results.

Think Critically

Describe two ways international trade is advantageous to Americans.

1._____

_____

2._____

_____

Describe two ways international trade is disadvantageous to Americans.

1._____

_____

2._____

_____

The Two-Way Street of Trade

In Chapter 1, you learned that people gain when they trade voluntarily. The bread you buy is brought into your household. It was baked by someone outside your household. You voluntarily purchased it from the producer. The bread is your gain from the exchange. However, the exchange is a two-way street. You must pay for it. That payment is your cost of the exchange. If you made a good decision, the money you gave up was worth less to you than the loaf of bread.

Most people sell their labor outside of their household to an employer. You voluntarily exchange your work for income, and your employer voluntarily hires you to do the work. Working is the cost you bear so you can receive income to purchase goods and services. Your income is the gain you receive from working. When you studied the Circular Flow of Money, Resources, and Products in Chapter 2, you learned about the exchanges between households and businesses. The Circular Flow did not include exchanges between people in different countries, although these exchanges are very similar to exchanges within one country. However, economists use special terms to help us understand international trade.

Figure 15-1: Two-Way Street of Trade

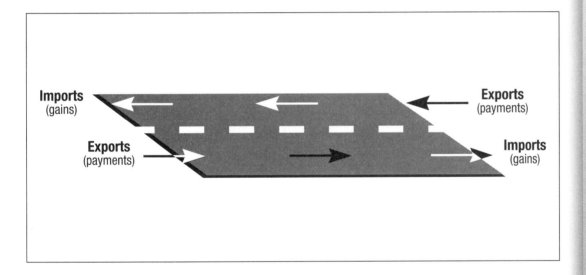

Check Your Understanding

Explain in your own words why international trade is described as a "two-way street."

_____

_____

_____

_____

Study the diagram in Figure 15-1 for a moment. In international trade, people in different nations make voluntary exchanges with one another. Goods and services traded internationally are called *exports* and *imports*. An **export** is a good or service sold to a buyer in another country. An **import** is a good or service purchased from a seller in another country. In the United States, we import into our households goods and services made by people who live in other countries. Foreign sellers then earn income that can be used to purchase United States exports.

When United States goods are sold in another country, we, as a nation, are paying for our imports by exporting goods and services. Indeed, one country's imports are another country's exports. People in one country earn money to import only because people in other countries buy what they export. International trade is a two-way street.

1. export 2. import

An Export or an Import?

Next to each item below, indicate whether the item is a United States export or import.

_____ A calculator made in China

_____ Wheat sold to Japan

_____ Furniture bought in Canada

_____ Perfume made in France

_____ A Ford car made in Detroit and sold in Italy

The Benefits of Trade

The value of United States imports per year does not always equal the value of United States exports. Exports and imports do not have to be equal for the economy to function well. Trade is a two-way street because imports and exports generally depend on one another, not because they equal one another. As people in the United States have imported more goods and services over the years, people in other countries have purchased more exports from the United States. Figure 15-2 is a graph that shows U.S. imports and exports as a percent of gross domestic product from 1970 to 2005.

Figure 15-2: U.S. Trade in Goods and Services as a Percent of GDP

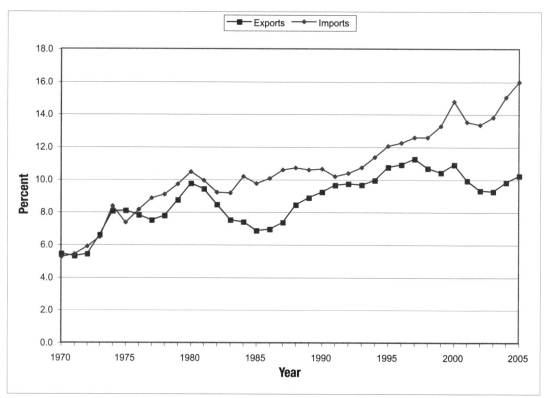

Sources: U.S. Census Bureau, *Foreign Trade Statistics, Historical Series.*
Website: http://www.census.gov/foreign-trade/statistics/historical/gands.pdf
Economic Report of the President, 2006, Table B-1.

U.S. seaports serve as points of entry and departure for imports and exports.

iStockphoto '07

Check Your Understanding

Study Figure 15-2. In one or two sentences, describe the story of U.S. imports and exports from 1970 to 2005.

_____

_____

_____

_____

266

While the two measures, imports and exports, are not always equal and have not been equal for many years, they have generally risen together over time. International trade does change the tasks you and others perform. By importing goods and services and not making them yourself, you can specialize in your own production. This means that you can concentrate on your most productive activity and gain greater income than if you had not specialized. Greater income allows you to enjoy a higher standard of living. For example, suppose you are a teacher, a profession that requires advanced education and day-to-day planning. Teaching is your specialty. Your income from teaching allows you to buy imported goods and services.

In the same way, international trade allows people within a nation to give up certain jobs at which people in other nations specialize. **Specialization** is the concentration of productive efforts of individuals or business firms on a limited number of activities. Specialization allows people to concentrate on the tasks at which they are most productive.

Many people in Asia, for example, no longer produce farm products. Instead, they have concentrated on the computer industry. In fact, many computer software call centers, established to help consumers understand how to use software, employ English-speaking workers in India to provide this service. Your toll-free call from the United States is routed internationally to India. You may never know you are speaking to someone from India because the speaker's language and technical skills are excellent.

China, India, and other Asian countries now have many productive people who specialize in understanding technology. They earn higher incomes than they did as farmers. Asian companies export many technology goods and services to gain income. Then they import other goods and services that are produced more efficiently by people in other countries. As a result, people around the world have become more productive, and the world economy has become capable of producing and consuming more goods and services. Why has this happened? The answer lies in two important economic concepts—*absolute advantage* and *comparative advantage*.

Pause to Predict

What do you think "absolute advantage" means?

_____

_____

_____

What do you think "comparative advantage" means?

_____

_____

_____

Analysis of Figure 15-2

Review Figure 15-2, and use the information in it to answer the questions below.

1. Describe the relationship between exports and imports between 1970 and 1974.

_____

2. Exports were what percentage of GDP in 1992? _____

3. Exports were what percentage of GDP in 2005? _____

4. Imports were what percentage of GDP in 1984? _____

5. Imports were what percentage of GDP in 2005? _____

6. Between 2000 and 2005, what was the relationship between exports and imports?

_____

3. specialization

Absolute and Comparative Advantage

Absolute advantage is the ability of a person or a nation to produce a good at a lower cost than another person or a nation. Suppose you and your friend Andrea decide to earn some extra money by ironing shirts and typing term papers. You can iron three shirts per hour or type three pages per hour. Andrea, on the other hand, can iron five shirts per hour or type five pages per hour. Clearly, Andrea is more productive than you in both ironing shirts and in typing. Andrea has an absolute advantage over you in ironing and in typing. Should Andrea be self-sufficient because she has an absolute advantage in ironing and typing, or would you both be better off if you specialized?

Countries have had to face this same problem for years. Should they remain self-sufficient, or should they specialize in producing a few products and trade for products that other countries produce? Comparative advantage will help us understand the answer to this question.

Comparative advantage is the ability of an individual or nation to produce a product at a lower opportunity cost than another individual or nation. Here is an example of an individual situation. Suppose Oprah Winfrey has excellent accounting skills, as well as her high-paying skills as a talk show host. Does this mean that she should do her own accounting? Think about what she would give up—her opportunity cost—if she did her own accounting. She would give up income from being a talk show host, a high opportunity cost. If she hired an accountant, she would have a much lower opportunity cost by paying the accountant.

The same kind of thinking applies to nations. The country of Kuwait could produce both solar energy and oil. Kuwait would have a high opportunity cost if it chose to produce solar energy, as the country has not produced solar energy in the past. However, its lower opportunity cost would be in producing oil rather than solar energy. Kuwait is very good at oil production. The country of Singapore could produce both manufactured goods and forest products. As you may know, Singapore has a small land area, and its opportunity cost of producing forest products would be very high. Singapore has a lower opportunity cost in producing manufactured goods, and it would be better off to trade with Canada or Russia for forest products.

To gain a comparative advantage, an individual or a nation should produce and sell a product at a lower opportunity cost than another individual or nation. Then the individual or nation can trade its lower opportunity cost products for higher opportunity cost products. This is the real meaning of comparative advantage. In 1776, Adam Smith, in *The Wealth of Nations,* stated the idea this way: "It is the maxim of every prudent master of a family never to attempt to make at home what it will cost him more to make than to buy." Since 1776, economists have told us that increased trade and specialization among people, even if they live in different countries, generally increases the amount of goods and services produced and sold in the world economy.

Apply Your Understanding

Now that you have read more about absolute and comparative advantage, refine and rewrite your understanding of the two concepts.

Absolute advantage

_____

_____

_____

Comparative advantage

_____

_____

_____

4. absolute advantage   5. comparative advantage

What Did Adam Smith Mean?

Adam Smith stated, "It is the maxim of every prudent master of a family never to attempt to make at home what it will cost him more to make than to buy." In your own words, what does this statement mean?

_____

_____

_____

Productivity, Wages, and Trade

When trading internationally, many poorer nations in the world have worried that they would not be able to compete with wealthier nations whose productivity is so much higher. People in these nations have often argued that the more productive workers in wealthier nations would take jobs away from less productive workers in their nations. However, economists have explained that even if countries are less productive at making every possible product, they can still compete and gain from trade. Even poorer nations have some comparative advantage with respect to producing some products.

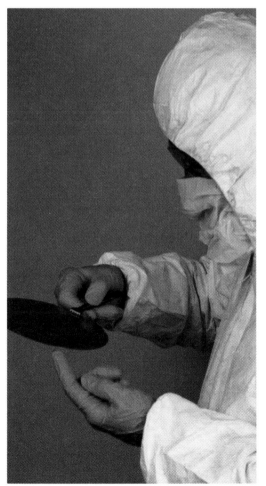

iStockphoto '07

The opposite fear is sometimes expressed by American workers about international trade. Their fear concerns the ability of higher-paid United States workers to compete successfully with lower-paid workers in other nations. However, economists point out that the main reason for the higher pay of U.S. workers is their higher productivity. American workers generally produce more than workers in poorer countries because of many years of American industry's investment in capital resources, as well as Americans' higher levels of education, skills, knowledge, and work values.

This discussion points out the importance of maintaining a high level of productivity in the economy. As you learned in Chapter 10, productivity determines our wages and standard of living. Suppose that U.S. workers are generally four times more productive as workers in another country where wage rates are much lower. This means the average U.S. wage can be up to four times higher than wages in another country without hurting U.S. trade possibilities.

Think Critically

Economists believe that high productivity will continue to allow American workers to make high wages, even if workers in less-developed countries are paid lower wages to do similar work. How does productivity affect wages?

_____

_____

_____

Classical Champion of Free Trade

David Ricardo lived in a time of profound change, a time of revolution in France and America, of Napoleon and war, and of radical transformations in farming and manufacturing. While he lived only 51 years, he filled those years with extraordinary accomplishments.

When only 14 years old, he went to work for his father, a stockbroker, and he quickly learned the ins and outs of the financial world. By the time he was 30, Ricardo had made a fortune. He eventually became a member of England's Parliament, but it was in the fledgling area of economics where he made a lasting contribution. Heavily influenced by Adam Smith's *The Wealth of Nations*, he studied economics on his own and corresponded with other economists of the time. Then, in 1817, he completed *The Principles of Political Economy and Taxation*.

iStockphoto '07

With brilliant perception, Ricardo was the first to explain the difference between absolute and comparative advantage. Using an exchange of English cloth for Portuguese wine to make the point, he observed, "This exchange might even take place notwithstanding that the commodity imported by Portugal could be produced there with less labour than in England." This statement means that making cloth in England has a lower opportunity cost to the English than making wine in England.

Ricardo praised the advantages of free trade and attacked the barriers that England had legislated against grain imports. He explained that England could buy its grain from France more cheaply than it could produce the grain itself. By importing grain, England could free some of its resources from growing grain, produce other items, and end up with more grain and other products besides.

As a member of Parliament, Ricardo pressed the government to abandon its policy of trade barriers. Though he did not live to achieve that goal, his efforts bore fruit in the 1840s when England became the first industrial power to adopt a policy of free trade. Then came 70 years of economic growth, during which England became the world's wealthiest industrial power.

Barriers to International Trade

People have often become uncertain and concerned about the benefits of international trade. If people believe they will lose more than they may gain, they will oppose free-trade agreements between two countries. If these people can gain enough political support, they can get the national government to establish barriers to free trade, even if the country as a whole might benefit from the trade. Indeed, most countries, including the United States, have put up barriers to trade, which keep competitors out of local markets.

For example, in 2006, representatives from the United States and South Korea met in Seattle to negotiate changes in South Korean trade barriers. Hundreds of protesters opposed the talks. The United States wanted South Korea to reduce its high tariffs on U.S. automobiles, agricultural products, and pharmaceuticals. The government representatives of both countries agreed that a free-trade agreement would help drive economic growth and increase the income of each country by billions of dollars. However, American labor groups worried about companies moving jobs to Korea, while Korean farmers feared they would be unable to compete with American agricultural products.

In 2006, South Korea had a 40 percent tariff on beef imports. A **tariff** is a duty, or tax, on imports. Tariffs increase the price of an imported product. A Korean government representative argued that eliminating the beef tariff would mean that not only would the Korean livestock farmers go out of business, but also the people in the industries related to livestock farming would suffer. The representative felt that for the South Korean government to pursue this trade agreement without thinking of alternatives for the farmers would be irresponsible. By early 2007, the final outcome of the agreement was still undecided.

What are the major barriers to trade? There are four: tariffs, quotas, preservation of standards, and export subsidies. We discuss each of these, briefly, next.

Pause to Predict

What kinds of barriers to trade do you think countries can set up to keep some competitors out of specific markets? Name two.

_____

_____

_____

_____

Finding a Compromise

In the appropriate spaces below, describe the concerns expressed by both the South Korean and the United States representatives to a new trade agreement between the two countries.

South Korean Representatives   United States Representatives

_____   _____

_____   _____

What compromise would you propose to encourage both countries to sign a new trade agreement?

_____

_____

6. tariff

271

Show Your
Understanding

Underline one sentence
about each barrier that
will help you remember
key information about it.

Tariffs

You learned that a tariff is a duty, or tax, on imports. There are two basic types of tariffs—revenue tariffs and protective tariffs. Revenue tariffs are levied as a way to raise money for the government. Like sales taxes, they are usually low in cost relative to the price of an item. If revenue tariffs are set too high, they discourage buyers and don't raise revenue for the government. Until 1910, revenue tariffs were the principal source of income for the U.S. government. The passage of the 16th Amendment in 1913 gave Congress the ability to collect income taxes that surpassed revenue tariff as the main source of U.S. government income.

Protective tariffs are levied to protect a domestic industry from foreign competition, rather than to raise money. The South Korean beef tariff is a good example of a protective tariff. These tariffs discourage buyers from purchasing the foreign product by making it more expensive than a similar item produced in the country.

Quotas

A **quota** is a restriction on the amount of a specific good that can enter the country from abroad. Like protective tariffs, quotas limit the amount of foreign competition that a domestic industry will have to face. By restricting imports, quotas reduce the supply of particular items in domestic markets and cause their prices to rise. For example, the United States had quotas that restricted imports of textiles and apparel.

Preservation of Standards

Government rules and regulations can make it difficult to import goods. For example, the government may require people in other nations to meet certain labor standards that require higher pay, benefits, or work safety conditions. A government also may require producers in other countries to meet strict environmental standards. The main purpose of the standards may be to preserve the quality of people's lives, but they also restrict market competition. This occurs because producers in those nations who are unable to meet the standards will be prohibited from exporting their products to a country that does have the standards.

Export Subsidies

Think Critically

Some critics claim that
export subsidies are merely
a form of welfare to farmers
and others who receive the
subsidies. What do these
critics mean when they
make this claim?

_____

_____

Why do you agree or
disagree with the critics?

_____

_____

An **export subsidy** is a payment by a country to its exporters, enabling them to sell their products abroad at a lower price than at home. For example, European governments and the U.S. government subsidize their farmers, who are then able to undersell other farmers in the world market. Export subsidies are a way to keep family farms in business. This is especially the case in France in the dairy and wine industries.

iStockphoto '07

Governments may subsidize agricultural products to help family farms stay in business.

Trade barriers are controversial. Several arguments both for and against barriers to trade are discussed next.

7. quota   8. export subsidy

Barriers to Trade

Match the example on the right with the barrier to trade on the left.

____ Tariff

____ Quota

____ Standards

____ Export subsidy

1. Limit of 1,000 Austrian-made skis allowed for import

2. Giving U.S. pig farmers $50.00 per pig they sell in Italy

3. Refusal to import athletic shoes because they are made with child labor

4. Charge of a 5 percent duty on an imported purse

Arguments for Barriers to Trade

The effect of tariffs, quotas, and other trade restrictions is to make imported goods and services less available and more costly than they would be otherwise. With fewer goods and services to go around, living standards are reduced for many people. What arguments, then, could be used to restrict trade?

The cheap foreign labor argument. This argument may be the most frequently heard argument in the United States in favor of protective trade barriers. People who make this argument claim that some foreign countries can undersell U.S. goods because their workers are paid much less. As a result, U.S. workers in the same industry, if they are equally productive as foreign workers, have to accept lower wages or lose their jobs to foreign competition. They argue that the government, therefore, should protect U.S. workers by placing restrictions on the goods produced by "cheap foreign labor."

Restrictions to protect the environment argument. Many people argue for import restrictions that prevent U.S. companies from moving to other nations that have lax environmental rules and then shipping their goods back to the United States. These people believe this restriction yields a cleaner world environment.

The national defense argument. Certain industries are vital to the nation's security—industries such as aircraft and weapons manufacturing. If they were replaced by foreign competitors, they might not be available in times of war. During the 1950s, for example, the United States initiated oil import quotas, hoping to encourage oil exploration in our country so that we could produce our own oil during a war. Interestingly, the result of this policy was a higher price of oil in the United States, increased profits for domestic oil producers, and more rapid use of lower-cost oil reserves in our country.

iStockphoto '07

Preventing U.S. companies from producing goods in countries with lax environmental rules may result in a cleaner world environment.

Think Critically

Some people believe environmental protection is a national issue. Others believe that it is a global issue.

Which do you believe and why?

_____

_____

_____

Infant industry argument. Nations that are beginning to industrialize often impose tariffs and create other trade restrictions to protect their new and fragile industries. The belief is that once an industry has had an opportunity to grow, it will be able to compete with rivals in other nations, and the restrictions can be lifted. In 1791, Alexander Hamilton used this argument to support protective tariffs for the United States so that the new nation could industrialize with less threat from more industrialized European nations.

Economic diversity argument. This argument is similar to the infant industry argument. The economies of some developing countries depend almost entirely on single crops or products. Their economic welfare could be dramatically affected if crops fail or prices fall. To prevent such a situation, some argue that the governments in these countries should support (with tariffs and subsidies) new industries to diversify their economies. An unintended outcome, however, may be that the nation wastes scarce resources and blocks the very development it seeks.

Retaliation argument. Some people argue that the United States should retaliate against any country that limits the import of U.S. goods by restricting imports of that country's goods to the United States. The Bush Administration in 2004 applied this policy to the sale of Canadian wood products in this country. The European Union, another trading entity, threatened retaliation restrictions if the U.S. government opposed the protection of Europe's farm industry.

Arguments Against Barriers to Trade

Many people, both in business and in government, advocate free trade without any barriers. They generally argue that free trade increases production, employment, and the general welfare. Advocates of free trade believe trade barriers should be removed.

Benefit a few workers argument. Economists are generally critical of the argument that trade barriers protect a country's workers from "cheap foreign labor." U.S. workers, economists claim, can compete successfully with lower-paid workers abroad when their superior productivity supports their higher wages and benefits. With trade barriers, protected workers can raise their wages and benefits above their productivity. When this occurs, people in other countries pay artificially high prices for imported goods.

There is yet another unseen cost. Suppose the trade barrier requires workers in poorer countries to meet higher wage standards to sell their products in a nation that demands the standards be met. The requirement would prevent these workers from receiving the lower wages that compensate for their lower productivity. The producers who employ the workers would then be unable to compete successfully in the world marketplace. Once again, protected workers gain at the expense of workers elsewhere.

Cleaner environment argument. Proponents of free trade argue that evidence refutes the claim that businesses move to other countries because of lower environmental restrictions. Instead, free-trade advocates claim that trade barriers block a cleaner environment because they prevent the trade that would help reduce poverty in lower-income countries. As a result, incomes fail to rise to levels where people willingly make sacrifices for a cleaner environment. They argue that poverty is never kind to the environment.

Apply Your Understanding

Rank order the six arguments for barriers to trade to indicate which arguments you believe are most persuasive. Make the argument you believe is strongest #1 and the one you think is least persuasive #6.

1 _____

2 _____

3 _____

4 _____

5 _____

6 _____

Why do you feel the argument you ranked #1 is most persuasive?

_____

_____

Harming consumers argument. Opponents of trade barriers point out that the biggest sufferers of a nation's trade barriers are its own consumers. These citizens must pay higher prices for a lower quality and quantity of goods and services. Put another way, a nation's consumers gain if trade barriers are eliminated. Adding more producers to the marketplace creates an increase in supply, which, in turn, leads to greater production and lower prices. Consumers receive a higher quality and quantity of goods and services at a lower cost. For this reason, foes of trade barriers often say that a nation would be better off even if it acted independently to eliminate its trade barriers, regardless of what other nations do.

Out of concern that trade restrictions have reduced general economic prosperity, nations have acted to open up international trade. One organization that promotes free trade is the World Trade Organization.

Think Critically

Having read arguments both for and against trade barriers, which position do you support?

_____
_____

Why? _____
_____
_____
_____

For or Against a Trade Barrier?

The quotations below are typical comments about trade barriers. On the line before each quotation, indicate whether you believe the quotation speaks for or against the barrier to which it refers.

_____ "The cheap labor in that country will hurt us."

_____ "This quota will punish our consumers."

_____ "We must protect our new widget industry."

_____ "The tariff will keep our economy diversified."

_____ "Poverty is never kind to the environment."

The World Trade Organization

There are a few historical cases where nations have taken unilateral action to reduce trade barriers. England took such a step in 1846 when it eliminated laws against grain imports, and Hong Kong and South Korea took similar steps in more recent years. More commonly, however, nations have tried to promote free trade by jointly agreeing to reduce their trade barriers.

Multilateral agreements, trade agreements that involve three or more countries, can magnify the benefits of freer trade by including more participants in larger markets. Multilateral agreements may also find acceptance if people give up their own barriers when they see other nations following suit. Today, the main organization promoting multilateral efforts is the World Trade Organization (WTO).

The roots of the WTO reach back to the end of World War II. Having just suffered the horror of this war, representatives of 23 countries created the General Agreement on Tariffs and Trade (GATT) in 1947. Its purpose was to promote a more peaceful world by encouraging increased trade among nations. Through a series of meetings, or "rounds,"

GATT enabled member nations to agree on substantial reductions in tariffs. The lower tariffs applied to goods, because trade in goods dominated international commerce in the years following World War II. Since then, trade in services, such as banking, telecommunications, insurance, and finance, has grown considerably. Also growing rapidly has been trade in ideas or intellectual property, such as inventions, designs, computer software, and entertainment.

In a major effort to extend trade agreements to these areas, GATT began its eighth series of negotiation rounds in 1986. After years of conferring, more than 100 nations agreed in 1994 on the most significant revision of international trade rules since the formation of GATT. This agreement produced the World Trade Organization and new rules relating to trade in services, intellectual property, and other areas:

- Eliminate or cut tariffs on various products, such as construction equipment, agricultural equipment, pharmaceuticals, and electronic products.

- Phase out import quotas on textiles and clothing.

- Reduce import quotas and government export subsidies on farm products.

- Protect intellectual property rights, such as patents, copyrights, and trademarks.

In 1994, the U.S. Congress approved the new WTO, but only after a heated national debate. Opponents argued that freer trade with lower-wage countries would reduce jobs and wages in the United States. Some claimed that freer trade would undermine efforts to protect the environment.

The discontent festered and came to a head in 1999, when representatives of 135 nations met at a WTO summit in Seattle, Washington, to consider another round of trade negotiations. Numerous contentious issues topped the list of items to negotiate. For example, the United States, Canada, Australia, and other countries objected to European government subsidies on farm exports. Many developing countries objected to U.S. import quotas for textiles and apparel.

Meanwhile, the United States and Europe wanted to consider linking trade to environmental and labor standards, a demand also voiced by crowds of protestors that had gathered in Seattle to oppose the WTO and its meeting. Yet many representatives of developing nations strongly objected to linking such standards to trade. They feared that such attempts were disguised trade barriers. Because of these deep disagreements and the turmoil of angry protestors, the meeting failed to launch another round of trade negotiations. Free trade, said many observers, had lost the "Battle in Seattle."

However, the WTO did not disappear. After the Seattle meeting, the WTO continued to fulfill its original purpose to supervise the trade agreements reached by member nations and to provide a forum to negotiate further reductions in trade barriers. The organization continues in these activities today. It provides a means of settling trade disputes between WTO members. Member nations also act together to accomplish these goals, making the WTO a many-sided, or multilateral, force to produce freer trade throughout the world.

iStockphoto '07

The World Trade Organization is the main organization promoting trade between multiple countries.

Imagine that you had been a United States representative to the Seattle WTO Summit in 1999. What position would you have taken on the following issues?

Import quotas   _____

Environmental standards   _____

Labor standards   _____

Export subsidies   _____

Generally expanding global trade   _____

Generally limiting global trade   _____

Regional Trade Agreements

In contrast to the worldwide, multilateral efforts of the World Trade Organization, some nations have formed regional agreements to reduce trade barriers. Such efforts occur as _free-trade associations_, customs unions, and common markets. A **free-trade association (FTA)** is an agreement among countries to remove the barriers to trade among themselves. The member countries remain free to maintain whatever barriers they choose against nonmember countries. Two examples of important regional trade agreements are the European Union and the North American Free Trade Agreement.

The European Union (EU)

The origin of the European Union goes back to 1957, when France, Germany, Italy, Belgium, the Netherlands, and Luxembourg signed the Treaty of Rome and created the European Community (EC), as it was known at that time. In later years, Denmark, Ireland, the United Kingdom, Greece, Spain, and Portugal became members. In 1995, Austria, Finland, and Sweden joined, bringing the total membership to 15. Ten more nations joined in 2004-2005. They are Cyprus (the Greek section), the Czech Republic, Estonia, Hungary, Latvia, Lithuania, Malta, Poland, Slovakia, and Slovenia.

By the early 1990s, members of the European Community had eliminated most barriers to the movement of goods, services, people, and capital. However, there still remained the problem of separate national currencies that restricted European trade. Imagine, for example, if the dollar was not the universal money in the United States, but instead each state had its own currency. This would be most confusing and make trade very difficult.

To facilitate trade in Europe, therefore, the governments of the EC agreed to create a single currency by proposing an Economic and Monetary Union (EMU). Representatives of European countries met in Maastricht, Netherlands, where they developed a plan, the Maastricht Treaty, that would create such a currency before the turn of the century. In 1995, the countries in the European Union agreed to a single currency, called the euro,

Check Your Understanding

What is the difference between the WTO and an FTA?

_____

_____

_____

9. free-trade association

Think Critically

When the euro was proposed as the currency to be used throughout all European Union countries, people in many EU nations opposed the idea. Why do you think they objected?

_____

_____

which eliminated the use of other currencies in the countries in the European Union. The euro was expected to benefit trade among member nations in many ways, such as the four described below.

- **Easier comparison shopping.** A single currency would make shopping easier by enabling consumers to compare prices in different nations. As a result, companies would compete more intensely among one another and would try even harder to be efficient producers.

- **Lower trading costs.** Buying and selling between nations would no longer require converting one currency into another. The costs of making trades would be much lower.

- **Less uncertainty.** A single currency would eliminate uncertainty about future rates of exchange between currencies. For example, an investor in one country would no longer worry that exchange rate changes would reduce the value of an investment in another country.

- **More efficient financial markets.** Smaller national stock and bond markets could merge into larger, more efficient markets that promote a freer and more efficient flow of financial capital among European nations.

In economic terms, the European Union has been successful. The EU has the largest economy in the world, with prospects of steady economic growth and good expectations for job creation.

The North American Free Trade Agreement (NAFTA)

Another regional trade agreement is the North American Free Trade Agreement (NAFTA). NAFTA is an effort to create a single open market among the three countries in North America. Stretching from the Yukon to the Yucatan, NAFTA unites Canada, Mexico, and the United States in the world's largest market. Canada and the United States created the free-trade accord in 1989. Then, on January 1, 1994, Mexico signed the agreement. On that day, NAFTA eliminated many trade barriers between Mexico and the United States. Most remaining tariffs and quotas have been phased out, and most citizens of all three countries now experience important economic benefits.

- Individuals and businesses have more freedom to trade industrial and agricultural products and telecommunications and insurance services.
- Patents on pharmaceuticals and other research-intensive products are respected, and copyrights on sound recordings, computer programs, and other intellectual property are enforced.
- NAFTA makes it easier for people in one country to invest in the other countries.

Since NAFTA was first proposed, it has been controversial. Opponents are convinced that it reduces total employment and wage levels in the United States and undermines U.S. efforts to protect the environment. Ross Perot, a presidential candidate in 1992, became famous for his description of NAFTA. He said it would create "a great sucking sound" from Mexico as U.S. jobs and businesses fled to Mexico to take advantage of Mexico's cheaper labor costs. The prediction was incorrect, since the real consequence of the treaty was to draw millions of Mexican workers north to job opportunities in the United States.

Meanwhile, the people who supported NAFTA expected reduced prices and increased variety of goods and services for U.S. consumers, increased employment in technology and other U.S. industries, and increased growth of Mexico's economy. All of their expectations were met, but not to the degree they had hoped. In particular, Mexico's economy has grown, but not fast enough to provide employment opportunities for large numbers of its population. For that reason, many Mexican citizens have come to the United States to find employment.

International Trade Organizations

Indicate whether the statements below are true (T) or false (F).

__ 1. The WTO includes at least 135 nations.

__ 2. The WTO grew out of the General Agreement on Tariffs and Trade (GATT).

__ 3. One argument in the "Battle in Seattle" was over export subsidies.

__ 4. The European Union includes Israel and Saudi Arabia.

__ 5. NAFTA includes the United States, Canada, and Mexico.

Financing International Trade

Money can be a barrier to trade. If you have the wrong type of money, you cannot trade. Money tends to be worthless if people cannot use it to exchange goods and services. For this reason, euros are very valuable in Europe but not valuable in the United States. If you attempt to buy a hamburger in your town with euros, the manager of the store will probably tell you that the store does not accept that currency.

The same behavior occurs in international transactions. Japanese producers may wish to sell products in the United States, but they want to be paid in yen, the currency of Japan. In the same manner, U.S. businesses selling in Mexico want to receive dollars, while Mexican consumers want to pay Mexican pesos. How do people get foreign currencies to facilitate trade? There is an easy and efficient method to exchange currencies. It is called the foreign exchange market. It follows the same laws of supply and demand that you learned about in Chapters 3, 4, and 5.

Exchange Rates and the Foreign Exchange Market

Bankers and currency dealers provide a market for foreign currencies, called the foreign exchange market. In reality, the foreign exchange market is composed of many small markets operating throughout a country. In these markets, each currency has a price called an *exchange rate*. An **exchange rate** is the value of one nation's currency stated in terms of the value of another nation's currency. For example, the U.S. dollar has an exchange rate with the European euro, the Mexican peso, the Canadian dollar, and every other currency. Each market is separate from the other, so the market for U.S. dollars and the European

Apply Your Understanding

Since the implementation of NAFTA in 1994, illegal immigration from Mexico has increased. Do you think increased immigration is an indication that NAFTA is:

__1. effective

__2. ineffective

__3. unrelated to NAFTA

Explain your choice.

_____

_____

Think Critically

If currency exchange markets didn't exist, how would a merchant who serves people from many nations make sales?

_____

_____

_____

Why do exchange markets make trade easier?

_____

_____

euro will have a different exchange rate than the market for Mexican pesos and U.S. dollars. The exchange rate is given either as the price of the dollar in terms of another currency or as the price of the other currency in terms of the dollar. The table in Figure 15-3 shows both units of foreign currency per U.S. dollar and U.S. dollars per unit of foreign currency for six countries on June 20, 2006.

Figure 15-3: Selected Exchange Rates, June 20, 2006

Foreign Currency	Foreign Currency Units per U.S. Dollar ($)	U.S. Dollars ($) per Foreign Currency Unit
British Pound (£)	0.543	1.843
Canadian Dollar ($)	1.118	0.895
Chinese Yuan Renminbi (π)	8.003	0.125
European Union Euro (€)	0.795	1.258
Japanese Yen (¥)	114.930	0.009
Mexican Peso ($)	11.475	0.087

Source: *The Wall Street Journal*, June 21, 2006, p. B9.

Since 1971, most trading nations have used a system of "floating" exchange rates. This means they allow the exchange rate of a currency to move up and down as its demand or supply in the foreign currency market changes. Simply stated, the price of one country's currency changes almost daily in terms of the price of another country's currency.

Apply Your Understanding

Suppose in June 2006, you were planning a trip to one of the regions listed in Figure 15-3. You decide to travel to the area in which you would get the most value for your U.S. dollars. Where would you have traveled?

_____

_____

Why? _____

_____

_____

Applying Exchange Rates

Use the exchange rate table in Figure 15-3 to answer the problems below.

1. You have $50 in Canadian currency. How much is this in U.S. dollars? _____

2. You have $75 in U.S. currency. How much is this in British pounds? _____

3. You have $75 in U.S. currency. How much is this in Mexican pesos? _____

4. You have 200 euros. How much is this in U.S. currency? _____

The price of one country's currency changes almost daily in relation to the price of another country's currency.

iStockphoto '07

280

The graph in Figure 15-4 should look familiar to you. It illustrates the supply and demand relationships for the market of European euros and U.S. dollars. The demand for euros comes from U.S. citizens, governments, and businesses. These buyers may be taking a trip to Italy, buying cars from Germany, or buying investments in European projects. In each case, they are offering U.S. dollars in exchange for euros. At low prices for euros, they demand more euros than they demand at high euro prices. The demand for foreign currency is consistent with the law of demand.

Figure 15-4: Supply and Demand of Euros

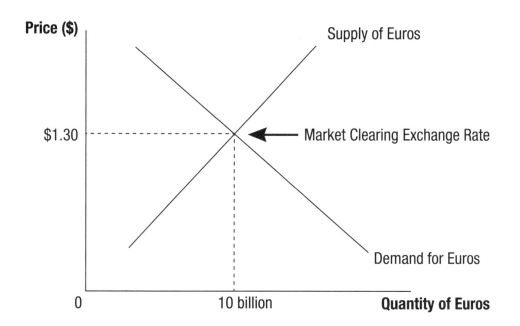

Check Your Understanding

Examine Figure 15-4 to answer the questions below.

1. The market clearing exchange rate for euros is

_____

2. At this rate, how many euros would be exchanged?

_____

3. How many euros could you buy for $9.10?

_____

The supply of euros comes from the demand of Europeans for U.S. goods and services. Europeans might want to buy U.S. vacations, airplanes, wheat, or movies. To do so, they must supply euros to the exchange market to obtain U.S. dollars. If the dollar price for euros is high, Europeans will sell more euros. If the dollar price for euros is lower, Europeans will sell few euros. The supply of currency to the foreign exchange market is consistent with the law of supply. That is, if the price of euros is increasing, more euros will be offered for sale. In Figure 15-4, the market clearing price of $1.30 purchases one euro.

If the demand for a currency suddenly increases (shifts to the right), its exchange rate can rise. In other words, it would take more U.S. dollars to buy one euro. For example, if the demand to buy European investments, automobiles, and airplanes increased next year, then the demand for euros would also increase as U.S. citizens attempt to buy the currency necessary to purchase the European goods and services. On the other hand, if its demand drops in the world currency market (demand shifts to the left), the euro's exchange rate can fall.

Many nations try to control the rise and fall of their currencies by trying to control currency supply and demand. These attempts do not work well. Most exchange rates "float" up and down in the world currency market today, just as most prices of goods and services "float" up or down with demand and supply.

Check Your
Understanding

Read the four factors that
can affect the demand
or supply for a currency.
Then explain below why
nations' efforts to control
the rise and fall of their
currencies generally don't
work well.

_____

_____

_____

_____

Apply Your
Understanding

When the U.S. dollar rises
against other countries'
currencies, who gains
and why?

_____

_____

Who loses and why?

_____

_____

Many factors can affect the demand or supply for a currency and cause its exchange rate to increase or decrease.

Imports and exports of goods and services. If people in a country import more goods and services, they will send more of their currency to the world's currency market. As the supply of the currency increases, its price (exchange rate) is likely to fall. If people in other countries begin buying more of that nation's exports, they will demand more of its currency to pay for those imports, and the price of the currency is likely to increase.

Monetary policies. The monetary policies of a nation's central bank can influence the currency's exchange rate. Rapid money creation, for example, can increase the world supply of a currency and cause its exchange rate to fall. If such rapid increases in the money supply produce higher inflation, people in other nations may also demand less of the currency.

Differences in interest rates. If interest rates rise in one nation compared with those in others, savers around the world may demand more of the currency to buy financial assets like stocks and bonds. As a result, the currency's exchange rate can rise. If interest rates in the nation fall compared with those abroad, the currency's price can fall.

Expectations. Expectations of the future value of a currency also influence its exchange rate today. For example, if savers and investors throughout the world believe that a nation's government will follow inflationary policies in the future, they may buy less of the currency today and cause its exchange rate to fall.

Whatever the reason for an increase or decrease in an exchange rate, the change affects many people. For example, if the U.S. dollar rises against other currencies, U.S. importers, tourists, and anyone else wanting another currency will be able to buy more of it with their dollars. Consumers in this country will find that goods made abroad are less expensive than they once were. U.S. exports, however, are likely to fall because the rise of the dollar against other currencies makes U.S. goods more expensive to people in other nations.

The opposite also can take place. When the dollar falls against other currencies, exports of U.S. goods will increase because people in other nations will be able to buy more dollars with their currencies. At the same time, imports will become more costly to Americans, so they will buy fewer of them.

Foreign exchange operates on the basis of supply and demand, except that the currencies involved are different. If a foreign country, say Britain, demands more and more United States products, it will need United States dollars to buy our products. As the demand for our products goes up, so does the demand for our dollars. This means that more British currency, the pound, must be paid for a dollar. On the other hand, if United States citizens demand more and more British products, we have to pay for those products in British pounds. As a result, our demand for British pounds increases, and we much pay more dollars for the pounds.

A Traveler's Cheat Sheet

When people travel to other countries, they often create their own exchange rate table or "cheat sheet" to help them as they pay for food, housing, and souvenirs. At the exchange rate for euros, create your own cheat sheet.

Exchange rate: 1 euro = $1.25 dollars

2 euros = _____   100 euros = _____

5 euros = _____   175 euros = _____

10 euros = _____   250 euros = _____

25 euros = _____   400 euros = _____

50 euros = _____   1,000 euros = _____

The United States Balance of Payments

The flow of trade between the United States and the rest of the world affects everyone. For that reason, many people keep close tabs on international trade and what is called the *balance of payments*. A nation's **balance of payments** is a record of all exchanges between its residents and those of other nations over some time period. Each transaction always has two sides. Something is gained, and something is paid. The balance of payments records both sides of each exchange, so the balance of payments must always balance.

iStockphoto '07

To illustrate, apply the "balance of payments" idea to buying pizza. If you spend $10 for a pizza, you receive a pizza worth $10. Your balance of payments includes both sides of this exchange—your receipt of a pizza worth $10 and your payment of $10. The same thing occurs when people in different nations trade. For example, suppose someone in the United States buys $200 worth of computer software from Canada. The U.S. balance of payments would then record the receipt of software worth $200 and also the payment of $200 in its currency. Similarly, every international exchange has two equal sides that are recorded in the balance of payments. Each country's balance of payments always balances.

Think Critically

Is there one country whose products you favor over U.S. products?

What country? _____

What products? _____

Why do you favor the products?

_____

_____

The Balancing Act

While the overall balance of payments must balance, its individual parts may be out of balance. For example, consider the *balance of trade,* a measure often reported in the daily news. The **balance of trade** is the value of goods and services bought and sold on the world market.

Figure 15-5: U.S. Balance of Payments, 2004
(Billions of Dollars)

Check Your Understanding

Answer the questions below with information from Figure 15-5.

1. What is the current account balance?

_____

2. What is the capital account balance?

_____

3. What is the balance of payments balance?

_____

Current Account	Plus	Minus	Balance
Exports of goods	$807.5		
Exports of services	$343.9		
Imports of goods		−$1,472.9	
Imports of services		−$296.1	
Trade Balance			−$617.6
Income receipts on U.S.-owned assets abroad	$379.5		
Income payments on foreign-owned assets in the U.S.		−$349.1	
Unilateral transfers		−$80.9	
Current Account Balance			−$668.1
Capital Account			
Capital flow into the U.S. (foreign loans and investments in the U.S.)	$1,440.1		
Capital flow out of the U.S. (loans and investments in other countries)		−$855.5	
Statistical discrepancy	$83.5		
Capital Account Balance			$668.1
Balance of Payments			0

Source: *Statistical Abstract of the United States*: 2006, Table 1273.

In 2004, U.S. imports of goods and services exceeded exports of goods and services by $617.6 billion (−$617.6). This amount represents a trade deficit. With such a big trade deficit, this part of the balance of payments was obviously not balanced. However, there are other parts of the balance of payments, which are summarized in the table in Figure 15-5. One of them is the balance on **current account**, a nation's balance of payments that includes exports and imports of goods and services, net investment income, and net transfers. Net investment income is income paid and received on U.S. investments abroad and on other countries' investments in the United States. The current account includes unilateral transfers, which are mostly grants and pensions from the U.S. government to people in other countries.

Figure 15-5 shows that in 2004, the current account had a deficit of $668.1 billion. What offset this deficit so that the overall balance of payments was in balance? The answer is the **capital account**, an account in a nation's balance of payments that shows the flow of

12. balance of trade   13. current account   14. capital account

financial capital into and out of a nation. The U.S. capital account surplus in 2004 was a surplus of $668.1 billion. This amount exactly matched the current account's deficit.

The capital account includes loans and investments flowing into and out of the United States. For example, suppose you spend $100 this month to "import" goods and services into your household. During the month, you also "export" your labor at a job but earn only $75 to pay for your purchases. This means you have a deficit on your current account equal to $25. How could you pay for the difference? You could borrow the money or use some of your savings. In either case, a surplus in your capital account would exactly match the deficit in your current account. As a result, your overall balance of payments would balance.

This is what Figure 15-5 shows for the United States in 2004. In that year, a surplus in the country's capital account of $668.1 billion offset the deficit in its current account. As a result, the minuses of some parts of the balance of payments canceled the pluses of other parts, and the overall balance of payments balanced.

The balance of payments is a very useful accounting tool. It helps a nation keep track of where it stands in its trading relationship with the world.

Think Critically

Is it better for a nation to have a positive or a negative trade account?

_____

Why? _____

_____

_____

Calculating a Balance of Payments

 Below is a simplified U.S. balance of payments statement. Use the information to calculate the trade balance, the current account balance, the capital account balance, and the balance of payments.

Current Account

Exports of Goods and Services	$350
Imports of Goods and Services	$450
Trade Balance	_____
Net Receipts on U.S. Owned Assets Abroad	$(50)
Current Account Balance	_____

Capital Account

Capital Flow into the United States	$200
Capital Flow out of the United States	$150
Capital Account Balance	_____
Balance of Payments	_____

Summary

Instead of each of us trying to produce everything we consume, we concentrate our work on tasks we do best. We specialize. Then we use our earnings to buy the goods and services we want. In this way, we "import" more goods and services for a given "export" of labor. World trade takes place in the same manner. The only difference is that the goods and services travel across geographic boundaries. In both domestic and international trade, our ability to buy or import products depends on our ability to sell or export to earn the money required for payment. In international trade, this means that a country's ability to export is dependent on purchasing imports.

For example, when people in Canada and Mexico buy products from people in the United States, they provide the United States with the foreign currency necessary to buy Mexican and Canadian products.

When making these exchanges with one another, some nations have an absolute advantage in the production of particular things. An absolute advantage is the ability to produce something with fewer resources. Most important for trade, however, is comparative advantage, which occurs when a producer has a lower opportunity cost of producing a given good or service than another good or service. By concentrating their production on those products for which they have comparative advantages, nations can then trade and increase their standards of living.

In the second half of the 20th century and the first part of the 21st century, there were many efforts to tear down trade barriers to enable people of different nations to exchange more freely. Leading these efforts was the General Agreement on Tariffs and Trade (GATT), which was replaced by the World Trade Organization (WTO) after 1994. The activities of GATT and the WTO were multilateral, since they involved joint efforts of many nations to reduce trade barriers. In contrast, regional organizations, such as the North American Free Trade Association (NAFTA) and the European Union have taken steps to reduce trade barriers among nations in a particular area of the world.

Trading among nations requires the exchange of national currencies. In the foreign currency market, the selling price of one nation's currency in terms of the currencies of other nations is its exchange rate. Exchange rates fluctuate according to changes in supply and demand for different currencies.

The balance of payments summarizes the exchanges that have taken place in international trade over a period of time. Each exchange has two sides that are recorded, so the balance of payments always balances. Despite the overall balance, individual parts of the balance of payments may not be balanced. When these various pluses and minuses are added up in both the current account and the capital account, the result is a balance of payments that balances.

Looking Ahead
The next chapter will investigate the impact of globalization on different economies and the role of markets in dealing with issues of population growth, economic growth, and environmental protection.

Our Globalized World

Read to Find Out

As you read this chapter, look for answers to the following questions:

What is globalization?

What worldwide changes have occurred as a result of globalization?

What is the relationship between economic development and population growth?

How has China changed its economy to achieve greater prosperity?

What are the concerns about income growth in less-developed countries?

What role can property rights and markets play in the protection of environmental resources?

How can government use market incentives to protect the environment?

Why It Matters

When you started this course, you began a journey of economic thinking. One of the first lessons you learned was that people cannot have everything they want. Scarcity influences all our decisions. Another lesson you have learned is that scarcity does not mean people have to be poor. It just means we must make choices about what to produce, how to produce, and who will receive what is produced. There are resources available to help people live well. The key is to coordinate the use of these resources so that they provide appropriate living standards for everyone.

We make choices as part of a world economy, a web of human activity in which our individual choices affect others, and their choices affect us. A businessperson may make a choice to produce cornflakes, but no one individual or group has all the required knowledge to produce cornflakes. Instead, that knowledge is spread among many different people and groups, each performing specialized tasks. That same observation is true for many products we use today. The production and use of cell phones, computer software, and Global Positioning Systems (GPS) are some obvious examples of how people from several continents help provide the products and services we use. Because we now rely on others around the world for many goods and services, it is important to understand how a global economy works.

Mark to Remember

* *This is important.*

? *I have a question about this.*

! *This is a surprise.*

Chapter 16

Our Globalized World

Building On What You Know

No doubt you know about the Olympic Games, held every four years, in which athletes compete in several sports. You've probably seen the opening or closing ceremonies with athletes from around the world parading in very colorful costumes that reflect their unique cultures. We know the results of Olympic competition in real time through worldwide television transmission. This kind of television transmission brings the world into your living room, not just for the Olympics but for many of the other natural, political, and cultural events that happen around the globe. Perhaps you have heard the expression that "our world is getting smaller," that we are becoming a global community. What does this mean? What happens to international trade in a smaller world? What about international travel? What are the effects of a smaller world—a global community—on richer countries and on poorer countries?

Many people worldwide are using their specialized knowledge to produce complex goods and services, such as aircraft or international bank accounts. Internationally, people are also producing many things others want, such as electronic appliances, music, clothes, sports, and entertainment. Working in gigantic teams, international producers fit things together economically, like pieces of a puzzle. We also communicate with each other—almost instantaneously. Our world is becoming more and more globalized.

Think Critically

At least one expert has claimed that the two technological advances which have most advanced globalization are wireless communication and the airplane. Explain why you agree or disagree.

_____

_____

_____

Globalization

Globalization is a relatively new term, and it has become more widely used today. **Globalization** is the process in which countries and their citizens becoming increasingly interdependent. Defined this way, globalization includes international trade, international travel, and tourism, as well as the spread of movies and music, information via the Internet, sports, disease, terrorism, and religious conflicts.

Globalization since World War II has been driven by advances in technology. These advances have reduced the costs of international trade. As you learned in Chapter 15, international trade negotiations have led to a series of agreements to remove restrictions on free trade. Trade agreements, such as the North American Free Trade Agreement (NAFTA), have pursued the goal of reducing tariffs and barriers to trade.

Many people have come to agree that our world is increasingly confronted by problems that cannot be solved by individual nations acting alone. Examples include cross-boundary air and water pollution, overfishing of the oceans, regulation of outer space, global warming, international terrorist networks, and global trade and finance. Since World War II and the beginning of the United Nations, there has been an explosion in the expansion of transnational corporations and in the spread of democracy worldwide.

Worldwide Changes as a Result of Globalization

The United Nations and other global organizations, such as the World Bank, have begun keeping statistics on different dimensions of globalization related to the quality of people's lives. Here are some highlights of quality-of-life changes that these organizations claim.

- Life expectancy has almost doubled in the developing world since World War II, and the gap is starting to close in the less-developed world where the improvement has been smaller. Infant mortality has decreased in every developing region of the world.

- Democracy increased dramatically from almost no nations with universal suffrage (the right to vote) in 1900 to 62.5 percent of all nations in 2000.

- Between 1950 and 1999, global literacy increased from 52 percent to 81 percent of the world. Women made up much of this gap; female literacy as a percentage of male literacy increased from 59 percent in 1970 to 80 percent in 2000.

- The percentage of children in the world labor force fell from 24 percent in 1960 to 10 percent in 2000.

- Current trends indicate increased availability in many countries of electric power, cars, radios, and telephones per capita.

- An increased percentage of the world's population has access to clean water.

Check Your Understanding

How does clean water improve the quality of life in a country?

_____

_____

_____

How Does Globalization Help?

The text lists six areas in which globalization has improved the quality of life in less-developed countries. Choose three of the areas and explain how globalization has helped bring about improvements.

1. _____

_____

2. _____

_____

3. _____

_____

Antiglobalization

Critics of economic globalization claim that it does not always flow naturally from the needs of everyone, nor does globalization always serve everyone's needs. These critics argue that globalization serves corporate interests. The critics also maintain that the poor and working classes throughout the globe are kept poor by corporate interests.

Antiglobalization critics state that unrestricted free trade benefits those who are better off financially (the rich) at the expense of the poor. That is, all the benefits of free trade accrue to the rich, and the poor are not better off.

Some antiglobalization groups argue that globalization is imperialistic, meaning that more-powerful countries try to dominate or exercise some authority over less-powerful countries. They state that imperialism was one of the driving forces behind the United States' invasion of Iraq and that the resulting war caused savings to flow into the United States from developing nations. The critics state that globalization is just another term for Americanization. These critics also say that the United States could be the only country to profit from globalization.

However, it is hard to argue with the improvements in peoples' quality of life worldwide. Improvements in life expectancy, democracy, literacy, and other trends represent significant improvements, whether or not they have come about solely because of globalization. This is not to say that the entire world is well off. There are still significant differences between the lives of people in richer, more-developed countries and those in poorer, less-developed countries.

Economic Development

In general economic terms, *development* means "to grow or to expand." For an economy to grow and expand, its gross domestic product must increase without significant inflation. In addition, economists consider per capita income a good measure of how well a country has developed and how its standard of living has grown.

In the 21st century, globalization is an economic fact of life. Not all countries have embraced it or want it to expand. Countries such as Iran, Venezuela, and Ecuador have resisted globalization, and high oil prices in the global market helped them maintain their economic standards of living while they resisted other opportunities to open their economies to international trade. Most countries, some reluctantly, others enthusiastically, embraced the new world economy. The new century and millennium began with widespread confidence that open markets and free global trade would offer great opportunity for higher productivity and living standards in developed countries. Leaders in less-developed countries could see the higher incomes in developed economies, and they too wanted growth in productivity and living standards for their citizens. They welcomed open markets and increased international trade activity.

According to the World Bank, in 2000 low-income, or less-developed, nations were those with per capita GDPs between $760 and $9,360. High-income, or more-developed, nations had per capita GDPs of $9,361 and higher. Based on these per capita income criteria, the countries of Yemen, Tanzania, Malawi, Afghanistan, Uganda, Mongolia, and India were considered less-developed nations. More-developed nations included Russia, South Korea, Australia, Canada, the United States, Germany, and Norway.

Check Your Understanding

Describe three arguments critics make against globalization.

1._____

_____

2._____

_____

3._____

_____

Do you think these arguments are persuasive enough to slow the growth of globalization? Why or why not?

_____

_____

_____

While levels of income and production are lower in less-developed nations, their growth rates of production today are generally higher than more-developed countries. This growth will likely result in much improved living standards over time.

More or Less Developed?

Use the World Bank criteria for identifying low-income, less-developed nations. Beside each country listed below, indicate whether the country's 2005 per capita GDP put it in the more-developed or the less-developed nation category.

Country	Per Capita GDP	More Developed or Less Developed
Bangladesh	$2,011	_____
Denmark	$34,740	_____
Japan	$30,615	_____
Peru	$5,983	_____
El Salvador	$4,518	_____
Chile	$11,937	_____

Economic Development and Population Growth

It is wise to remember that meaningful economic growth is a recent event. Per capita income remained virtually unchanged for the first millennium and changed little for much of the second millennium. Not until the last two centuries has there been much growth of per capita production and income. Compared to earlier times, the last 200 years have brought remarkable advancements in people's lives, not just in production and income but also in life expectancy, health, knowledge, and even leisure.

Not surprisingly, the improved living standards over the past 200 years have also brought a faster growing population. People are living longer, so death rates have fallen compared to birth rates. If one compares population and production between the more-developed economies of Europe, North America, and Japan on the one hand and the less-developed economies on the other, there is a major difference in population. The more-developed economies have bigger increases in per capita production, but smaller increases in population. As production and living standards rose ever higher in Europe, North America, and Japan, birth rates began to equalize with death rates. When birth and death rates in a country become equal, there is no net growth in the country's population. Nations pass through this change, referred to as the "demographic transition." In this transition, as parents' incomes rise, they have fewer children.

iStockphoto '07

Think Critically

Why do you think an increase in a country's per capita production often happens together with a decrease in the country's birth rate?

_____

_____

_____

291

Figure 16-1: Rates of Birth, Death, and Population Growth by Region, 2002

Check Your Understanding

Show the calculation you would do to obtain the rate of natural increase for North America in Figure 16-1.

_____

Region	Births per 1,000 population	Deaths per 1,000 population	Rate of natural increase (percent)
World	21	9	1.2
Demographic Transition Mostly Over			
Europe and the New Independent States	11	11	0.0
North America	14	8	0.6
Oceania	17	7	1.0
Demographic Transition Occurring			
Africa	36	14	2.2
Asia	19	8	1.2
Latin America and the Caribbean	21	6	1.5

Source: *U.S. Census Bureau, Global Population Profile: 2002,* Table A-3.
Website: http://www.census.gov/prod/2004pubs/wp-02.pdf

The table in Figure 16-1 illustrates the demographic transition that has occurred in various regions of the world. In Europe, North America, and Oceania, birth rates have plummeted and are equal or close to death rates, thus greatly reducing the yearly growth of population. In some European nations, birth rates are falling so low that populations could decline. Because of low birth rates in Europe and North America, elderly people comprise a larger percentage of these nations' populations. In the United States, for example, people age 65 and over are expected to represent about 20 percent of the population in the next 30 years, up from about 12 percent in 1999.

Birth and Death Rates

Refer to Figure 16-1 to answer the following questions.

1. What continent has the highest birth rate? _____

2. What continent has the lowest birth rate? _____

3. What continent has the highest death rate? _____

4. What is the world's birth rate? _____

5. What is North America's death rate? _____

Productivity and Population in Less-Developed Countries

For living standards to continue to rise in less-developed nations, production must rise faster than the increase in the number of people. The demographic transition is in its early stages in these nations. While population growth rates are higher in Asia, Africa, and Latin America than in other regions, they have still declined over the last two decades as birth rates have fallen.

Figure 16-2: Fertility Rates, 1990–2050

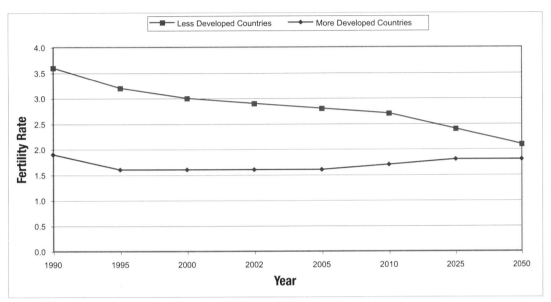

Unequal time intervals on the horizontal axis. Population replacement fertility rate is 2.3.
Source: U.S. Census Bureau, *Global Population Profile: 2002,* Table A-9.
    Website: http://www.census.gov/prod/2004pubs/wp-02.pdf

The graph in Figure 16-2 shows that the *fertility rate* has been falling significantly for less-developed nations since 1990. The **fertility rate** is the average number of births during a year to women of childbearing age. If per capita incomes continue to rise in less-developed economies, they are likely to pull these regions farther through the demographic transition. Population growth in these regions and throughout the world would then continue to fall.

Analyzing Fertility Rates

Use the information in Figure 16-2 to answer these questions.

1. What was the fertility rate in less-developed countries in 2000? _____

2. What was the fertility rate in more-developed countries in 2000? _____

3. Describe what the graph suggests about the projected trend in fertility rates of less-developed countries for the period 2005 to 2050.

_____

Show Your Understanding

Using a pen, follow the trend lines in Figure 16-2 to the point where they come together.

If the trends continue as they are currently going, about how many years will it be before less-developed and more-developed countries have approximately the same fertility rates?

_____

2. fertility rate

China: A Case Study in Development

Not long ago, China had a very poor economy. It had a rapidly growing population mostly living on farms, which made the country vulnerable to food shortages. It was a communist country, in which the economy was coordinated through central government planning. People were not allowed to own their own property, nor were they allowed to travel freely.

In the 1980s, things began to change. Even though the political leadership of China still refers to itself as communist, it has allowed the country's economy to change so it more closely resembles a market economy. It allows ownership now. As you know, private ownership is a key to economic progress in a free enterprise economy. First, farms were allowed to be owned privately, and within a short time China was producing enough food for its citizens, as well as exporting food to other countries. Next, it allowed people to start and own businesses. It also sold some of the government-operated businesses to private owners.

By 2005, 70 percent of China's GDP was coming from the private sector of the economy. It had a population of 1.3 billion people, and its per capita income was approximately $7,200, making it a less-developed nation. This income was low by United States standards, but it is rising rapidly. Chinese officials have claimed that the GDP has increased by a factor of ten since 1978. All this change seems to have resulted from the Communist Party's decision to reform the economy. It became more market-oriented, yet political control is still exercised by the Communist Party. The system is called "Socialism with Chinese Characteristics" and mixes government-controlled businesses with private business. In particular, the government has focused on foreign trade as the major vehicle for economic growth. The United States has become one of China's largest trading partners.

The changes in China have brought on problems, as well as improvement of living conditions. The government has been criticized for human rights violations, for not moving toward a democratic form of government, for conducting unfair trade practices, and for creating a large gap between rich and poor citizens. However, the net effect of the economic reform seems to be positive. In 1980, China and its population were desperately poor. Now, by embracing trade and economic freedom, it has improved the living conditions of its people and contributed significantly to the growth of the world economy.

Check Your Understanding

When China's leaders decided to try to raise their citizens' standard of living, how did they start the process?

_____

_____

_____

Why do a communist government and a free-market economy seem an unlikely combination?

_____

_____

_____

Chinese Imports

The number of products imported from China into the United States has dramatically increased in the past decade. With three or four other students, compile a list of all the made-in-China products you can identify on the lines below. Do a satisfaction rating by having the owners of the products that you identify state whether the product is *satisfactory* or *unsatisfactory*. Use additional paper if needed. To create a more comprehensive list, compile the lists of all the groups in your class.

Made-in-China Product	Satisfactory or Unsatisfactory?
_____	_____
_____	_____
_____	_____

Economies of Other Countries

As China has reformed into the 1990s, Russia and other former communist countries have attempted to move toward democracy and free markets. In these former communist economies, it was difficult to establish a rule of law, property rights, and other necessary conditions for markets to rise and flourish. As most of these economies struggled to make the transition toward markets, they often stumbled. The unfortunate result was a negative growth rate in many of these economies as shown in the table in Figure 16-3 for the time period 1990–2001. Negative growth rates mean that a country's people are becoming less fortunate financially because fewer goods and services are being produced and consumed.

Figure 16-3: Average GDP Growth, 1990–2001

Country	Growth Rate (Percent)
Armenia	-0.7
Azerbaijan	2.7
Belarus	-0.8
Bulgaria	-1.5
Estonia	0.2
Georgia	-5.6
Kazakhstan	-2.8
Latvia	-2.2
Lithuania	-2.3
Moldova	-8.4
Poland	4.5
Romania	-0.3
Russian Federation	-3.7
Slovak Republic	2.3
Slovenia	2.9
Tajikistan	-8.7
Turkmenistan	-2.8
Ukraine	-7.9
Uzbekistan	0.0
World	**2.7**

Source: *World Development Report, 2003*, Table 3 (World Bank).

Check Your Understanding

Use information in Figure 16-3 to answer this question:

Which three countries had the greatest negative GDP growth rates during the period 1990 to 2001?

_____

_____

_____

In the widely read newsmagazine, *The Economist*,[1] GDP growth forecasts for 2007 were reported. For four former communist countries, the report forecasted GDP growth rates that are close to or that exceed 10 percent. They are Azerbaijan (18 percent), Kazakhstan (10 percent), Armenia (9 percent), and Estonia (9 percent). Clearly these four countries have been able to turn around their economies.

Many countries throughout Asia have been promoting rapid economic growth. During the 1970s and 1980s, Japan, South Korea, Hong Kong, Singapore, Taiwan, and other Asian nations looked to markets and international trade to promote economic growth. In many cases, they also accepted democracy and political freedom. The rapid, sustained growth of Asia's economies did not escape the world's attention. Government leaders elsewhere turned away from central planning and looked toward markets to grow their economies. In nation after nation, governments trimmed their budgets, sold government-owned resources to private individuals, and opened their markets to greater competition, both at home and abroad.

What Has Happened to Russia, China, and Japan Today?

After the end of World War II, the United States developed an adversarial relationship with Russia and China. Although enemies during the war, the United States and Japan became allies and trading partners. In the past 50 years, much has happened in the three countries. Describe the status of each country's economy today.

Russia _____

_____

China _____

_____

Japan _____

_____

Pause to Remember

In Chapter 15, you learned about some arguments that critics make against free trade. Recall and explain two of those arguments.

1. _____

_____

2. _____

_____

Income Growth in Less-Developed Economies

Economic growth may continue to raise living standards in today's less-developed nations, but this growth depends partly on whether people will be free to trade openly with others in the global marketplace. Governments opened their markets and promoted free trade during the second half of the last century. Yet, serious opposition to foreign ownership of businesses and labor migration from one country to another still exists. One major obstacle to increasing free trade is that wealthier nations are insisting that labor and environmental standards be part of further trade agreements. Most developing nations view such standards as disguised trade barriers that close world markets to them. This disagreement has threatened to reverse decades of progress toward freer global trade.

1 "The Times They Are A-Changin'." *The Economist* (vol. 36, January 7, 2006).

Labor Standards

Many who want future trade agreements to include strong labor standards offer at least two arguments. First, they believe that without such standards, further opening of global markets will cause a "race to the bottom." Workers' wages and benefits will fall in advanced economies as their higher-paid workers are forced to compete with lower-paid workers in less-developed nations. Chapter 15 explained why economic thinking flashes a warning light in front of this argument. Wages and benefits are generally higher in more-developed economies. When higher wages are accompanied by higher productivity, they don't raise per unit labor costs.

Second, proponents of strong labor standards believe the standards are necessary to improve wages and working conditions in less-developed nations. Again, economic thinking flashes a warning light. Over time, wage levels depend on the productivity of people's labor. Wages in less-developed nations tend to be low because productivity in these nations is usually much lower than in more-developed economies. With productivity low in these nations, could their workers compete successfully in the global economy if they had to meet labor standards similar to those in more productive, wealthier nations? It seems unlikely.

This worry is nothing new to people in less-developed nations. They have long wondered how their less-productive workers could possibly compete against more-productive workers elsewhere. The best chance these workers have of competing successfully is to work for lower wages that compensate for their lower productivity. It shouldn't be a surprise, then, that less-developed nations strongly oppose putting tough labor standards in future trade agreements.

iStockphoto '07

Proponents of strong labor standards believe the standards are necessary to improve wages and working conditions in less developed nations.

Think Critically

In your own words, explain what "race to the bottom" means.

_____

_____

_____

Muhammad Yunus
Marcus Brandt/Getty Images

Micro-Credit Pioneer, Muhammad Yunus

Bangladeshi economist Muhammad Yunus and the Grameen Bank he created won the 2006 Nobel Peace Prize for leveraging small loans into major social change for impoverished families.

The Grameen Bank's pioneering use of micro-credit has been duplicated across the globe since Yunus started the project in his home village more than three decades ago. Loans as low as nine dollars have helped beggars start small businesses and poor women buy cellular phones and basket-weaving materials.

The Nobel committee praised Yunus as "a leader who has managed to translate visions into practical action for the benefit of millions of people, not only in Bangladesh but across cultures and civilizations."

After he won the award, "I was trying to find people to tell, and the phone kept buzzing, so I could hardly tell anybody," said Yunus, from his home in Dhaka, the capital of Bangladesh. "Then people started coming and bringing flowers." Still exuberant after hours of telephone calls and hundreds of visitors, Yunus said, "This prize is so overwhelming, it will affect our work tremendously. It will bring the issues I'm raising to the attention of people who can make a difference in the world."

Yunus said he believed the Nobel committee endorsed his view that bridging the gap between rich and poor countries in an age of increasing globalization is critical to reducing conflict around the world.

"You cannot go on having absurd amounts of wealth when other people have problems of survival," he said. "If you can bring an end to poverty, at least from an economic point of view, you can have a more livable situation between very rich people and very poor people, very rich countries and very poor countries. That's our basic ingredient for peace."

Source: *Washington Post Foreign Service*, October 14, 2006, by Molly Moore (excerpted)

Economic Growth and the Environment

In the years following World War II, the United States' economy grew at an astonishing rate. With the increase in goods, services, incomes, and living standards came a variety of new environmental problems. In 1948, a "killer smog" in Donora, Pennsylvania, took 20 lives and demonstrated the reality of air pollution. Other events, like a burning river in Cleveland and air pollution so thick that cars drove with headlights on during the day, demonstrated the water and air quality problems of the 1960s. In the 1970s, incidents at Love Canal in New York and elsewhere brought public attention to the consequences of improper disposal of toxic wastes. Today, the impact of human activity on changing the world's climate is receiving global attention.

There is no doubt that markets have sometimes failed to promote careful and efficient use of environmental resources. Yet markets have motivated and coordinated people to use other resources wisely. Why do they sometimes fail to do the same for environmental resources? Economists suggest there may be an interesting answer to this question, and it begins with the following fable.

Think Critically

Air and water are essential to life. Yet they are our most often polluted natural resources. Why do you think this is the case?

_____

_____

_____

The Cow and the Buffalo

A long time ago, there was a cattle ranch that belonged to a family named Burger. The Burgers took great care to raise their steers and keep them well-fed and healthy. They ringed their ranch with barbed wire to keep their cattle in and trespassers out. The family's stewardship of the herd caused its size to grow over the years. Beginning with only 50 steers, the herd eventually grew to 5,000.

The Burgers' ranch was near buffalo country, where these wild beasts roamed freely across acres and acres of land that no one owned. People valued the buffalo for their meat and hides, so they killed them. Then, they killed many more. "It's like a race to take as many as you can," said grizzly old Will Hunt. "If I didn't take 'em, someone else would. So I took 'em while the takin' was good." While cattle thrived and multiplied on the Burgers' ranch, buffalo disappeared on the wide-open range.

Resources and Incentives

The point of the fable is that people have incentives to care for resources they own. The Burgers took good care of the cattle because they could benefit from that stewardship. A healthy, large steer brings a better price in the marketplace than a smaller animal. They also knew they could incur the cost of caring for the cattle because no one was allowed to take the cows from them. They owned the cattle, and their ownership was protected.

In contrast, buffalo were common property; they were resources with access open to everyone. Here, the incentive was not careful stewardship but, as Will Hunt put it, a race to use resources before someone else got them first. No one owned the buffalo until the animal was killed. At that point, the animal belonged to the hunter. People ignored the cost of destroying the valuable resource because it was external to their decision making. Ecologist Garrett Hardin called the wasteful result "the tragedy of the commons." We still see this behavior with regard to the atmosphere and the oceans. Both areas are used to dump our wastes because the atmosphere and the oceans belong to no one person. They are owned in common.

Economic reasoning suggests that environmental destruction usually happens because of an absence of clearly defined rights to private property. There are no market prices for many environmental resources, so people lack accurate information about their scarcity, and they lack strong incentives to use these resources carefully. Is there a way to provide the missing information and incentives? The story of the African elephant may hold an answer.

Elephants and Ownership

Between 1979 and 1994, the number of elephants in 14 African nations dwindled by nearly 60 percent, from 1.3 million to 543,000. The decline occurred because people slaughtered the animals for ivory and other products. To save the elephants, the Convention on International Trade in Endangered Species (CITES) of Wild Fauna and Flora banned all international trade in ivory and other elephant products in 1989. The result was that a large illegal market for ivory thrived because poachers killed elephants and sold the ivory to dealers who sold the product internationally. The number of elephants in countries like Kenya continued to decline despite the government's attempt to protect them in national parks.

South Africa and Zimbabwe took a different approach. Under a program called CAMPFIRE (Communal Areas Management Program for Indigenous Resources), communities located near the elephant herds received limited property rights to the elephants in their regions.

Check Your Understanding

Describe what the expression "tragedy of the commons" means.

_____

_____

_____

_____

299

iStockphoto '07

Apply Your Understanding

Air is something we all use, but there is no market price for air. Why?

_____

_____

If you had to set a price for air, how might you go about it?

_____

_____

_____

As "owners" of the elephants, the communities were allowed to legally earn money from tourists and hunters and from the sale of meat, hides, ivory, and other elephant products. With market incentives similar to those of the Burgers in the fable, the communities now view elephants as valuable investments to protect. Elephant populations are increasing in South Africa and Zimbabwe, two countries that have turned toward property rights and markets as a means of protection. Meanwhile, the number of elephants has continued to decline in nations that rely solely on banning the sale of ivory and other elephant products.

The elephant story illustrates two approaches to reducing environmental destruction. In this instance the problem concerns protecting and preserving the elephant population. The ban on selling ivory products tried to reach that goal through government controls. In contrast, nations creating property rights to the elephants in certain regions sought to create market incentives to care for the animals.

A similar conflict exists between government control and voluntary markets over the protection of other environmental resources (such as fresh air, forests, and fish). Like elephants and wild buffalo, these resources are generally common property with open access to all. For example, from a worldwide viewpoint, fresh air is a global commodity that people everywhere have been using and abusing with little or no thought to the cost. The reason has been an absence of private ownership and markets. Can markets truly promote the careful use of air, water, fish, and other open-access resources? The next section will help you decide.

Human Motivation

The elephant story in the text describes two ways to motivate people to change their behavior: disincentives (fees or punishments) and incentives (opportunities to personally benefit). Explain the pros and cons of disincentives and incentives in solving public problems.

	Pros	Cons
Disincentives	_____	_____
	_____	_____
Incentives	_____	_____
	_____	_____

Markets or Government Regulations?

 Government agencies usually are given responsibility to protect the environment and regulate those producers who use environmental resources. In the 1960s and 1970s, the United States Congress enacted important environmental protection laws such as the Clean Air Act, the Clean Water Act, and the Endangered Species Act. In the subsequent decades, water quality and air quality improved in the United States. However, the consequences of the laws' enforcement had unfortunate results for many businesses. For some, the costs of conforming with environmental legislation outweighed its benefits. Businesses used legal challenges to avoid some of the high costs of cleanup. In other cases, firms went out of business because they could not afford the costs imposed by the laws.

Economists have suggested a variety of governmental policies to change the incentives involved in the decision to pollute or clean up. These incentive-based solutions create prices so polluters can estimate their cost of pollution control and evaluate the costs of different methods to reduce their pollution output. These solutions rely on the information received from different prices, rather than government regulations, to reduce pollution. Below are a few examples.

Fees and Pollution

Government can now levy taxes or fees that rise or fall with the amount of pollution a business emits. The less pollution a business produces, the lower the fee. By linking the fee to the amount of pollution generated, firms are given an incentive to find the most efficient ways to reduce pollution.

Environmental fees or taxes can also work for resources other than air. For example, many local governments in the United States set the price of trash collection below the real costs of providing this service. They often charge fixed fees that don't vary with the amount of collection services that a household uses. Some communities have changed that policy. Now they charge people fees based on the amount of solid waste that households discard. To avoid higher fees, people curb their waste creation and recycle more material. Similarly, drivers in Singapore and in Stockholm, Sweden, pay higher tolls to drive during rush hour. To avoid this higher toll, people drive at different times, take a bus, or find a different way to make their commute. The rush-hour fees reduce the traffic congestion in both cities, and they reduce the air pollution levels.

Tradable Permits

Another governmental method of using limited market incentives to reduce air pollution and other environmental harm is tradable permits. Here, government officials sell or distribute permits that allow businesses (or individuals) to emit a fixed amount of pollution. The total level of pollution allowed by the permits is less than the current level of pollution. The permits are tradable, however, so a business able to reduce pollution at a small cost can do so and then sell some of its permits to other firms for whom pollution control is more costly.

The business selling the permit gains money from its sale, but it must reduce its pollution emissions enough so it equals the amount of reduction required by both firms. The business buying the permit must bear the costs of polluting by paying the market price for the permit, but it gains by being allowed to continue producing. The community gains because it sacrifices fewer resources when meeting an environmental goal. The sacrifice is

Think Critically

Why would a government levy a tax that can rise or fall based on the amount of pollution a business emits?

_____

_____

Do you think this is an effective way to limit pollution? Why or why not?

_____

_____

_____

301

smaller because the businesses reducing pollution are the ones able to do so at the lowest opportunity cost. In other words, businesses with a comparative advantage in pollution reduction are the ones who specialize in that activity.

In the United States, the Environmental Protection Agency uses tradable permits to reduce sulfur dioxide emissions to meet the standards set by the Clean Air Act. Tradable permits are even used to reduce over-catching of Alaskan halibut and other fish. As part of the international effort to reduce global warming, an international tradable permit system has been proposed to help reduce emissions of carbon dioxide and other noxious gases.

Tradable Parking Permits

The principal of an inner-city high school received many complaints from neighbors around the school about the noise and air pollution created by the cars that students drive to school. He decided to respond to the complaints by reducing the number of student parking spaces from 400 to 100 and selling permits for those 100 spaces. The parking permits could be traded, but the price for a permit was quite high, $300.

Mario had $300 in savings that he could use to buy a permit. However, if he used that money, he wouldn't have any money left for gas or entertainment. How might Mario buy the permit and use it to make money to pay for his other needs? Name at least three possibilities.

_____

_____

_____

Think Critically

Imagine that your city has a river running through the center of it. The river has become very polluted and unattractive. A company with a plant along the river has agreed to buy the river and clean it up, if the city will grant the company the rights to unlimited water from the river at no cost. Do you think the city council should make this agreement with the company?

_____ *Why or why not?*

_____

_____

Our Global Cupboard

Efforts to create or strengthen markets can help preserve or improve environmental resources while also promoting economic growth. Indeed, the objective of economic growth is to increase, not decrease, the contents of our global economic cupboard, which include such natural resources as fresh air and clean water. Markets can work on behalf of all these resources by requiring people to choose carefully when using them. Markets can also encourage people to add value to the economic cupboard over time.

From 1900 to 2005, real (inflation-adjusted) prices for commodities such as farm products, metals, minerals, and energy (excluding oil) declined, meaning that these commodities were becoming more plentiful in the global economic cupboard, despite increasing world production, incomes, and population over the period. In late 2005 and 2006, many commodity prices, especially petroleum, increased dramatically because of the increased demand coming from China and India as their economies grew rapidly. Economists anticipate these prices will stabilize or fall as producers respond to the higher prices by increasing the long-term supply of these materials.

New Research and Technology

Why did the price of these commodities decline? One important reason was the development of new resources and the discovery of new technologies that got more mileage out of existing ones. For example, finding ways to produce twice as much from a given quantity of a resource is much like having twice as much of it. The World Bank describes the process this way:

"Substitution between commodities has been an important element of commodity demand during the twentieth century. This has included increased substitution between commodities such as aluminum and other metals. But in addition, synthetics such as plastics and other man-made materials displaced traditional commodities. Synthetic rubber production, for example, now exceeds natural rubber production. Man-made fabrics such as nylon and polyester have replaced cotton in clothing and other fiber uses, and now account for about half of all fiber use. Non-caloric sweeteners have replaced sugar in some drinks. New man-made materials continue to be developed and are likely to further displace commodities during the twenty-first century." [1]

The kinds and quantities of resources are continually changing. People persistently search for new resources and methods when markets give them incentives and when markets provide accurate information about the scarcity of particular resources. For example, there are many historical examples of instances when an increasing scarcity of a resource (like wood or whale oil) increased its market price and thus encouraged people to develop substitute resources (like coal or oil). Similarly, businesses today know they can reduce their costs and earn more money if they can discover ways of using fewer resources while also maintaining or improving product quality.

The Future

Our globalized world does not, and will not, stand still. Too much trade activity, worker immigration, and flows of financial capital occur between countries. In mid-2016, the U.S. economy had a very low unemployment rate of 4.7 percent of the labor force—relatively full employment. The Dow Jones Industrial Average continued its climb into record high territory, indicating an optimistic outlook about the economy.

In spite of a sound internal economy, many Americans today believe that free trade with other countries costs more jobs than it creates. This concern may have some basis in fact. One prediction is that by the year 2030, total world trade will triple to $27 trillion. Much of the world trade growth will take place outside the United States. Insecure U.S. workers, concerned about losing their jobs to other countries, include white-collar service industry workers (such as hotel managers), computer programmers, software engineers, radiologists, and accountants. United States union officials are considering tougher labor standards in other countries as part of trade agreements. Other officials are concerned about weak environmental standards abroad and want stricter environmental standards in trade agreements. Additional globalization concerns are likely to surface almost every month. We can be sure that the next two decades will witness significant changes in how our globalized world works.

Apply Your Understanding

Many people worry that the United States will run out of oil and gas to fuel our cars and trucks. Some people argue that the government should invest more money in developing substitutes for the oil and gas we currently use. Others argue that the government should place stricter limits on fuel consumption and increase the price of fuel.

Which do you think would be the more effective way to solve the fuel problem?

_____

Explain your answer.

_____

_____

_____

1 Source: The World Bank *Global Economic Prospects 2006* (Washington, DC, 2006).

Summary

Our world is becoming more and more globalized. Globalization is the process of increasing interdependence among countries and their citizens. While some argue against globalization, it cannot be denied that significant improvements in peoples' quality of life have been made in the past 50 years.

For purposes of analysis, the world's countries are categorized as less-developed and more-developed, based on each country's per capita gross domestic product. Economic growth rates of less-developed countries have improved markedly the past 200 years. Better living standards mean that economic productivity must increase faster than increases in population. China is a good case study of increasing productivity through markets since the 1980s.

Economic growth may continue to raise living standards in less-developed countries. However, an obstacle to opening up free trade with these countries may be their willingness to institute fair labor standards and environmental protections.

The worldwide environment is of major concern to economists and policymakers. Rather than instituting a wide range of government regulations to try to stop environmental destruction, market incentive-based solutions have been tried with some successes. Similarly, new research and technology may help reduce the overuse of scarce natural resources.

iStockphoto '07

Bibliography to Support JA Economics

Online Resources

The resources cited are mainly sources of statistical data, many of which were used in the *JA Economics* chapters. These sources are useful in updating the tables and graphs in the text.

U.S. Census Bureau................................... www.census.gov

Bureau of Labor Statistics .... www.bls.gov or stats.bls.gov

Department of Commerce .... www.commerce.gov

Economic Report of the President............. www.gpo.gov/fdsys/browse/collection.action?collectionCode=ERP

Occupational Outlook Handbook............. www.bls.gov/ooh

Small Business Administration .... www.sba.gov

Statistical Abstracts of the United States .... www.census.gov/library/publications/time-series/statistical_abstracts.html

Resources of the Federal Reserve System

Each Federal Reserve Bank publishes several useful and easy-to-read documents on various aspects of our economy and monetary system for high school students and general audiences. For example, the Dallas Fed publishes *Free Enterprise: The Economics of Cooperation*. The New York Fed publishes *The Story of Money*. The San Francisco Fed publishes a history of the Federal Reserve.

To access the Board of Governors of the Federal Reserve System site go to:
www.federalreserve.gov
This site will present the websites of all the federal reserve banks.

For a listing of educational resources of the Federal Reserve, go to:
www.FederalReserveEducation.org

Current News Sources

Two current news sources are recommended, *The Wall Street Journal* and *The Economist*. Their access information appears below.

The Wall Street Journal services: www.wsj.com, or call 1-800-568-7625
For information on the WSJ Student Journal, go to student.wsj.com

For subscription information on *The Economist*, call 1-800-456-6086 or visit the website:
www.economist.com
E-mail is: customerhelp@economist.com

Basic Economics Library

A basic economics library is recommended. The volumes cited below will provide sound economics content, as well as a range of policy positions on the economy.

Friedman, Milton. *Capitalism and Freedom*. 40th Ed. Chicago: University of Chicago Press, 2002.

Friedman, Milton, and Rose, Friedman. *Free to Choose: A Personal Statement*. Orlando, Florida: Harcourt Brace and Company, 1980.

Gwartney, James D., et al. *Economics: Private and Public Choice*. Australia; Mason, Ohio: South-Western, Cengage Learning, 2012.

Heilbroner, Robert L. *The Making of Economic Society*. 13th Ed. Upper Saddle River, New Jersey, 2012.

Heilbroner, Robert L. *The Worldly Philosophers*. 7th Ed. New York: Simon and Schuster, 1999.

Mankiw, N. Gregory. *Principles of Macroeconomics and Principles of Microeconomics*. 3rd Ed. Mason, Ohio: Thompson/Southwestern, 2004.

McConnell, Campbell R., and Stanley L. Brue, and Sean M. Flynn. *Economics: Principles, Problems, and Policies*. 20th Ed. New York: McGraw-Hill Education, 2015.

Samuelson, Paul A., and William D. Nordhaus. *Economics*. 19th Ed. Boston: McGraw-Hill Irwin, 2010.

Silk, Leonard. *Economics in Plain English*. New York: Simon and Schuster, 1986.

Glossary of Key Terms

401(k) plan – A for-profit company's retirement plan that allows an employee to save up to a certain amount of income per year and avoid paying taxes on the income until it is withdrawn.

A

Ability-to-pay principle – A principle stating that government should tax people in proportion to their ability to pay the tax.

Absolute advantage – The ability of a person or a nation to produce a good at a lower cost than another person or nation.

Annual percentage rate (APR) – The cost of credit calculated as an annual percentage rate of the principal borrowed.

Asset – Anything of monetary value owned by an individual or company.

Average fixed costs – Total fixed costs divided by quantity produced.

Average total costs – The sum of average fixed and average variable costs.

Average variable costs – Total variable costs divided by quantity produced.

B

Balance of payments – A record of all exchanges between a country's residents and those of other nations over some time period.

Balance of trade – The value of goods and services bought and sold on the world market.

Balance sheet – A report of a company's, or an individual's, assets, liabilities, and net worth on a specified date.

Bank – A financial institution that accepts demand deposits and makes commercial loans.

Barter – An exchange of goods and services without using money.

Benefits – The gains that result when a choice is made.

Benefits-received principle – A principle stating that government should tax people in proportion to the benefits they receive from a government good or service.

Bond – A promise to repay borrowed money to a lender at a fixed rate of interest at a specified time.

Break-even point – The point of production at which income from sales equals total fixed and total variable costs.

Budget – A financial plan that summarizes an individual's planned income and spending over a specific time period.

Glossary of Key Terms

Business cycle	–	A measure of recurring ups and downs in the level of economic activity over time.
Buying power	–	The quantity of goods and services a person can buy with a given amount of money.
Capital	–	The buildings, tools, and machines people create and use to produce final goods and services.
Capital account	–	An account in a nation's balance of payments that shows the flow of financial capital into and out of a nation.
Certificate of deposit (CD)	–	A receipt issued by a bank to a person depositing money in an account for a specified period of time at a fixed rate of interest.
Charter	–	A document that states the nature of the business, the initial owners of the stock, and the types of stocks to be sold.
Collateral	–	The capital acceptable to a lender for a loan.
Collective bargaining	–	A process in which union and company representatives meet to negotiate a new labor contract.
Collusion	–	An agreement in which companies restrict production to raise prices and profits.
Command economy	–	An economic system in which the government holds most property rights.
Common stock	–	A claim to a share of the profits of a company after all expenses and taxes are paid.
Comparative advantage	–	The ability of an individual or nation to produce a product at a lower opportunity cost than another individual or nation.
Complementary goods	–	Products that often are used together.
Compound interest	–	Interest calculated on the sum of savings plus the accumulated interest, provided the interest earned is kept in savings.
Concentration ratio	–	The percentage of an industry's sales accounted for by its four largest firms.
Conglomerate merger	–	The combination of two or more unrelated companies under a single management.
Constant dollars	–	The term used to reflect the changes in the purchasing power of the dollar from a base year.

C

Glossary of Key Terms

Consumer price index (CPI)	–	An index that measures the prices of a market basket of 300 goods that typical consumers purchase.
Consumption	–	The process of using a product or service.
Corporation	–	A business organization managed on behalf of its owners, who provide the funds.
Co-signer	–	A person who has a good credit rating and who guarantees to pay off your loan if you cannot.
Cost-push inflation	–	A situation of rising prices resulting from increases in the cost of production.
Costs	–	The losses that result when a choice is made.
Credit	–	The ability of a customer to buy goods or services before paying for them, based on an agreement to pay later.
Currency	–	Paper money and coins.
Current account	–	An account in a nation's balance of payments that includes exports and imports of goods and services, net investment income, and net transfers.
D **Demand**	–	Quantities of a particular good or service that consumers are willing and able to buy at different prices at a particular time.
Demand deposits	–	Checking accounts held by the public at commercial banks.
Demand-pull inflation	–	A situation of rising prices in which there is too much money "chasing" too few goods.
Deposit multiplier	–	The total possible increase in the money supply calculated by dividing 100 by the reserve ratio.
Derived demand	–	Demand for a resource, such as labor, based on the demand for the goods and services that the resource produces.
Diminishing marginal utility	–	The point reached when an additional unit of a product consumed is less satisfying than the one before it.
Discount rate	–	The interest rate charged by the Federal Reserve on its loans to banks and other financial institutions.
Disincentives	–	Negative or withdrawn rewards.
Disposable income	–	The money you take home after taxes are paid.

Glossary of Key Terms

Distribution	–	The process of getting a product or service to consumers.
Dividends	–	Profits distributed to stockholders.
Durable good	–	A consumer good that is expected to last three years or more.
E **Economic equity**	–	A condition of economic fairness and impartiality.
Economic freedom	–	A condition in which individuals and businesses have freedom of choice in employment, buying, selling, use of time, and other economically related decisions.
Economic growth	–	A condition in which the output of goods and service in an economy increases over the period of a year.
Economic indicators	–	Measures of different parts of the economy that are used to determine what has happened and what is likely to happen in the economy.
Economic security	–	A condition in which the basic needs of every person should be met.
Economics	–	A social science that studies how people, acting individually and in groups, decide to use scarce resources to satisfy their wants.
Economies of scale	–	Reductions in cost resulting from large-scale production.
Efficiency	–	A condition in which maximum output is obtained from the resources used to produce goods and services.
Elastic currency	–	The supply of currency that expands and contracts with the needs of business.
Employee stock ownership plan	–	An employer-sponsored retirement plan that allows employees to purchase the employer's stock, often at a reduced stock price.
Enterprise	–	A term for a business organization.
Entrepreneurship	–	The imagination, innovative thinking, and management skills needed to start and operate a business.
Exchange rate	–	The value of one nation's currency stated in terms of the value of another nation's currency.
Export	–	A good or service sold to a buyer in another country.
Export subsidy	–	A payment by a country to its exporters, enabling them to sell their products abroad at a lower price than at home.
Externality	–	An economic side effect of producing or consuming a good or service that generates benefits or costs to someone other than the person who decides how much to produce or consume.

Glossary of Key Terms

F | **Factors of production** | – | The land, labor, and capital resources used to produce goods and services.

Federal Reserve System | – | The nation's central bank.

Fertility rate | – | The average number of births during a year to women of childbearing age.

FICA | – | An acronym that stands for Federal Insurance Contributions Act, which directs the taxes people pay for Social Security and Medicare.

Finance charge | – | The total amount paid to use credit.

Fiscal policy | – | The use of government spending and taxation to stabilize the economy.

Fiscal year | – | A 12-month period that can begin on any date. The U.S. federal government's fiscal year starts October 1 and ends September 30 of the next year.

Fixed costs | – | Costs that remain the same regardless of the amount of product a firm produces.

Fractional reserve banking | – | When banks withhold a percentage, or fraction, of depositors' money and then lend the remainder of the deposits.

Franchise | – | A license that entitles its holder to operate his or her individually owned business as if it were part of a large chain of stores.

Free enterprise | – | The condition that allows people to freely make choices in their economic roles.

Free-trade association (FTA) | – | An agreement among countries to remove the barriers to trade among themselves.

Full employment | – | A condition in which almost all people in the labor force are able to find work.

G | **GDP deflator** | – | A price index that reduces the current gross domestic product prices into prices of a base year.

Globalization | – | The process of countries and their citizens becoming increasingly interdependent.

Grievance | – | A formal complaint made by a union if it feels that one member or a class of its members have been treated inappropriately under the terms of a contract.

Gross domestic product (GDP) | – | The final value of all goods and services produced within a country in a year.

Glossary of Key Terms

Gross national product (GNP)	–	The total market value of all final goods and services produced annually by American residents, whether these residents are located in the United States or in another country.
H **Horizontal merger**	–	The combination of two or more companies engaged in the same business.
I **Import**	–	A good or service purchased from a seller in another country.
Incentives	–	Positive rewards that result from making a choice or behaving in a certain way.
Income statement	–	A statement of earnings or a profit-and-loss statement.
Index	–	A combination of different numerical data, such as prices, into one measure that is reported over time.
Individual retirement account (IRA)	–	A kind of retirement account that an individual can establish with a bank, an insurance company, or a brokerage firm.
Industry	–	A group of one or more firms that produce identical or similar products.
Inflation	–	A general rise in overall prices.
Initial public offering	–	A company's first sale of stock to the public.
Injunction	–	A court order to keep a union from striking and picketing.
Interest	–	Income earned from allowing someone else to use your financial capital.
J **Job discrimination**	–	The practice of favoring one person over another for reasons that have nothing to do with ability to perform a job.
Joint venture	–	Two companies that keep their independence while cooperating on a particular project.
L **Labor**	–	The physical and mental efforts people use to create goods and services.
Labor force	–	All the people not in institutions who are 16 years of age or older and who are currently employed or who are unemployed and looking for work.
Labor productivity	–	The amount of goods and services the workforce can produce during a given time period—an hour, a week, a month, or a year.
Labor union	–	An association of workers that seeks to improve its members wages, working conditions, and benefits.

Glossary of Key Terms

Land	–	Natural resources that are unaltered gifts of nature, such as soil, minerals, timber, and fresh water.
Law of demand	–	An inverse relationship between the quantity demanded and the price of a product.
Law of diminishing marginal returns	–	An economic principle which holds that as more and more variable resources are added to a fixed amount of other resources, the additional amount produced eventually decreases.
Law of supply	–	A positive relationship between the quantity supplied and the price of the product.
Liability	–	Anything of monetary value owed by an individual or company.
Line of credit	–	An agreement a business makes, usually with a bank, to borrow up to a certain amount of money for ongoing cash needs.
Liquidity	–	The ease with which any asset, such as savings or a stock, can be converted to cash.
Lockout	–	The closing down of a business to pressure a union into accepting employment conditions.
Macroeconomics	–	The study of the economy as a whole.
Marginal	–	The extra or additional costs or benefits of a decision.
Marginal analysis	–	Decision making that involves comparing marginal benefits and marginal costs.
Marginal cost	–	The additional cost of increasing one unit of production.
Marginal revenue	–	The additional revenue generated from the sale of an additional quantity of the product.
Market	–	An arrangement that allows buyers and sellers to make exchanges.
Market-clearing price	–	The price at which the amount supplied is equal to the amount demanded.
Market competition	–	Rivalry among businesses for resources and customers.
Market demand	–	The total of all individual demands in a given market at a particular time.
Market economy	–	An economy that relies on voluntary trade as the primary means of organizing and coordinating production.

Glossary of Key Terms

Market risk	–	The potential decrease in the value of a stock in a stock market.
Market structure	–	A set of conditions that describes the characteristics of a market in which a business firm competes. The characteristics are the number of firms, differentiation of products, control over prices, and barriers to entering the marketing.
Market supply	–	The total of all individual suppliers' products in a market at a particular time.
Marketing	–	In economics, everything that takes place in a company between product production and purchase.
Merger	–	The purchase of one business by another business. The term *buyout* is sometimes used instead of merger.
Microeconomics	–	The study of individual consumers and businesses.
Mixed economies	–	Economic systems that blend voluntary exchange, government command, and traditional elements of economic choice making.
Monetary policy	–	Regulating the money supply to help the economy achieve a full-employment, noninflationary level of total output.
Money	–	Anything that is generally accepted as final payment for goods and services.
Money supply	–	The total amount of money in circulation within a country at some time period.
Monopolistic competition	–	A market structure with many firms that offer similar but not identical products.
Mutual fund	–	A pool of money used by a company to buy assets, such as stocks or bonds, on behalf of its shareholders.

N

National debt	–	The cumulative sum of all federal government borrowing used to finance annual deficits.
Near monies	–	Assets that can easily be converted into cash.
Net worth	–	An individual's wealth after debts and other obligations have been subtracted.
Nominal GDP	–	Gross domestic product reported in current prices.

Glossary of Key Terms

O   **Oligopoly**   –   A market structure in which a few large firms supply most or all products in a market.

Open-market operations   –   The purchase and sale of government securities by the Federal Open Market Committee.

Opportunity cost   –   The highest valued alternative given up as a result of making a choice.

P   **Partnership**   –   A business organization owned by two or more people who share ownership and control over the business.

Peak   –   A phase in the business cycle during which business activity is at a temporary maximum, and the economy is close to full employment.

Perfect competition   –   A market structure in which a large number of firms all produce the same product.

Picketing   –   The act of employees carrying signs that call attention to a labor strike with the goal of arousing public sympathy.

Predatory pricing   –   Selling a product below its cost with the goal to drive competitors out of business.

Preferred stock   –   Ownership shares issued as nonvoting stock.

Price effect   –   The inclination of people to buy less of something at higher prices than they would buy at lower prices.

Price elasticity of demand   –   A measure of the impact of the price effect.

Price-fixing   –   An action in which all businesses in a market agree to charge the same or similar prices.

Price stability   –   An economic condition in which prices of goods, services, and resources do not fluctuate significantly, either up or down, in a short period of time.

Price system   –   An arrangement that uses monetary prices as messages to facilitate exchanges between buyers and sellers.

Principal   –   An initial amount of savings or an original amount of money borrowed.

Private property   –   Resources and products owned by individuals or businesses.

Production   –   A process that combines economic resources so the result is a good or service that is available for sale.

Productivity   –   The output of goods and services measured per unit of input by labor, capital, or land.

Glossary of Key Terms

Profit	–	A positive difference between total sales and total costs.
Progressive tax	–	A tax that takes a higher proportion of income from higher income earners than from lower income earners.
Proportional tax	–	A tax for which the percentage of income paid in taxes is the same for all income levels.
Public good	–	Something that, once provided, is available to anyone without additional cost.
Public property	–	Resources and products owned by government.
Public sector	–	The part of the economy that involves the transactions of government.
Purchasing power	–	The value of money for purchasing goods and services.
Pure monopoly	–	A market structure with only one seller in the market.
Q **Quota**	–	Restriction on the amount of a specific good that can enter the country from abroad.
R **Rate of return**	–	The percentage of interest or the amount of dividends paid on savings or on an investment.
Rationing	–	Distributing or allocating a product by a price system.
Real GDP	–	Gross domestic product adjusted for inflation.
Real per capita GDP	–	Real gross domestic product divided by a country's population.
Recession	–	A period of time, six months or longer, in the business cycle during which total GDP output declines.
Recovery	–	A phase in a business cycle during which output and employment expand toward full employment.
Regressive tax	–	A tax for which the percentage of income paid in taxes decreases as income increases.
Rent	–	Payment for the use of someone else's property.
Reserve ratio	–	The percentage of total deposits held in reserve by a bank.
Retained earnings	–	The amount of money that has been saved over the year for reinvestment.

Glossary of Key Terms

S

Salary	– Earnings paid weekly, monthly, or on a yearly basis.
Scarcity	– An inequality that exists between wants and the resources available to satisfy them.
Seniority	– A worker's length of service with an employer.
Share of stock	– A share of ownership in a corporation.
Shortage	– The difference between the amount supplied and the amount demanded when the asking price is less than a market-clearing price.
Sole proprietorship	– A business owned by one person.
Specialization	– A process in which businesses and people focus on producing one or a few parts of an entire product; also the concentration of productive efforts of individuals or business firms on a limited number of activities.
Stock	– Ownership in a corporation.
Stock exchange	– A market in which the public buys and sells shares of stock.
Stock market	– A market in which the public is able to buy or sell stock.
Strike	– A withholding of labor services by a union.
Substitute	– A good or service that can replace another good or service.
Supply	– The quality of a good or service that producers are willing and able to sell at different prices at a particular time.
Surplus	– The difference between the amount supplied and the amount demanded when the asking price is greater than a market-clearing price.

T

Tariff	– A duty, or tax, on imports.
Tax deferment	– The payment of taxes on interest after the interest is earned, often upon retirement.
Total costs	– The sum of total fixed costs and total variable costs.
Total revenue	– A calculation of revenue that is determined by price times the quantity of units sold.
Trade	– Exchanging something for something else.

Glossary of Key Terms

Traditional economy	–	An economic system in which people rely on traditions or customs to make the what, how, and for whom choices.
Trough	–	A point in a business cycle in which output and employment reach their lowest level.
U **Unemployment rate**	–	The number of people looking for work divided by the number of people in the labor force.
Union shop	–	A factory, business, or agency operating under a contract in which nonunion members can be hired but only on the condition that they join the union after they are hired.
V **Variable costs**	–	Costs that change with changing amounts of production.
Venture capitalists	–	Investors who make loans to new companies.
Vertical merger	–	The combination of two or more companies involved in different steps of a production process.
W **Wage**	–	Earnings paid by the hour or unit of production.
Wealth	–	The value of the things you own.
Y **Yield**	–	The percentage return actually earned over time on a bond investment that is figured by dividing the annual interest by the price paid.

Index

Index

Index

Index

Index

Index

Index

Index

Index

Index

Index

M

Index

Index

Index

Index

Index

Index